This major work in the history of ethics is the first study of early modern British moral philosophy in several decades. Its aim is to uncover the roots of the contemporary thesis known as *internalism* – the idea that the practical 'ought' must be based in the motives of a deliberating agent – as this developed in the thought of British philosophers writing in the period from Hobbes to the appearance of Hume's *Treatise* in 1740.

Stephen Darwall discerns two different ways this idea was worked out, within two distinct traditions. On the one hand, an empirical naturalist tradition, comprising Hobbes, Locke, Cumberland, Hutcheson, and Hume, argued that obligation is the practical force that empirical discoveries acquire in the process of deliberation. On the other, a group including Cudworth, Shaftesbury, Butler, and in some moments Locke viewed obligation as inconceivable without an autonomous will and sought (well before Kant) to develop a theory of the will as self-determining and to devise an account of obligation linked to that.

Questions about the relation between obligation and motivation are central to contemporary ethics, so this outstanding work of scholarship not only reshapes our appreciation of the early modern British moralists but also discloses the philosophical sources of some of the liveliest debates in present-day ethics.

The British moralists and the internal 'ought':
1640–1740

The British moralists
and
the internal 'ought':
1640–1740

STEPHEN DARWALL

THE UNIVERSITY OF MICHIGAN

CAMBRIDGE
UNIVERSITY PRESS

Published by the Press Syndicate of the University of Cambridge
The Pitt Building, Trumpington Street, Cambridge CB2 1RP
40 West 20th Street, New York, NY 10011-4211, USA
10 Stamford Road, Oakleigh, Melbourne 3166, Australia

First published 1995

Printed in the United States of America

Library of Congress Cataloging-in-Publication Data
Darwall, Stephen L., 1946–
The British moralists and the internal 'ought': 1640–1740 /
Stephen Darwall.
p.   cm.
Includes bibliographical references and index.
ISBN 0-521-45167-1. – ISBN 0-521-45782-3 (pbk.)
1. Philosophy, British – 17th century. 2. Philosophy,
British – 18th century. 3. Ethics, Modern – 17th century. 4. Ethics,
Modern – 18th century. I. Title.
B1131.D37   1995
170'.941'09032 – dc20   94-21945
CIP

A catalog record for this book is available from the British Library.

ISBN 0-521-45167-1 hardback
ISBN 0-521-45782-3 paperback

To my family:
Rosemarie, Julian, and William

Contents

Acknowledgments

In 1986, having spent the preceding fifteen years thinking about foundational issues in ethics as they arise in contemporary debates, I began to try to uncover the roots of these discussions in the seventeenth- and eighteenth-century British moralists. Although I had read in this area for years and taught courses using Raphael's and Selby-Bigge's anthologies, I was unprepared for the gold mine of philosophical ideas to be found when these materials are studied seriously and systematically. If nothing else, I hope the present volume may lead others to these wonderful texts as well.

Throughout this project, I have been helped by many people and institutions in many ways – more ways, I'm sure, than I can remember. It is a great pleasure to be able to thank publicly those I do remember. I hope those I do not will forgive me.

To J. B. Schneewind I owe my first introduction to Hobbes and Hume in graduate school, the example of how to do history of ethics in a historically and philosophically engaged way, and much support and encouragement during the current project. From the late W. D. Falk I received an almost spiritual sense of ethical internalism's deep appeal and the importance of the British moralists. To him I owe perhaps the greatest debt: the conviction that led me to this study in the first place. Since I have been at the University of Michigan, I have had the benefit of W. K. Frankena's great wisdom and learning in ethical theory and the history of ethics, and about the British moralists in particular. He has been an invaluable resource, critic, and interlocutor.

From my colleagues at Michigan, both faculty and students, I have had a wonderfully stimulating and exciting environment in which to think about moral philosophy, as well as much help in formulating my ideas about the British moralists. I am indebted particularly to

Acknowledgments

Elizabeth Anderson, Richard Brandt, Edwin Curley, Allan Gibbard, Daniela Gobetti, Donald Herzog, David Hills, Louis Loeb, Peter Railton, Donald Regan, David Velleman, and Nicholas White, as well as David Aman, David Anderson, David Cummiskey, Justin D'Arms, Richard Dees, David Nagle, Connie Rosati, and Sigrun Svavarsdottir.

I have read papers on which parts of this book are based at Bowling Green State University, the Chapel Hill Colloquium, Harvard University, a Hume workshop at the University of North Carolina at Chapel Hill, Northwestern University, the University of Pittsburgh, the University of Wyoming, and Hume Society meetings at the 1992 Central Division meetings of the American Philosophical Association in Louisville, Kentucky, and in the summer of 1992 at the University of Nantes, in France. I am greatly indebted to commentators and members of these audiences and, especially, to Annette Baier, Kurt Baier, Charlotte Brown, Rachel Cohon, John Deigh, Rosalind Hursthouse, Christine Korsgaard, Ned McClennen, Jan Narveson, David Fate Norton, Gerald Postema, Connie Rosati, T. M. Scanlon, J. B. Schneewind, Robert Shaver, and Nicholas Sturgeon.

Various people read parts of the book in draft and gave me very helpful comments, including William Frankena, Louis Loeb, S. A. Lloyd, J. B. Schneewind, Robert Shaver, Nicholas Sturgeon, Gregory Velazco y Trianosky, and Nicholas White. I am also indebted to Kenneth Winkler, who read the manuscript for the Cambridge University Press, for his suggestions. Terence Moore of Cambridge University Press also provided much-appreciated encouragement and good counsel. And Eric and Jane Van Tassel gave valuable editorial advice.

The National Endowment for the Humanities awarded fellowship support at two critical stages: in 1986–87, when I was beginning serious research, and in 1993–94, when I finished the book. The College of Literature, Science, and the Arts of the University of Michigan provided paid research leaves in 1986–87, the winter of 1991, and 1993–94. In 1991 I also received from the Office of the Vice-President for Research a summer research grant that, together with sabbatical leave in the winter of 1991 and relief from teaching one course in the fall of 1991, funded through the James B. and Grace J. Nelson Philosophy Endowment, enabled me to write a virtually complete first draft of the manuscript. During this period, Louis Loeb took over my duties as chair of the Philosophy Department. I am also indebted to the Horace Rackham School of Graduate Studies and to the Office of the Vice-President for Research at the University of Michigan for a grant to Richard Dees and myself to work on

Cudworth's manuscripts. Without the generous support of these individuals and institutions, I could not possibly have conducted this project.

During my research year in England, 1986–87, I was very much helped by the expert staff at the British Library, especially in the North Library and Manuscripts Room, at the Bodleian Library, Oxford, the Senate House Library of the University of London, and Dr. Williams's Library, London. I also thank D. A. Lloyd-Thomas and his colleagues at King's College of the University of London, and James Griffin and his colleagues at Keble College, Oxford, for their generous hospitality and philosophical stimulation.

Two chapters of this book, those on Butler and Hume, are based on previously published essays: "Conscience as Self-Authorizing in Butler's Ethics," in *Joseph Butler's Moral and Religious Thought: Tercentenary Essays,* edited by Christopher Cunliffe (Oxford: Clarendon Press, 1992), and "Motive and Obligation in Hume's Ethics," *Nous* 17 (1993): 415–48. I thank the respective editors and publishers for permission to make use of this material.

Finally, I want to thank my family, to whom this book is dedicated, who have sustained me in all ways during the whole project – Julian and William and my wife, Rosemarie, whose patience and support have been unfailing.

Abbreviations

A	Butler, *The Analogy of Religion*
Char	Shaftesbury, *Characteristics*
DC	Hobbes, *De Cive*
Dis	Culverwell, *A Discourse of the Light of Nature*
DV	Butler, *A Dissertation of Virtue*
ECPM	Hume, *An Enquiry Concerning the Principles of Morals*
Elements	Hobbes, *The Elements of Law*
EPA	Hutcheson, *An Essay on the Nature and Conduct of the Passions*
Essay	Locke, *An Essay Concerning Human Understanding*
FMG	Balguy, *The Foundation of Moral Goodness*
FW	Cudworth, *A Treatise of Freewill*
IMS	Hutcheson, *Illustrations on the Moral Sense*
In	Hutcheson, *An Inquiry into the Original of Our Ideas of Beauty and Virtue; In Two Treatises . . . II. Concerning Moral Good and Evil*
Lev	Hobbes, *Leviathan*
Life	Shaftesbury, *Philosophical Regimen* and letters (in Benjamin Rand, *The Life of Shaftesbury*)
S	Butler, *Fifteen Sermons Preached at the Rolls Chapel*
Sys	Hutcheson, *A System of Moral Philosophy*
TEIM	Cudworth, *A Treatise Concerning Eternal and Immutable Morality*
THN	Hume, *A Treatise of Human Nature*
TIS	Cudworth, *The True Intellectual System of the Universe*
TLN	Cumberland, *A Treatise of the Laws of Nature*

The British moralists and the internal 'ought':
1640–1740

Chapter 1

The British moralists: inventing internalism

Ever since Selby-Bigge published his anthology almost a century ago, the term *British moralists* has come to refer to moral philosophers writing in Britain from roughly the time of Hobbes in the middle of the seventeenth century through that of Bentham at the end of the eighteenth.[1] This was a time of extraordinary ferment and creativity throughout Europe, no less in philosophy than in other areas. We call the period "early modern" to mark it as a point of departure, as one that broke in significant ways with forms of thought and organization of earlier periods and to which we can trace many of the terms in which we still encounter issues of intellectual, moral, and political life. No doubt all epochal categories are crude and distorting. Still, it seems undeniable that what we now think of as science, for example, is much more like what Boyle and Newton were engaged in than anything in the ancient world or in what came in between. Similarly, thanks to fundamental changes in political organization and thought just before and during this period, we are far likelier to find problems of political life posed in terms that are recognizably *ours* in the writings of Hobbes, Locke, and Rousseau than in Renaissance, medieval, or ancient texts, continuing interest in Aristotle notwithstanding.[2]

The same is true, in large measure, in ethics, especially in *moral* philosophy. Questions about how to live a human life or about what

1. L. A. Selby-Bigge, ed., *British Moralists, Being Selections from Writers Principally of the Eighteenth Century*, 2 vols. (Oxford: Oxford University Press, 1897), reprinted in one volume, with a new introduction by Bernard H. Baumrin (Indianapolis, Ind.: Bobbs-Merrill, 1964). See also D. D. Raphael, ed., *British Moralists: 1650–1800*, 2 vols. (Oxford: Clarendon Press, 1969); reprint, Indianapolis, Ind.: Hackett, 1991. Selections from many of the British moralists are also included in J. B. Schneewind, ed., *Moral Philosophy from Montaigne to Kant: An Anthology*, 2 vols. (Cambridge: Cambridge University Press, 1990).
2. Consider the problem of political obligation, for example.

1

does or should matter to us are, naturally, nearly as old as philosophy itself. But it is arguable that only in the early modern period (or just before) did a number of features coalesce into the idea of *morality*, the notion that there exist requirements or *demands* that are binding on all rational persons, even though the conduct demanded may lack any necessary connection to the good of the person obligated.[3] Of course, this idea was not universally received; neither is it now. However, it came during this period to be widely thought a very important idea, one many philosophers wanted to understand and defend. And this forced a fundamental question: In what might the universal bindingness of morality consist? What makes morality obligating? And that question forced another even more fundamental: What is it for anything to be binding? What is bindingness, obligation, or, as moral philosophers are inclined to say these days, *normativity* itself? In what does an *ought to do* consist?

THE BACKGROUND

Why was the *general* issue of normativity a special focus for the seventeenth century, however? Even if the conception of morality is an early modern discovery or construction, fundamental questions of justification were staples of ethical thought from ancient times. The difference was the *way* the issue arose. To put the matter much too simply, ancient ethics and its premodern successors assumed a *unified practical object*, the *good*, which, because it is uniquely given *as end*, structures all rational deliberation, and whose status as end is guaranteed *metaphysically*, since it is intrinsic to human nature or part of the basic structure of reality. Presently, I shall describe how these assumptions worked within the classical theory of natural law, deriving from Saint Thomas. But it is perhaps clearest in Aristotle, whose *Nicomachean Ethics* begins with the declaration that, as every action aims at some good, the task of ethics is to discover the chief or

---

3. On the idea that modern moral philosophy differs from ancient ethics in respect of the idea of *demandingness*, see Henry Sidgwick, *The Methods of Ethics*, 7th ed. (London: Macmillan, 1967), p. 106; and Nicholas White, "The Imperative, the Attractive and the Repulsive: Sidgwick and Modern Views of Ancient Ethics," in Bart Schultz, ed., *Essays on Henry Sidgwick* (Cambridge: Cambridge University Press, 1992).

most final good.[4] By such a good, Aristotle says he means 'the good for man', that is, for the person himself or herself, not any Platonic form.[5] Deliberation thus makes sense only in relation to this chief good: *eudaimonia*, or a flourishing life for the agent. Moreover, Aristotle's teleological metaphysics assures that this end is given metaphysically, as final cause.[6] For Aristotle, therefore, practical normativity can be understood only through relation to the agent's good; it is uniquely given *as end*. Against this background, to be something an agent ought to do *just is* to be something that furthers her good.[7] The main difference from Plato was that Plato believed the good to be person-neutral: Reasons for action are determined by *the* good.

The idea that rational action aims (even uniquely) at the agent's good was hardly absent in the seventeenth century, of course. On the contrary, it was, if anything, the default view. But philosophers could not both reject Aristotelian, teleological metaphysics, as increasingly many did, and claim a *metaphysical* basis for this view.[8] They could no longer simply assume that there being reason *to do* something, or an action's being something an agent *ought* to do, is *the same thing as* the action's furthering the agent's good. What is more, without teleological metaphysics a harmony of individuals' goods is not metaphysically guaranteed. The possibility that persons' goods might conflict deeply was not only thinkable but urgent. And the question could now be raised: What should a person do if his good does conflict with those of others or, more to the point, with demands general compliance with which is mutually advantageous? Should he promote his own good? Or that of others or of all? More specifically, should he comply with mutually advantageous demands even when it is contrary to his good to do so? These are genuine questions

---

4. Aristotle, *The Nicomachean Ethics*, I.1–2, trans. W. D. Ross (New York: Oxford University Press, 1980). For a discussion of this aspect of ancient ethics in general, see Julia Annas, *The Morality of Happiness* (New York: Oxford University Press, 1993), esp. pp. 3–43.
5. *Nicomachean Ethics*, I.4.
6. On this point, see T. H. Irwin, "The Metaphysical and Psychological Basis of Aristotle's Ethics," in Amèlie Oksenberg Rorty, ed., *Essays on Aristotle's Ethics* (Berkeley and Los Angeles: University of California Press, 1980), pp. 35–53.
7. This is, of course, consistent with the chief good's being an "inclusive" end, in Hardie's sense, including various intrinsic goods as part of it. See W. F. R. Hardie, "The Final Good in Aristotle's Ethics," *Philosophy* 40 (1965): 277–95.
8. Alasdair MacIntyre has famously argued, of course, that this doomed the "enlightenment project" to failure. See *After Virtue* (Notre Dame, Ind.: University of Notre Dame Press, 1981), esp. pp. 49–59.

only if practical normativity is a different thing from relation to the agent's good. And even if the right answers must still be based on egoistic concerns, as many thought, this would now have to be defended as an independent normative thesis without a basis in teleological metaphysics. So the more fundamental question could now arise: In what could the truth of such a thesis consist?

The modern conception of morality developed as a solution to the problem of conflicting interests, especially the problem of conflict among persons who cannot expect to share a common confession or religious discipline. In some ways, its solution is as old as Glaucon's suggestion in the *Republic* that the unrestricted pursuit of self-interest is collectively disadvantageous, and that mutual advantage is served by everyone's acknowledging and following requirements that restrict individuals' pursuit of self-interest.[9] For Glaucon, though, these demands are simply a modus vivendi that individuals rightly seek to evade when they can get away with it. But among the writers we shall be considering, even Hobbes, who is closest to this view, thinks that morality has a more secure normative status than that. And so the question arises, What gives morality this status? And again, What (in general) *is* normative status anyway?

CLASSICAL NATURAL LAW VERSUS MODERN NATURAL LAW

Philosophically, the modern conception of morality developed first within the seventeenth-century natural law tradition of Grotius, Pufendorf, and Cumberland, as well as, more generally, Hobbes and Locke.[10] To understand its novelty, we need to survey briefly the classical, Thomistic theory of natural law against which the modern tradition reacted. The idea that there are norms or laws to which all rational human beings are subject – a natural law or law of nature –

9. *Republic*, 358e-360b.
10. The main works here are Hugo Grotius, *De Jure Belli ac Pacis* (Amsterdam, 1625), translated as *The Law of War and Peace* by Francis W. Kelsey (New York: Carnegie Endowment for International Peace, 1925); Samuel Pufendorf, *De Jure Naturæ et Gentium* (Lund, 1672), translated as *On the Law of Nature and Nations* by C. H. Oldfather and W. A. Oldfather (Oxford: Oxford University Press, 1934); Bishop Richard Cumberland, *De Legibus Naturæ Disquisitio Philosophica* (London, 1672), translated as *A Treatise of the Laws of Nature* by J. Maxwell (London, 1727); Thomas Hobbes, *Leviathan* (London, 1651); and John Locke, *Essays on the Law of Nature*, edited and translated from the Latin by W. von Leyden (Oxford: Oxford University Press, 1954). Locke's *Essays* were probably composed in the 1660s; see Chapter 2, note 1.

goes back as far as the Stoics. Not until Thomas Aquinas in the thirteenth century, however, was it developed systematically. For Thomas, natural law is a formulation of 'eternal law', God's ideal or archetype for all of nature – "the exemplar of divine wisdom . . . moving all things to their *due end*."[11] Eternal law specifies the distinctive perfection or ideal state of every natural thing. But while all things are "ruled and measured" by eternal law, rational beings are subject to the law in a distinctive way, since they have "a share of the eternal reason."[12] Uniquely, they are bound by what Aquinas calls 'natural law' – a law that they, unlike nonrational creatures, can follow or flout. Natural law is simply eternal law as applied and made accessible to rational creatures.[13]

Thomas's theory of the good was perfectionist: The good of each being is its perfection.[14] It follows that individuals can realize their respective goods only if they function properly in the overall scheme specified by eternal law. Any deep conflict between their goods is thus ruled out – harmony is guaranteed by perfectionist/teleological metaphysics.[15] It is a consequence also of the way Aquinas based natural law on eternal law that following *natural* law (morality) must lead each to his greatest good. Finally, like Aristotle, Aquinas took each agent's good to be part of his nature *as end*. The normativity of the agent's good is thus built into what he is. Its having intrinsic practical normative relevance – relevance to what he *ought* to do – that the goods of other persons cannot have (for him) is assured metaphysically. This "egoism" is, of course, entirely benign, since an agent will realize her good only if, through following eternal law, she acts in ways that enable others to realize theirs. And they will presumably realize theirs only if she does what will realize hers.

Contrast this with the picture presented by Grotius in *The Law of War and Peace*, the founding work of modern natural law, published in 1625. Grotius begins by considering a skeptical objection to natural

11. *Summa Theologica*, XCIII, 1 (emphasis added), in Anton C. Pegis, ed., *Basic Writings of Saint Thomas Aquinas*, (New York: Random House, 1945).
12. Ibid., XCI, 3.
13. Ibid., XCI, 2.
14. *Summa Contra Gentiles*, III, 16, in *Basic Writings of Saint Thomas Aquinas*.
15. For the question of human law and governance, Aquinas recognizes that important issues of conflict arise. See, e.g., *De Regno*, I.1, in Saint Thomas Aquinas, *On Law, Morality, and Politics*, ed. William P. Baumgarth and Richard J. Regan, S.J. (Indianapolis, Ind.: Hackett, 1988). Although these might be raised well enough, consistently with the doctrines relating eternal law and the good just mentioned, in terms of conflicting *beliefs* about the good, Aquinas does speak there about conflicting interests.

law that simply could not have arisen on the classical view: "[T]here is no law of nature, because all creatures, men as well as animals, are impelled by nature towards ends advantageous to themselves . . . [C]onsequently, there is no justice, or if such there be, it is supreme folly, since one does violence to his own interests if he consults the advantage of others."[16] This objection can be raised only if interests can conflict deeply and if the requirements of natural law can diverge from what would advance the good of those it purports to obligate. On the classical theory, it wouldn't get off the ground.

In fact, Grotius shares his objector's assumption that deep conflict between individuals' goods is possible. And he does not question that natural law may require real sacrifice. It may occasionally be more in an agent's interest, he is willing to allow, to violate norms the collective following of which is best for all. Grotius's response is rather to criticize the assumption that the desire for their own good is the only "impelling desire" rational human beings have. Human nature also includes, he argues, "an impelling desire for society," and the collective following of certain norms (natural laws) is essential to social order. Had Grotius accepted the Thomist picture, however, he could hardly have argued just that we have a desire for peaceful society *along with* the desire for own good, since he would have had to admit the normative priority of the latter. Now, on the classical theory these two desires cannot deeply conflict. There is, indeed, a crucial interdependence between the classical doctrines that the agent's own good is the unique source of practical normativity and that the goods of all are metaphysically harmonized. Grotius denies both doctrines. He assumes that deep conflict is possible and that natural law is required to enable human agents to deal with it peaceably. And he supposes that being an action an agent ought or has reason to do is not the same thing as being an action that furthers the agent's good. So he must face the skeptical objection: Why suppose there are norms by which rational persons are bound requiring them

---

16. *The Law of War and Peace*, Prolegomena, pp. 10–11. For a discussion of Grotius as responding to the skeptical challenges posed by Montaigne and Charron, see Richard Tuck, "Grotius, Carneades, and Hobbes," *Grotiana*, n.s. 4 (1983): 43–62, and "The 'Modern' Theory of Natural Law," in Anthony Pagden, ed., *The Languages of Political Theory in Early-Modern Europe* (Cambridge: Cambridge University Press, 1987), pp. 99–122. Tuck argues that Grotius's response anticipates Hobbes. For a different view, see Robert Shaver, "Grotius on Skepticism and Self-Interest," *Archiv für Geschichte der Philosophie*, forthcoming.

  Grotius puts this objection in the mouth of the Academic skeptic Carneades. Locke considers the very same objection, using Grotius's formulation, in *Essays on the Law of Nature*. See Chapter 2 below.

to act against their good? And again: What is it, in general, to be under an 'ought'?

THE BRITISH MORALISTS AND
THE INVENTION OF INTERNALISM

WHY BRITAIN?

These questions were at the very center of early modern British moral thought and debate from Hobbes on. The influence of an emerging non-Aristotelian science during this period was as great in Britain as anywhere, creating a widespread belief that any defensible moral philosophy, including any acceptable account of moral obligation, must be consistent with modern science, if not itself scientific. These days, we are likely to regard Hobbes's most enduring contribution as the positive account of political and moral obligation he was able to ground on lean epistemological and metaphysical assumptions. His contemporaries, however, widely read him as a nihilist and moral skeptic (as well, of course, as a political absolutist), and many conceived their task as trying to vindicate morality in the face of the Hobbesian challenge. Hobbes had made his contempt for the teleological metaphysics of the schools evident enough. But, with few exceptions, his opponents did not respond by trying to defend Aquinas and Aristotle. They agreed with Hobbes that the schools had been discredited and, therefore, that any acceptable view of the normativity of morals would have to be based on different grounds.

At the same time, Britain was undergoing profound social and political struggle over issues of toleration, liberty, and autonomy during the period of the Civil War and Glorious Revolution, and on into the eighteenth century. In 1689 the Toleration Act was passed, and in 1718 the Schism and Occasional Conformity acts were repealed. These struggles profoundly affected and reshaped the way people thought about moral obligation. A passage from Saint Paul's Epistle to the Romans was widely cited (and variously interpreted) in support of the idea that morality obligates all rational persons, even those not bound together by a common faith, because of a common moral capacity: "For when the Gentiles, which have not the law, do by nature the things contained in the law, these, having not the law, are a law unto themselves" (2:14). This text had been used for centuries to justify moral community beyond the boundaries of

7

revelation.[17] What was new in early modern Britain was the use made of it by philosophers trying to work out a conception of the *autonomy of the moral agent* and to argue that obligation can be understood adequately only if it is properly linked to that.[18]

This book is a study of the British moralists' efforts to come to grips with the issue of obligation. Despite its fundamental importance to the early moderns, as well as to moral philosophers of our own period who have inherited it from them, the early history of this problematic has been relatively little studied. The question of *political* obligation as it arises, for example, in the works of Hobbes and Locke has been much discussed. But though more fundamental normative and metaethical issues lying in the background of these discussions are sometimes brought to the fore, they are rarely the central focus. And, in any case, much of the most interesting early modern work on these fundamental issues was done by "lesser" British thinkers – or by greater ones in lesser-known works – that have come to be studied in this century only lately with the recent flowering of the history of modern moral and political thought.[19] No serious study of the

17. On this point, see J. B. Schneewind, "The Use of Autonomy in Ethical Theory," in Thomas C. Heller, Morton Sosna, and David E. Wellbery, eds., *Reconstructing Individualism: Autonomy, Individuality, and the Self in Western Thought* (Stanford, Calif.: Stanford University Press, 1986), pp. 64–65.

18. Schneewind's category of philosophers who form a tradition of "autonomy and responsibility" (in *Moral Philosophy from Montaigne to Kant*) is broader than I here intend, since he includes philosophers who shared the idea that moral knowledge and motivation are universally available to moral agents. This brings in a number of thinkers, Hutcheson and Hume being prominent examples, who did not think that the capacity for self-determining moral agency has anything to do with obligation itself. See *Moral Philosophy from Montaigne to Kant*, vol. 1, pp. 26–29.

19. In addition to an almost breathtaking increase in the level and depth of scholarship on Hobbes, Hume, Locke, and Kant. Among the most important work on lesser-known early modern ethical writers, I would include Richard Tuck, *Natural Rights Theories* (Cambridge: Cambridge University Press, 1987), in addition to his work on Grotius (mentioned in note 16); J. B. Schneewind, "Kant and Natural Law Ethics," *Ethics* 104 (1993): 53–74, "Pufendorf's Place in the History of Ethics," *Synthese* 72 (1987): 123–55, and "Natural Law, Skepticism, and Method," *Journal of the History of Ideas* 52 (1991): 289–308; Knud Haakonssen, "Divine/ Natural Law Theories in Ethics," in M. Ayers and D. Garber, eds., *Cambridge History of Seventeenth-Century Philosophy* (Cambridge: Cambridge University Press); "Moral Philosophy and Natural Law: From the Cambridge Platonists to the Scottish Enlightenment," *Political Science* 40 (1988): 97–110, and "Natural Law and Moral Realism: The Scottish Synthesis," in M. A. Stewart, ed., *Studies in the Philosophy of the Scottish Enlightenment* (Oxford: Oxford University Press, 1990); Wolfgang Leidhold, *Ethik und Politik bei Francis Hutcheson* (Freiburg: Alber, 1985); David Fate Norton, *David Hume: Common-Sense Moralist, Sceptical Metaphysician* (Princeton: Princeton University Press, 1982), also on Hutcheson. An important

wealth of significant work by the early modern British moralists on
the problem of obligation can fail to take account of Balguy, Cudworth, Cumberland, Shaftesbury, Hutcheson, and Locke's *Essays on
the Law of Nature*, as well, of course, as Hobbes, Hume, Butler, and
Locke's *Essay*.

INTERNALISM AND EXTERNALISM

Actually, our scope will be narrower even than a general study of the
British moralists on obligation. To delimit it properly, however, I
need first to say something about the moral philosophy of our own
period. Many of the most important debates in contemporary ethical
theory have come to turn on the issue of whether *internalism* is true.[20]
In fact, 'internalism' refers in contemporary discussions to a host of
positions on a host of issues. What these have in common is the
assertion of a necessary connection between either the having or the
truth conditions of ethical or normative thought (or language) and
motivation.

Sometimes internalism is asserted as a view about the nature of
normative thought or language. What I call *judgment internalism* is
the position that it is a necessary condition of a sincere or genuine
ethical or normative utterance, thought, or conviction – for instance,
that one should x – that one would, under appropriate conditions,
have some motivation to *x*.[21] According to judgment internalism,
nothing counts as a genuine normative or ethical thought or utterance unless it has the appropriate connection to motivation. Internal-

stimulus to much of this work, at least on the side of political philosophy, was
Quentin Skinner's monumental *The Foundations of Modern Political Thought*, 2
vols. (Cambridge: Cambridge University Press, 1978). Many important ethical
texts of this period are collected and illuminatingly introduced in J. B.
Schneewind's *Moral Philosophy from Montaigne to Kant..*

20. The term 'internalism' derives from W. D. Falk's "'Ought' and Motivation,"
Proceedings of the Aristotelian Society 48 (1947–48): 492–510, reprinted in *Ought,
Reasons, and Morality: The Collected Papers of W. D. Falk* (Ithaca: Cornell University
Press, 1986). Other important discussions include William Frankena, "Obligation
and Motivation in Recent Moral Philosophy," in A. I. Melden, ed., *Essays in Moral
Philosophy* (Seattle: University of Washington Press, 1958); Thomas Nagel, *The
Possibility of Altruism* (Oxford: Clarendon Press, 1970), pp. 3–12; Bernard
Williams, "Internal and External Reasons," in *Moral Luck* (Cambridge: Cam-
bridge University Press, 1981), pp. 101–13; Stephen Darwall, *Impartial Reason*
(Ithaca: Cornell University Press, 1983), pp. 51–61; Christine Korsgaard, "Skepti-
cism About Practical Reason," *Journal of Philosophy* 83 (1986): 5–25; and Stephen
Darwall, "Internalism and Agency," *Philosophical Perspectives* 6 (1992): 155–74.
21. In *Impartial Reason*, p. 54.

ism of this sort has loomed large in twentieth-century arguments for ethical noncognitivism – that is, for the view that ethical judgments have no cognitive content and so cannot literally be true or false, but rather express noncognitive (in this case motivation-laden) mental states.[22]

The other main category of internalisms I call *existence internalisms* because they are concerned with what must be the case for an ethical or normative proposition to be true or for an ethical or normative fact to exist.[23] On all such views, it is a necessary condition of its being the case that someone should *x* that *that person* would, under appropriate conditions, have some motive to *x*. There is, however, an important distinction between two fundamentally different kinds of existence internalism. According to one sort, although motive is in no way intrinsic to ethical facts themselves, it is a necessary consequence of *perceiving* or *knowing* them. This, perhaps, was Plato's position. One cannot know the Good without being moved, although motivation is not itself part of what one knows. Motivation is an effect of the knowing encounter with normativity, not part of normativity itself. It was also the position of the eighteenth-century British rational intuitionists: Samuel Clarke, John Balguy, and, later, Richard Price. And, in a quite different way, it is the view of contemporary "sensibility" theorists, such as David Wiggins and John McDowell.[24]

Internalism of this sort, however, does not help us understand what normativity itself is. This was no oversight for the intuitionists, since they thought there is nothing to be said about that. Ethical facts

---

22. See, for example, Charles Stevenson, *Ethics and Language* (New Haven: Yale University Press, 1944); R. M. Hare, *The Language of Morals* (Oxford: Clarendon Press, 1952); and Allan Gibbard, *Wise Choices, Apt Feelings* (Cambridge, Mass.: Harvard University Press, 1990).
23. In *Impartial Reason*, p. 54. For a fuller discussion of the two kinds of existence internalism I am about to distinguish, see my "Internalism and Agency," 157–60, 162–69.
24. See especially John McDowell, "Values and Secondary Qualities," in Ted Honderich, ed., *Morality and Objectivity: A Tribute to John Mackie* (London: Routledge & Kegan Paul, 1985), pp. 110–29, and *Projection and Truth in Ethics*, Lindley Lecture, University of Kansas, 1987; and David Wiggins, "Truth, Invention, and the Meaning of Life," "Truth, and Truth as Predicated of Moral Judgments," and "A Sensible Subjectivism?" reprinted in his *Needs, Values, and Truth: Essays in the Philosophy of Value* (Oxford: Blackwell Publisher, 1987). For a discussion, see Stephen Darwall, Allan Gibbard, and Peter Railton, "Toward *Fin de siècle* Ethics: Some Trends," *Philosophical Review* 101 (1992): 115–89, at 152–65; and Darwall, "Internalism and Agency," 159–60.

concerning the reasonable and unreasonable, obligatory and pro-
hibited, fit and unfit are sui generis – a metaphysical order existing
independently of moral agency or the knowing mind. Such a view
can seem mysterious on a number of counts, however. How could
there be such a nonnatural metaphysical order, and how could it be
known? Moreover, if, as the intuitionists believed, the faculty
through which we can know this order is no different from that
through which we know mathematical facts, what explains why we
are necessarily moved in the former case but not in the latter?

A very different sort of existence internalism, hoping to understand the nature of normativity itself, claims that the existence of
motive, perhaps of a certain kind or under certain circumstances, is
(at least part of) what it is for a normative proposition to be true.[25]
Obligation, this sort of internalism holds, consists in something internal to the moral agent in some suitable sense; it can be realized only
in motives available to a deliberating agent, from a *practical* point of
view. A valid or binding 'ought' is ultimately an *internal 'ought'*. This
is the version of internalism that will be most relevant to our concerns. *From this point on, I shall use 'internalism' to refer specifically to it,
except when I note otherwise.*

Whether internalism is true is at the heart of a great number of
present-day debates in ethical philosophy – for example, those concerning moral realism and irrealism, relativism and absolutism, and
whether moral demands are categorical imperatives. J. L. Mackie's
famous argument that ethical properties are too "queer" to be real
turns on an assumption of internalism.[26] So too does Gilbert Harman's argument for moral relativism.[27] And internalism is fre-

25. In "Internalism and Agency" (162) I call this *constitutive internalism*.
26. Although probably something closer to the other kind of existence internalism. J.
    L. Mackie, *Ethics: Inventing Right and Wrong* (Harmondsworth: Penguin, 1977),
    pp. 39–40. For moral realism, see Peter Railton, "Moral Realism," *Philosophical
    Review* 95 (1986): 163–207; David O. Brink, *Moral Realism and the Foundations of
    Ethics* (Cambridge: Cambridge University Press, 1989); and the articles in Geof-
    frey Sayre-McCord, ed., *Essays on Moral Realism* (Ithaca: Cornell University Press,
    1988). Brink discusses the relation between the question of whether internalism is
    true and moral realism throughout chap. 3 of *Moral Realism and the Foundations of
    Ethics*. The relevant kind of internalism is what he calls "agent internalism"; see
    p. 40. This is what I have called *existence internalism*.
       For general discussion of internalism's role in recent moral philosophy, see
    Darwall, Gibbard, and Railton, "Toward *Fin de siècle* Ethics," passim.
27. "Moral Relativism Defended," *Philosophical Review* 84 (1975): 3–22, at 8–9. I argue
    that internalism does not lead to this conclusion, in "Harman and Moral Relativ-
    ism," *Personalist* 58 (1977): 199–207.

quently in the background of arguments that moral imperatives can be only hypothetical and not categorical.[28] At the same time, there are moral realists who accept versions of internalism.[29] Moreover, one of the most powerful interpretations of Kantian ethics is an internalist one, and philosophers of this persuasion are among the most ardent defenders of the absolute and categorical character of moral demands.[30]

Thus, whether internalism is true and what the consequences would be for ethics if it were are among the most vigorously debated questions in contemporary moral philosophy. But although internalism has wide appeal, little systematic work has been done to try to understand the sources of its appeal. More frequently than not, its proponents appear simply to take it for granted. But the same is often true of those who deny internalism. *Externalists* (of the relevant sort) hold that the truth of a normative claim does not depend on its being the case that the person to whom the claim applies would be motivated under any conditions other, of course, than those in which she is moved as she ought to be. And they are no less likely to assert externalism as self-evident than are internalists so to treat internalism. Thus, although the dispute between internalists and externalists is vigorous, it also frequently stalls frustratingly. And because the issue is so central for so many other important debates, this has had unfortunate consequences for fundamental moral philosophy generally.

INTERNALISM AMONG THE BRITISH MORALISTS

This book was born of two convictions: first, that more systematic exploration of the rationales for (and species of) internalism in ethics would be desirable; and, second, that British moral philosophy of the early modern period saw the development of some of the first inter-

28. For a recent example, see Samuel Scheffler, *Human Morality* (New York: Oxford University Press, 1992), pp. 33n, 74, 90, 135. Scheffler does not actually claim that moral imperatives are *not* categorical – in the sense of providing any agent overriding reasons that are unconditional on any aspect of her psychology other than what makes her subject to them – just that internalism makes it implausible that this is so.
29. Peter Railton accepts it for the case of intrinsic, nonmoral value. See "Facts and Values," *Philosophical Topics* 14 (1986): 5–31, at 9.
30. See, for example, Christine Korsgaard, "Kant's Analysis of Obligation: The Argument of *Foundations* I," *Monist* 73 (1989): 311–40, esp. p. 311, and *The Sources of Normativity*, Tanner Lecture on Human Values, Clare Hall, Cambridge University, November 1992.

nalist theories of moral obligation and practical normativity in the history of ethics. I hope that the first conviction will be evident enough to contemporary readers. Regarding the second, my aim is not so much to prove it as to illustrate it in detail by examining the way different internalist accounts of moral obligation and the normative, and different rationales for such accounts, function within the ethics of British moralists as diverse as Hobbes, Cudworth, Cumberland, Locke, Shaftesbury, Hutcheson, Butler, and Hume. Only through such an examination, I believe, can a similar conviction arise in the reader.

My objective is thus less a comprehensive study of early modern British theories of obligation than an investigation of the origins (and differing natures) of the various internalisms found in these British writers.[31] Morality obligates, they variously argued, through the motives of a deliberating moral agent – perhaps inescapable, perhaps conclusive, perhaps intrinsically moral. Insofar as we may be said to "experience" the pull or bindingness of obligation, they held, it is from a practical point of view, as *agents*. Again, this view is not to be confused with a different kind of existence internalism that holds the knowledge or perception of value and normativity to be inherently practical. Versions of that view are as old as the ancients. And, as I mentioned, it was also the position of the British rational intuitionists. What was new with the early modern British internalists was a view about the metaphysics of the normative, namely, that what obligation itself consists in is inherently practical: a motive for an agent deliberating about what to do. On this view, the normative's very way of being is practical, via its role within rational deliberation from the agent's point of view. This anticipates Kant's distinction between two viewpoints: theoretical and practical, or observer's and agent's.[32]

---

31. Thus the period 1640–1740, which appears in the title of this book, is meant to cover the time from the appearance of Hobbes's *Elements of Law* in 1640 and *De Cive* in 1642 to the publication of the ethical parts of Hume's *Treatise* in 1740. (I do, however, also discuss some ideas in Hume's second *Enquiry*.)
32. Immanuel Kant, *Groundwork of the Metaphysics of Morals*, Ak. pp. 450–53. In *On the Law of Nature and Nations* (1672), Pufendorf makes a distinction between "physical entities" and "moral entities" that is in the same neighborhood. Moral aspects of situations are, he says, distinct and underivative from "the intrinsic nature of the physical properties of things" (1.i.4). The latter compose a realm of things "already existent and physically complete," to which the moral realm is entirely additional. Physical entities are distinguished by their varying capacities directly "to produce physical motion or change," whereas the "active force" of moral entities consists "only in this, that it is made clear to men along what line they

What led these writers to attempt to explain moral obligation and normativity in internalist terms? And how did these different rationales lead to different internalist theories? Since early modern philosophers were rarely much better at spelling out their most fundamental philosophical motives than are contemporary thinkers, answering these questions is a delicate and complicated task of interpretation. We must attempt to tease out assumptions and draw inferences (sometimes intricate) to make the best philosophical sense of texts, both of what is said and what is not. Answering these questions, however, promises dividends of two sorts. First, it will help us better to understand and appreciate one of the most exciting periods in the history of ethical thought. And second, since these are some of the first attempts to think through the relation between 'ought' and motivation in the way that that issue still presents itself on the current philosophical scene, understanding what lies behind them should also shed significant light on the present-day debate concerning internalism, and on the many other issues that currently depend on it.

TWO INTERNALIST TRADITIONS: EMPIRICAL NATURALIST AND AUTONOMIST

EMPIRICAL NATURALIST INTERNALISM

One of the most remarkable features of the early history of internalism is that it developed within two very different traditions of British moral thought, for very different reasons. An *empirical naturalist* tradition, comprising Hobbes, Cumberland, Hutcheson, Hume, and, in most moods, Locke, was driven primarily by the desire to account for normativity in a way consistent with an empiricist epistemology and naturalist metaphysics. In calling this tradition naturalist, I do not mean to imply that all these philosophers believed that nothing exists that is not natural, that there is no supernatural realm.[33] Rather, philosophers of this tradition had an empirical naturalist *element* to their ethics – namely, the desire to account for normativity

should govern their liberty of acting" (1.i.4). At the same time, however, Pufendorf holds that morality, natural law, is created by the "imposition" of God's superior will, and that we are obligated because, owing to God's authority, His sanctions are justified. Thus, he is not an internalist in our sense. For an excellent discussion, see Schneewind, "Pufendorf's Place in the History of Ethics."
33. On this, see Chapter 4, note 8.

in fully natural terms, without reliance on supernatural posits and without attributing to reason any powers beyond those involved in empirical inquiry. For example, whereas Locke says clearly that moral obligation would be unthinkable without God's superior *authority* and supernatural sanctions, "authority" functions as a fifth wheel in his moral psychology, as we shall see. The normative force of morality ultimately depends for him on there being conclusive motives for being moral, albeit guaranteed by the Deity.

Cumberland is perhaps the clearest example of this strategy, since he wears his reductionist aims on his sleeve. His object, he says, is to "resolve . . . [t]he Whole of *moral Philosophy* . . . into *natural Observations* known by the Experience of all Men, or into Conclusions of true *Natural Philosophy*."[34] Cumberland complains that what philosophers and legal theorists have said about obligation or bindingness is confused, unempirical, and "somewhat *obscure* from Metaphors; for the mind of man is not properly tied with bonds" (*TLN*.233). Since nothing "can superinduce a *Necessity* of doing or forbearing any thing, upon a Human Mind deliberating upon a thing future" other than (naturally) inescapable *motives,* Cumberland concludes that obligations cannot consist in anything other than motives that are unavoidable for agents deliberating rationally (*TLN*.233).

The empirical naturalists were anxious not to rely on any view of reason's powers extending beyond what is necessary for empirical inquiry. But there was a difference of emphasis, at least, between those, like Hobbes, who stressed a purely *instrumental* conception and those, like Cumberland and Hutcheson, who argued that the calm, reflective use of theoretical reason can lead creatures with our psychological constitution to new ends, in particular to universal benevolence. Both views agree with the common thesis of empirical naturalist internalism that *obligation consists in motives raised through the use of theoretical reason.* The *instrumental reason* view of normativity holds that moral demands are binding just in case following them is necessary to accomplish ends that inescapably (if contingently) structure human deliberation – for Hobbes, self-preservation. The *calm reflective deliberation* view, by contrast, agrees that reason's powers are exclusively theoretical – by itself, reason

34. Richard Cumberland, Bishop of Peterborough, *A Treatise of the Laws of Nature,* trans. John Maxwell (London, 1727), p. 41; originally published in Latin as *De Legibus Naturæ Disquisitio Philosophica* in 1672. Hereinafter, references will be placed in parentheses in the text, preceded by '*TLN*' when context requires. For full reference, see Chapter 4, n.3.

15

dictates no ends – but holds that it is nonetheless possible for beings with our psychology to come to desire new ends through calm, reflective appreciation of what theoretical reason enables us to know.[35]

In addition to these approaches, another empirical naturalist theory of obligation was developed by British moralists that is internalist in a broad sense, although not in the specific sense of our study, namely, the sentimentalist theories of Hutcheson and Hume.[36] Since moral sentiment can provide no direct motive for morality according to Hume and Hutcheson, their theories of moral obligation are not internalist in our sense. This reveals a deep feature of their ethics. For neither Hutcheson nor Hume does ethics fundamentally concern *regulation of conduct*, not to mention *self*-regulating moral agency.[37] Moral obligation consists in an *observer's* responses when contemplating traits or motives (usually desires for natural goods) *in* moral agents, rather than agency itself. Nor can this response play any direct role in deliberation. Even so, there is an obvious sense in which moral obligation is internal for Hume and Hutcheson as well.

AUTONOMIST INTERNALISM

The other major internalist tradition approaches the problem of obligation from the perspective of what I just remarked is largely absent from the ethics of Hutcheson and Hume, namely, the idea that anyone subject to morality must be a *self-determining moral agent*. Whereas empirical naturalist internalism is inspired by the belief that any acceptable account of obligation must be consistent with what empirical science tells us about the world (including about us), *autonomist internalism* arises from the conviction that a satisfactory theory of obligation must be consistent with the *autonomy of the moral agent*. Broadly speaking, it holds that *obligation consists in conclusive motives raised through the exercise of autonomous practical reasoning* (that is, the

35. It might be held that Cumberland believes that one *formal* dictate is inherent in practical reason, namely, "Pursue the *best* end." See Chapter 4, "The Practical Dictates of Reason, Agreement, and the Best End."
36. Although Hutcheson got the idea of a moral sense from Shaftesbury, Shaftesbury did not attempt to base an account of moral *obligation* directly on it, as did Hutcheson and Hume. There are other reasons for not including Shaftesbury under this heading. First, whereas Hutcheson's (and Hume's) theories of moral sense are empiricist, Shaftesbury's is most usefully viewed as rationalist. And second, although an account of self-determining agency is central to Shaftesbury's account of the obligation to be moral, it is not for either Hutcheson or Hume. Chapter 6 includes a discussion of these points.
37. With the important exception, for Hume, of justice, as I argue in Chapter 10.

practical reasoning that realizes autonomy). We should not suppose, however, that there was a well-developed concept of autonomy available for philosophers of this tradition to make use of in their thinking about obligation. On the contrary, one of the most significant developments of this period was the fashioning of the concept of autonomy *in tandem with* philosophical speculation about moral obligation.

One strand of autonomist internalist thought, the *accountability* view, begins by pondering the connection between obligation and accountability. For Cudworth and Locke, especially, it is distinctive of moral obligation that agents are thought to be accountable for violations. Not just any kind of intelligent being can intelligibly be held accountable – only a being who can determine herself to act as she is obligated. Thus, Locke wrote that he did not see "how any thing can be capable of a Law, that is not a free Agent."[38] And beginning with the second edition of the *Essay*, he worked out an account of the capacity for free, self-determining agency to demonstrate how, on his theories, a moral agent is obligated to do only what she herself would choose to do through the exercise of this capacity. There are places, moreover, where Locke suggests that that is all that obligation really is – a conclusive motive for acting that arises through autonomous practical reasoning.

In Locke, these ideas are placed within an empiricist framework with its distinctive conception of theoretical reason. Lockean self-determination involves a stepping back from present desire so that the agent can then use theoretical reason, and her powers of imagination, vividly to consider the various objects of her desires, and come to a judgment of which course of action promises the greatest long-run pleasure. So understood, "autonomous practical reason" simply puts the agent in contact with independently standing motives; it has no motive power of its own. Thus, for Locke, the internalist formulas "motive raised through the use of theoretical reason" and "motive raised through autonomous practical reasoning" *coincide*. It is with Ralph Cudworth, from whom Locke arguably got many of his ideas about self-determination, that we find the first rationalist autonomist internalism of a sort that looks forward to Kant. Like Kant, Cudworth holds that ethics must be grounded in pure practical reason. But whereas Kant would hold that this motivation must be *formal*,

38. John Locke, *An Essay Concerning Human Understanding*, ed. Peter H. Nidditch (Oxford: Clarendon Press, 1975), p. 74.

Cudworth believed it to be a kind of *love*. Cudworth, however, thinks that to be *obligated* to be moral, to follow a "law of love," agents require not only this source of motivation but a power to draw on it in autonomous deliberation. At this point, Cudworth's ideas are more like Locke's than like the sort of autonomist internalism later to be found in Kant. "Autexousy," as Cudworth calls it, is the agent's capacity to step back from current desires, to survey and draw upon standing motives, which are themselves independent of the exercise of this capacity, including the motive of universal love that pure intellect includes, and to make a motivating judgment of her good on the whole. Only imperfect rational beings have or need the "autexousious power," and only they can be obligated. God is ruled by pure practical reason, by love. He has no need for autexousy, and neither does morality *obligate* Him.

Autonomist internalisms like Locke's and Cudworth's might be called theories of self-*determination* in contrast to self-*regulation*. Both Locke and Cudworth hold that autonomous agents determine conduct by comprehensive, self-reflective judgments of the good – their own good.[39] They require no conception of the normative, as distinct from a concept of their own good, to guide conduct. In particular, autonomous agents need no conception of the *authority* of any motives (for example, of the desire for their own good). By contrast, first Shaftesbury and then, more emphatically, Butler argue that autonomous agency must be self-*regulating*. Rational will and agency require the capacity for self-*governance*, and that demands that the agent be able to distinguish between the "power" and the "authority" of her motives, as Butler puts it.[40] At this point an important difference opens up between Shaftesbury and Butler, since Shaftesbury thinks that agents rightly regard self-love as uniquely authoritative, and Butler stresses that genuine autonomy requires that authority be accorded to motives that root the very possibility of autonomy itself – conscience or the "principle of reflection."

What lies behind autonomist internalisms of the sort represented by Shaftesbury and Butler (and later by Kant) is a *normative theory of the will*. It is a condition of the very possibility of autonomous will,

39. There are important differences, again. Locke is a hedonist about the good, and Cudworth is not. And Cudworth holds, as against Locke, that reason is itself practical and that exercising the loving motive of pure reason is intrinsically good.
40. Joseph Butler, *Fifteen Sermons Preached at the Rolls Chapel* (London, 1726), Sermon II, para. 14.

18

according to these thinkers, that reason be purely practical by enabling a form of *normative judgment* that is intrinsically motivating.[41] As with Locke and Cudworth, obligation for Shaftesbury and Butler consists in conclusive motives raised through exercising the power of autonomy. But there remains a substantial difference that I have masked (and will frequently continue to mask) by the ambiguous phrase "conclusive motive." If we give that phrase a de facto reading, we end up with Locke and Cudworth's view. It is no part of their accounts of autonomy that a self-determining agent herself acts on a normative conception, and so, in order for a motive to be obligating, it is not necessary that the agent *regard it as authoritative,* as being one on which she should act. Rather, a motive inherits normativity by winning a contest of *strength* – not in the agent as she *happens* to be, but as she *would* be were she fully to exercise her power for autonomous practical thought. Locke believes that autonomous practical thought is like what Richard Brandt has called "cognitive psychotherapy" and believes that were a human being fully to engage this process, she would want to perform actions in proportion to her estimate of their expected long-run happiness.[42] What makes her greatest happiness *obligating* is that this would be most compelling in fact were she to deliberate fully in the way that realizes autonomy.

For Shaftesbury and Butler, however, it is critical to autonomy that the agent herself be guided by a normative conception. But this does not mean that, for them, "conclusive motive" in the autonomist internalist formula "conclusive motive raised through autonomous practical reasoning" should be given a fully de jure reading. As it happens, the de jure reading would be true, by their lights. The problem is that a fully de jure reading cannot explicate normativity or its source, since the de jure notion of a conclusive motive – a conclusive *reason* – is itself a normative idea. The formula is thus fully consistent with externalism of the sort represented by rationalist intuitionists such as Clarke, Balguy, and Price, who believe in a nonnatural order of normative facts, independent of the operation of practical rea-

41. Thus Kant: "Everything in nature works in accordance with laws. Only a rational being has the power to act *in accordance with his idea* of laws – that is, in accordance with principles – and only so has he a *will*. Since *reason* is required to derive actions from laws, the will is nothing but practical reason." *Groundwork of the Metaphysics of Morals,* Ak. p. 412, trans. by H. J. Paton (New York: Harper & Row, 1964), p. 80.
42. Richard Brandt, *A Theory of the Good and the Right* (Oxford: Oxford University Press, 1979), pp. 11–12.

son.[43] To get the distinctive character of Shaftesbury's and Butler's autonomist internalism, we need the following: *Obligation consists of motives the agent would herself regard as conclusive (de jure) were she fully to exercise the capacity for autonomous practical reasoning.* For internalism of this sort, the source of genuine normativity is what would have this status in an autonomous agent's own practical reasoning.[44]

It might be argued that in advancing a normative theory of the will, Shaftesbury and Butler were drawing out implications already there in ideas of Locke and Cudworth. Both Cudworth and Locke sharply distinguish between any desire or preference an agent might happen to have and her *will*, which is more properly *hers*. Unlike the former, they argue, volition involves a kind of *command* the agent issues to herself. And both use normative terms in attempting to characterize this idea. Here, for example, is Locke: "*Volition*, 'tis plain, is an Act of the Mind knowingly exerting that Dominion it takes it self to have over any part of the Man."[45] But if this is right, then will itself requires some notion of *internal authority*.

It is interesting to speculate that it can hardly be an accident that this conception of the will, as the capacity to make demands *of oneself*, should arise in the attempt to understand and defend the distinctively modern conception of morality, namely, that of a set of demands that are binding on all rational moral persons. How else, after all, *could* demands necessarily bind any rational agent unless they were somehow rooted in autonomous rational will itself?

A NEW HISTORIOGRAPHY?

I hope the reader has been convinced, by this point, that a study of the British moralists on obligation might yield significant philosophical benefits, including, perhaps, some clarification of the issues underlying contemporary debates about internalism. Such a study also promises substantial historiographical insights. As reflected in the structure of Selby-Bigge's original anthology, the history of this

43. In Chapter 11, I contrast this sort of view, which agrees with Butler and Shaftesbury (and Kant) in having a normative theory of rational will, with their strain of autonomist internalism.
44. It would, however, still be true that an agent would have motivation to do what is obligatory were she fully to exercise her power of autonomous practical thinking. According to autonomist internalism of this sort, the autonomous normative judgment of conclusive reason in which obligation consists is itself intrinsically motivating.
45. *Essay*, pp. 240–41.

period has most frequently been construed as a debate between rationalists ("intellectualists" or "intuitionists") and empiricists ("sentimentalists"). But although this framework is useful for certain purposes, it is also distorting in crucial respects, some of which can be brought out by focusing on the issue of internalism. To begin with, of course, there are important seventeenth-century British empirical naturalists who are not sentimentalists: for example, Hobbes, Cumberland, and Locke. This is no objection to Selby-Bigge's scheme, since it was concerned with the eighteenth century. But there are other, more worrisome problems. Cudworth, for example, is usually classed along with Clarke, Balguy, Price, and Wollaston as rationalist/intellectualist. Clarke, Balguy, and Price make up a recognizable group. But whereas Price borrows a good deal from Cudworth's general critique of empiricist epistemology, Cudworth differs from these thinkers radically on fundamental issues of the metaphysics of morals. As I shall seek to show, Cudworth, unlike the rational intuitionists, holds a rationalism of *practical* reason. His is a position much closer to Kant's (and, actually, to Shaftesbury's) than anything in Clarke.[46]

The orthododox classification of Shaftesbury as a sentimentalist is appropriate in one way, but his moral sense theory is radically different from Hutcheson's, even if Hutcheson got the basic idea from him. Shaftesbury's fundamental philosophical orientation has more affinities to Stoicism, Neoplatonism, and Cambridge Platonism, especially as represented by Cudworth, than to Hutcheson. His is actually a kind of rationalist sentimentalism. For him, moral sense is no contingent response, but the sharing, by a rational being, of the same ordering principle involved in rationally creative (moral) action.

Most important, I think, this study reveals within British moral philosophy an autonomist internalist tradition that has never before been described. Particularly in the form advanced by Shaftesbury and Butler – interconnecting obligation with a normative theory of the will – this tradition constituted the most important steps taken before Rousseau in the direction of Kant's idea that the bindingness of moral demands is entailed by the autonomy of the will.

Finally, I hope this study will help put into the hands of readers several fascinating philosophical texts they might not otherwise

46. And Wollaston is yet another kind of rationalist, a *reductive* rationalist who attempts to show that actions express propositions and that all immoral actions express false ones. See Chapter 11.

have encountered. Hutcheson has recently been rediscovered, and interest in Hobbes, Locke, Butler, and Hume has remained steady or increased in the last several decades, but the works of Cudworth, Cumberland, and Shaftesbury continue to be largely unread by all but the most dedicated specialists. It is my hope to make evident, however, both how central these texts are to one of the most exciting periods in the history of ethical thought and how enduring their intrinsic philosophical interest continues to be.

Chapter 2

Culverwell and Locke:
classical and modern natural law

An excellent way to begin to appreciate the profound changes that philosophical thinking about obligation was undergoing in seventeenth-century Britain is to juxtapose Nathaniel Culverwell and John Locke. Here are two thinkers whose views are superficially very similar, at least when we compare Culverwell to the Locke of *Essays on the Law of Nature*.[1] Indeed, it has been argued that Culverwell's *Discourse of the Light of Nature* is an important source of Locke's main doctrines in the *Essays*.[2] But though similar on the surface, their views have utterly different philosophical underpinnings. Whereas Culverwell writes still within the classical tradition of natural law, Locke is a modern. He rejects the natural teleology necessary both to ensure a coincidence between duty and interest and to give classical natural law its normativity. And so he has to confront the modern problematic of moral obligation.

Beginning with this comparison requires us to proceed out of

1. Composed in the 1660s, and deposited in the Lovelace Collection in the Bodleian Library at Oxford, Locke's manuscripts on natural law were first published as *Essays on the Law of Nature*, translated and edited, with an introduction, by W. von Leyden (Oxford: Clarendon Press, 1954). A more recent translation is *Questions Concerning the Law of Nature*, translated and edited, with an introduction, by Robert Horwitz, Jenny Strauss Clay, and Diskin Clay (Ithaca: Cornell University Press, 1990). Because von Leyden's translation is more familiar, I will refer to it hereafter, parenthetically in the text, as *Essays* when context requires it. See the translators' introduction to *Questions*, however, for a critique of some aspects of von Leyden's translation.

   There are three manuscripts, which von Leyden labeled A, B, and C. Von Leyden and Horwitz, Clay, and Clay agree that C, which is largely an error-ridden copy of A and B made by Locke's amanuensis, probably around 1681, is useless for purposes of establishing a text. (For C's probable date, see *Questions*, p. 69.) And they agree that B was composed in 1664, and A some time between 1654 and 1664, but probably close to the latter date.

2. By von Leyden. See *Essays*, pp. 41–43.

chronological order. Hobbes is the earliest (and, in many ways, most radically original) of the writers we shall be considering, whereas Culverwell's *Discourse of the Light of Nature* was published in 1652, one year after the appearance of Hobbes's *Leviathan* and ten years after the first Latin edition of *De Cive*. But Culverwell's *Discourse* was largely unaffected by the main seventeenth-century philosophical currents – in particular, by the powerfully influential Hobbesian project of an empirical-naturalist ethics without final causes, drawing "consequences from the passions of men."[3] Culverwell's main source of inspiration was Suarez, not Hobbes, Selden, or even Grotius, although he frequently referred to him.[4] Comparing Culverwell with Locke will help us grasp at the outset, therefore, the sea change taking place in early modern thinking about obligation.

Like Suarez, Culverwell aimed to steer a middle course between "realist" natural lawyers who argued that a natural moral law exists that obligates intrinsically, independent of its relation to the dictates of any superior authority, and voluntarists who maintained that obligation depends entirely on God's arbitrary will. But where Suarez's polar opponents had been Catholic thinkers such as Vasquez and Ockham, Culverwell found himself flanked by Protestant realists such as Grotius and Hooker, on the one side, and Calvinist voluntar-

---

3. Thomas Hobbes, *Leviathan*, chapter IX, para. 4. No doubt this is partly explained by the fact that it was written more than six years before publication, in the years 1645–46. See Nathaniel Culverwell, *An Elegant and Learned Discourse of the Light of Nature*, ed. Robert A. Greene and Hugh MacCallum (Toronto: University of Toronto Press, 1971), p. xiii, for evidence of the date of composition. This is a very useful edition, with helpful notes and an informative introduction. The *Discourse* was originally published (in 1652) together with "several other treatises." A facsimile edition was published by Garland (New York and London) in 1978. Knud Haakonssen, "Moral Philosophy and Natural Law: From the Cambridge Platonists to the Scottish Enlightenment," *Political Science* 40 (1988): 97–110, is also helpful on Culverwell and the early modern context; see esp. pp. 104–5.

   References to the *Discourse* will hereafter be to chapter and page number from Greene and MacCallum and will be placed parenthetically in the text, preceded by *Dis* when context requires.

   The quote from Hobbes is from Hobbes's table of the "several subjects of knowledge" in *Leviathan* I.xi.

4. Francisco Suarez's great work was *De Legibus ac Deo Legislatore* (1612). For an English translation, see *A Treatise on Laws and God the Lawgiver*, trans. Gwladys L. Williams, Ammi Brown, and John Waldron, rev. Henry Davis., S.J., with intr. by James Brown Scott, in *Selections from Three Works of Francisco Suarez, S. J.*, vol. 2 (Oxford: Clarendon Press, 1944), reprinted by Carnegie Endowment for International Peace. Selections from this are included in Schneewind, *Moral Philosophy from Montaigne to Kant*, vol. 1, pp. 67–87, which contains a very helpful introduction to modern Continental and British moral philosophy.

   Richard Tuck discusses John Selden in *Natural Rights Theories*, pp. 82–100.

ists, on the other. Culverwell's middle course, like Suarez's before him, was to hold that the existence of genuine moral law, and hence of moral *obligation*, depends on the commands of a superior authority, on God's will, but that God's dictates are inherent in the metaphysical nature of His creation, hence of His subjects, and thus are not imposed arbitrarily from the outside. Human acts can accord or conflict with human rational essence independently of any positive command, therefore, and the grounds for God's commands derive entirely from this "conveniency" or "disconvenience." Only because God actually commands us to perform the former and forbear the latter are we "formally" or "morally" *obligated* to do so, but even without authoritative edict these would be no less intrinsically compelling or repellent to our rational nature. Culverwell notes without dissent Suarez's terming the latter a "natural obligation," but he is careful to stress that, strictly, it constitutes only a "just *foundation* for a Law" and nothing with the "height and perfection" or the "formality" of a law itself (VI.51).[5]

As I have said, this view is superficially very similar to the position that Locke takes in his *Essays*. In fact, Locke held consistently throughout his mature philosophical life that, as he put it in the *Essay*, "the only true touchstone of *moral Rectitude*" is "that Law which God has set to the actions of Men" (352).[6] God can create this law because of His superior authority: "He has a right to do it, we are his Creatures" (352). And this authority makes His law obligating for us. However, because God's commands are not groundless, moral obligation has a natural basis. Moreover, in the *Essays* Locke adopts some of the same technical vocabulary Suarez and Culverwell had used to express this idea. Rational human nature gives rise, he writes, to a *debitum naturale*, Suarez's phrase, which his translator renders as "natural obligation" (*Essays*. VI.180–1). And, Locke adds, it follows "just as necessarily from the nature of man that, if he is a man, he is bound to love and worship God and also to fulfil other things appropriate (*convenientia*) to the rational nature" (*Essays*. VII.199).[7]

---

5. *A Treatise on Laws and God the Lawgiver*, p. 225.
6. John Locke, *An Essay Concerning Human Understanding* (1690), ed. Peter H. Nidditch (Oxford: Clarendon Press, 1975). References hereafter will be given parenthetically, preceded by *Essay* when context does not make it superfluous.
7. 'Convenientia' is used by Suarez and Grotius (Culverwell uses 'conveniency'; see below) to express the idea that an act can be in harmony or conformity with rational human essence. Grotius's "realist" definition of the law of nature is "a dictate of right reason, which points out that an act, according as it is or is not in

But appearances here are deceiving, as we shall see. Culverwell's view is largely cast within a Thomistic metaphysics and epistemology, with some Christian Platonist elements mixed in. It postulates a perfectionist/teleological human essence – in effect, a final cause – and epistemic access to this essence as the basis for human knowledge of natural law. Locke could hardly accept these metaphysical and epistemological ideas. He agreed with Culverwell that the law of nature binds us formally because it is God's will and God has authority over us. And he also agreed that God's law can be obligating only if moral agents are guaranteed a conclusive rational motive for following it in the fact that doing so is for their own good. But what secured the latter connection for Culverwell was a teleological metaphysical order implicit in the Thomistic conception of eternal law, mediating the relation between natural law and the goods of individuals subject to it. Since natural law is an expression of eternal law, and eternal law specifies the harmoniously ordered perfections, and thus goods, of each, both natural law's normativity and its coincidence with interest are guaranteed by final causes. This Locke could not accept, and so he was forced to rethink the fundamental relations between morality, obligation, interest, and rational motive.

NATHANIEL CULVERWELL

ETERNAL LAW

A good way into Culverwell's thought is through his use of the Thomistic idea of *eternal law*, since this joins together his teleological metaphysics of nature with his theory of law. The eternal law is, Culverwell writes, "the spring and original of all Lawes" including natural law (*Dis.* v.34). Culverwell quotes with approval Thomas's doctrine that since natural law is "nothing but *participatio Legis aeternae in Rationali creatura* [the participation of the eternal law in the rational creature],"[8] this "imprinting" of eternal law "upon the

> conformity [convenientia] with rational nature, has in it a quality of moral baseness or moral necessity; and that, in consequence, such an act is either forbidden or enjoined by the author of nature, God" (Hugo Grotius, *The Law of War and Peace*, pp. 38–39). To this Grotius adds: "[T]he acts in regard to which such a dictate exists are, in themselves, either obligatory or not permissible, and so it is understood that necessarily they are enjoined or forbidden by God" (39).

8. The quote from Aquinas is from *Summa Theologica*, Ia IIae, 91.2, as translated in Anton C. Pegis, ed., *The Basic Writings of Saint Thomas Aquinas*, p. 750. It is also quoted in Suarez, *De Legibus*, I,iii,9.

breast of a Rational being" means that "eternal Law was in a manner incarnated in the Law of Nature" (v.34).

Thomistic eternal law, we recall, is the "exemplar" or archetype of the natural order existing in God – an ideal or "model" of each natural thing harmoniously ordered with every other thing. This qualifies as law by Aquinas's most general definition: "a rule or measure of acts, whereby man is induced to act or restrained from acting."[9] The relevant inducement is guaranteed metaphysically; eternal law specifies for each a perfection (and good) essential to its nature *as end*. "[T]he exemplar of divine wisdom, as moving all things to their due end, bears the character of law. Accordingly, the eternal law is nothing else than the exemplar of divine wisdom, as directing all actions and movements."[10]

We shall consider presently Culverwell's claim that, by itself, eternal law is insufficient to create genuine obligation. At this point, however, I want to stress his agreement with the teleological metaphysics inherent in Thomas's notion of eternal law. Every natural thing has an intrinsic end it naturally seeks in a teleological order ordained by God. "At the command of this Law," Culverwell writes, "all created beings took their several ranks and stations, and put themselves in such operations as were best agreeable and conformable to their beings. By this Law all essences were ordained to their ends by most happy and convenient means" (v.36).[11] This includes rational beings. They too have ends that are no less intrinsic to their nature.

[Grant] only the being of man, and you cannot but grant this also, that there is such a constant conveniency and Analogy, which some objects have with its Essence, as that it cannot but encline to them, and that there is such an irreconcileable Disconvenience, such an Eternal Antipathy between it and other objects, as that it must cease to be what it is before it can come neer them. (VI.51)

Culverwell is a classical natural lawyer in respect of holding that both the content and the inherent *practicality* of natural law derive from eternal law. Eternal law specifies an ideal for each being, its good, that is built into its essence as end. Since the good of each is defined in relation to this perfectionist/teleological scheme, a harmony of goods and, given the relation between natural and eternal

9. *Summa Theologica*, Ia IIae, 90.1, *Basic Writings*, p. 743.
10. *Summa Theologica*, Ia IIae, 93.1, *Basic Writings*, p. 763.
11. Note that Culverwell here drops his scruples about the use of 'law'.

law, a coincidence between duty and the interest are metaphysically guaranteed. Moreover, since this ideal is included in the essence of each person as end, it is inherently practical: It structures agents' deliberations as something *to be sought*.

OBLIGATION

But while eternal law determines the content and inherent practicality of natural law, it does not, Culverwell thinks, explain any obligation to follow it. And, for this reason, it does not yet account for its formal character *as law* – its "binding vertue," which, he says, is the "sinew," "life[,] and soul of a Law" (IV.30). Eternal law is "a binding determination" for all natural creatures, but it can only *"fortiter inclinare* [strongly incline]" irrational beings. (V.36). As promulgated to rational beings through their natural reason, however, it can *"formaliter obligare* [formally bind]" (V.36). Only rational beings can genuinely be obligated through the eternal law, since only they can grasp it and their relation to its author, and obligation is "the very forme and essence of a Law" (IV.30).

Culverwell follows Suarez in rejecting Vasquez's view that "the formality of this Law [of Nature] consists only in that harmony and proportion, or else that discord and disconvenience, which such and such an object, and such and such an action has with a Rational Nature" (VI.49).[12] No "naked Essence," Culverwell writes, can "lay a Moral engagement upon it self, or binde its own being" (VI.49). Law and obligation presuppose *superior authority*. We cannot be bound by our essence, for "this would make the very same being superior to it self, as it gives a Law, and inferiour to it self, as it must obey it" (VI.49). The "binding vertue" of law requires a superior's will. "The will of a Law-giver makes a Law" (IV.31). God's nature is no less a standard for His acts than human nature is for ours, but God cannot be obligated. He could be only if He were subject to the authority of some other being, as we are to Him (VI.49).

When Culverwell writes that the law of nature is both "intrinsecal and essential to a rational creature," he means to stress both 'rational' and 'creature' (VI.39): "[F]or such a creature as a creature has a superiour to whose Providence and disposing it must be subject, and then as an intellectual creature 'tis capable of a moral government"

---

12. Presumably Culverwell is using Vasquez at least partly as a stand-in for more contemporary Grotian realists.

(VI.39). Both elements are necessary. God has supreme authority over us because we are "totally dependent" on Him as His creatures (VI.53). But God's authority can only obligate beings who "are capable of a moral government." The law "God has set . . . to the waves" and other nonrational entities are "at the most but *inclinationes, & pondera* [tendencies and gravitations], and not the fruits of a legislative power" (IV.28).

In arguing that the capacity for "moral government" is necessary for a being to be subject to obligation, Culverwell sounds an important theme for our study. This idea, put together with the notion that moral government must be *self*-government – autonomous or self-determining – constituted the core of one significant tradition of seventeenth- and eighteenth-century thought that sought to understand obligation *internally*, in this case through its role in the practical reasoning of a free or self-determining rational agent. Culverwell suggests central elements of this tradition when he writes:

Law 'tis founded in intellectuals, . . . it supposes a Noble and free-borne creature, for where there is no Liberty, there's no Law, a Law being nothing else but a Rational restraint and limitation of absolute Liberty. Now all Liberty is *Radicaliter in Intellectu* [rooted in the intellect]; and such Creatures as have no light, have no choice. (VI.42)

For Culverwell, however, "moral government" is more like obedience to a wise parent than mature self-regulation. The relevant capacity lies in the ability to follow God's orders, "to be guided and commanded by one that is infinitely more wise and intelligent than it self is; and that mindes its welfare more than it self can" (VI.39). Only by using our intellectual capacity to discover the commands of a superior authority, he thinks, can we regulate our conduct by a conception of law.

Culverwell notes that Suarez had called the "conveniency" and "disconvenience" that can obtain between acts and an agent's rational essence – quite independently of any consideration of authoritative command – a "natural obligation." "Everything," Suarez had written, "has towards itself, in a sense, the obligation of doing nothing inconsistent with its own nature."[13] "But," Suarez then added, "in addition to this, the law imposes a special moral obligation which we speak of as an effect of that law."[14] Culverwell endorses the second thought: "[M]oral obligation" requires "a Com-

13. *A Treatise on Laws and God the Lawgiver*, p. 225.
14. Ibid., pp. 225–26.

mand from some Superiour Powers" (VI.51). But he is evidently less than fully comfortable calling a "conveniency" between an act and the agent's rational essence an *obligation*, even in a sense. At best, it is "a just foundation for a Law." Genuine obligation and law cannot exist without authoritative command.

Even so, Culverwell is committed to thinking that human beings would have roughly equally weighty rational motives for doing what natural law demands whether or not an obligating law required it of them. Some goods have "such a Magnetical power . . . as must needs allure and attract a Rational Being" (VI.50). This "intrinsical loveliness . . . does not depend upon an external command, but by its own worth must needs win upon the Soul" (VI.50). And contrariwise for the evils natural law proscribes. Natural *law* requires God's commands, but these simply indicate what we already have sufficient rational motive for doing by virtue of our rational essence without any "external command." God's command does add *some* reason, since we are obligated, inter alia, to obey God (VI.52). But even without this motive, the "conveniency" with rational essence that provides natural law's "just foundation" already gives us adequate reason.

Since Culverwell conceives of rational essence in teleological terms, he believes that what God commands of each agent is simply what is requisite to the agent's own good or happiness: "such acts as should be advantageous" (VI.52). Thus God does no more than "binde man to his own happinesse" (VI.52).[15] Guidance by God's commands involves no motives, therefore, other than those supplied by the agent's own rational good. It follows that the capacity to govern oneself by following a law, which Culverwell holds to be necessary for obligation, is itself effected entirely through motives provided by one's good.

Culverwell evidently accepts the classical natural law tradition's assumption of a metaphysically guaranteed harmony of human interests. If God commands each to do what will achieve her good, this must be because the goods of each are in harmony with the goods of others. So Culverwell can say, indifferently, either that natural law requires what is for the agent's good or, as in his rendering of Saint Thomas's definition, that natural law is "a rational Ordinance for the advancing of the publike good" (IV.31). The two must ultimately coincide.

15. See also VII.57.

NATURAL LAW

Natural law obligates agents only if they can discover it. But how does Culverwell think we do this? Commentators have noted that, despite his frequent talk of God's "imprinting" eternal law on rational beings, Culverwell quite explicitly rejects innate knowledge and, moreover, suggests an epistemology based more on sense experience and "discoursive" reason (xi.81, 83). In fact, this is sometimes indicated as evidence of fundamental agreement with, indeed influence on, Locke.[16] It is impossible, however, to piece together any systematic epistemology from Culverwell's scattered remarks about the sources of knowledge. He rejects what he identifies as the Platonic notion of "connate Ideas" and the doctrine of reminiscence (xi.81–82). And he endorses what he presents as Aristotle's view that "the windows of sense" must be "set open" before the "many sparks and appearances fly from variety of objects to the understanding," making knowledge possible. "Thus," he writes, "the Candle of knowledge is lighted" (xi.81).

Fortunately, we need not worry about the details of Culverwell's view of how the understanding, prompted by sense and working in a "discoursive way," grasps natural law (xi.83). More important for our purposes is what Culverwell thinks the understanding can grasp, namely, the eternal law and, with it, rational human essence. Culverwell distinguishes three categories of natural moral precept we can know. Among the "fresh springs of Common and Fountain-Notions [that] are in the Soul of Man, for the watering of his Essence," are included, first, the "first and Radical Principles" (vii.54). As examples he gives Aquinas's "good is to be sought, evil avoided," along with "happiness is to be striven for" and the negative form of the golden rule, "[D]o not do to others, what you do not wish to have done to yourself" (vii.54). Reason derives a second rank of "particular and more defined principles" from these fundamental principles:

16. First, by von Leyden, *Essays*, pp. 40–1. Greene and MacCallum take note of von Leyden's claims in the course of a very helpful and balanced discussion of Culverwell's epistemological views. They do not comment specifically on the similarities of Locke's and Culverwell's views in this respect. Despite some "minor doubts," however, they accept von Leyden's claim that Locke's and Culverwell's theories of natural law are fundamentally similar. See Greene and MacCallum, pp. xxix–xxxiv.

In *John Locke and the Way of Ideas* (London: Oxford University Press, 1956), John Yolton argues that Culverwell should be interpreted as rejecting only a naive form of the theory of innateness, while retaining some version of the theory: see pp. 41–3.

for instance, that "we must maintain justice, we must worship God, we must live temperately" (vii.55).[17] Finally, there comes a third rank of "conclusions, clearly inferences which, however, cannot be known without intellectual effort; as that lying, theft and the like are wicked" (vii.55). Why it is worth remarking that the third takes intellectual effort to grasp, if our knowledge of any rank requires a discursive inference, Culverwell does not say.

What philosophical work does the concept of obligation actually do in Culverwell's thought, if he thinks we have compelling reasons to act as we are obligated independent of our being obligated to do so? If, to take one of Culverwell's examples, a person has conclusive reasons not to lie that are independent of her obligation not to, why does it matter whether she is obligated? Or, to put the question in Suarez's terms, what does *moral* obligation matter if we already have natural obligation? Culverwell's answer, I believe, has to do with *accountability* and with justified punishment. A person can have conclusive reasons for doing something and still not be accountable to anyone for not doing it. This is God's situation, according to Culverwell. If God makes a promise, He will have conclusive reason to keep it. Indeed, "we may justly conceive him necessitated to [do so], by vertue of that indissoluble connexion and concatenation between these two Acts, which does in a manner knit and unite them into one" (vi.52). Nonetheless, God is not accountable to anyone; He could not be. He could be, Culverwell thinks, only if there were some being with the authority to punish Him, or in whose name He could be punished. Likewise, neither can a being obligate itself. If it could, it would have to be able to "inflict upon it self such a punishment as is answerable to the violation of it" (vi.50). But no being "would be willing or able to punish it self in so high a measure as such a transgression would meritoriously require" (vi.50).

ACCOUNTABILITY

What moral obligation adds for Culverwell, then, is accountability. Without it, we would not lack reason, say, to tell the truth, but we could nonetheless lie with impunity. We could lie and rightly think we were responsible to no one, not even ourselves, for so acting. This

17. This is Greene and MacCallum's translation of Culverwell's Latin, as is the next passage quoted in the text.

is what God's obligating commands provide: the necessary conditions for the possibility of moral accountability:

[T]he Light of Nature will reveal and disclose thus much: That a being totally dependent upon another, essentially subordinate and subject to it, must also be accountable to it for every provocation and rebellion: And for the violation of so good a Law, which he has set it. (vi.53)

As we shall see, the relation between moral obligation and accountability was a significant strand of the autonomist internalist tradition in early modern British moral thought. Cudworth and, in some moments, Locke were especially concerned to arrive at an understanding of obligation that would guarantee that moral agents can reasonably be held accountable for doing what they are obligated to do. And both held that this could be so only if it is guaranteed that moral agents can freely determine themselves so to act. Because connection to self-determining practical reasoning is necessary to reasonable accountability, in their thinking, so also is self-determination connected to moral obligation. Indeed, there are points where both seem to be suggesting that obligation just consists in the existence of motives engaged through self-determining deliberation.

Although he holds no brief for the idea of autonomy, Culverwell clearly feels the pull of the idea that agents can be obligated only if they can govern themselves by law, and that this requires that they be guaranteed rational motives to do so. But although he says that this involves the law's presenting itself as a "rational restraint" (vi.42), his view entails that the motives be provided by considerations of the agent's good entirely independent of any issue of law, obligation, or accountability.

JOHN LOCKE

The theory of the source and nature of moral obligation that Locke advances in his *Essays on the Law of Nature* bears several obvious resemblances to Culverwell's. Locke holds that human beings are bound by a law of nature; that this law derives from God's will because of His superior authority; that it is, nonetheless, also based on human nature; and that God has given humanity cognitive access to this law, not innately but through the capacity to reason from sense experience. As striking as these similarities are, they are underlain by deep differences. It is a symptom of these that the Thomistic notion of eternal law, so central in Culverwell's thought, is almost entirely absent from Locke's.[18] Let us begin, however, with the similarities.

THE RIGHT TO RULE AND THE OBLIGATION TO OBEY

For Locke, as for Culverwell, the power of the law of nature to obligate those subject to it derives from the *authority* of its source. God is our superior by Whom we are ruled with *right*. His commands create obligations. "It is pretty clear," Locke writes,

that all the requisites of a law are found in natural law. For, in the first place, it is the decree of a superior will, wherein the formal cause of a law appears to consist; . . . Secondly, it lays down what is and what is not to be done, which is the proper function of a law. Thirdly, it binds men, for it contains in itself all that is requisite to create an obligation. (111–13)[19]

And Locke more or less agrees with Culverwell's thesis that God's right to rule derives from His creatures' being entirely dependent on Him. We discover this authority, Locke says, when we see that "there exists another more powerful and wiser agent who at his will can bring us into the world, maintain us, and take us away" (153). Inferring "this on the evidence of the senses, reason lays down that there must be some superior power to which we are rightly subject,

18. Locke does mention Saint Thomas's notion of eternal law in the course of giving his third argument for the existence of natural law. Indeed, he appears to *rely* on it, arguing that it would be odd if God had prescribed the "form and measure" of all other beings sufficient for their being governed by eternal law, and not also have done so for human beings (*Essays.*117). In his very next argument, however, Locke asserts that human "social intercourse or union" depends on "the fulfilment of pacts" and "a definite constitution of the state and form of government," and that both require an obligation that depends on external authority (*Essays.*119). Evidently, in whatever sense Locke thinks eternal law establishes a "form and measure" of human conduct, it is insufficient to give agents reasons to cooperate with each other without actual command (backed, as we shall see, by sanctions).
19. "[T]his law contains all that is necessary to make a law binding. For God, the author of this law, has willed it to be the rule of our moral life. . . . The result is that, since nothing else is required to impose an obligation but the authority and rightful power of the one who commands and the disclosure of his will, no one can doubt that the law of nature is binding on men" (187). This theme is sustained throughout Locke's writings; in the *Essay*, e.g., "what Duty is, cannot be understood without a Law; nor a Law be known, or supposed without a Lawmaker" (74).

namely God" (153–55).[20] We not only were first made by God but also are "constantly preserved" by Him (185). God has a "right of creation" to our obedience[21] (185).

Sometimes Locke seems to hedge on the claim that God's authority consists in this right. Just after having asserted the right in the *Essay,* he adds that God "has Goodness and Wisdom to direct our Actions to that which is best" (352). And in the *Essays,* he says that the obligation of the law of nature "seems to derive partly from the divine wisdom of the law-maker, and partly from the right which the Creator has over His creation" (183). Locke may be introducing an independent element here, but God's wisdom would play an important role in creating obligation even if the latter derived solely from a right of creation. This will be clearer when we consider Locke's views of the interrelations between God, humanity, and natural law below, but even here we can note that, for Locke (at least in his early writings), a person can discover the content of the law of nature through inferring God's will only because he can also infer others of His features, for example, His omniscience. "Knowing god to be a wise agent," Locke writes, a person "cannot but conclude y^t he has that knowledge & that faculty wch he finds in himself above other creatures given him for some use & end."[22] To attribute a specific will to God, we must be able to attribute specific beliefs to Him as well.

Locke makes clear in a variety of places that he takes relation to God's law, and hence to His superior authority, to be necessary not just for moral *obligation,* but for morality to exist in any fashion at all. Indeed, he begins the *Essays* by announcing his assumption that "there will be no one to deny the existence of God, provided he recognizes . . . that there is a thing that deserves to be called virtue or vice" (109). And he adds that "moral good or virtue" can be identified with lawful conduct (109).[23]

---

20. In a later manuscript, Locke says even more explicitly that "the originall & foundation of all Law is dependency. A dependent intelligent being is under the power & direction & dominion of him on whom he depends & must be for the ends appointed him by y^t superior being." "Ethica B," Lovelace Collection (MS c28, fol. 141), quoted by John Colman, *John Locke's Moral Philosophy* (Edinburgh: Edinburgh University Press, 1983), p. 46. This is a superb work, to which I am very much indebted.
21. The idea of God's "right of creation" can be found in Calvin's *Institutio Christianae Religionis* (Geneva, 1559), II.ii.2; *The Institutes of the Christian Religion,* trans. F. L. Battles (Philadelphia: Westminster, 1961).
22. This is from a journal entry dated July 15, 1678. MS f3, pp. 201–2; quoted in Colman, p. 45.
23. Also: "[W]ithout natural law there would be neither virtue nor vice" (119).

Similar remarks can be found throughout Locke's writings, connected, in later years, with a hedonistic theory of the good.[24] Thus, in the *Essay*, Locke contrasts moral good and evil with good and evil *simpliciter*, saying that whereas the latter "are nothing but the Pleasure or Pain, or that which occasions, or procures Pleasure or Pain to us," "*Morally Good and Evil* . . . is only the Conformity or Disagreement of our Voluntary Actions to some Law, whereby Good or Evil is drawn on us, from the Will and Power of the Law-maker" (351).[25]

CONFLICT, RATIONAL MOTIVE, AND DIVINE SANCTION

Already this provides a glimpse of deep disagreements with Culverwell. For Culverwell, God simply commands what accords with the eternal law incorporated in our rational essence. Without His command there would be no obligation to live up to this standard, and we could not be justly punished for failing to do so, but the standard would still exist, intrinsic to our rational essence. To take one of Culverwell's examples, one that is particularly salient for comparison with Locke, stealing another's property is something we have preponderant reason not to do, quite independent of any command of God's. God's commandment simply codifies what is already inherent in His eternal law; owing to our rational essence,

24. An earlier remark, in the same vein as the *Essays*, from Locke's *First Tract on Government* (finished in 1660): "[W]ere there no law there would be no moral good or evil, but man would be left to a most entire liberty in all his actions." *Two Tracts on Government*, ed., trans., and with an introduction by Philip Abrams (Cambridge: Cambridge University Press, 1967), p. 124. Von Leyden maintains that the first place a hedonist theory of the good appears in Locke's writings is in a journal entry of 1676 (which von Leyden reprints), and that he probably developed the view as a result of contact with Gassendists during his time in France in the mid 1670s. See *Essays.*71–73, 263–72. See also Edward A. Driscoll, "The Influence of Gassendi on Locke's Hedonism," *International Philosophical Quarterly* 12 (72): 87–110.
25. A similar remark can be found in "Of Ethick in General," probably composed in the late 1680s: "The difference between moral and natural good and evil is only this; that we call that naturally good and evil, which, by the natural efficiency of the thing, produces pleasure or pain in us; and that is morally good or evil which, by the intervention of the will of an intelligent free agent, draws pleasure or pain after it, not by any natural consequence, but by the intervention of that power." Later in the same work, Locke makes it clear he still believes that such an intervention must be authoritative: "To establish morality, therefore, upon its proper basis . . . we must first prove a law, which always supposes a law-maker; one that has a superiority and right to ordain." Peter King, *The Life of John Locke, with Extracts from His Correspondence, Journals, and Common-Place Books*, vol. 2 (London: Henry Colburn & Richard Bentley, 1830), pp. 128–29, 133. On "Of Ethick in General," see von Leyden's introduction to p. 69.

there is "an inseparable deformity and malignity" in theft, "so that Reason must needs loath it and abominate it" (*Dis*.VI.50).[26] Locke, however, regards moral evil as entirely due to God's command

There are two distinct but related features of Locke's central idea here. One has already been mentioned, namely, that every aspect of Lockean morality derives from God's authoritative will. It is no distortion to say that, for Locke, the idea of morality is a fundamentally *juridical* notion, essentially involving authority, or the right to rule. God's authority is rock bottom, and the notions of moral obligation, moral good, virtue, and vice are all understood in relation to it. The second, which we must now explore, is that God's commands provide agents with reasons for acting that they would otherwise lack. They make theft, for example, unreasonable for agents when it might have been reasonable otherwise. That God's commandment creates a moral obligation not to steal, and in that sense a *moral* reason against theft, follows directly from the first feature. But as we shall see, Locke also thinks both that a moral reason in this sense is nothing an agent can rationally act on – it is not a reason *for acting* – *and* that God's commands must decisively affect agents' rational deliberations; they must give agents reasons for acting that they otherwise would not have had, making choices rational that otherwise would not have been. At just this point, we encounter what is most distinctive about Locke's view, namely, that although what makes God's commands morally obligatory appears (as with Culverwell) to have nothing intrinsically to do with what makes them rationally compelling, *and vice versa*, the two are, nonetheless, necessarily related, since, Locke thinks, the only form in which God *can* make His demands is by providing agents with rational motives to obey them.

We can begin to see how Locke is thinking if we consider the role of divine sanctions in his theory. In the course of arguing that the law of nature cannot be known by "the general consent of men" in Essay V, Locke remarks that it is not "surprising that men think so differently about what is right and good," since they differ even in fundamental metaphysical views, and thus "doubt is thrown upon God and the immortality of souls" (173). Both "God and the soul's immortality," Locke declares, "must be necessarily presupposed if natural law is to exist." We can well understand why Locke must

---

26. This remark is not made about theft in particular, but Culverwell is committed by his general theory to regarding theft in something like this way.

think there can be no law of nature without God, but why is the immortality of the soul necessary? Locke's answer is that "law is to no purpose without punishment." Indeed, he evidently thinks that law is to no purpose without *supernatural* punishment, after death. That is what makes immortality necessary.

This is only implicit in the *Essays*, but Locke makes it quite explicit in the *Essay*. In arguing there against the innateness of moral principles, he says that since "duty cannot be understood without a Law; nor a Law be known, or supposed without a Law-maker, or without Reward and Punishment," it is impossible to suppose innate moral principles "without supposing the *Ideas* of God, of Law," or "of a Life after this, innate" (74). And, in the course of there defining *divine law*, he adds that God, in addition to having "Goodness and Wisdom to direct our Actions to that which is best," also has "the Power to enforce it by Rewards and Punishments, of infinite weight and duration, in another Life." "This," he concludes, "is the only true touchstone of *moral Rectitude*" (352).

Although punishment and reward are central to Locke's theory of natural law in the *Essays*, their theoretical role is made much clearer in his later writings. The *Essay*'s definition of moral good and evil, we recall, brings sanction centrally into account: "the Conformity or Disagreement of our voluntary Actions to some Law, whereby Good or Evil is drawn on us, from the Will and Power of the Law-maker" (*Essay.*351). Locke also indicates there why he thinks this is necessary. The "free Actions of Man" aim at good and the avoidance of evil for himself. Thus,

it would be in vain for one intelligent Being, to set a Rule to the Actions of another, if he had it not in his Power, to reward the compliance with, and punish deviation from his Rule, by some Good and Evil, that is not the natural product and consequence of the Action itself. For that being a natural *Convenience, or Inconvenience, would operate of it self without a Law.* This, if I mistake not, is the true nature of all *Law*, properly so called. (351–52; emphasis added)

For Culverwell, since the law of nature simply replicates an eternal law incorporated in an agent's rational essence – a natural "convenience" and "inconvenience" – it is sufficient that the agent discover eternal law to see conclusive motives for obedience. Granted, Culverwell also thinks that the notion of obligation requires that of liability to punishment for its distinctive sense. But the presence of rational motives for compliance, necessary for an agent to be obligated, does not importantly depend on sanctions. Locke obviously disagrees. He shares Culverwell's view that an agent can be obligated by the law of nature only if discovering it can rationally motivate compliance. What he denies is that, without hope of a good or threat of an evil deriving from *obedience*, and not just as a "natural product and consequence of the Action it self," agents will be guaranteed any such motive.

There are two reasons why this is so. One is that, unlike Culverwell, Locke does not believe that the law of nature simply directs agents to what is for their own good. To the question that forms the basis for Essay VIII, "Is Every Man's Own Interest the Basis of the Law of Nature?" Locke gives a resounding "No" (205). By this he means not what he has already argued in Essay VII, that an act's being obligatory is a different thing from its being in the agent's interest. Culverwell agrees with that. In Locke's words, "all obligation binds conscience and lays a bond on the mind itself, so that not fear of punishment, but a rational apprehension of what is right, puts us under an obligation" (185). For both Culverwell and Locke, obligation must be understood through the juridical notion of superior authority. What Locke is concerned with in Essay VIII is whether *what* God commands, the content of the natural law, is always what furthers the agent's good. Sometimes Locke's negative answer appears to mean just that agents are not free to do whatever they *"judge"* advantageous or whatever will lead to *"immediate* personal advantage" (*Essays*.207; emphases added). But he also makes it clear that he thinks the natural law requires genuine sacrifice. "A great number of virtues," he writes, "and the best of them, consist only in this: that we do good to others at our own loss" (207).

Locke's ultimate position in Essay VIII is that, although what natural law requires is often enough something that would involve genuine sacrifice absent God's commands, nonetheless, *in every case*, the hope of divine reward and fear of punishment make obedience be in the agent's rational interest. Let me quote it at some length.

Utility is not the basis of the law or the ground of obligation, but the consequence of obedience to it. Surely, it is one thing for an action of itself to yield some profit, another for it to be useful because it is in accordance with the law, so that if the law were abolished it would have in it no utility whatever: for example, to stand by one's promise, though it were to one's own hindrance. In fact we must distinguish between an action as such and obedient action, for an action itself can be inexpedient – for example, the restitution of a trust that diminishes our possessions – whereas obedient action is useful in so far as it averts the penalty due to a crime. But this penalty would not be due and hence need not be shunned, if the standard of rightness were immediate advantage. And thus the rightness of an action does not depend on its utility; on the contrary, its utility is a result of its rightness. (215)[27]

Although it is already more or less implicit in the *Essays*, it is only in later writings that Locke makes the second reason explicit. This is that agents can rationally be motivated only by their own good, or, as his later hedonism requires, their own pleasure, and, therefore, that "moral rectitude" can motivate only by being connected to the agent's good.[28]

The pleasure that a man takes in any action or expects as a consequence of it is indeed a Good in it self able & proper to move the will. But the Moral Rectitude of it considered barely in it self is not good or evill nor in any way moves the will but as pleasure & pain either accompanies the action it self or is looked on to be a consequence of it. W^{ch} is evident from the punishments & rewards wch god has annexed to moral rectitude or pravity as proper motives by ye will wch would be needless if moral rectitude were it self good & moral pravity evil.[29]

27. These are, quite literally, Locke's last words on the subject in the *Essays*. He follows them, and concludes the work, with the authoritative closing, "Thus thought, J. Locke, 1664."

28. What von Leyden claims were Locke's earliest thoughts on pleasure and pain are contained in a journal entry for July 16, 1676, which advances a hedonistic theory of desire and the good (MS. Locke f1, pp. 325–47; reprinted in *Essays*.263–72). On Gassendi's influence on Locke in this connection, see E. A. Driscoll, "The Influence of Gassendi on Locke's Hedonism."

   Locke's egoistic hedonism in the *Essay* will be discussed much more fully in Chapter 6. That egoistic considerations are at least powerful human motives and that their direction would not agree with that of natural law without supernatural sanction are evidently presupposed already in the *Essays*. For a general discussion of Locke's ethics that stresses his egoistic hedonism, see Jurgen Sprute, "John Lockes Konzeption der Ethik," *Studia Leibnitiana* 17 (1985): 127–42.

29. Locke titles this 1693 entry to his Commonplace Book "Voluntas." MS C28, fol. 114. It is quoted in Colman, *John Locke's Moral Philosophy*, pp. 48–49. Colman's discussion is especially apt at this point: "'Right' is the central concept in Locke's natural law doctrine, but the law could have no purchase on human conduct unless that which is right were in some way productive of good. 'Good' is the central concept in his moral psychology."

   There are a number of other places where Locke makes similar remarks. Thus: (1) "Nothing can attract a rational agent nor be a cause to it of action but good. That good is only pleasure or greater pleasure or the means to it" ("Ethica" (1692), MS C42, B, fol. 224; quoted in Driscoll, p. 102). (2) "If this [perception of Delight] were wholly separated from all our outward Sensations, and inward Thoughts, we should have no reason to preferr one Thought or Action, to another" (*Essay*.129). (3) "Things then are Good or Evil, only in reference to Pleasure or Pain. That we call Good, which is apt to cause or increase Pleasure or diminish Pain in us; or else to procure, or preserve us the possession of any other

Since agents can be rationally motivated only by their own good, and since the law of nature frequently requires them to sacrifice this good, the law would be vain if it did not supply them with additional interests to obey it (*Essay*.351–52). This explains why both in the *Essay* and in the slightly earlier work "Of Ethick in General" Locke explicitly brings into his definitions of moral good and evil the good and bad consequences of an act (for the agent) caused "by the intervention of the will of an intelligent free agent" ("the Law-maker").[30] And it also explains why, in the *Essays*, Locke assumes that the soul's immortality is entailed by the law of nature (173). Without an immortal soul, reward or punishment beyond the grave would be impossible, and only a "vain" law could issue from God's will. So even in the *Essays* we find Locke writing, "Without natural law there would be neither virtue nor vice, neither the reward of goodness nor the punishment of evil. . . . [M]an would not be bound to do anything but what utility or pleasure might recommend" (*Essays*.119–21). Partly, of course, Locke's point is that without demands with an authoritative source no one would be obligated to do anything (otherwise) inconsistent with his own good. But it is also part of his meaning that without reward and punishment for obedience, any such demand, from an authoritative source, would be "vain" and "to no purpose," even if, per impossibile, it came from God.

Culverwell agreed entirely with Locke's thought that an agent can only be obligated to do what she can have good and sufficient reasons for doing. And they agreed also that such reasons are provided only by the agent's good. Where the disagreement between Locke and Culverwell is primarily located is over the nature of the good and its relation to the law of nature. For Culverwell, a person's good is the chief end intrinsic to her essence, an integral part of an organized whole of goods embodied in eternal law. And the law of nature is simply the eternal law publicized, dictating to each what will achieve her own good in common with others. For Locke, however, there is no such metaphysically assured community of interests. In-

Good, or absence of any Evil" (*Essay*.229). (4) "Men have a natural tendency to what delights, and from what pains them. This universal observation has established past doubt. That the soul has such a tendency to what is morally good, and from what is evil has not fallen under my observation, and therefore I cannot grant it for as being" (Noah Porter, "Marginalia Locke-a-na," *New Englander and Yale Review* 47 (1887): 38). (5) "[N]oe thing could be a rule or a law to them whose observation did not lead to happynesse & whose breach did [not] draw misery after it" (MS C28, fols. 139–40).

30. See King, *The Life of John Locke*, vol. 2, p. 128–29; and *Essay*.351.

deed, Locke believes that the distinctive function of the law of nature is to enable mutually advantageous collective action when it would otherwise be impossible. It is worth seeing why this is so.

In the course of arguing in Book I of the *Essay* that there are no innate practical principles, including moral ones, Locke grants that "Principles of Actions indeed there are lodged in Men's Appetites, but these," he writes, "are so far from being innate Moral Principles, that if they were left to their full swing, they would carry Men to the over-turning of all Morality" (*Essay*.75). "Moral Laws," therefore, must be "set as a curb and restraint to these exorbitant Desires, which they cannot be but by Rewards and Punishments" (75).

That there can be real conflicts between individuals' goods is not merely a position Locke was required to hold by the hedonist theory of good he adopted after the *Essays*. He was deeply committed to it already in his earlier work. The second reason he gives in Essay VIII for holding that the natural law cannot be based on the agent's interest is that if it were, then, because people's interests conflict, this would make it impossible for people jointly to obey it, but "it is impossible that the primary law of nature is such that its violation is unavoidable" (*Essays*.211). The reason is scarcity. The goods nature provides "have been bestowed in a definite way and in a predetermined quantity; they have not been fortuitously produced nor are they increasing in proportion with what men need or covet. Clothes are not born with us, nor do men, like tortoises, possess and carry about shelters" (211). There is, unhappily, no "extension, then and there, of the world's limits" when human need increases. And when one person takes from the common stock of goods the world provides, "he takes away from another man's heap the amount he adds to his own" (211). These themes are more maturely articulated in the *Second Treatise*, but it is evident that Locke is already in the *Essays* preoccupied with issues centering on appropriation and conflict.

Indeed, it is in the preservation of property, in his broad sense, that he there holds the benefits of the law of nature primarily to reside. "The strongest protection of each man's private property," he writes, "is the law of nature." Only if this is observed can a person "be master of his property and . . . pursue his own advantage" (207). Locke concludes that "nothing contributes to the general welfare of each and so effectively keeps men's possessions safe and secure as the observance of natural law" (207).[31]

31. It is useful to compare this with the familiar passage from section 57 of the *Second*

Until he became more pessimistic about the prospects later in his life, Locke held that human beings can infer both the content and the form of the law of nature from materials provided by sense experience. And we can now see fairly well how he must have thought such an inference would go. From the manifest design of the universe, we can infer the existence of a supremely wise and powerful Creator (*Essays*.151–55). Since "it is contrary to such great wisdom to work with no fixed aim," and since human beings have a variety of faculties, instincts, and needs, we may assume that these are all to some purpose (157). We may therefore conclude from our need and propensity to live "in society with other men" that it is God's will that we do so.[32]

This is as far as Locke's explicit remarks go, but we can fill in with what is implied in his remarks elsewhere. God may will us to preserve ourselves and society, but how *can* we do so if there is scarcity, if He also wills that we make use of the goods He has given us for our "use and convenience," and if, as Locke also believes, self-interest is the only rational motive? At this point we are faced with the *problem of collective action*, familiar in present-day theory, which also defines the fundamental problematic of morality for the modern tradition of natural law.[33] We can see that God wills that we conform to principles to which it is in the interest of each that all (or almost all) conform. And we also see that, for each, *his* conformance may involve sacrifice of his own rational interests. But on Locke's theory of action this is impossible. Agents can not act contrary to their interests, at least when they are acting for reasons.[34] God, however, does

Treatise: "For law . . . prescribes no farther than is for the general good of those under that law: could they be happier without it, the law as an useless thing would of itself vanish; and that ill deserves the name of confinement which hedges us in only from bogs and precipices."

    It is worth remarking that Locke sets out his remarks in Essay VIII as a response to a skepticism about natural law rooted in rational egoism. Like Grotius before him, Locke uses Carneades as a stand-in for contemporary skeptics. See Richard Tuck, "The 'Modern' Theory of Natural Law," in Anthony Pagden, ed., *The Languages of Political Theory in Early-Modern Europe* (Cambridge: Cambridge University Press, 1987), pp. 99–119, for an excellent discussion of this general strategy and its relation to the historiography of the period.

32. In supposing that there are deep and natural sources of interpersonal conflict, Locke is not, it should be pointed out, assuming any sort of asocial, atomistic picture of individuals.

33. See, e.g., Mancur Olson, *The Logic of Collective Action* (Cambridge, Mass.: Harvard University Press, 1971).

34. Locke revises this theory in the second edition of the *Essay*, but the revision would not help here, since what he comes to hold is that action always results from the greatest "present uneasiness." See, e.g., p. 249.

not will in vain, so He must have made it possible for us rationally to conform to these principles. Therefore, He must have created super-natural benefits for compliance and burdens for noncompliance beyond their normal natural consequences, sufficient to make the former always in the agent's interest and the latter always against it.[35] Voilà, a deduction of the immortality of the soul and the doctrine of eternal delights and torments as necessary conditions for the very possibility of morality and reasonable social unity.

DEMONSTRATION AND MORAL IDEAS

It is clear enough, I think, that something like this line of thought is involved in Locke's understanding of how it is that human beings can know the form and content of the law of nature and, indeed, in his famous claim that the truths of morality are capable of demonstration.

> The *Idea* of a supreme Being, infinite in Power, Goodness, and Wisdom, whose Workmanship we are, and on whom we depend; and the *Idea* of our selves, as understanding, rational Beings, being such as are clear in us, would, I suppose, if duly considered, and pursued, afford such Foundations of our Duty and Rules of Action, as might place *Morality amongst the Sciences capable of Demonstration*. (*Essay*.549)

Lying behind his claim that moral truths can be known with certainty is the important Lockean thesis that moral notions are archetypes, not ectypes. They are complex ideas fashioned by the mind and refer simply to a combination of features. In Lockean terms, their nominal essence is their real essence. Our ideas of real substances, on the other hand, are ectypal. They refer not just to some combination of features through which we identify a substance, its nominal essence, but to the real essence of what we thereby identify. The function of archetypal notions, however, is to combine features for a different purpose than the representation of reality. The function of ethical archetypal notions is *practical*. In terms of present-day philosophy, they aspire to a different "direction of fit" than do repre-

---

35. As Charles Taylor puts it, "Eternal life, in a world beyond, is something super-added . . .; but it is so fitted on that it too conduces to the proper running of this early order." *Sources of the Self* (Cambridge, Mass.: Harvard University Press, 1990), p. 244.

sentative notions.[36] Whereas the attribution of an ectypal concept will be faulted if it fails to fit the world, failure of fit between an archetypal notion and, say, an action in the world is occasion for criticism of the world – specifically, the action in question.

ETHICS AS INHERENTLY PRACTICAL

In the final chapter of the *Essay*, Locke proposes a three-way division of knowledge, corresponding, roughly, to theoretical, practical, and logic and semantics (720). The practical concerns "that which Man himself ought to do, as a rational and voluntary Agent, for the Attainment of any End, especially Happiness" or "[t]he Skill of Right applying our own Powers and Actions, for the Attainment of Things good and useful." And he there defines "Ethicks" as "the seeking out those Rules, and Measures of humane Actions, which lead to Happiness, and the Means to practise them." Its end, he remarks, is not "bare Speculation, and the Knowledge of Truth; but Right, and a Conduct suitable to it" (720). In fashioning moral notions, we therefore seek a way of thinking about our relations to each other and to the world that can enable us rationally to achieve our ends. Moreover, we know that God shares this aim, and we may infer that the "Rules and Measures of humane Actions" general conformance to which would preserve society and the general good are those He Himself eternally sanctions, thereby giving practical force to the complex ideas (theft, for example) that appear therein.

We can, of course, construct in any way we please the complex ideas through which we conceive ourselves and our conduct. Locke frequently criticizes Aristotle's and other ancient ethics, however, by saying that the terms identifying their favorite virtues are mere "names." It is only when the complex features of character and conduct that putative praising and condemnatory terms collect can be related to interests making their pursuit inescapably rational that they will be of any concern for ethics:

But whilst they discourse ever so acutely of temperance or justice, but show no law of a superior that prescribes temperance, to the observation or breach of which law there are rewards and punishments annexed, the force of

36. I am indebted to Ned McClennen for reminding me of this. On "direction of fit," see G. E. M. Anscombe, *Intention*, 2d ed. (Ithaca: Cornell University Press, 1963); Mark Platts, *Ways of Meaning* (London: Routledge & Kegan Paul, 1979), pp. 256–57; Michael Smith, "The Humean Theory of Motivation," *Mind* 96 (1987): 36–61; I. L. Humberstone, "Direction of Fit," *Mind* 101 (1992): 59–83.

morality is lost, and evaporates only into words, disputes, and niceties. And, however Aristotle or Anacharsis, Confucius, or any one amongst us, shall name this or that action a virtue or a vice, their authorities are all of them alike, and they exercise but what power every one has, which is to show what complex ideas their words shall stand for: for without showing a law that commands or forbids them, moral goodness will be but an empty sound.[37]

What makes the conceptions that figure in natural law, indeed the very notion of moral good and evil itself, more than mere names, therefore, is their practical "force." God's sanctions make them universally practically relevant by connecting them to every agent's sole rational end. Only so do we acquire motives to make the world fit archetypal moral notions through our actions.

Locke contrasts the intrinsically practical knowledge at which ethics aims with knowledge of "the Nature of Things, as they are in themselves, their Relations, and their manner of Operation" (*Essay*.720). In particular, he believes that knowledge of morality – at least, presumably, of the most general laws of nature – does not require knowledge of the real essences of substances: most important, of human agents themselves. "For as to Substances, when concerned in moral Discourses, their divers Natures are not so much enquir'd into, as supposed; v.g. when we say that *Man is subject to Law*: We mean nothing by *Man*, but a corporeal rational Creature: What the real Essence or other Qualities of that Creature are in this Case, is no way considered" (*Essay*.516). The basis for the law of nature, therefore, is nothing about the real essence of human beings.

37. "Of Ethick in General," in King, *The Life of John Locke*, vol. 2, pp. 129–30. See also *Essays*.129–31. Also: "[Ancient] philosophers seldom set on their rules on men's minds and practices, by consideration of another life. The chief of their arguments were from the excellency of virtue; and the highest they generally went, was the exalting of human nature, whose perfection lay in virtue . . . Before Our Savior's time, the doctrine of a future state, though it were not wholly hid, yet it was not clearly known in the world . . ." The "beauty of virtue," however, did not elicit rational commitment. "The generality could not refuse her their esteem and commendation, but still turned their backs on her, and forsook her, as a match not for their turn." With Christ's coming, however, and evidence of a life after death secured, "there [was] put into the scales, on her side, 'an exceeding and immortal weight of glory,' . . . virtue now is visibly the most enriching purchase, and by much the best bargain." "Upon this foundation," he concludes, "and upon this only, morality stands firm, and may defy all competition. This makes it more than a name." John Locke, *The Reasonableness of Christianity*, ed. I. T. Ramsey (Stanford, Calif.: Stanford University Press, 1958), pp. 69–70. It should be noted that in this work, first published in 1695, Locke retreats from the view that the form and content of the natural law can be known by natural reason without revelation.

Locke writes that there is such a "harmony [*convenientia*]" between human nature and the law of nature that it follows "as necessarily from the nature of man that, if he is a man, he is bound to love and worship God and also to fulfil other things appropriate to the rational nature, i.e. to observe the law of nature, as it follows from the nature of a triangle that, if it is a triangle, its three angles are equal to two right angles" (*Essays*.199). And he also defines the "bond of the law" as "the bond of natural law whereby one is bound to discharge a *natural obligation*, that is, to fulfil the duty which it lies upon one to perform by reason of one's nature, or else submit to the penalty due to a perpetrated crime" (181; emphasis added). But it should now be clear that by "natural obligation [*debitum naturale*]" here he could not have meant what Suarez or Culverwell meant, and that by "harmony [*convenientia*]" he could not have been referring to what Vasquez, Suarez, Grotius, and Culverwell had in mind. What Locke obviously means is that the content of natural law derives from the human condition: corporeal rational beings placed in circumstances of relative scarcity requiring some means for mutually advantageous collective action, but unable, without God's sanctioned law, rationally to undertake it. He decidedly does *not* mean, as Vasquez and Grotius had, that there is such a direct connection between what the law of nature requires and our essential rational ends that we would be obligated by it without God's sanctioned commands. Nor does he mean what Suarez and Culverwell meant: that, although there is no obligating law without God's commands, nonetheless we have conclusive rational motives for doing what such a law requires independent of its existence.[38] As he says, the *debitum naturale* is a bond of *the*

---

38. Von Leyden argues at some length in the Introduction to *Essays* both that there is a deep and unresolved tension in Locke's views between Grotian "realism" and theological voluntarism *and* that Locke was deeply influenced by Culverwell's *Discourse of Nature* on key points (*Essays*.39–43, 51–60). See Colman for effective criticisms of von Leyden's claim that there are realist strains in Locke (*John Locke's Moral Philosophy*, pp. 32–50). It is worth adding to Colman's arguments that a passage on which von Leyden's case partly depends actually tells against it when read in context. The passage is this: "Hence, this law of nature can be described as being the decree of the divine will discernible by the light of nature and indicating what is and what is not in conformity with rational nature, and for this very reason commanding or prohibiting" (*Essays*.111). Colman remarks that the passage is ambiguous, both in Latin and in von Leyden's translation. He omits to note, however, the sentence that directly follows: "It appears to me less correctly termed by some people the dictate of reason, since reason does not so much establish and pronounce this law of nature as search for it and discover it *as a law enacted by a superior power* and implanted in our hearts" (111). On this, see John

law by which one must obey "or else submit to the penalty due to a perpetrated crime."

EXTERNAL AUTHORITY AND MORAL AGENCY

In one currently familiar sense, both Culverwell and Locke would properly be called externalists about moral obligation. They locate what constitutes obligation firmly outside the moral agent in a juridical relation of authority obtaining between God and humankind. But both have a story to tell about why it is that anyone has rational motives for discharging the obligation laid on by the law of nature. Culverwell's is a Thomist narrative that guarantees motivation through a final cause. The mystery on this philosophical narrative is what the law's being obligatory has to do with its being rationally compelling, and vice versa. As Vasquez realized, we can ask why, if (almost) all the reason we have to do what God prescribes is independent of His prescribing it, should its being obligatory have anything to do with command? For Culverwell, the concept of obligation functions in a circle of concepts, including accountability, punishment, responsibility, and guilt, that make no direct connection with what justifies or rationally motivates agents to follow the law.

Locke's story is very different. With Culverwell he shares the belief that only rational agents can be subject to law and, even then, only if they can rationally govern themselves by it. But this creates a problem for Locke that it did not for Culverwell. As he can accept no Thomist eternal law that determines the content of natural law, together with its associated idea that rational human beings have an essence that guarantees rational motives for following it, he must seek an account of the capacity of rational agents to govern them-

Lenz, "Locke's Essays on the Law of Nature," *Philosophy and Phenomenological Research* 17 (1956): 111.

The points on which von Leyden claims close similarity between Locke and Culverwell are (1) their views about the nature of obligation and the basis for the law in rational nature, (2) their rejection of innate ideas and embrace of an epistemology based on sense experience and discursive reason, and (3) their "dismissal of every attempt to show that the law of nature becomes known to men by tradition." There is no doubt that there are intriguing similarities in all three of these areas. On the other hand, there is, as I have argued, a deep difference between the ways each relates the content of natural law to human nature. At best, it is misleading to say that "they both recognized the existence of what Suarez has termed 'natural' obligations" (40).

selves by the law elsewhere. Otherwise, he will not be able to show how moral obligation fails to be vain, or how 'obligation' is anything other than a mere name. He denies, moreover, that the acceptance of moral right or even, for that matter, the belief that one is obligated can provide or entail any motivation by itself; the only source of rational motive is the agent's own interest or pleasure. The only recourse, Locke believes, is that motives are provided by divine sanctions annexed beyond the "natural product and consequence" of the commanded action.

This might be called, without prejudice, an "artificial" solution to the problem, but it is not ad hoc. As Locke thinks of it, saving human beings from their inability, left to their own devices, rationally to settle problems of collective action is precisely God's purpose in laying down and sanctioning the law of nature; artifice from Him is required beyond the creation of human agents and the natural order. "If man were independent he could have noe law but his own will noe end but himself. He would be a god to himself, & ye satisfaction of his own will the sole measure & end of all his actions."[39] And the very evidence we have for inferring God's demands also licenses the inference that they are backed by the appropriate eternal sanctions, since we cannot reasonably believe that God's demands are to no purpose, as they would have to be if they were left unsanctioned.

The mystery that arose for Culverwell's view, however, arises also for Locke: What does the fact that something is morally obligatory have to do with its being rationally compelling, and vice versa? Indeed, it arises more pointedly. The problem can be put (somewhat tendentiously) in the following way. Locke judges it a great triumph of his view over earlier theories of ethics such as Aristotle's that he can explain what he calls the "force" of morality. But what, it might be asked, does the "force" of morality have to do with its being *morality* (insofar as this is determined by a juridical relation obtaining between us and God)? The force of moral demands, on Locke's view, consists entirely in the inescapable rational motives God's sanctions give us to comply with them, and not at all in their being moral. The latter derives from the juridical relation obtaining between their author and the agents to whom they are addressed. But this fact, in itself, can provide these agents with no reason to *follow* them. Sharply distinguishing in the *Essays* between the source and nature of obliga-

39. "Ethica B," MS C28, fol. 141, quoted in Colman, *John Locke's Moral Philosophy*, p. 46.

tion and what can motivate the rational will, Locke writes that "all obligation binds conscience and lays a bond on the mind itself, so that not fear of punishment, but a rational apprehension of what is right, puts us under an obligation" (185). It is no exaggeration, therefore, to say that for Locke in his *Essays*, whereas obligation lays a bond on the mind, it does not, in itself, lay any bond on the *will*.

I have said that for Locke obligation is a fundamentally juridical notion; it is defined by its place in a circle of concepts including authority and right. But in what, exactly, does a fact about authority, right, or obligation consist? The question is not what grounds God's authority. We know Locke's answer to that question; God has the right to obedience (and we the obligation to obey) because we are totally dependent upon Him. The question rather is, What is the nature of the fact that our total dependence on God grounds? In what does the juridical fact of God's authority itself consist? Presumably, God's authority, and our obligation to obey, entails (the normative fact) that we ought to do what God commands. But in what does *this* normative fact consist?

Locke actually faces two problems here. One is to account, within his epistemological and metaphysical framework, for the juridical facts of divine authority and human obligation. We know the natural and supernatural facts in which Locke thinks the *ground* of these facts to consist, namely, our total dependence on God. But what about the juridical facts themselves? We cannot, it seems, simply identify these with their ground without robbing them of normativity.

The second problem is that Locke compounds this difficulty by maintaining that the facts of right and obligation (not to mention their grounds) can play no intrinsic role whatsoever in the deliberations of a rational agent. The only considerations that can rationally motivate are facts about the agent's good. The obligatoriness of an act or the "moral rectitude of it considered barely in it self is not good or evill nor in any way moves the will."[40] But what can a practically normative fact conceivably be if it can neither play any role in rational deliberation nor be grounded in anything that can – what can practical normativity be if it is no guide to the will? The problem is not just that Locke provides no account that guarantees normative facts an action-guiding role. It is that the account he provides explicitly *excludes* their having any such role.

40. See note 29.

A LOCKEAN EMPIRICAL NATURALIST
INTERNALISM?

Locke never faces these questions directly, but he does give them a very interesting indirect response, as we have seen. Although there is no necessary intrinsic connection between obligation and action-guidance, there is a necessary extrinsic one. It would be contrary to God's nature vainly to command; thus, if He commands, it must be that He also provides us with rational motives to obey. So although the fact of obligation is neither itself action-guiding nor grounded in anything that is, it is nonetheless necessarily connected to super-natural sanctions that can rationally motivate. Locke stops short (at least in the *Essays*) of holding that motivation must enter into our understanding of obligation itself. Nevertheless, it is not unlikely that the problems his view was left with made the latter alternative seem more eligible to later writers and, indeed, to himself in later moments.[41]

I said in Chapter 1 that two different traditions of early modern British moral thought put forward the idea that the normativity of morality must be understood *internally*, through the force of motives from the agent's point of view – or, as we might also put it, that morality's 'ought' is internal. On its surface, nothing might seem farther from this idea than Locke's doctrine that morality obligates because it consists of a law imposed by an external, superior author-ity. As we have seen, however, the notion of authoritative command, central as it is to Locke's rhetoric, does no real work in explaining what gives morality what Locke calls "force" or what makes its value-laden, archetypal categories, such as theft or murder, more than mere "names," and thus part of "ethics." Locke explains these entirely in terms of their *practical* role, by their relevance to a person "as a rational and voluntary Agent, for the Attainment of . . . Happi-ness." (*Essay*.720). Their normative hold is thus accounted for in terms of an empirical naturalist conception of reason's instrumental powers to discover necessary means to accomplishing an agent's ends. At this deeper level, therefore, Locke advances a generalized form of the characteristic thesis of naturalist internalism: namely, that practical normativity consists in motives from an agent's deliberative point of view, raised through the use of theoretical rea-son. Morality, he believes, has normative force if, and only if, such

41. See Chapter 6.

motives are guaranteed invariably to recommend doing what morality demands. Of course, moral demands are not guaranteed on Locke's view to be *intrinsically* motivating. And the externally guaranteed motives themselves depend on supernatural sanctions. Nonetheless, it is clear that in his most fundamental thinking about ethical or normative force, Locke takes the empirical naturalist view that these consist in motives that ordinary empirical knowledge raises in a deliberating agent in exhibiting necessary means to ends she inescapably (if contingently) has.

ACCOUNTABILITY, AGAIN

In discussing Culverwell's linking of obligation, accountability, and "moral government" above, I said that when "moral government" is interpreted as *self*-government this becomes a core theme of a different, autonomist internalist tradition of early modern British moral thought and that, in some moments, elements of this tradition can be found in Locke's thinking. We have seen the central role that accountability – or punishment, at least – plays in Locke's moral philosophy, but not yet his later conclusion that these must be connected to a distinctive kind of freedom (a capacity for self-determination) that moral agents must have to be morally obligated. I shall discuss this in Chapter 6. It will thus turn out that although Locke's official account of obligation might be offered as a textbook example of an externalist theory, different elements of his thinking represent the two major internalist traditions of early modern British moral thought.

Chapter 3

Hobbes: ethics as "consequences from the passions of men"

John Locke was not the first seventeenth-century philosopher to attempt to find a place for morality and politics within the framework of the emerging science, without final causes. No doubt the most original and influential in this respect was Thomas Hobbes. Indeed, Hobbes calls moral philosophy itself a science, the "science" of good and evil.[1] Since he insists that English language users invariably employ 'good' and 'evil' simply to refer to objects of their desires and aversions, respectively – there being no "common rule of good and evil, to be taken from the nature of the objects themselves" – Hobbes holds that ethics can equivalently be defined as the science whose subject is "consequences from the *passions* of men" (*Lev.*VI.7; IX.4). Simplifying greatly, ethics is the subject that works out what people should do from premises about their desires and aversions, that is, from what they hold to be good and evil.

At the same time, Hobbes also says that "the true and only moral philosophy" is the science of the laws of nature (*Lev.*XV.40). This invites the obvious question of what earns something the status of law, and precisely what this status is. Sometimes – for example, in his initial statements of the right of nature and definition of a law of nature – it can seem as if Hobbes is simply assuming fundamental normative truths, whose normativity he takes for granted as addi-

1. Thomas Hobbes, *Leviathan*, XV.40. Because there are various scholarly editions of *Leviathan* currently in use, I refer hereafter to chapter and paragraph number, placed parenthetically in the text (after *Lev*, when context requires it). In addition to the version in Sir William Molesworth, *The English Works of Thomas Hobbes*, vol. 3 (London: John Bohn, 1839), there is a recent edition edited by Richard Tuck (Cambridge: Cambridge University Press, 1991), and one edited by Edwin Curley (Indianapolis, Ind.: Hackett, 1994). Curley's edition has the great virtue of including translations of the Latin edition of *Leviathan* when this differs from the English text.

tional to anything science might discover about human beings, their passions, and their situation vis-à-vis another. This, together with Hobbes's statements that the laws of nature are "immutable and eternal" (for example, *Lev*.xv.38), has led some writers to conclude that Hobbes really held such a view, perhaps because he accepted some form of theological voluntarism.[2] By far the dominant view among commentators, however, is that such a position would be inconsistent with Hobbes's whole method (as suggested here) and that it fits the text very badly in any case.[3] After having delineated the laws of nature, Hobbes remarks that, strictly speaking, they are called laws "but improperly." What they really are, he says, are "but conclusions, or theorems concerning what conduceth to the conservation and defense" of any person (*Lev*.xv.41).[4] But if this is so, Hobbes must explain why we might reasonably substitute these theorems for what people have improperly called laws. What is lawlike about them?

There is a second issue related to this one. Hobbes defines 'obligation' as abandoning or granting away a *right* (for example, in a contract), and he explicitly distinguishes between an obligation to keep a contract and any motive to do so. So again the question arises, In what do obligation and right, respectively, consist? And how are these to be accounted for in a naturalistic science that aims to work out "consequences from the passions of men"?

2. This is known as the Taylor–Warrender Thesis. See A. E. Taylor, "The Ethical Doctrine of Hobbes," in Keith Brown, ed., *Hobbes Studies* (Oxford: Blackwell, 1965), pp. 35–55; and Howard Warrender, *The Political Philosophy of Hobbes* (Oxford : Clarendon Press, 1957). For a more recent defense of the claim that Hobbes was a theological voluntarist, see A. P. Martinich, *The Two Gods of "Leviathan": Thomas Hobbes on Religion and Politics* (Cambridge: Cambridge University Press, 1992).
3. To this we might add that it would certainly have come as a surprise to Hobbes's contemporaries, many of whom roundly rejected him as an atheist, that he was a theological voluntarist. For a review and assessment of the case for this orthodox view (and the controversy), see Edwin Curley, "Reflections on Hobbes: Recent Work on His Moral and Political Philosophy," *Journal of Philosophical Research* 15 (1990): 169–250, esp. pp. 187–94. This also has an extensive bibliography of recent work on Hobbes.
4. Granted, he goes on to say that "if we consider the same theorems, as delivered in the word of God, that by right commandeth all things; then are they properly called laws" (xv.41). But this passage was dropped from the Latin edition of *Leviathan* (see Curley's edition, pp. 100–101). See also *Lev*.xxvi.8. I think Hobbes did believe that *were* there to exist a being such as God, whose power is so great that we must utterly despair of resisting it and, therefore, have no alternative but to yield to it, this would obligate us to obedience, but I agree with commentators who hold that the proposition that such a being in fact exists does no work in his system.

Consider, in this second connection, two different things Hobbes says about why covenants should be kept in civil society and in the state of nature where there is no reasonable suspicion of nonperformance by others. First, in *Leviathan*, the *obligation* to keep covenant is analytic, following directly from Hobbes's definitions of 'covenant' and 'obligation.' Covenant is a special case of *contract*, which Hobbes defines as a "mutual transferring of right," where at least one of the parties takes on faith the other's expressed intention to perform at some future time (xiv.9,11). And obligation, as Hobbes there defines it, is the condition that obtains when "a man hath . . . abandoned, or granted away his right" (xiv.7). When a right is transferred, a man "is said to be OBLIGED, or BOUND, not to hinder those, to whom such right is granted, or abandoned, from the benefit of it" (xiv.7). The obligation to keep covenant is therefore analytic: To have covenanted is to have transferred a right not to perform, and this condition is just what being obligated to perform is.

But, second, Hobbes also says that *"that men perform their covenants made"* is a substantive law of nature – a "dictate of reason" whose validity depends on important (if contingent) facts about the human condition, specifically concerning covenant's critical role in self-preservation (*Lev*.xv.1–9, 40–41). And in both *De Cive* and *Leviathan*, Hobbes distinguishes the fact of obligation from its "tye" (*De Cive*) or "bond" (*Leviathan*). "Contracts oblige us," Hobbes says in *De Cive*, but, he goes on, "Lawes *tie* us fast, being obliged."[5] He elaborates: "[A] man is obliged by his contracts, that is, that he ought to performe for his promise sake; but that the Law tyes him being obliged, that is to say, it compells him to make good his promise, for fear of the punishment appointed by the Law" (*DC*.xiv.2). And, in an analogous definition from *Leviathan*, "the BONDS, by which men are bound, and obliged: bonds, that have their strength, not from their own nature, for nothing is more easily broken than a man's word, but from fear of some evil consequence upon the rupture" (*Lev*.xiv.7).

That Hobbes is saying two different things here can be obscured by the fact that he sometimes also says that the laws of nature oblige. In *Leviathan*, he comments on his definitions of the law and right of

5. Howard Warrender, ed., *Thomas Hobbes: De Cive, the English Version, Entitled in the First Edition, Philosophicall Rudiments Concerning Government and Society* (originally published in Latin in 1642; first English edition published in 1651) (Oxford: Clarendon Press, 1983), p. 169. Further references will be to chapter and section number, preceded by *DC* when context requires it, and placed parenthetically in the text. Thus, the present reference is *DC*.xiv.2.

nature respectively, saying that they "differ as much, as obligation, and liberty" (xɪv.3). And he famously distinguishes there between the laws' obliging *"in foro interno;* that is to say, the[ir] bind[ing] to a desire they should take place,"* and their obliging *"in foro externo,"* that is, to conduct, in conditions where others are prepared to act similarly (xv.36; see also *DC.*ɪɪɪ.27). However, although he does not hesitate to say that natural law obliges, Hobbes almost always reserves 'obligation' for the state that results from the voluntary laying down or transferring of right. "All obligation derives from Contract," he writes in *De Cive* (vɪɪ.3).[6] And, in *Leviathan:* "[T]here [is] no obligation on any man, which ariseth not from some act of his own" (xxɪ.10).[7]

Here we have what look like two free-standing lines of thought. The obligation to keep covenant is apparently located within a space of interdefinable but, it may seem, irreducibly normative concepts: right, covenant, and obligation. On the other hand, Hobbes recognizes a sense in which it is far from analytic that people ought to keep covenant. We might call these the *obligation 'ought'* and the *law 'ought'*, respectively.[8] If it is analytic that covenants ought to be kept in the obligation sense, that they ought in the law sense is a substan-

6. This remark is actually misleading in the context of *De Cive,* since, as we shall see below, Hobbes recognizes something he there calls "naturall obligation" that is completely unrelated to any laying down of right. (xv.7).
7. This might be seen as some evidence of the force that the autonomist internalist line had, even for Hobbes. A number of writers have noted the difference between Hobbes's official use of 'obligation' and its contrast with the "obligingness" of natural law. See, e.g., Brian Barry, "Warrender and His Critics," *Philosophy* 43 (1969): 117–37; and David Gauthier, *The Logic of Leviathan* (Oxford: Clarendon Press, 1969), pp. 40–44. A failure to note this distinction infects Richard Tuck's discussion of Hobbes's theory of obligation in *Natural Rights Theories,* pp. 119–42.
8. Kavka makes a similar distinction between obligations and 'ought' principles. See Gregory Kavka, *Hobbesian Moral and Political Theory* (Princeton: Princeton University Press, 1986), pp. 303–14.
   S. A. Lloyd suggests to me that Hobbes need not be read as supposing there is a distinct obligation 'ought'. Perhaps Hobbes intends 'obligation' to function not as a normative concept at all but just as a term that refers to a kind of debt of which it is not analytically true that it ought to be kept, even prima facie. Lloyd notes that whereas Hobbes says the obligation concerns the *covenanted act,* he says also that what the person *ought* to do is "not to make void that voluntary act of his own," i.e., not to break his covenant (*Lev.*xɪv.7). As will become clear below, I agree that the only independent normative concept Hobbes has at his disposal is what I am calling the law 'ought'. And thus I agree that Hobbes can only make good the claim that, having laid down a right in covenant, a person ought to keep his covenant in terms of this fundamental normative concept. At the same time, Hobbes seems clearly to be supposing at *Lev.*xɪv.7 that it *follows* from the fact that a person has covenanted that he ought to keep his covenant. And so the question remains, What can ensure this connection?

tive normative thesis. It is this latter claim, moreover, that Hobbes attempts to secure by providing a novel, naturalistic account of normativity. Law 'oughts' are, Hobbes says, "dictates of reason." But he also says, again, that they are called "laws, but improperly," being "theorems concerning what conduceth to the conservation and defence of" any person (*Lev*.xv.41). For Hobbes, as we shall see, the normativity of the "laws" of nature consists in their role in rational deliberation from an agent's point of view, indicating necessary means for an inescapable end.

In moving along these two different lines, Hobbes's argument is not unlike Locke's. For Locke, the independent order within which genuine obligation is rooted is a juridical one; natural law obligates because God wills it and He has authority over us. At the same time, it is central to Locke's view that God's obligation-creating commands would be impossibly empty if He did not also give us rational motives to obey. Otherwise, 'obligation' would be no more than a "name" with no interest for ethics. In this chapter, I shall argue that Hobbes's views have a similar structure. Although Hobbes *defines* 'obligation' independently of motive, it is critical to his view that obligation connect up with the agent's rational will, nonetheless. What appear to be two completely free-standing lines of thought must ultimately be connected.

RIGHT REASON AND NATURAL LAW: NORMATIVITY AS INSTRUMENTAL REASON

Surely the most remarkable transformation the natural law tradition received in Hobbes's hands was that of its fundamental notions of law and right reason. Even when they disagreed about whether God's authoritative will is required to ground the formality of law and obligation, natural lawyers before Grotius were unified on the proposition that reason itself dictates the content of natural law. According to Saint Thomas's definition, "law is nothing else than an ordinance of reason for the common good, promulgated by him who has the care of the community."[9] And even Grotius defined the law of nature as a "dictate of right reason."[10] Hobbes retains this traditional thesis (*Lev*.xv.41). But he does so by altering the concept of a rational *dictate* in a fundamental way, thereby providing a radically

9. *Summa Theologica*, Ia IIae, 90.4.
10. Grotius, *The Law of War and Peace*, p. 38.

57

different, and utterly novel, account of the normativity of natural law.

Hobbes, too, wants to be able to say that natural laws are rational dictates. In *De Cive*, he defines a law of nature as a "Dictate of right Reason, conversant about those things which are either to be done, or omitted for the constant preservation of Life" (*DC*.II.1), and in *Leviathan*, as "a precept or general rule, found out by reason, by which a man is forbidden to do that, which is destructive of his life, or taketh away the means of preserving the same; and to omit that, by which he thinketh it may be best preserved" (*Lev*.XIV.3). But he also makes it clear that, for him, reason is not a faculty through which we intuit normative facts, or ends intrinsic to our metaphysical nature. "By Right Reason in the naturall state of men," Hobbes says, "I understand not, as many doe, an infallible faculty, but the act of reasoning, that is, the peculiar and true ratiocination of every man concerning those actions of his which may either redound to the dammage, or benefit of his neighbours" (*DC*.II.1). Reason is "nothing but *reckoning*," a power of inference (*Lev*.V.2).[11] But if this is so, how can reason *dictate* any action? At the most, it would seem that reason can dictate only theoretical conclusions, if even that.

This problem is compounded by Hobbes's materialist metaphysics and philosophy of language. To enter properly into our reckoning, words or "names" must refer to things for which we can appropriately "account" (*Lev*.IV.13–14). Hobbes lists four possibilities. A word may refer to some matter or body, to some "accident" or "quality" in a body, to some property in our own body by which we distinguish the accidents in external bodies (for example, "fancy" that gives us the idea of color), or to other names (IV.15–18). "All other names," he writes, "are but insignificant sounds" (IV.20). The only propositions that can enter into our reasoning, therefore, are those concerning the properties of natural (material) bodies. How, then, can the idea that reason dictates some action or other even have content?

Familiar as it is to us, it may be difficult to appreciate how radical a departure Hobbes's answer to this question was. Reason dictates action just insofar as an agent already has ends, ends that do not derive from reason but that provide the background necessary to give right (*theoretical*) reasoning practical "force." It is in the transfer

---

11. See Gregory Kavka's very helpful "Right Reason and Natural Law in Hobbes's Ethics," *Monist* 66 (1983): 120–33.

of motive force from end to means by right reasoning that reason's dictates consist. We may call this the *instrumental reason* view of normativity.

Any agent has desired ends. "To lack desire, is to be dead" (*Lev*.viii.16). And "the thoughts are to desires, as scouts, and spies, to range abroad, and find the way to the things desired" (*Lev*.viii.16). Reason, again, is a power of "reckoning" or inference. So it can recommend no conduct or end directly or intrinsically. Its practical function is purely instrumental, to work out the means or "way to the things desired." Reason makes "science" possible, projecting beyond the "knowledge of fact" provided by experience and memory to "knowledge of consequences, and dependence of one fact upon another" (*Lev*.v.17). This enables us to discover how to achieve our desired ends, "because when we see how any thing comes about, upon what causes, and by what manner; when the like causes come into our power, we see how to make it produce the like effects" (*Lev*.x.17).

Moreover, there is one end that all human beings cannot help desiring, as a matter of their contingent makeup, and this forms the basis of the science of the laws of nature (the "true moral philosophy"): self-preservation (*Lev*.xv.40). We shun death "by a certain impulsion of nature, no lesse than that whereby a Stone moves downward" (*DC*.i.7).[12] It is part of the human psyche, moreover, that knowledge that something is a necessary means to this end leads us to desire it as well. Right reasoning about "those things which are either to be done, or omitted for the constant preservation of Life" (*De Cive*'s definition of a law of nature) thus transfers motive force from end to means. "By *naturall necessity*" a person comes "to intend the procurement of those things which are necessary to his own preservation" (*DC*.iii.9; see also ii.18).

The end of self-preservation, inescapable for human beings, thus gives practical force to truths about its necessary means. Viewed

---

12. For parallel passages in *Leviathan*, see xv.17 and xviii.11. S. A. Lloyd argues in *Ideals as Interests in Hobbes's Leviathan* (Cambridge: Cambridge University Press, 1992) that, whatever desire for self-preservation Hobbes takes human beings to have, he also attributes to them "transcendent interests," e.g., interests in their own salvation. A problem emerges when these desires conflict, therefore, since presumably whatever force an instrumental 'ought' has depends on what an agent desires, "all things considered." However this problem is resolved, I take it that Hobbes is assuming "all men agree on this, that peace is good," and that he thinks the normative force of the laws of nature derives from their being necessary means to this end (*Lev*.xv.40). I am indebted to Lloyd for discussion of these points.

purely theoretically, from an observer's perspective, these truths have no particular practical relevance. Reasoning rightly, we can determine what we must do in order to survive. But in itself this is no more inherently normative than a fact about what must happen if water is to boil. Viewed, however, from the perspective of a rational human *agent* who *has* this end, it has an inescapable practical force. Right reason(ing) transfers the motive force of an inescapable end to its necessary means. In defining a law of nature as a "Dictate of right Reason, conversant about those things which are either to be done, or omitted for the constant preservation of Life" (*DC*.II.1), therefore, Hobbes evidently identifies the law's normativity or "dictating" quality with this inescapable transfer of motive force by right reasoning.

It is usual these days to call "Humean" the constellation of propositions (1) that reason is purely instrumental, (2) that what a person ought to do depends only on what will achieve her ends, and (3) that (1) and (2) follow from a philosophical naturalism that adequately respects the workings and findings of modern science. As we shall see in Chapters 10 and 11, it is far from obvious that Hume himself actually held this view. But, in any case, it should be clear that a far earlier impetus for the *instrumental reason* view came from Hobbes.

OBLIGATION INTRODUCED

Viewed against this background, Hobbes's remarks about contract and obligation in *Leviathan* may seem puzzling at first sight. 'Contract', again, he defines as "the mutual transferring of right" (XIV.9). And the condition of being "OBLIGED, or BOUND, not to hinder those, to whom such a right is granted" he treats as a direct consequence of such a transfer (XIV.7). On the face of it, the concepts of right, obligation, justice, and injury seem to move in their own normative space in *Leviathan*, connected only extrinsically to the naturalized normativity of the law of nature through the third law, "that men perform their covenants made" (XV.1). It seems almost as if Hobbes wants to make two distinct normative claims about the violation of contracts – that it violates obligation (and right) and that it violates a rational dictate – only one of which he is prepared to account for naturalistically.

But Hobbes really has no place for a source of normativity that cannot be given a naturalistic grounding. So, if he is to retain a distinction between the obligation that follows analytically from contract (the obligation 'ought') and its being unavoidably rational to keep covenant given the (inescapable) end of self-preservation (the law 'ought'), he must provide some alternative naturalistic account of the former. Moreover, because normativity as instrumental rationality is clearly most fundamental to his picture, he must also relate the former to the latter.

Now, in fact, Hobbes attempts to do just this. Indeed, he makes two different attempts, although this has not been noticed by commentators. He tries first, in *The Elements of Law* and in *De Cive*, to account for the distinctive bond created by contract in terms of a naturalistic theory of deliberation and freedom of the will. By the time of *Leviathan*, however, he has had what he must have thought was a better idea: Although not everything one ought to do is an obligation, the normativity of obligation derives from the same source as any practical 'ought,' namely, instrumental reason.

OBLIGATION IN *THE ELEMENTS* AND *DE CIVE*

Although Hobbes may sometimes seem to be appealing to an independent order of right, he makes it clear in *De Cive* and in *The Elements* that claims of right themselves depend on reason's dictates. To ease exposition, I primarily present the argument as it appears in *De Cive*, noting passages from *The Elements* when they are especially of interest.

It is therefore neither absurd, nor reprehensible; neither against the dictates of reason for a man to use all his endeavours to preserve and defend his Body, and the Members thereof from death and sorrowes, *but that which is not contrary to right reason, that all men account to be done justly and with right.* (DC.1.7; emphasis added)[13]

Having defined 'Right' as "that liberty which every man hath to make use of his naturall faculties according to right reason," Hobbes then formulates what he calls "the first foundation of naturall *Right* . . . , That *every man as much as in him lies endeavour to protect his* life and members" (1.7). Several pages later he repeats the thought,

13. For a parallel passage, see Thomas Hobbes, *The Elements of Law, Natural and Politic*, ed. Ferdinand Tönnies, 2nd ed. (London: Frank Cass, 1984), p. 71. Further references will be to part, chapter, and paragraph number, preceded by *Elements* when necessary. Thus, the present reference would be *Elements*.1.xiv.6.

just before he defines the law of nature. "But since all doe grant that is done by RIGHT, which is not done against Reason, we ought to judg those Actions onely *wrong*, which are repugnant to right Reason, (i.e.) which contradict some certaine Truth collected by right reasoning from true Principles" (II.1).[14] He concludes with *De Cive*'s definition of "The *Law of Nature*": "the Dictate of right Reason, conversant about those things which are either to be done, or omitted for the constant preservation of Life, and Members, as much as in us lies" (II.1).

The right of nature, therefore – the "liberty" each has to use his faculties according to right reason to preserve himself – has no independent normative basis. That each so acts with right derives entirely from the fact that reason determines this to be necessary for the (naturally inescapable) end of self-preservation. The right's "foundation" is simply this end which each has by a necessity of nature: the "endeavour to protect his life and members" (1.7). The normative basis of the right, as well as of the law of nature, is normativity as instrumental rationality.

At the same time, Hobbes is concerned to argue in *De Cive* that parties who contract with each other "mutually conveigh" their rights and, in so doing, become *obligated* to fulfill the contract. Moreover, he insists, the obligation deriving from contract is a different thing from reason's dictating that the contract be fulfilled. (Obligation 'ought' is distinct from law 'ought'.) The latter is expressed by a law of nature requiring that contracts be kept (the second law in *De Cive*) and consists simply in the necessity of keeping contracts to promoting self-preservation. "A Contract," however, "obligeth of *it self*." "Contracts oblige us," but "Lawes *tie* us fast, being obliged" (XIV.2).[15]

To be obliged, and *to be tyed being obliged*, seems to some men to be one, and the same thing, and that therefore here seems to be some distinction in words, but none indeed. More cleerly therefore, I say thus, That a man is obliged by his contracts, that is, that he ought to performe for his promise sake; but that the Law tyes him being obliged, that is to say, it compelles him

14. Cf. "Reason is no less of the nature of man than passion, and is the same in all men, because all men agree in the will to be directed and governed in the way to that which they desire to attain, namely their own good, which is the work of reason. There can therefore be no other law of nature than reason" (*Elements*.I.xv.1).
15. A somewhat parallel passage occurs in *Elements*.II.x.2.

to make good his promise, for fear of the punishment appointed by the Law. (xɪv.2)[16]

The rational dictate to keep contract is different from the obligation that contract itself creates.[17] The former is what "tie[s] us fast, being obliged"; the latter, our being obliged in the first place.

Before we consider how Hobbes tries to account for obligation's distinctive bond in *De Cive*, we must first note that he there recognizes another species of obligation, which he calls "naturall obligation." Hobbes introduces this idea in his discussion of God's right of sovereignty over His creatures, which, he is concerned to argue, derives from His almighty power over them. All of creation lies under a natural obligation "of yeelding him obedience."

But there are two Species of *naturall obligation*, one when liberty is taken away by corporall impediments, according to which we say that heaven and earth, and all Creatures, doe obey the common Lawes of their Creation: The other when it is taken away by hope, or fear, according to which the weaker despairing of his own power to resist, cannot but yeeld to the stronger. (xv.7)

In the first sense, natural obligation is just natural necessitation. This sense is irrelevant to any question of obligation arising in morals and politics, since, Hobbes thinks, every voluntary action is naturally necessitated, but, in any sense of interest to ethics and political philosophy, not all are obligatory.[18] The second sense is relevant, however. Agents are obligated naturally to obey another when the other's power is *irresistible*.

We can see what Hobbes has in mind here if we contrast the situation of human agents with respect to each other in the state of nature with their situation in relation to God. Whatever differences

16. The primary object of Hobbes's remarks here is civil law, but he also mentions "the Lawes of Nature" in the same context (xɪv.2).
17. But note that Hobbes also says that "the Law holds the party obliged by vertue of the universall Contract of yeelding obedience" (xɪv.2).
18. "Because every act of man's will, and every desire, and inclination proceedeth from some cause, and that from another cause, in a continual chain, whose first link is in the hand of God the first of all causes, proceed from necessity" (*Lev.*xxɪ.4). This passage is from *Leviathan*, but it expresses no change in view from *De Cive*. Care is needed in stating the role of natural necessity in Hobbes's view of normativity. That an act required by a law of nature is one that an agent would, as a matter of natural necessity, have a predominant motive to perform *if* she used right reasoning is what gives the laws normative force. That the decision to take a particular action is necessitated naturally does not distinguish it, by Hobbes's lights, from any other decision. Hobbes wants to be able to maintain a version of the view that laws of nature are dictates of right reason. Compare Schneewind, "Kant and Natural Law Ethics," 64–65.

of power exist in the state of nature, Hobbes is clear that no one's power there is irresistible. Indeed, no one's power is irresistible by *any other person*, since even "the weakest man [can] kill the strongest" (*DC*.1.3). Rough equality of power gives rise to a rough equality of hope in attaining ends. When two want what only one can have, neither need despair of attaining it simply by virtue of the fact that the other would have it also. But this would not be true of our relation to a being as powerful as God is conceived to be. We would have to despair of successfully contravening His will. A being like God would have irresistible power, since it is from Him that we would derive our very capacity to resist anything.[19]

But what leads Hobbes to call this relation a kind of obligation? What does it have in common with the sort of obligation that contract creates? We can begin to understand this, and see as well how Hobbes is thinking of contract's bond, by reflecting on the fact that he sees both as restrictions of *liberty*. Because we cannot help despairing of resisting irresistible power, our "liberty is taken away." It is a corollary that, since roughly equal power gives every human being in the state of nature reasonable hope in opposing any other, no person's presence restricts the liberty of any other person. This, we should note, is tantamount to the right of nature. No one is antecedently obligated to anyone else in the state of nature, because, as Hobbes sees it, if she were, her liberty would be restricted. In explaining how obligation derives from contract, Hobbes writes, "[F]or where Liberty ceaseth, there beginneth Obligation" (*DC*.11.10).[20] In the state of nature, everyone is at liberty until, somehow, he voluntarily restricts himself through contract. But how does Hobbes think this can be done?

And what, then, is *liberty*, if it can be restricted both by contract and by irresistible power? Hobbes's theory of liberty in *De Cive* is connected to the view he there takes of deliberation and the will.[21] His ideas on these subjects underwent significant elaboration (and some change) in the years following the publication of *De Cive*, espe-

---

19. Some might be tempted to discount this passage on the grounds that Hobbes was most likely an atheist. The passage's interest, however, does not depend on assuming that God exists; rather, it asserts what would be true if He existed. It is important here that the obligation that would exist would derive from *irresistible power*, not from any independently grounded superior authority.
20. A similar passage from *Elements* occurs at 1.xv.9.
21. For a discussion of some aspects of Hobbes's theory of deliberation and liberty, see W. von Leyden, *Hobbes and Locke: The Politics of Freedom and Obligation* (New York: St. Martin's, 1982), pp. 3–61.

cially in the course of his extensive exchange with Bishop Bramhall.[22] We need not, however, take account of these. Our concern is to understand how what Hobbes thought about liberty, deliberation, and the will in *De Cive* led him there to conclude that contract obligates by restricting the liberty of the contracting agent.

Deliberation, for Hobbes, is a process made up of an agent's thoughts of the good and evil consequences of possible future courses of action.[23] "Deliberation is nothing else but a weighing, as it were in scales, the conveniencies, and inconveniencies of the fact we are attempting; where, that which is more weighty, doth necessarily according to its inclination prevaile with us" (*DC*.XIII.16). This is basically the same theory advanced in more familiar form in *Leviathan:*

When in the mind of man, appetites, and aversions, hopes, and fears, concerning one and the same thing, arise alternately; and divers good and evil consequences of the doing, or omitting the thing propounded, come successively into our thoughts; so that sometimes we have an appetite to it; sometimes an aversion from it; sometimes hope to be able to do it; sometimes despair, or fear to attempt it; the whole sum of desires, aversions, hopes and fears continued till the thing be either done, or thought impossible, is that we call DELIBERATION. (*Lev*.VI.49)

In *Leviathan* Hobbes characterizes will as the "last appetite" of deliberation; in *De Cive* he calls it "the last act of him who deliberates" (*DC*.II.14).[24] There is no difference for Hobbes. The last act of deliberation is the last thought of good or evil consequence that determines action. Since "*Good* and *Evill* are names given to things to signifie the inclination, or aversion of them by whom they were given," the last thought of good or evil consequence just *is* the last desire or aversion (*DC*.III.31)

Now the connection Hobbes draws between deliberation and liberty is this: So long as an agent is deliberating about whether or not to do something, she is at liberty to do or not to do it. Once, however, deliberation is terminated and the will determined, let us say, to act, then the agent no longer has liberty not to act. "He that deliberates, is

22. Hobbes's contributions to that exchange are contained in *A Treatise of Liberty and Necessity*, in Molesworth, *English Works*, vol. 4, pp. 229–78; and *The Questions Concerning Liberty, Necessity, and Chance*, in *English Works*, vol. 5.
23. Since it concerns what is to be done, it can only "concerne things possible, and to come" (*DC*.II.14). Cf. *Elements*.I.xv.18.
24. Cf. *Elements*.I.xv.7.

so farre forth free" (*DC*.II.8).[25] And the "last act of deliberating" is that "whereby the liberty of non-performance is abolisht" (*DC*.II.10).[26]

In *De Cive*, Hobbes defines liberty as "nothing else but an *absence of the lets, and hinderances of motion*" (*DC*.IX.9). Some "lets are externall, and absolute," physical impediments like the stone wall that prevents a prisoner from walking more than a few feet from the center of his cell.[27] But in *De Cive* Hobbes adds that there are also *internal* impediments, obstacles he calls "arbitrary" (because they are chosen), "which doe not absolutely hinder motion, but by accident; to wit, by our own choyce, as he that is in a ship is not so hindered, but he may cast himselfe into the Sea, if he will" (*DC*.IX.9). Choices impede action because the will is then determined in a direction different from (earlier) alternatives. The ship's captain may not be so hindered that, *if he will*, he can cast himself upon the sea. Nonetheless, since he will not, Hobbes appears to hold in *De Cive*, his determination not to is an impediment to his doing so and, therefore, a restriction of his liberty to do so.

But if terminating deliberation restricts liberty, so also is liberty restricted by other impediments to action that make deliberation impossible with respect to it – obstacles, that is, to a path of deliberation terminating in the action. This is how God's power restricts human liberty. It is irresistible, so we reasonably despair of opposing it. By taking away any hope of doing so, God's power excludes resistance as a genuine option and thereby excludes the possibility of successfully concluding a deliberation with the will to resist. Because we cannot hope to oppose Him, we cannot deliberately choose to do so.

Hobbes's reason for saying we have a natural *obligation* to obey God, then, is that God's irresistible power restricts our liberty. But how does contract limit liberty? Hobbes's answer in *De Cive* is that the conclusion of a contract is the conclusion of a deliberation that limits the liberty of the agents not to perform.

The *promises* therefore which are made for some *benefit* received (which are also Covenants) are Tokens of the Will; that is, . . . of the last act of deliberating, whereby the liberty of non-performance is abolisht, and by consequence

25. Cf., from *Questions*, "Of a voluntary agent, it is all one to say he is free, and to say he hath not made an end of deliberating." *English Works*, vol. 5, p. 363.
26. Cf. *Elements*.I.xv.7.
27. In *Leviathan* Hobbes counts only external impediments as restrictions of liberty; internal impediments are a lack of power, not of freedom (*Lev*.xxi.1).

are obligatory; for where Liberty ceaseth, there beginneth Obligation. (DC.II.10)[28]

If an agent's liberty not to perform is to be restricted by concluding a deliberation, it is necessary that the last act of deliberating be not a volition to contract to do something but a will *to perform*. Otherwise, the only restriction of liberty will be a restriction of the liberty not to contract. And, in *De Cive*, this is what Hobbes in fact says. When a contract is concluded, the parties end their deliberations by *willing to perform*.[29] If this is not already implicit in the passage above, Hobbes makes it explicit elsewhere: "For by contracting for some future action, he wills it done" (DC.III.3).[30] By determining to perform, contracting agents limit their liberty not to perform, and this is what their being obligated not to perform *is*.

It might be thought that what Hobbes is saying in the first passage quoted in the last paragraph is not that a contract always ends a deliberation with the will to perform, but that it always ends with a symbol or *token* of such a will. But even if this has a far better chance of being true, it will provide no explanation of an obligation to perform. At best, the token of the will to perform will be a token that the agent's will is restricted, and hence that he is obligated. But there would remain a gap between such a token and actual obligation. Obligation begins "where Liberty ceaseth," not where there is a token of liberty's ceasing.

Hobbes distinguishes the declaration of a deliberation-concluding – hence obligating – will in contract from a promise of future free gift, which fails to obligate. When one person promises to benefit another in future, receiving nothing now in return, not even a reciprocal promise, "a promiser in this kind, must be understood to

28. Cf. "Promises therefore, upon consideration of reciprocal benefit, are covenants and signs of the will, or last act of deliberation, whereby the liberty of performing, or not performing, is taken away, and consequently are obligatory. For where liberty ceaseth, there beginneth obligation" (*Elements.*I.xv.9).
29. Note how different is the analogous passage in *Leviathan:* "He that promiseth only, because he hath already received the benefit for which he promiseth, is to be understood as if he intended the right should pass" (*Lev.*XIV.16). The implied will is not one to perform, but simply to *contract:* to obligate oneself to perform.
30. Also "Covenants are made of such things onely as fall under our deliberation, for it can be no Covenant without the Will of the Contractor, but the Will is the last act of him who deliberates" (DC.II.14). "Will of the Contractor" cannot here refer simply to consent to the contract, since, unless willing the contract involves willing performance, needing the "Will of the Contractor" for covenant would have no tendency to show that only performances (believed to be) within the contractors' power can be objects of covenant.

have time to deliberate, and power to change that affection as well as he to whom he made that promise, may alter his desert" (*DC*.II.8).[31] And since "he that deliberates, is so farre forth free," he cannot be considered to be obligated. Describing this situation in *The Elements*, Hobbes writes that "he that deliberateth hath not yet willed, because the will is the last act of his deliberation."[32] Such a promise does not obligate, therefore, because it does not declare the promiser's will. But the reverse is true with contract. Contract obligates, Hobbes apparently thinks, precisely because it ends deliberation.

Hobbes underscores the claim that contract involves a will to perform by drawing an analogy between *injury*, the breaking of contract, and *absurdity*, the maintaining of contradictory propositions in disputation. The analogy is carried through in *Leviathan*, but in tellingly different terms and with a different argumentative purpose. In *Leviathan*, Hobbes speaks of violating contract as a "voluntary undo[ing]" of "that, which from the beginning he had voluntarily done" (*Lev*.XIV.7). This must refer to a doing and undoing of the contract. In *De Cive*, however, he says clearly that the absurdity consists in the fact that a contracting party wills *performance* when the contract is concluded, and nonperformance when it is violated: "For by contracting for some future action, he wills it done; by not doing it, he wills it not done, which is to will a thing done, and not done at the same time, which is a contradiction" (*DC*.III.3).[33] He describes the violation as deriving from "weaknesse of mind."[34]

31. Cf. "He that promiseth to give, without any other consideration but his own affection, so long as he hath not given, deliberateth still, according as the causes of his affections continue or diminish" (*Elements*.I.xv.7).
32. Ibid.
33. Cf. "For he that covenanteth, willeth to do, or omit, in the time to come; and he that doth any action, willeth it in that present, which is part of the future time contained in the covenant; and therefore he that violateth a covenant, willeth the doing and the not doing of the same thing, at the same time, which is a plain contradiction" (*Elements*.I.xvi.2).
34. Richard Tuck claims that the central idea of Hobbes's account of the obligation of covenant in *The Elements* is "the claim that if it is rational to *make* a promise, then it is rational to *keep* it: no separate source of obligation is needed" (*Natural Rights Theories*, p. 127). And as evidence he cites a passage according to which the law of nature "*That every man should divest himself of the right*, &c. were utterly vain, and of none effect, if this also were not a law of the same Nature, *That every man is obliged to stand to, and perform, those covenants he maketh*" (*Elements*.I.xvi.2). This idea may well play a role as a basis for the law of nature governing covenant, but it is not what grounds the *obligation* of contract (in Hobbes's technical sense), which results directly from transferring right, and which has already been secured in the preceding chapter. Tuck suggests that the idea he mentions is what "led [Hobbes] to the curious doctrine, perpetuated in *De Cive*, that to break a

De Cive's account of the obligation created by contract, then, is – if implausible and somewhat simple-minded – fully naturalistic. The bond of obligation does not derive from some independent normative source. It is constituted by the fact that, as Hobbes there believes, a contract involves a deliberate determination to perform, and this restricts the liberty of an agent not so to act. Hobbes must have known that this account was unsatisfactory. It was hardly lost on him that people do voluntarily violate contract and are not prevented from doing so by their having agreed not to. Moreover, Hobbes had no convincing story to tell about how being obligated to keep a contract, in this sense (obligation 'ought'), relates to the dictates of reason (law 'ought'). If "that is done by right, which is not done against reason," what does the fact that the will has already been determined to keep a contract have to do with whether in so acting one will act with right?[35]

OBLIGATION IN *LEVIATHAN*

By the time of *Leviathan*, these ideas are nowhere in evidence. Hobbes retains the thesis that the conclusion of deliberation brings an end to the liberty to act otherwise, but his description of when this occurs is notably more cautious: "Every *deliberation* is then said to *end*, when that whereof they deliberate, is either done, or thought impossible; because till then we retain the liberty of doing, or omitting; according to our appetite, or aversion" (*Lev.*vi.52). It follows that the only kind of contract that could possibly bring deliberation to a close, thereby ending the liberty to act otherwise, is one to perform immediately, and even then only when the will to contract coincides with the will to perform. So long as "that whereof they deliberate" (the performance) remains undone, the deliberation is not yet ended.

Gone also is any talk of natural obligation.[36] Nor do we find

promise is equivalent to a contradiction." But surely what lies behind that doctrine is the view about the relation between will and contract described above.

35. Hobbes was aware of this even in *De Cive:* "[I]f what they *Vow* be contrary to the Law of Nature, they are not tyed by their *Vow*, for no man is tied to perform an unlawfull act; but if what is vowed, be commanded by some *Law* of nature, it is not their *Vow*, but the *Law* it self which ties them" (*DC.*ii.13).

36. On this, see both Brian Barry, "Warrender and His Critics," pp. 118–19, and F. C. Hood, *The Divine Politics of Thomas Hobbes* (Oxford: Clarendon Press, 1964), pp.

Hobbes saying in *Leviathan* that contract ends deliberation, thereby limiting the liberty of the parties and thus obligating them. The contrast between nonobligating promises of free-gift and obligating contract is described without any mention of their respective relations to deliberation and freedom. As previously noted, the analogy between injury and absurdity is repeated, but in more cautious terms (*Lev.*xiv.7). Hobbes no longer says that the absurdity consists in both willing and not willing the contracted action, and the passage leads immediately into a discussion of declaration and signification in the renunciation and transfer of rights. Moreover, the passage occurs in a revealingly different place. It is now located relatively early in Chapter XIV as part of the explication of conveying right – before the discussion of contract and before the discussion of the law of nature that contracts be kept. In *De Cive*, however, it had been placed at a point that is analogous to the crucial juncture of Chapter XV in *Leviathan*, just after the statement of the law of nature governing contract, where Hobbes makes his critical argument against the fool that injustice is contrary to reason (*DC.*iii.3; *Lev.*XV.4). I shall argue that this argument, which did not appear in *De Cive*, provides the key to understanding how Hobbes conceives of obligation's bond in *Leviathan*.

Another important difference between the two works is that in *Leviathan* Hobbes gives what approaches a formal definition of obligation, namely, the condition that results when a person has "abandoned, or granted away his right" (*Lev.*xiv.7). Since contract is itself defined as "the mutual transferring of right," it follows analytically that contract creates obligation. And it seems to follow quite independently of whether or not there is any dictate of reason requiring that contracts be kept. Hence our recurring puzzle: What can Hobbes be understanding obligation to be if its existence is thus independent of his central, naturalistically based normative concept? What, we might ask, can the force of an obligation 'ought' consist in, if it is the different idea of a dictate of reason (a law 'ought') that does the fundamental normative work in his system? Hobbes writes that "the BONDS, by which men are bound, and obliged . . . have their strength, not from their own nature, for nothing is more easily broken than a man's word, but from fear of some evil consequence upon the rupture" (*Lev.*xiv.7). But what can an obligation be if its bindingness is,

45–53, which discuss Hobbes's dropping of natural obligation and some texts from *Questions* in which Hobbes replies to relevant criticism from Bramhall.

as it seems, only extrinsically connected to it? The answer, I think, is that whereas having an obligation to perform is not, in the framework of *Leviathan*, the very same thing as performance's being required by a dictate of reason (the law of nature), it can nonetheless turn out to be true in that framework that joint undertakings are valid contracts, and hence obligating, if, and only if, performance is dictated by the law of nature. An obligation 'ought' will exist only if a law 'ought' does.

Obligation results from contract because contract is a transfer of right, and obligation just is the state resulting from granting away a right. But how is it possible to grant away or transfer a right? The relevant right is one deriving from the right of nature, the liberty each has to use anything he will, so long as "in his judgment, and reason" it will aid self-preservation. And each has this liberty, presumably, because so acting is consistent with what right reason (instrumentally) dictates in pursuit of self-preservation. But how can such a liberty, a permission located not in any owned privilege but in circumstances, be transferred or laid down? The liberty just consists in its being the case that one does no wrong in making use of anything judged necessary for self-preservation. Of course, if one is permitted to do something in this sense, one may consistently not do it, but this is not the same thing as granting away the permission to do it. The permission is not something one *owns*, in any obvious sense.

Because this is so, it is easy to feel that Hobbes allows the rhetoric of rights to drive his argument in ways to which he is not really entitled. If the right of nature is no more than a reflection of the fact that an agent acts with right (not wrongly) when she does what reason recommends in the service of self-preservation, how can any voluntary declaration or promise affect that? After all, the law of nature (or, more accurately, the general form of a law of nature) will continue to hold. And no matter what assurances agents give to each other about their future actions, it will still be true that they are bound by "precept[s] or general rule[s], found out by reason, by which a man is forbidden to do that, which is destructive of his life, or taketh away the means of preserving the same" (*Lev*.XIV.3).

Suppose, for instance, that two parties in the state of nature give assurances one to the other of future performance. One (we need not worry how) performs first on the expectation that the other will perform. Now, whereas before the performance of the first, there was a real question as to whether either was obligated to perform,

Hobbes clearly states that once the first party has performed, the second party is obligated to perform, even in the state of nature. Failure to do so, indeed, is one of the instances of injustice that Hobbes assumes the burden of demonstrating to the fool to be contrary to reason (*Lev*.xv.5).[37] Any "reasonable suspicion" voids contract, but in this case the first party has already performed (*Lev*.xiv.18). Consequently, the contract is in force; the second party no longer has any right not to perform and so is obligated to do so.

But, we may now wonder, how *can* the agent have no right not to perform? For Hobbes, what it is right for the agent to do, what he should do, is always determined by what reason in the service of self-preservation directs. But nothing has yet been said about that. Granted, contract is *defined* as the obligating laying down of a right. So *if* there is a contract between the two parties, then both must have laid down their rights, and the second must now be obligated. But that just raises the same question in another form: Can there be contracts in this sense? The puzzle is how Hobbes can *both* understand contract in terms of obligation and transferring right and *also* hold that what a person ought to do is determined always by the direction of reason for the preservation of the agent. And the remarkable thing is how close Hobbes *can* legitimately get to combining these, at least when he is granted some substantial empirical assumptions that, though questionable, are not outlandish.

The core text for something approaching a solution to this puzzle is Hobbes's reply to the fool. It goes beyond what is fully warranted by the text, however, to call it "Hobbes's solution." The most that can be claimed is that it is a solution that is made available by resources that Hobbes himself brings to bear, that it is the only solution to a problem Hobbes recognizes in earlier works, and that it appears in the dialectical place where Hobbes's earlier solution had appeared. It will be useful to quote Hobbes's description of the fool's position at some length.

The fool hath said in his heart, there is no such thing as justice; and sometimes also with his tongue; seriously alleging, that every man's conservation, and contentment, being committed to his own care, there could be no reason, why every man might not do what he thought conduced thereunto: and

37. "For the question is not of promises mutual, where there is no security of performance on either side; as when there is no civil power erected over the parties promising; for such promises are no covenants: but either where one of the parties has performed already; or where there is a power to make him perform."

therefore also to make, or not make; keep, or not keep covenants, was not against reason, when it conduced to one's benefit. He does not therein deny, that there be covenants; and that they are sometimes broken, sometimes kept; and that such breach of them may be called injustice, and the observance of them justice: but he questioneth whether injustice . . . may not sometimes stand with that reason, which dictateth to every man his own good. . . . And if it be not against reason, it is not against justice; or else, justice is not to be approved for good. (*Lev*.xv.4)

We should note that Hobbes *agrees* with the fool about this last matter. If violating an agreement is not against reason, then "it is not against justice; or else, justice is not to be approved for good." And Hobbes also agrees that whether an action is in accord with or contrary to reason depends on whether it accords with right reasoning in the service of self-preservation. Hobbes must agree with both of these if he is to solve the puzzle of obligation. What then is at issue? Hobbes disputes two claims he takes the fool to assert: first, that it is not contrary to reason for an agent to violate covenant whenever *the agent thinks* it will promote self-preservation ("There could be no reason, why every man might not do what *he thought* conduced thereunto"); and, second, that it is not contrary to reason for an agent to violate covenant whenever this will *in fact* promote self-preservation ("[w]as not against reason when it conduced to one's benefit").

On any reasonable interpretation, Hobbes's argument against the fool rests on the significant dangers, some of them potentially calamitous, that a person brings upon herself by violating contract. In the state of nature, no one can hope to defend herself without help from confederates, but confederacy relies on covenant and is impossible without it. The growth of confederacy, moreover, may be the best hope there is to escape the terrors of the state of nature.[38] And once the commonwealth has been founded, because it rests on covenant those who violate covenants are likely to be treated as public menaces and thereby risk being returned to the state of nature.

He therefore that breaketh his covenant, and consequently declareth that he thinks he may with reason do so, cannot be received into any society, that unite themselves for peace and defence, but by the error of them that receive him; nor when he is received, be retained in it, without seeing the danger of their error. (*Lev*.xv.5)

38. On this point, see Kavka, *Hobbesian Moral and Political Theory*, pp. 157–71.

Being known to have violated covenant therefore puts at risk the most valuable means available for survival. If a person is in the state of nature, she risks the loss of confederacy and, with it, the possibility of withstanding other united confederates. And if outside it, she risks return to its terrors.

It has been usual for philosophical commentary on Hobbes during the past twenty-five years to discuss the choice facing covenanters, both in the state of nature and in civil society when punishment can be evaded, in terms of the theoretical game of Prisoner's Dilemma.[39] Two parties face a Prisoner's Dilemma when each profits most by a course of action by which the other profits least (say, when one violates the covenant and the other keeps it), but when both profit more if they agree in doing one thing rather than another (say, by both keeping covenant rather than both violating it). Each party orders his outcomes thus: first: I violate, he keeps; second: we both keep; third: we both violate; and fourth: I keep, he violates. In such a situation, instrumental reason seems unambiguously to recommend breaking covenant, since, whatever the other does, one comes out better. If the other keeps the contract, one achieves one's best outcome by violation; if the other violates, one avoids one's worst outcome by violation.

As some writers have pointed out, however, it is probably more accurate to see the dynamic of Hobbesian covenanters not as a one-shot Prisoner's Dilemma, but as an iterated form of the game. When whether to keep a given covenant is seen as a move in a potential series of covenants, either with the same person or with others who can be expected to have some knowledge of one's past performance, the question of whether to perform is radically transformed.[40] Although whether the other party keeps the present covenant will be

---

39. See, e.g., Gauthier, *The Logic of Leviathan.* For a short introduction to the Prisoner's Dilemma, see Brian Barry and Russell Hardin, ed., *Rational Man and Irrational Society* (Beverly Hills, Calif.: Sage, 1982), pp. 11–12, 24–25.

    Jean Hampton argues that the strategic situation in the state of nature is not one of pure rational conflict, like Prisoner's Dilemma; rather, conflict results from various irrationalities, such as short sightedness. See her *Hobbes and the Social Contract Tradition* (Cambridge: Cambridge University Press, 1986). Kavka argues, on the other hand, that conflict becomes rational in the state of nature, on the reasonable Hobbesian assumption that *some* people are "dominators" (i.e., that they desire power over others for its own sake), even if the great majority of people are "moderates," desiring power only as a means. See Kavka, *Hobbesian Moral and Political Theory*, esp. pp. 96–125. For a discussion of this dispute, see Curley, "Reflections on Hobbes," pp. 175–87.

40. So long, that is, as there is no foreseeable determinate end to the series of

---

independent of what one does, whether future covenanters (the current other or some one else) do so, or whether they will even be willing to covenant with one, is unlikely to be. Since what hangs in the balance are the inestimable benefits of society and of an escape from the state of nature, Hobbes argues, not without some plausibility, that breaking valid contract always threatens dangers that are too great to risk.

Now, it is important to see that Hobbes does not deny that contract violations can, on occasion, actually benefit the agent. What he denies is that in such cases the agent violates with reason: "[W]hen a man doth a thing, which notwithstanding any thing can be foreseen, and reckoned on, tendeth to his own destruction, howsoever some accident which he could not expect, arriving may turn it to his benefit; yet such events do not make it reasonably or wisely done" (*Lev*.xv.5). The crucial thought here is that whether an action is done with reason depends not on the objective circumstances but on what an agent is in a position to "reckon on." If, by some accident that the agent could not expect, violating contract actually brings net benefit, that does not mean it was recommended by right reason. Hobbes writes of "attaining sovereignty by rebellion": "[T]hough the event follow, yet because it cannot reasonably be expected, but rather the contrary; and because by gaining it so, others are taught to gain the same in like manner, the attempt thereof is against reason" (*Lev*.xv.7).

The fool is also reported as believing that it is not contrary to reason to violate contract when the agent *thinks* it will benefit him to do so. We can extend the reasoning of the last paragraph to construct Hobbes's reply to this position. A person may think that violating contract promises net benefit when he is no position to reason on that belief – for example, when he cannot reasonably expect that violation will pay. Given evidence, it might be most reasonable for him to believe that violation will not pay. This, Hobbes thinks, is the usual situation. We may assume that in such cases right reasoning in the service of the agent's good will recommend not what the agent *thinks* it recommends, but that he keep his contract.

It might seem that Hobbes is committed by the logic of this argument to the position that the agent should do (that right reasoning would recommend that she do) whatever she would most reasonably believe, on the available evidence, leads to her greatest expected

contracting opportunities. See Kavka, *Hobbesian Moral and Political Theory*, pp. 129–56. (This includes a discussion of Hobbes's reply to the fool in this context.) See also Hampton, *Hobbes and the Social Contract Tradition*, pp. 75–78.

benefit (in the current decision-theoretic sense, say) or gives her the greatest likelihood of self-preservation. If, consequently, Hobbes is to hold that reason always dictates keeping valid covenant, it may appear he must hold that the belief that a violation will maximize the agent's expected benefit, or her chances for self-preservation will never be reasonable on available evidence. But this is not so. We know that much of what we most reasonably believe on available evidence turns out to be false. It can happen, therefore, that although an agent reasonably believes on evidence that violation will pay, this is disastrously mistaken. If she acts on this belief, the fact that her belief was a reasonable one will then be cold comfort. Moreover, whereas the standard of reasonable belief relative to available evidence may rule out wishful underestimation of the likelihood of discovery or its costs, or overestimation of the short-term benefits of violation, shortsighted self-interest may also affect what evidence is likely to be available to the agent. Given that what hangs in the balance is the very possibility of escape from (or prevention of return to) the terrors of the state of nature itself, Hobbes may consistently hold that the costs are sufficiently high that right reasoning in pursuit of self-preservation does not recommend violating covenant even when what it would be most reasonable for the agent to believe is that violation would benefit (even, indeed, when she takes account of her own fallibility).

The problem with agents' doing what seems best by the light of available evidence is that poor evidence sheds poor light. Hobbes seems to be willing to grant the fool that if we could *know* that violating contract would be best for our self-preservation or good, then we should violate – it would be contrary to reason not to. The problem, he appears to be saying, is that we are never in a position to know this, and that the potential costs are so high that no matter how close to knowledge we may seem to be, we are never close enough to warrant taking the chance. To put the point in today's decision-theoretic terms, Hobbes's position appears to be that when it comes to keeping or breaking covenant, rational deliberators will treat the problem not as a decision under conditions of *risk*, where they attempt to estimate and take account of the likelihood of various outcomes, but as one of *uncertainty*, where they cannot rationally take such estimates into account.[41]

41. This point is stressed by Gregory Kavka; see *Hobbesian Moral and Political Theory*, pp. 137–56. See also Kavka, "The Rationality of Rule-Following: Hobbes' Dispute with the Foole," *Law and Philosophy*, in press.

If we interpret Hobbes in this way, his reply to the fool will run as follows. Although it would not be against reason to violate contract if we could know that this would be for our good or preservation, we never do know this. Moreover, the costs of being wrong are so extreme that the only reasonable strategy to follow in promoting our good or self-preservation is always to keep valid contracts, even when we think violating will pay, and even when available evidence supports this belief. Normally, right reasoning recommends whatever action an agent reasonably believes most likely to promote self-preservation, but the special circumstances surrounding covenant make the agent's reckoning and choosing on this basis decidedly less advisable, from the point of view of his own preservation, than keeping covenant, regardless of his estimate of the benefits of doing so. When it comes to covenant, the latter and not the former is dictated by right reasoning. In effect, the latter recommends (includes?) a form of practical reasoning in which agents treat covenants as categorical constraints. The case for their so deliberating derives not from any magical normative force of covenanting but from human fallibility and the potentially disastrous consequences of being wrong about the costs of violation in particular cases.

So far we have an argument for the third law of nature, "that men perform their covenants made." But how does all this relate to the *obligation* that contract creates? To answer this we must return to consider the right an agent is said to lay down in contracting in the state of nature: the right of nature. This, we recall, is "the liberty each man hath, to use his own power, as he will himself, for the preservation of his own nature" (*Lev*.XIV.1). This means, Hobbes adds, the liberty "of doing any thing, which *in his own judgment, and reason, he shall conceive* to be the aptest means thereunto" (XIV.1; emphasis added). But we now see that, because of the central role covenant plays in extricating human beings from the state of nature and keeping them in civil society, the *law* of nature dictates the keeping of covenants, even when contracting parties (perhaps reasonably) believe their interests would be better served by violating them.[42] *It follows that the right of nature must be qualified for the case of contract in the state of nature.* When a contract is involved, right reasoning in the

---

42. Note, however, that Hobbes also says that a law of nature is "a precept or general rule, found out by reason, by which a man is forbidden to do that, which is destructive of his life, or taketh away the means of preserving the same; and to omit that, by which *he thinketh* it may be best preserved" (*Lev*.XIV.3; emphasis added).

service of the agent's good is not the same thing as what the agent "in his own judgment, and reason, . . . shall conceive to be the aptest means thereunto." In this case, right reasoning recommends keeping contract regardless of what the agent believes the relation to be between doing so and his own preservation or good. It follows, therefore, that when an agent contracts, it then becomes true that the full and unqualified right of nature no longer applies to the act he has contracted to perform. It is no longer true that he may do what he believes to be the best means to his self-preservation, for this might include violating the contract, and Hobbes's reply to the fool entails that a person should not violate a valid contract on this belief, even if the belief is reasonable. By covenanting, a person does something that makes it no longer advisable for him to base his determination whether or not to do the covenanted thing, and thereby perform as covenanted, upon whether doing so is likeliest to promote his own preservation or good. Covenant so raises the ante that it is invariably true that a person ought (in the law-'ought' sense) to act as covenanted, regardless of whether doing so (reasonably) seems best on available evidence. And since this is what a person ought to do, he may not act on his best judgment in this case. The "in his own judgment, and reason" part of the right of nature no longer applies.

We might say, then, meaning no more, that when an agent contracts, *she lays down her right* not to do what she has contracted to do.[43] She alters her decision situation in a way that makes it true that she should perform the contracted act, whether she thinks (even reasonably) it best to do so or not. And if laying down a right, by definition, puts her into a state of obligation, she will have obligated herself. The normative force of this obligation, however, will be no different from that of the dictate of reason to keep covenants. Indeed, as we have just seen, it is only because instrumental reason dictates always keeping covenant as a general rule or policy, regardless of how instrumental reasons appear to stack up in the individual case, that contracting creates an alteration of the right of nature with respect to the covenanted action and therefore, on the *Leviathan* definition, an obligation to perform it. An obligation 'ought' exists with respect to the covenanted act only if a law 'ought' obtains with respect to it. Still, the obligation to keep a covenant is a different thing from reason's dictating doing so. Whether something is an obligation

---

43. On this interpretation, Hobbes must define contract in some way other than via the transfer or granting away of a right.

depends, analytically, on whether it results from the laying down of a right. Whether an action is dictated by reason, however, does not.

CONCLUSION

Although the concept of obligation seems to function within its own normative dialectical space in *Leviathan*, Hobbes can reasonably be interpreted as aiming to provide it with the same naturalistic grounding that anchors the law of nature. Both the obligation 'ought' and the law 'ought' ultimately derive their normativity, therefore, from the same source: right (theoretical) reasoning in the service of the necessary end of self-preservation. In other words, appearances to the contrary, each 'ought' turns out to be *internal*. Their force derives from an *instrumental reason view* of normativity.

Hobbes is undoubtedly unable, finally, to construct a concept with all the features he thinks he requires. On the present interpretation, for example, we still have no explanation of how rights and obligations can be held by and owed to specific individuals, respectively. And, as we shall better appreciate when we consider this terrain again in the form of Hume's theory of justice in Chapter 10, it is far from clear that covenant will even be generally possible unless agents have available some motivational resource for keeping covenant other than self-preservation or self-interest, specifically, the capacity to follow a rule. Nonetheless, were his empirical arguments to work, Hobbes could still be read as having provided an account of how human agents might come to have compelling instrumental reasons for acting in mutually agreed and agreeable ways, reasons they would have lacked without an agreement. In any case, *Leviathan* stood for his contemporaries, as it still stands today, as a vivid example of what a morality whose normative grip derives entirely from *instrumental reason* in the service of the agent's own ends might look like.

Chapter 4

Cumberland: obligation naturalized

As we have seen, Hobbes would not have said that an agent is obligated to do something simply by virtue of the fact that action is necessary to achieve an inescapable end. He was prepared to say that the laws of nature *oblige* on these grounds, or that this is how obligation *binds*, but he reserved 'obligation' for the state a person enters by laying down a right. By the turn of the century, however, many British moralists would come to find this way of thinking and speaking both sensible and familiar. They frequently posed the question Why be moral? by asking whether there is an obligation to be virtuous. And they often sought the answer to this question in whether or not the virtuous life conduces most to an agent's interest, taking for granted that this is an end all rational human beings seek.[1] His diction notwithstanding, Hobbes was firmly behind this phenomenon.[2] But another, insufficiently appreciated, source was Richard Cumberland.

1. John Gay was an especially clear example, holding that "obligation is the necessity of doing or omitting any action in order to be happy." *A Dissertation Concerning the Fundamental Principle and Immediate Criterion of Virtue. As Also, the Obligation to, and Approbation of It. With Some account of the Origin of the Passions and Affection,* "prefix'd" to William King, *Essay on the Origin of Evil* (London, 1731), sect. II, p. xviii. Almost all of this work is included in Schneewind, *Moral Philosophy from Montaigne to Kant,,* vol. 2, pp. 399–413. I discuss this aspect of Shaftesbury's, Hutcheson's, and Hume's thought in Chapters 7, 8, and 10.
2. Tuck argues that, before Hobbes, John Selden had taken the position that obligation consists in a motive of rational self-interest, albeit one created by external command (*Natural Rights Theories,* pp. 90–100). Tuck notes that Selden's position might be interpreted as a not unusual instance of seventeenth-century divine voluntarism, but he argues that this would be a bad mistake. It must be granted that Selden holds that threat of sanctions is "a necessary correlative of obligation," but whether he holds, as Tuck suggests, that obligation is *constituted by* fear of sanctions or by a rational motive to avoid such sanctions is highly questionable. Indeed, in no passage that Tuck quotes does Selden actually say this. One formulation of the position Tuck attributes to Selden – "obligation is *constituted* by fear of a

Hobbes aimed to understand morality's normative grip in entirely naturalistic terms. The laws of nature are dictates of reason, but this does not mean that they structure an independent, irreducible normative order grasped by an intuitive faculty. Right reason is right *reasoning* – the correct use of calculative, theoretical reason. And it dictates not by discovering norms but through the practical force of its discoveries from an agent's deliberative point of view, indicating unavoidable means to an inescapable end. The practicality of its dictates is carried, we might say, not in the content of what it discovers, but by the unavoidable relevance that content has from a human agent's perspective in deliberating about what *to do*. Reason discovers, for instance, that keeping covenants is essential to maintaining peace, which is necessary to self-preservation. So far, this is a matter of natural necessities, causal connections we observe in nature. As human agents, however, we encounter it as a *practical* necessity – we see ourselves *obliged* to keep covenants – because we aim inescapably at self-preservation and see keeping covenants to be necessary for that. Ultimately, for Hobbes, there is nothing more to its being the case that we ought to keep covenants than this. Morality's normative grip is accounted for by instrumental rationality, owing to the fact that following moral demands is necessary, in uncertain human circumstances, to achieve an end we cannot escape.

Similar ideas are at work in Cumberland's *Treatise of the Laws of Nature*, but with extremely important and interesting differences.[3] Originally published in Latin in 1672, the same year as Pufendorf's *The Law of Nature and Nations*, the *Treatise* was regarded as one of the three great works of the modern natural law tradition, along with Grotius's *On the Law of War and Peace* and Pufendorf's *Law of Nature*. It was widely read, and it substantially influenced British moral and political thought – most significantly and prominently, that of

prospective punishment administered by . . . a superior" – combines two quite independent ideas (p. 93). If superiority is not itself to be understood in terms of power to make inescapable threats (and Tuck quotes no passage in which Selden says that it is), then obligation will have two quite distinct necessary aspects: a motive, first, which is related in the right way to superior authority, second. As I have understood him, this is also what Locke requires if obligation is not to be "vain." Tuck gives Locke, however, as an example of the sort of voluntarist position with which he claims Selden is to be contrasted (p. 93).

3. Originally published in Latin as *De Legibus Naturæ Disquisitio Philosophica* in 1672. I shall refer to the English translation by John Maxwell (London, 1727), of which a facsimile was published by Garland (New York, 1978). Excerpts are included in Schneewind, *Moral Philosophy from Montaigne to Kant*, vol. 1. References will be in parentheses in the text, preceded by *TLN* when context requires.

Hutcheson, as we shall later appreciate. Indeed, it can reasonably be claimed that Cumberland's *Treatise* marked the beginning of a tradition of naturalistic utilitarian thought leading to Bentham and Mill in the nineteenth century.[4] Our interest is less in Cumberland's relation to utilitarianism, however, than in his views on the foundations of morality.

Historians of ethics often duly note that Cumberland anticipated utilitarianism by attempting to resolve morality into the single principle of promoting the good of "all rationals," but they have taken much less account of his foundational views.[5] No doubt this derives, at least in part, from the facts that these must be pieced together from the *Treatise* taken as a whole and that it is no easy task to do so. Readers of the last century seem generally to agree with Sidgwick's opinion that, although "Cumberland is a thinker both original and comprehensive, who has furnished material to more than one better-known moralist[,] . . . his academic prolixity and discursiveness, his academic language, and a want of clearness of view in spite of an elaborate display of exact and complete demonstration, have doomed his work to oblivion."[6] But if Sidgwick's judgment of the *Treatise*'s fate beyond the mid eighteenth century is apt, his assessment of the clarity of Cumberland's views, once they have been fully worked out, is decidedly less fair. Cumberland asks his reader "not [to] pass a severe *Censure* upon this work, before he has thorowly *read the Whole, and compared all its Parts together*" (36). No less is necessary to see shape in what will otherwise seem a formless collection of ideas.[7] In order to understand Cumberland's views, we must

4. Ernest Albee called Cumberland "the true founder of English utilitarianism." *A History of English Utilitarianism* (London: Allen & Unwin, 1957; originally published 1901), p. 1.
5. See Albee, *A History of English Utilitarianism*, pp. 1–51. See also Henry Sidgwick, *Outlines of the History of Ethics for English Readers*, 6th ed., enlarged (Boston: Beacon, 1964), pp. 173–75; Frank Chapman Sharp, "The Ethical System of Richard Cumberland and Its Place in the History of British Ethics," *Mind* 21 (1912): 371–98; Tuck, *Natural Rights Theories*, pp. 165–68; Murray Forsyth, "The Place of Richard Cumberland in the History of Natural Law Doctrine," *Journal of the History of Philosophy* 20 (1982): 23–42; Linda Kirk, *Richard Cumberland and Natural Law: Secularisation of Thought in Seventeenth-Century England* (Cambridge: James Clarke, 1987); and Haakonssen, "Moral Philosophy and Natural Law," 99–104.
6. Sidgwick, *Outlines*, p. 174. Cf. Albee: "Cumberland is so utterly lacking in a talent for exposition that the adequate presentation of his views is a matter of peculiar difficulty" (*History of English Utilitarianism*, p. 14).
7. It is also necessary to take account of political factors that might bear on the way Cumberland formulates his ideas. This is especially true of his view of the obligation to follow the laws of nature.

read him comprehensively. Since he remains largely unread, and his work is largely unavailable, in what follows I shall frequently quote him at length.

There is something ironic, actually, in the perception of Cumberland as having only antiquarian interest, since no other philosopher of the period was closer to several important strains of contemporary ethical and political thought. It is arguable, for example, that Cumberland was the first writer to introduce quantitative probabilistic techniques into ethical thought to take account of risk (*TLN*.257n). And no one of the period may be a clearer advocate of naturalistic reduction, a project that retains substantial support on the philosophical scene in our own time.

Cumberland characterized the *Treatise* as a consideration and refutation "of the Elements of Mr. Hobbes's Philosophy." He wished to prove what he took Hobbes to deny, namely, that there are "certain *Propositions of unchangeable Truth, which direct our voluntary Actions, about chusing Good and refusing Evil; and impose an Obligation to external Actions, even without Civil Laws, and laying aside all Consideration of those Compacts, which constitute Civil government*" (39). Cumberland realized, of course, that Hobbes held that laws of nature apply to human beings even in the state of nature. His complaint was twofold. First, without the security provided by the sovereign, only Hobbes's first law (to "endeavour peace" if there is hope of achieving it, otherwise to seek "all advantages of war") binds to external actions, the rest binding only *in foro interno*. And under such circumstances, even the first law usually prescribes prosecution of war rather than concrete steps in the promotion of peace. Cumberland believed, however, that the law of nature can be summarized as a prescription to promote "the common Good of the whole System of rational Agents" (16) and that this binds to concrete actions. Second, Hobbes had said that the practical generalizations with which he was concerned are only improperly called laws. Strictly, they are "theorems concerning what conduceth to the conservation and defence" of human agents. And he refused to say that they create obligations of obedience. Against this, Cumberland aimed to show that the prescription of universal benevolence is a law in the only way in which there can be practical law, and that it therefore creates a real obligation.

Cumberland makes clear at the outset that he intends to argue these points within an empiricist epistemology and naturalist metaphysics that, though not materialist, are not otherwise dissimilar from Hobbes's. "The Whole of *moral Philosophy*, and of the Laws of Nature," he writes, "is ultimately resolv'd into *natural Observations* known by the Experience of all Men, or into Conclusions of true *Natural Philosophy*" (41).[8] Cumberland's is an explicitly *reductionist* program. He believes not only that all knowledge, including moral knowledge, proceeds from experience of the natural realm, but also that what we thereby know, the moral laws themselves, are nothing but "conclusions of true *Natural Philosophy*." Ultimately, Cumberland's position is that universal benevolence's being a law, its normativity or obligatoriness consists in facts of natural philosophy knowable by empirical methods.

If we recall Cumberland's initial formulation of the kind of practical law he hopes to establish, we shall notice that he makes an apparent distinction between two elements. First, natural laws are immutably truths *"which direct our voluntary Actions"* to universal benevolence. And, second, they *"impose an Obligation to external Actions, even without Civil Laws."* A necessary condition of the success of Cumberland's project, therefore, is that he be able to present naturalistic accounts of both of these. He must show that truths of natural philosophy *direct* human action to universal benevolence and that they demonstrate the *obligatoriness* of this direction. On the face of it, Cumberland offers distinct naturalistic reductions of these different elements. A more probing inquiry, however, will reveal a unified account lying behind.

On any view, it seems clear that Cumberland regards his statement of the law of nature as providing not simply the content of rational dictate and obligation – namely, universal benevolence – but the key to benevolence's being both dictated by reason and obligatory.[9] We should begin, therefore with a statement of the law of nature: *"The greatest Benevolence of every rational Agent towards all, forms the happiest State of every, and of all the Benevolent, as far as is in their Power; and is necessarily requisite to the happiest State which they can attain"* (41). However this is to be read, it asserts a connection between states of

---

8. See also, e.g., p. 201. Unlike Hobbes, Cumberland does not take this restriction to entail materialism: "*Natural Philosophy*, in the large Sense I now use it, does not only comprehend all those *Appearances of natural Bodies*, which we know from Experiment, but also inquires into the Nature of our *Souls*, from Observations made upon their Actions and distinguishing Perfections, and at length leads Men, by the Chain of natural Causes, to the Knowledge of the *first Mover*, and acknowledges him to be the Cause of all necessary Effects" (41).
9. Cumberland will ultimately identify these two – that is what makes his position internalist – but he distinguishes them superficially, as did Hobbes and Locke.

affairs in nature. It will take some work to see exactly which connection or connections are in question, why Cumberland thinks they
exist, and what their relevance is, but it is clear enough that some
relation is being asserted between a rational agent's (or all rational
agents') acting with *"the greatest Benevolence"* and the *"happiest State"*
of all who act with this motive.[10] One burden that Cumberland is
evidently undertaking is to show that these states "are necessarily
connected," that is, that the thesis that these states are generally
causally related in nature is a *"true* Proposition" (42). But he also
intends to show that it is "practical," that it directs action, and that it
has "the force of a *Law"* – in other words, that it obligates (42).

PRACTICAL PROPOSITIONS

To direct human action, natural philosophy must establish what
Cumberland calls *"practical propositions."* All action, he believes, aims
at some end or good.[11] An *end* is simply an *"Effect"* the idea of which,
"preconceiv'd in the Mind, first moves a Rational Agent to intend the
producing it, and afterward limits his actions in order thereto"
(196).[12] Cumberland calls a proposition *"practical"* when it "pro-
nounc[es] concerning the Consequences of human Action" (18). By
this test, the law of nature is practical, but so also is any proposition
concerning any consequence of any action. That the law of nature is a
practical proposition, therefore, does not show that it *directs* a rational agent to be universally benevolent. Cumberland indicates
what he takes the difference to be between the law of nature and
other, idle practical propositions, such as those that concern the
effects of certain geometrical constructions, as follows:

10. Other formulations (for example, that on p. 18) do not restrict the consequential
    benefits to the benevolent, but include "every Part" "of the whole System of
    rational Agents" (16).
11. See pp. 168, 173, 213, 220, 233. This idea will be explored in some detail further
    on.
12. "[B]ecause the words, *End* and *Means,* are of very doubtful signification, and
    suppose the *free,* the *mutable,* intention of a rational Agent, which can *never be
    certainly known;* and because they, consequently, present to our Minds a matter
    not so *proper for Demonstration;* I thought it fit, *without changing* the matter in hand,
    to consider it *under another notion;* that is, because the *connexion* is more *con-
    spicuous,* and perfectly *inseparable,* between *Efficient Causes,* and their *Effects.* . . .
    By this means, *Moral and Political Questions* are converted into Terms in use
    among *Natural Philosophers,* Whether these Efficient Causes can produce this
    Effect, or no?" (196).

[T]he true *Reason*, why *this practical Proposition*, and all those which may be deduc'd from thence, oblige all rational Beings who understand them; whilst *other practical Propositions*, (suppose Geometrical ones,) equally impress'd by Nature, and consequently by God, upon the Mind of Man, *do not oblige* him to conform his Practice to them; but may *safely be neglected* by most, to whom the Practice of Geometry is not necessary: Which is wholly owing to the *Nature of the Effects*, arising from the *one* and the *other* Practice. The Effects of the Practice of Geometry are such as most People may want [i.e., may lack] without Prejudice. But the Effects of a care of the common Good, do so nearly concern all, of whom we our selves are a part, and upon whose Pleasure the Happiness of each Individual does in some measure depend, that *such* care cannot be rejected, without the hazard of losing that Happiness, or the Hope thereof. (21)

When we turn later to consider the role of divine promulgation in Cumberland's theory of obligation, we shall appreciate why he feels entitled here to say that the law of nature *obliges* us to conform our practice to it, whereas other propositions asserting effects no less necessary do not. Our present concern, however, is not directly with obligation, but with the action-guidingness of the law of nature. And Cumberland writes that the law of nature "is, in its own Nature, a proper *Rule* to direct our Manners" quite independent of any knowledge of its authoritative source necessary to establish its obligation (49). The reason it directs us, though geometrical practical propositions do not, is that the effects included in the consequents of the latter are *optional*, whereas those of the law of nature are not. We are not free not to have the end they concern, since we have it as a matter of natural necessity.

Exactly what Cumberland supposes this naturally necessary end to be is a nice question. We may begin by assuming that he intends it to *include* the agent's own happiness; we shall have occasion further to elaborate this initial supposition later. Agents necessarily desire their own happiness, Cumberland believes. "[A]n *Action*," therefore, "is . . . *necessary to a rational Agent, when it is certainly one of the Causes necessarily requisite to that Happiness, which he naturally, and consequently necessarily, desires.*" (233). On the proposed reading of the law of nature, universal benevolence is "necessarily requisite to the happiest state which [the agent] can attain." Assuming it is within the agent's power to act on this motive (we shall see that Cumberland thinks it is), doing so is therefore an action that is "*necessary to a rational Agent.*" The law of nature thus directs agents to be benevolent by stating that their being so is necessary to an end they necessarily have.

"A *practical Proposition*," Cumberland writes,

is, sometimes, thus express'd. "This possible human Action" (universal Benevolence; for *instance*) "Will chiefly, beyond any other Action at the same time possible, conduce to my Happiness, and that of all others, either as an essential part thereof, or as a Cause, which will, some time or other, effect a principal essential part thereof." It is sometimes express'd in the *Form* of a *Command*. "Let that Action, which is in thy Power, and which will most effectually, of all those which thou can'st exert, promote the common Good in the present circumstances, be exerted;" often also, in the *Form* of a *Gerund*; "Such an Action ought to be done." In my Opinion, *these several Forms* of Speech, relating to the Law of Nature, mean the *same thing*. (180)

Thus the law of nature's being a conclusion of natural philosophy does not preclude its being, in Cumberland's view, either genuinely practical or normative. Its practical force, its power to motivate, derives from the fact that it asserts an action within the agent's power to be necessary for an end she necessarily has; it therefore necessarily has practical relevance from an agent's point of view. And as for its normative force, its asserting what an agent *ought* to do, Cumberland declares that the "*Fitness*, which is express'd by a *Gerund*, wants Explanation, which is to be fetch'd, either from the necessary *Connexion* of the *Means* with the *End*, or from the *Obligation of a Law*" (180). I have just mentioned what he takes to be the proper, naturalistic way of understanding the former, and I will discuss his proposed reduction of *obligation* presently. Whatever the details, however, it is evident Cumberland thought that natural philosophy can provide a satisfactory account of the practical and normative character of the law of nature.[13]

13. As will become clear only when we have fully analyzed Cumberland's account of obligation – specifically, his view of God's dominion or authority – it is artificial to separate normativity and practicality as though they were independent ideas. In the end, Cumberland unites them, or so I shall argue. So much, indeed, is entailed by his statement that declarative, imperative, and gerundive formulations of the law of nature "mean the same thing."

It is worth noting that Cumberland's statement that the gerundive form "wants explanation," as well as his related claim about the metaphorical character of the language of "ties" and "bonds" in connection with obligation, and his rationale for replacing 'end' with 'effect' (see note 12), all suggest that the naturalistic surrogates he offers should be viewed not as an attempt to capture everything speakers may mean when they use these words but as what some metaethical philosophers of our own century have called "reforming definitions." These

OBLIGATION

For Cumberland, the question of whether the law of nature obligates is the same as whether it is genuine law. His official view agrees with Locke's that obligation and law require the promulgation of *"competent Authority"* (14). It will be recalled, however, that whereas connection to authority is critical to obligation on Locke's official view, this juridical notion plays no role in his moral psychology and theory of action. Rational agents can act only for their good; the bare thought that conduct is obligatory cannot rationally motivate. In order, therefore, to avoid the promulgation of "vain" law, and to make obligation more than a mere "name," God must affix supernatural sanctions in addition to the natural consequences of contralegal actions, thereby giving rational human agents motives to comply that they would otherwise have lacked. Unlike Locke, Cumberland brings sanctions directly into his definition of law and obligation. Laws are "nothing but *practical Propositions, with Rewards and Punishments annex'd, promulg'd by competent Authority"* (14). And moral obligations ("the immediate *Effect* of Nature's Laws") are "resolve[d] . . . into their First and Principal *Cause,* which is the *Will* and Counsel of *God* promoting the Common Good; and, therefore, by Rewards and Punishments *enacting* into Laws the *Practical Propositions* which tend thereto" (225). To this Cumberland explicitly adds: "Mens *care of their own Happiness,* which causes them to *consider,* and be *moved* by, Rewards and Punishments, is no *Cause of Obligation;* That proceeds, wholly, from the *Law* and the *Lawgiver"* (225).

But if the connection between morality's practical force and its obligation, as a further feature, seemed indirect in Locke, it seems even less direct in Cumberland, despite the fact that Cumberland explicitly includes sanction in his definition of law and obligation. There are two reasons for this. One is that, according to Locke, God makes law and obligation effective by providing agents with motives for acting beyond the natural consequences of their actions. The promulgation of His will *as His will* plays an essential role in its accomplishment. As Locke sees it, human agents require additional, supernatural sanctions because natural ones leave them (as egoists)

philosophers, suspecting that at least some aspects of normative language are based on confusions, aim to reform it so that it can be, at once, clear and useful. See, e.g., Charles Stevenson, "The Emotive Meaning of Ethical Terms," in *Facts and Values* (New Haven: Yale University Press, 1963), pp. 10–15; and Richard Brandt, *A Theory of the Good and the Right* (Oxford: Clarendon Press, 1979), pp. 3–10. For further discussion, see Chapter 11.

with insoluble problems of collective action. Such motives play very little role in Cumberland's picture, however.[14] As he sees it, human beings can solve their collective problems with motives they already have at hand in knowing the natural consequences of their actions. The "rewards and punishments" through which God "enacts" the practical propositions that consist in, and derive from, the law of nature, are none other than those referred to in the law of nature itself. Cumberland does sometimes say that a necessary condition of the promulgation of natural law is that it be "known to proceed from God" (193). But while this plays an essential motivational role in Locke, this is not so for Cumberland. For him, the "rewards and punishments" of natural law are primarily, if not almost exclusively, the natural consequences of action.

The Knowledge (or Ideas form'd in the Mind) of *Human Actions*, of Consequences good or evil to human Nature, but especially, of *Rewards* and *Punishments* naturally connected with such Actions, and those Ideas reduc'd into the Form of *Practical Propositions*, such as I have describ'd, are all that is *essential* to a *Law*. (191)[15]

That the law of nature proceeds from God thus plays almost no role in making it true that agents have motives to follow it. If, mirabile dictu, the natural realm were to exist without God, human agents would have much the same reasons to be mutually benevolent.

The second reason why morality's obligation, as a distinct feature, has for Cumberland no direct connection to its practical force is that, despite his official view, it turns out not to be a substantially distinct feature for him after all. Officially, what makes the beneficial and harmful natural consequences of benevolence and contrary acts rewards and punishments, respectively, is that this natural order of sanctions is due to *"competent Authority."* I shall argue, however, that Cumberland believes that God's authority itself depends on (a proper understanding of) the law of nature itself. As he says at one point, "[I]t amounts to the same thing, when we *say*, 'That the Obligation is an Act of the Legislator,' or of the First Cause; as if in this place we had *call'd* it, 'An Act of the Law of Nature'" (234). It will turn out,

14. But they do play some role; see, e.g., pp. 267, 269.
15. This particular reductive account of law can be judged adequate by Cumberland's usual standards if we take the ideas of rewards and sanctions to presuppose their promulgation by competent authority. For other passages where Cumberland stresses the natural character of sanctions, see, e.g., pp. 53, 108, 192, 296. In addition, his argument for the truth of the law of nature – specifically, for the connection between benevolent action and the happiness of the agent – is conducted almost entirely in terms of natural consequences.

therefore, that morality's obligation is ultimately not a feature distinct from its inescapable practical force.

We must postpone the analysis necessary to establish that this is indeed Cumberland's considered view. We can, however, here note several indications that it is the tendency of his thought. In his discussion of the idea that obligation "binds" or "ties" agents, Cumberland remarks that these notions are metaphorical, and declares that nothing "can superinduce a *Necessity* of doing or forbearing any thing, upon a Human Mind deliberating upon a thing future, except Thoughts or *Propositions* promising Good or Evil, to ourselves or others, consequent upon what we are about to do" (233).[16] Of course, Hobbes distinguished obligation from its bond or "tie," so we cannot assume that Cumberland's account of the latter is also offered as an account of the former. But there are other passages where he seems almost to say that there is nothing to obligation beyond the motives that bind agents. Here are two:

[T]he Laws of Nature have an *intrinsecal* and essential *Proof* of their *Obligation*, taken from the *Rewards* or Increase of Happiness which attends the benevolent Person from the natural efficacy of his Actions . . .; and from the *Punishments*, or Degrees of Misery, which, whether they will or no, they call upon themselves, who either do not obey, or do oppose, the Conclusions of right Reason. (53)

[T]he *intrinsick Force of all those Arguments, with which the Legislator* (God) *uses to enforce Universal Benevolence*, is, in my opinion, all that is meant by the *Obligation of Laws.* (246)

For the moment, however, we may assume that Cumberland's official view is that neither the legality nor the obligatoriness of the law of nature can be understood as independent of the notion that it is promulgated by competent authority. This leaves the question, If all of moral philosophy is to be reduced to conclusions of true natural philosophy, to which such truths are facts of obligation and law to be reduced? The source and promulgation of the law of nature have clear naturalistic formulations for Cumberland. The "first cause" promulgates natural law by making the natural connections between acts and consequences sufficiently plain to our natural reason. Natural philosophy, concluding in the law of nature, is *itself* the process through which the law is promulgated. Thus is this *"Proposition, proposed to the Observation of, or impress'd upon, the Mind, with sufficient*

16. Note "to ourselves *or* others." It will be crucial to understanding Cumberland's fully articulated view to appreciate why he says this.

Clearness, by the Nature of Things, from the Will of the first Cause"
(189).[17] In order for it be fully promulgated as law, natural philosophy must be able further to conclude, as Cumberland believes it can,
that the natural connections the law asserts are themselves due to the
first cause.

The only remaining element necessary to naturalize fully the notions of law and obligation is that of *competent authority*. On Cumberland's official view, practically inescapable motives of self-interest
for being benevolent, known to derive from the will of the first cause,
are apparently insufficient by themselves to make it the case that
agents are *obligated* to be benevolent. It is also necessary that God's
will be *authoritative*. As we shall later appreciate, we are not yet in a
position to analyze Cumberland's view about God's authority. But
when we are, we shall see that despite the route Cumberland's official view takes through the notion of divine authority, this route is, in
fact, a circle. In the end, what makes the law of nature an obligating
law is the very same thing that makes it a dictate of practical reason.

EMPIRICAL GROUNDS FOR THE LAW OF
NATURE, UNDERSTOOD EGOCENTRICALLY

In our desire to understand why Cumberland thinks the law of nature action-guiding and obligating, we have said next to nothing
about why he thinks it is *true*. We have provisionally understood the
law to assert that all rational human agents are likeliest to have the
happiest lives within their power if they act with greatest benevolence "to all rationals" – to fellow humans and to God. Why does
Cumberland think this is so? All of his foundational theses will count
for nothing against Hobbes unless he can establish this apparently
unlikely empirical claim in the face of Hobbes's powerful arguments
against it. Of course, we should not make too much of this empirical
controversy, since even if Cumberland is wrong, there is still the
important question of how philosophically adequate (and histor-

17. This comes from Cumberland's definition of the law of nature at the beginning of
Chapter V: "a *Proposition, proposed to the Observation of, or impress'd upon, the Mind,
with sufficient Clearness, by the Nature of Things, from the Will of the first Cause, which
points out that possible Action of a rational Agent, which will chiefly promote the
common Good, and by which only the intire Happiness of particular Persons can be
obtain'd*" (189). For an interesting discussion of two different formulations of this
definition given in two different printings of the first (Latin) edition of 1672, see
Kirk, *Richard Cumberland and Natural Law*, pp. 31–32.
For other passages on natural promulgation, see, e.g., pp. 182, 192, 234, 296.

ically significant) an account of morality's normativity he would have provided were his empirical claims to have been correct. Nonetheless, we should try to understand why Cumberland thought they were.

Cumberland offers a barrage of empirical arguments, many of which depend importantly on what he takes a person's good to be. *"Natural good"* or happiness *"is that which preserves, or enlarges and perfects, the Faculties"* of a person (165).[18] "I have no inclination, very curiously to *inquire*," he writes at one point,

[w]hether the *Happiness* of Man be an Aggregate of the most vigorous *Actions,* which can proceed from our Faculties; or rather a most *grateful Sense of them,* join'd with Tranquillity and Joy, which by some is call'd *Pleasure.* These are inseparably connected, and *both necessary* to Happiness. (209)[19]

A person's happiness or natural good thus consists in some combination that includes the exercise of natural faculties, the enjoyment of good things, and such pleasurable awarenesses of these as tranquility and joy.

As we shall better appreciate in the next section, Cumberland believes he can reasonably claim that acting with universal benevolence is a more satisfying exercise of our powers than purely self-regarding action (23). An extensive benevolence is intrinsically satisfying in at least two different ways: It realizes the joy of love and the tranquility of a mind unconflicted between what it wills for itself and what it wills for others.[20] In addition to bringing these intrinsic psychic benefits, benevolence is also useful, making an agent less vulnerable to various maladies (psychological *and* physiological) that afflict the exclusively self-regarding. *"Hatred* and *Envy,* which fill the Mind of him who regards *his own Good only,* are necessarily accompanied with *Trouble* and *Sadness, Fear* and a *Solitary State,* which are evidently *inconsistent* with a *Happy Life"* (213). Egoism is, moreover, bad medicine:

In Envy, Hatred, Fear and Grief, the Motion of the Blood is retarded, and the Heart is clogg'd, so that it contracts, and expels the Blood, with difficulty;

18. Natural good contrasts with *moral good,* which Cumberland, like other writers in the modern natural law tradition, identifies by its relation to law. See, e.g., pp. 22, 166, 198, 203.
19. Again: "I care not in this Argument to *distinguish* between the *Health of Mind,* and the Consciousness, or *Enjoyment* thereof by *Reflexion,* since Nature has so intimately united these two, that the free Exercise of the Virtues, and the Perception or inward Sense thereof, are inseparable" (265).
20. See, e.g., pp. 207, 213, 224. Both themes will be further analyzed in the next section.

whence the Countenance of Man becomes pale, and numberless Mischiefs, and the whole Animal Oeconomy, but especially in the Functions of the Brain and Nerves, follow; such are the Distempers usually ascrib'd to the Spleen and Melancholy. (127)[21]

All these goods and evils are independent of the actions and attitudes of others. Benevolence requires others as object, of course, but the benevolent's peace of mind and its physiological correlates are not goods that need to be shared with others. Still, many of the most important goods *are* common goods, Cumberland thinks. Human beings are social by nature, not just in the sense that they depend on each other as means to their respective happiness, but in the sense that they figure *intrinsically* in each other's happiness.[22] Many of the powers we intrinsically enjoy are social powers, faculties that must be exercised in concert with others.

Part of Cumberland's disagreement with Hobbes, therefore, concerns the nature of human good. Hobbes sees the state of nature as one of conflict that can be roughly modeled as an n-person Prisoner's Dilemma, partly, at any rate, because he supposes there are enough people whose most highly valued outcome can be achieved only if others' are not. Desires for glory, power, and scarce resources, for example, tend to produce competition, since it is difficult if not impossible for them to be jointly satisfied. If we think of a simple version of the state of nature as a two-person game in which each can choose between aggression and nonaggression, at least a sizable minority, Hobbes supposes, will value most highly the outcome of their own *unopposed* aggression and value least highly the converse. For such persons, aggression cannot fail to be the course of action likeliest to achieve the agent's most preferred outcomes, assuming the game is played once and the action of each is independent of that of the other. An opponent has only two choices: If the other aggresses, the agent will have done better to have aggressed also; and if the other does not, the agent will have done better by aggression in that case as well. And if there are enough people like that, it will be rational for others to be aggressive preemptively.

This is not the way Cumberland sees things. For him, the peace that derives from mutual nonaggression and, even more, from mutual benevolence is not only the best outcome agents can rationally hope for given the power behind others' interests. Rather, Cumber-

21. Cumberland's physiological discussion even includes a fold-out diagram of the nerves in the human backbone, inserted between pages 150 and 151.
22. On mutual dependence, see, for example, pp. 60, 161, 237.

land supposes that in a two-person case each values these outcomes highest. And it is arguable that he thinks an agent will be worse off in the case where both are aggressive than in one where the other is aggressive and she is not. If human beings are like this, then the state of nature is more like what game theorists call a coordination problem than a problem of conflict. Moreover, since, whatever the other does, the best response is nonaggression, it is a game they can solve. Even if we suppose that human agents prefer the outcome of opposing aggression to what would result from not doing so, it will remain true that the most highly ranked outcome of each can be jointly achieved. So long as each can reasonably predict the other's values (and, of course, rely on her rationally pursuing them), nonaggression will remain, for each, the course of action most likely to achieve their ends.

Not even Hobbes thinks of the state of nature as a one-shot Prisoner's Dilemma.[23] Contracts in which the other has already performed should be kept, because this affects the future willingness of others to cooperate and thus the possibility of exit from the misery of the state of nature. To this thought Cumberland adds a distinctively Christian twist. Nothing is likelier to draw forth benevolence from others than love; and nothing more likely to incite hatred than violence.[24]

Cumberland recognizes, of course, that many of the goods we seek will be accomplished by benevolence only if others do in fact respond in kind, and that this response can hardly be assumed. With "future contingent" goods and evils, it is necessary to estimate their probability and discount them suitably.[25] All in all, he claims, human agents can expect to accomplish the greatest happiness within their power by a general policy of benevolence.

We need not worry much about the details of Cumberland's empirical arguments. Doubtless they prove too much. Cumberland is

23. See, for instance, Hampton, *Hobbes and the Social Contract Tradition*, pp. 75–78, 81–84. It is necessary, of course, and customary, to engage in some anachronistic counterfactual speculation at this point. There is an obvious sense in which Hobbes had no beliefs at all on this subject.
24. See pp. 63, 250, 273.
25. "Suppose a Man stealing *three* Pounds, is threaten'd by the Law with a *sevenfold* Restitution, that is, with a Fine of *Twenty-one* Pounds, and that the Chance of his escaping, is to that of his suffering, Punishment, as *four* to *three*, or that he has four Chances for escaping, and three for suffering, Punishment. That Fine of twenty-one Pounds, threaten'd with such a degree of Probability, is equal to *nine* Pounds certain; and, consequently, the *Motive to steal* is but as *three*, but the *Motive not to steal* is as, that is, thrice as great as the former" (257n).

no anarchist, after all, but we are apt to wonder what the need for civil power would be, except perhaps to provide coordinating salience, if he is right about the consequences of benevolence. Still, Cumberland is not without some powerful grounds for his claims.

In any case, whether the law of nature provides every agent with adequate reasons, based in his own good, for being benevolent may not matter as much to his overall argument as it may initially seem. Why this might be so can be initially glimpsed by noting several things. First, when Cumberland states the law of nature, he frequently includes within the consequences of benevolence not just the greatest happiness of the agent but that of *all*. Here is his first formulation: "The Endeavour, to the utmost of our power, of promoting the common Good of the whole System of rational Agents, conduces, as far as in us lies, to the good of every Part, in which our own Happiness, as that of a Part is contain'd" (16). Second, it may be recalled that in the passage, quoted in the last section, in which Cumberland analyzes the "bond" of the law of nature, he says that nothing can "superinduce a *Necessity*" of action on a deliberating agent "except Thoughts or *Propositions* promising Good or Evil to ourselves *or others*" (233; final emphasis added). And he adds that "we are *determin'd, by some sort of natural Necessity, to pursue Good foreseen*, especially the Greatest." In context, "the greatest" clearly cannot refer exclusively to the agent's good. Third, Cumberland remarks about his own account of obligation, "I do not deduce the *Obligation* of Laws, from this kind of Sanction, [here he adds a footnote: "The Happiness of a Particular Person"] (I have assign'd . . . another End, far greater) [footnote: "The Common Good"]" (248).

Up to this point, we have been assuming that the end relative to which the practical proposition of the law of nature directs benevolence is the agent's own good. These indications suggest, however, that this may not be the case, that practical reason recommends not just pursuing common good as a means to the *agent's* necessary end of his own good, but also, perhaps, *as an end in itself*.

PRACTICAL DICTATES OF REASON, AGREEMENT, AND THE BEST END

To explore this line of thought, we must begin with Cumberland's theory of the will. Cumberland assumes that benevolent, no less than self-regarding, action is within any human agent's power. "The *Truth* of *Moral Philosophy* is founded on" natural philosophy's discovery of "the *necessary Connexion* between the *greatest Happiness* human Powers can reach, and . . . Acts of universal Benevolence" (56). In order for this "speculative" truth to be a practical one, however, it must concern the consequences of something within the agent's power (42). It must be possible for agents to be benevolent, possible for them to take the good of others as end. In order for this speculative truth to found "the truth of moral philosophy," therefore, it must be *"suppos'd* as *Postulat[e]*, 'that [human agents] can exercise Love, not only towards themselves, but also towards God, and Men, partaking of the same rational Nature with themselves'" (56).[26]

In order to will an act, Cumberland holds, an agent must believe it promises good. But the good need not be the agent's; it may be the good of any rational being or of the system of rational beings. Sometimes Cumberland's claim seems to be that judging that an action will lead to some good for someone or other is a necessary condition for willing it; at other points, that it is sufficient to provide some motive, at least. In the first vein, he says such things as "a possible End is nothing else, than that Good or Happiness, which any one may propose to himself to pursue" (220). In the second: "'[T]he Understanding is capable of judging, what promotes the Good of others, as well as what promotes our own;' nor is there any *Reason*, 'Why we cannot will those same things, which we have judg'd to be good'" (173).[27]

There are three philosophically important moves here. One is that rational will is purely instrumental and exclusively "consequence-directed." The agent's end is always some (believed) *good effect* naturally producible by an action in his power.[28] This is hardly a trivial claim. It might be supposed, for instance, that a rational agent wills an act *as justified*, as supported by reasons, without necessarily supposing that the reasons she takes to justify it must derive entirely from the value of states of affairs that acting will realize. As we shall see, this is the thesis of the *normative theory of will* as advanced by Shaftesbury, Butler, and such rational intuitionists as Clarke and

26. See also, for example, pp. 54, 91, 160, 233.
27. See also pp. 168, 172. Sharp remarks that "the principle . . . that egoism and altruism have the same psychological root" "lies at the very foundation of [Cumberland's] system," since Cumberland believes that "the good as such, independently of its relationship to this or that possible possessor, tends to arouse the desire to realise it." See Sharp, "The Ethical System of Richard Cumberland," p. 380.
28. See pp. 168, 173, 196, 213–14, 220, 233.

Balguy. And it is, moreover, one of the things in contention between deontology and teleology throughout modern moral philosophy, which began to become apparent in the writings of Clarke, Butler, and Balguy.

This first move can be further analyzed into two distinct moments: first, the traditional doctrine that rational choice and will aim at the good and, second, the view that choice and agency have only *instrumental* value, that rational deliberation looks completely *through* agency, as it were, to the value of effects (states) it attempts to bring about. Together these moments yield the claim that the object of rational will is invariably some valuable effect within the agent's power.

The second fundamentally significant move is Cumberland's claim that the value of a consequential state must be resolvable into the *goods* of affected persons. This is the move characteristic of reductive naturalism, so long, that is, as it is supposed (as Cumberland evidently does suppose) that the good of a person can itself be naturalistically understood. It is a consequence of the first two moves that when an effect is aimed at *as good* (as Cumberland believes is true whenever an agent has an end), the will's object is the good *of someone.* Cumberland thus interprets the traditional doctrine that desire must be of the good as requiring that the object of desire always be the natural good of someone or other (168). In particular, he agrees with Hobbes and Locke that moral good cannot be desired intrinsically. For Cumberland, as for almost the entire modern natural law tradition, the idea of moral good derives from the more fundamental concept of law or right (166, 203). And only natural goods can be intrinsically desired. The belief that an action is unlawful or wrong cannot itself rationally motivate; only thoughts of naturally good and evil consequences of action can (246).

The third move is a departure from Locke, namely, that the good of others is no less eligible than the agent's good.[29] It follows, Cumberland argues, that since an agent has reason to will an end just insofar as it is a good effect, and since the good of others is no less good than the agent's own, the agent has the same reason to aim at the good of others that he does to aim at his own.

29. Although Cumberland takes the stronger position that an agent can will any action that he judges will realize good to some agent, it is more interesting to understand him as holding that benevolence is no less possible for us than is self-regard. So far as I can see, none of the arguments we are to consider depend on the stronger claim.

In order to will an act, therefore, an agent must be able to see some rationale for doing so in the thought that it will realize some good. And on this basis, human agents, at least, are capable of willing the good of any rational being. This being so, *it therefore arises as a practical question for us* not simply which act is likeliest to achieve *some single end* that is assumed exclusively to be the object of rational will (one's own good); rather, human agents face the questions, *Which* states *should* they make their ends? and Which acts are likeliest to achieve these? In the process of criticizing Hobbes's view that the right of nature follows from right reason, Cumberland makes just this point.

There is no doubt, but that Man has a *natural Power,* or *Will,* which he himself may *determine* to act which way he pleases. But when we are enquiring into the *Right* of Acting, the *Question* is, "Which, among those Actions which are in our *power,* are *lawful?*" . . . Any one *can* either hang, or throw down a Precipice, either himself, or any other innocent Person. (90).

A human agent *can* will to benefit *any* rational being. It is ultimately insufficient to establish a practical dictate of reason, therefore, to demonstrate that action is necessary to achieve the agent's own good, since we know that we can as well make the good of others our end, and their happiness is no less good than is ours.

This line of thought, which anticipates the rationale for half of what Sidgwick would later call the "dualism of practical reason," lies behind what might otherwise seem a puzzling series of remarks Cumberland makes about consistency and agreement.[30] We noted earlier, in passing, that Cumberland claims that the person who wills the same for himself that he does for others thereby has an " 'inward *Peace,* which arises from an uniform Wisdom, always agreeing with it self,' for it is *inconsistent* with it self, when it determines to act after *one manner in relation to itself,* and after *another manner in relation to others,* that partake of the *same Nature*" (44). But what sort of inconsistency does Cumberland here mean? It might be thought that he is referring to something that is more like conflicting desires than anything more deeply irrational. And for the purposes of his point about the agent's happiness, that appears to suffice. But other passages suggest he has some deeper kind of incoherence in mind.

Moreover, because of the *Likeness* of the Nature of other rational Agents. "To will *such* things to *them, as* we are naturally inclin'd to desire for *ourselves,*

30. Sidgwick, *The Methods of Ethics,* 7th ed., pp. 373–89, 507–9.

Reason cannot but judge more agreeable to our inward Principles of Action
. . . than to desire the *like* to Beings widely *different.*" (55)

It is difficult to understand Cumberland's comparison, but it is clear
enough that he thinks reason somehow recommends that we will the
happiness of all rational beings because we will our own and they
share our nature. Here is another passage to the same effect:

It is *evident,* "That *no Action relating to others* can be *consistent* with those
necessary and right *Actions conducing to our own Good,* unless the *Practical
Dictates of Reason,* by which we are determin'd to *that Action,* be plainly
conformable to those, by which we are directed in *pursuit of our own Happiness,*
that is, unless they enjoin us to *desire such things to them as to our-selves.*" (211)

Now, the thesis that consistency as a demand of practical reason
requires willing the same *states* with respect to all other rational
beings that one wills for oneself plainly differs from other similar
"agreement" theses Cumberland also advances. He formulates what
he calls "the fundamental *Corner-Stone* of the *Temple of Concord*" as
*"Whoever determines his Judgment and his Will by right Reason, must
agree with all others, who judge according to right Reason in the same
Matter"* (107). And he lists as a condition of "the perfection of the
Understanding" " 'That it *form like Judgments in like cases,* and alwaies
agree with it-self, after once it has form'd a right Judgment'" (208). The
judgment that each agent ought exclusively to pursue her own good
as end is consistent with both of these familiar and plausible latter
constraints, even though that judgment might involve an agent in
willing different *outcomes* for herself than she wills for other rational
beings. So why does Cumberland think the stronger constraint to be
warranted?

We can understand his thinking, I believe, if we consider an objection Cumberland makes to Hobbes's claim that agents in the state of
nature act with right when they act contrary to each other's goods.
"The reason of *Hobbes'*s making so gross a *Blunder* in this Argument,"
Cumberland says, "was, because he did not *observe,* 'That there was
the *same* Standard to *all,* by which the Reason of every one is to be
tried, whether it be right or no'" (106). There is a familiar sense, of
course, in which Hobbes agrees that right must be determined by the
same standard: each rightly does whatever tends to self-preservation.
But the problem, from Cumberland's point of view, remains. For if
we identify the agent's end with the effect at which he aims, since
different agents are aiming at different effects they are aiming at
different ends. And given his instrumentalist theory of agency and

what Cumberland means by 'standard', it follows that they act on *different standards*. Thus, Cumberland completes his criticism that what is wanting in Hobbes's scheme to provide a standard of right is an *"End* necessary to all rational Beings" (106). And it is clear he means to rule out any agent-relative end as a possible candidate. That gives each agent a different target effect or state, and so a different end. What is needed in order for there to be a common standard of practical reason is for there to be a *common end.*

As he puts his claim at another place,

Reason will not suffer, that the greatest *Private* Good should be propos'd as the *ultimate End.* For, since that *Action* is certainly *Good,* which will lead directly, or the shortest way, to that *End,* which is truly *ultimate;* supposing *different ultimate Ends,* whose Causes are opposite, *Actions* truly *Good* will be in *mutual opposition* to one another, which is impossible. (214)

Since this is so, he reasons, and "since there is no Cause, why the Happiness of one of these [say, the agent himself] should be [the agent's] ultimate End, rather than the Happiness of another should likewise be his ultimate End," he therefore concludes:

Reason dictates to neither, that he should propose to himself his own Happiness only, as his greatest End, but to every one, rather his own in conjunction with the Happiness of others; and this is that *Common Good,* which we contend is to be sought after. (214)

Cumberland's line of thought seems, then, much like Moore's famous "refutation of egoism" in *Principia Ethica*.[31] There is one fundamental ethical standard: the good. Therefore, whether conduct is justified – whether it is dictated by practical reason – depends not just on its aptitude for accomplishing some end or other but on whether it will accomplish ends that are really good. It cannot happen, therefore, that two "mutually opposing" actions, say, X and Y, are justified by their respective promotion of ends A and B, *irrespective* of the fact that each prevents the accomplishment of the *other* end – respectively, B and A. If X's promoting A can justify X, that is because A is good. And if Y's promoting B can justify Y, that is because B is good also. But then, that they will respectively prevent the accomplishing of B and A respectively must count *against* X and Y as well.

It follows, for Cumberland, that if another's good is no less good than the agent's, she has no less reason to aim at it than at her own.

31. G. E. Moore, *Principia Ethica* (Cambridge: Cambridge University Press, 1966), pp. 99–102.

Whether an agent's good is good has nothing to do with its being hers.[32] "Let *Hobbes* tell me," Cumberland writes, "what the addition of a *proper name* does, toward making the former Proposition [that each do what promotes her self-preservation] a *more evident* Dictate of Reason, that is, a Law of Nature, than the latter, which affirms the same with respect to *every one*" (216).[33] This is a familiar dialectic, the next move in which is usually for it to be pointed out that it might still be the case that, say, S's Xing's promoting A and, say, T's Ying's promoting B, respectively, justify S's Xing and T's Ying because A is an end which it is best for S to aim at (S ought to aim at A) and B is something which it is best for T to aim at (T ought to aim at B). But if the only thing that can rationalize action is the value of an effect that is naturally produced by an act (and not, say, the effect's being the object of a rational aim), then this move is unavailable.[34]

The "perfection of a rational Agent," therefore, requires not just instrumental rationality but *"that he should resolve upon the End before the Means"* (208). And so, Cumberland concludes "[t]hat *practical Reason* is then called *Right*, when it determines truly, or as the thing is in itself, in Propositions declaring what is every man's *best* and most necessary *End*, and what are the most proper *Means* of obtaining it" (105; emphasis added to "best").[35] Moreover, "the *Common Good* is the *only End*, in the pursuit whereof *all Rational Beings can agree* among themselves; because it comprehends the *greatest possible Happiness of all*; and it is most certain, that only *that* Practical Reason is true which discovers to *all* an *End* and *Means*, in which *all* who make a true Judgment *can agree*" (238).[36] The best end must be one on which all rational agents can agree; and the only such end is the common good.

32. See p. 273.
33. Evidently, what Cumberland means is not a proper name, but a reflexive or what Thomas Nagel has called a "free agent variable." See *The Possibility of Altruism*, p. 48.
    Cf. also p. 214, where Cumberland claims that if judgments of good signify or express some relation to the *judge's* desires, "the Terms, *Good* and *Evil*, will be *uncertain*, and altogether Equivocal, signifying *differently*, when they are made use of by *different* persons."
34. This amounts to the requirement that a theory of rational conduct be *agent-neutral*, "giving to all agents *common* . . . aims." *Agent-relative* theories give *"different* agents *different* [material] aims." See Derek Parfit, *Reasons and Persons* (Oxford: Clarendon Press, 1984), pp. 54–55.
35. As Albee remarks, "[R]ational character . . enables [a person] to apprehend and desire the Good, *qua* Good, quite independently of the question as to whose Good it may be." *History of Utilitarianism*, pp. 24–25.
36. See also, for example, pp. 141, 274..

Returning now to the law of nature, we should recall that it asserts a connection between a means, or "cause," and an end, or "effect." Our initial focus was on the connection between benevolence and the agent's own happiness. But Cumberland's usual formulation of the "effect" *combines* the happiness of the agent with that of all others. Thus, he first formulates the law of nature this way: "The Endeavour, to the utmost of our power, of promoting the common Good of the whole System of rational Agents, conduces, as far as in us lies, to the good of every Part, in which our own Happiness, as that of a Part, is contain'd" (16). The line of thought we have just been pursuing helps explain why this is so and, as well, why Cumberland says of this formulation, "[T]he foregoing *Proposition* . . . declares the *Cause* of the greatest and best *Effect*" (18).

What practical reason dictates is thus not simply the best means to whatever ends the agent happens to have or even, exclusively, to the agent's own good. The "dictates of practical reason . . . point out either the end, or the means thereto, in every man's power." And "that *practical Reason* is then called *right*, when it determines truly . . . what is every man's *best and most necessary End*" (105; emphasis added). Finally, "the common Good is the best and greatest End, which they [rational beings] can propose to themselves" (25).[37]

It might be thought that even if practical reason, faced with a choice between aiming at the end of the agent's own happiness and the greatest happiness of all, along with other possible ends, were to dictate the *best* end, it would not directly follow that practical reason dictates promoting the greatest overall happiness. There are, again, two steps that lead Cumberland to this further conclusion. The first is that the best end is the best *effect*, the best state of affairs producible by any act in the agent's power.[38] The second is the reductive naturalist move that the value of a state is constituted by the natural goods of affected parties. Thus, once he has established that practical reason aims at the best end, Cumberland thinks he has a very short argument for the conclusion that practical reason dictates promoting the greatest aggregate good:

"The Happiness of All is greater than the like Happiness of any smaller Number." But "that Happiness is the greatest, which is greater than any other assignable." Nor is it a different Judgment, that by which we *affirm*,

37. See also, for instance, pp. 30, 173, 186, 196, 201, 222, 296.
38. See note 29.

"The greatest Happiness of all Rational Beings is the greatest or chief End, which any Rational Agent can pursue." (220)

"The greatest overall happiness" is, if you like, the *naturalistic meaning* of "best end." This is why Cumberland says, quite early in the Introduction, and long before his readers can possibly understand what he means, that the *Method* is shown, "[h]ow to reduce whatsoever the Moralists have said concerning the Means of obtaining the best End into *Theorems* concerning the *Power* of human Actions in producing the Effects propos'd" (18).[39] Once "best end" is interpreted naturalistically, natural philosophy is able to establish truths concerning what will promote it.[40]

This leaves us with some puzzles about how exactly Cumberland conceives the relation between the best means and the best end, and between these and the agent's own happiness. If Cumberland believes he has a sound argument that practical reason (directly) dictates taking the greatest happiness of all as end, then what dialectical need is answered by his strenuous efforts to argue that every individual agent's interest is best served by benevolence? On the other hand, if the latter argument really is necessary to some important purpose, for example, to evidencing rewards and sanctions in order

39. "We must firstly distinctly know, what is the best effect in our power, before we can distinctly know the chief end we ought to regard" (47).
40. Exactly what naturalistic meaning Cumberland means to propose for the best end is hardly as clear as I have been suggesting. Sometimes, as in the passage above, it is referred to in net aggregative terms: "the greatest happiness of all rational beings." At other points, however, the best end is called the "common good," and some measure that takes account of the distribution of happiness throughout the system of rationals is suggested. For the latter, see, e.g., pp. 202, 203, 214.
    Haakonssen claims that Cumberland's "idea that the goods of all rational agents form a system is not an aggregative notion; it is not simply the sum of all individual goods." "Moral Philosophy and Natural Law," 100. Context suggests that by "individual goods" Haakonssen means not the goods of individuals but individually good things. If we take his claim to be that the best end is not simply the greatest sum of good things, whatever that might mean, that seems unobjectionable enough. It does not follow from this, however, that the best end is not an aggregative notion, since it could still be the greatest net aggregate happiness; and this may indeed be Cumberland's view. Whether or not it is, it is clear enough that Cumberland takes human goods to be commensurable, and hence susceptible to a quantitative treatment. See, for example, TLN.186–87: "The End is to be conceiv'd as the greatest Aggregate, or Sum, of good Effects, most acceptable to God and Men, which can be effected, by the greatest Industry of all our future Actions. . . . [I]f all Questions, concerning *Practice*, were handled *accurately*, they might be reduced to mathematical Evidence and Certainty; such are the determining the *Value*, both of Things and human Labour or Actions."

to establish an *obligation* to benevolence, then what exactly is the respective *force* of each argumentative prong? To say that Cumberland leaves these matters unclear is understatement. Perhaps his view is that whereas the best end is the greatest happiness of all, nonetheless the agent's happiness continues to make a claim as end that is not reducible to its being part of the happiness of all. If this were so, we could understand why Cumberland would still feel the need he so evidently does to establish a coordination between the greatest individual happiness and the greatest happiness of all. Exactly what rationale there could be for such a view, once it is supposed both that the only rational ends are (naturally) good effects and that the agent's happiness is no better an effect than the equivalent happiness of any other person, is, however, unclear.

Cumberland's remark, mentioned in passing above, that he "deduce[s] the *Obligation* of Laws" not from "the happiness of a particular person" but from the "common good" may now begin to take on something approximating sense. At least, we can now understand why he says, immediately thereafter:

In that most Universal Law [the law of nature], which I chiefly consider, concerning the pursuit of the most General Good, the Honour of God join'd with the Happiness of Men, it is evident, that the Action commanded, is not necessary to any superior or *greater Effect*, since no such there either is, or can be. (248)

The greatest happiness of all, Cumberland must be saying, is the best end, quite independent of whether pursuing it will best promote the agent's happiness. From this thought he proceeds, curiously, as follows. Were we to understand the law of nature as simply asserting a connection between benevolence and the greatest happiness of all, then it could not *incite* benevolent action, since we would already have to be benevolent, that is, to desire the greatest overall good, in order to have any motive to take the necessary means to it: benevolent action.[41] If, then, the law of nature is to be genuinely practical through directing or inciting to action, it must recommend benevolence as a means to some other end we can be supposed to have.[42]

41. This is not quite right, of course. Knowledge of this connection would at least disarm the thought that benevolence might have self-defeating side effects, and hence might lead the benevolent person actually to act.
42. But, then, how this could give rise to benevolence, as opposed to the desire to be benevolent, would be unclear. It could, however, clear away self-interested obstacles to the desire.

[T]herefore, the Pursuit or Production of this Effect (as far as we are able) is to be look'd on as necessary to some *lesser Effect* thence depending; that is, in order to procure, by the Assistance of all Causes, our own Happiness, which we are justly suppos'd to desire. The Proposition, understood so, does most powerfully excite to Action. (248)

OBLIGATION RECONSIDERED

If any idea is likely to be particularly resistant to Cumberland's project of naturalist reduction, it would appear to be the notion of Divine *authority* so seemingly central to his account of obligation. Even if the practicality of these prescriptions, their necessary connection to necessary ends, can be fully understood in naturalistic terms, and even if God's existence and will can be sufficiently established by naturalistic methods, in what proposition of natural philosophy can God's authority be thought to consist? And, hence, how can natural philosophy establish that the law of nature is a genuinely obligating law? Cumberland does not directly address this question until quite late in the *Treatise*, and his answer demonstrates that, despite appearances, he is in no sense a theological voluntarist. In discussing God's dominion or right to be obeyed, Cumberland says that he used, "as most others do, to deduce the Divine Dominion intirely from his being the Creator" (320). This, we recall, was Locke's view. But Cumberland tells us that he came to realize that "all Right is a Power granted or permitted by some Law. . . . But Law there is none prior to the *Natural* Law, or that *Dictate* of the Divine *Wisdom*, concerning the *Best End*, and the *Means* thereto *necessary*" (320). The ground for God's right that we obey the law of nature is simply *that it is the law of nature* – in other words, that it indicates the "*Best End*, and the *Means* thereto *necessary*." Indeed, Cumberland thinks we can judge the truth and bindingness of the law of nature for ourselves, without special reference to God's wisdom. "*God will determine the same End and Means to be best, which the Reason of any Man truly judges to be so*" (220). Once *we* have determined that the best end is the good of all, and that benevolence is the best means to our necessary ends,

there is no room to *doubt*, but that we shall *here also have God's Concurrence.* For, since He himself is *Rational*, and it cannot be conceiv'd, how he can act *rationally, without* proposing an *End* to himself, nor can there be a *greater* End than the aforesaid *Aggregate of all Good* Things; we cannot but think, he judges this to be the best End he can propose to himself. (220–21)

Cumberland even goes so far as to say that we "believe the sacred Scriptures to be the Word of God, the Author of Nature, *because* they every where illustrate, confirm, and promote the Law of Nature" (34).[43]

The only sense in which the law of nature obligates because it is prescribed by God, therefore, is that *it obligates because it is prescribed by practical reason,* and God is a (perfectly) rational agent. If, consequently, the idea of rational dictate can *itself* be understood naturalistically, no further naturalistic account of obligation is required. The *obligating* power of the law of nature *just is* its inescapable practical force for a rational agent.

CONCLUSION: NORMATIVITY AS CALM REFLECTIVE DELIBERATION

Cumberland thus follows Hobbes in attempting to provide a fully naturalistic account of the normative force of obligation and of the idea of a rational dictate, although he rejects Hobbes's theory that these derive entirely from instrumental rationality. Ends no less than means are within the scope of rational choice. Human rational will aims, by natural necessity, at ends (effects) as good, and therefore aims above all at the best end (effect) within its power. This is no less essential to human rational will, Cumberland evidently believes, than is instrumental rationality. A naturalistic account of the best end (best effect) is thus required, and one, he thinks, is to hand: the state realizing the greatest good of all rationals.

As human rational agents, Cumberland writes, "we are *determin'd, by some sort of natural Necessity, to pursue Good foreseen,* especially the Greatest" (233). Thus do "Thoughts or *Propositions* promising Good or Evil, to ourselves or others, consequent upon what we are about to do" "superinduce a *Necessity* of doing or forbearing . . . upon a Human Mind deliberating upon a thing future" (233). Normative force is thus practical force for an agent who deliberates rationally, with natural necessity determining what are ultimate ends for human rational agents.

---

43. As noted in Forsyth, "The Place of Richard Cumberland in the History of Natural Law Doctrine," p. 28. This article discusses Cumberland as a Baconian response to Hobbes.

This adds an additional empirical naturalist view of normativity to the instrumental reason view we encountered in Hobbes, one we might call a *calm reflective deliberation* view.[44]

What makes beneficence obligatory for Cumberland is that the greatest good of all rationals is what rational reflection leads a deliberating human agent to seek. This is a matter of *natural* rather than logical necessity. The idea is not, as we shall see it to be with Cudworth and Shaftesbury, that reason is a creative faculty, with ends internal to it. What we discover through the use of reason in ethics is no different from what empirical investigation yields in natural philosophy. Practical reason is nothing other than theoretical reason as it is relevant to an agent "deliberating upon a thing future." But neither is human deliberation restricted to instrumental reason. We can also ask what ends we should seek, and find that, given our psychological nature, we can desire the goods of others as well as our own. The fullest rational reflection, Cumberland argues, leads a human agent to seek the greatest good for all, and this, he concludes, makes universal benevolence obligatory. This choice is obligatory because it is what would eventuate from the fully calm, reflective use of (theoretical) reason.

Again, we should be clear that what makes this choice obligatory is not that *it* is naturally necessary but that, as a matter of natural necessity, it is the choice that would result from fully calm, theoretically informed deliberation. If a choice is a result of the "*Ignorance,* turbulent *Affections,* or *Rashness* of Men, like the *Fault in the Balance,*" it is not rationally binding (234). What makes a choice obligatory is that it is the one that would, by natural necessity, eventuate by the full use of theoretical reason in deliberation.[45]

This sketch of Cumberland's ideas leaves much unclear, but no doubts should remain about whether Cumberland's project, taken as a whole, was to provide an account of morality's normative grip in fully naturalistic terms, and to argue on this basis that morality genuinely obligates because it provides human agents with rationally inescapable motives. Later writers of the period were less likely than Cumberland to accept that benevolence is intrinsically rational be-

44. Schneewind rightly notes that Hobbes and Cumberland share the idea that obligation is to be understood in terms of motivational force. It should be clear from our discussion, however, how different their views are in other respects. See Schneewind, "Kant and Natural Law Ethics," p. 65.

45. On the importance of this point for Hobbes's theory of normativity, see Chapter 1, note 18.

cause it aims at the best end, but they were deeply influenced none-theless by his attempt to understand obligation itself as inescapable rational motive. By the turn of the century, this view would become orthodoxy.

Chapter 5

Cudworth: obligation and self-determining moral agency

For Hobbes and Cumberland, the rationale for the internal turn was philosophical naturalism. If ethics is simply the study of "consequences from the passions of men," and if "the Whole of *moral Philosophy*" is to be "resolv'd into . . . conclusions of true *Natural Philosophy*," then there may seem nothing plausible for morality's normative grip to be other than its motive power, viewed from the perspective of a rational human agent.[1] From an *agent's* point of view, empirical truths to which an observer is indifferent can present themselves as *demands* – as matters of *practical*, rather than merely natural, necessity. To the agent for whom self-preservation is an inescapable end, for example, facts about the natural necessities of survival have an unavoidable practical force; they present themselves as what *ought to* or must be done.

Empirical naturalist internalism of this sort exercised a continuing attraction throughout the early modern period, as it has, indeed, to the present day. At the same time, a second, quite different, internalist line of thought developed alongside it: an *autonomist internalism* or *internalism of practical reason*. We encountered elements of this line, in early form, in Culverwell's notion that only a being capable of "moral government" can be subject to obligation.[2] We shall return to it again in Locke's *Essay* thesis that moral government must involve *self*-government. Neither Culverwell nor Locke (at least in his earlier writings) proposed, however, that obligation itself be understood to consist in the motives of a self-determining agent, and so neither was an autonomist internalist. For both, the fact of obligation lay in a juridical relation of authority obtaining between Creator and created,

1. *Lev.*IX.4; *TLN*.41.
2. See Chapter 2, "Accountability."

and what guaranteed that human agents can determine themselves to act as they are obligated is extrinsic to that. For Culverwell, the guarantee derived from eternal law, from natural law's replicating what human beings already have adequate rational motives to do thanks to their final cause. And for Locke, it came from the vanity of any command without sanctions, and thus from the impossibility that God should command anything without also providing appropriate rational motives for obedience.

Taking the authority of morality to have an external source while maintaining that it can genuinely obligate only agents able autonomously to guide themselves by it is a position of doubtful stability, however. No inconsistency is involved, but it is hard to see how to hold these ideas together happily. Not surprisingly, some British moralists of the period began to feel that if morality can obligate no agent who cannot be autonomously moral, then the ground of moral obligation must be more closely linked to the capacity for self-government. And some effectively proposed that morality's normative grip must itself consist in morality's power to provide conclusive motives to an autonomous agent. This *autonomist internalism* was the second line of thought leading to the internal turn. Moral obligation must consist in a source of motivation available to autonomous moral agents as such, since otherwise agents could be bound contrary to what they can be autonomously motivated to do, and this is impossible. According to this view, a theory of moral obligation, of *subjection* to morality, must be made to fit with an adequate account of the self-determining moral *subject* and the *will*.

Now, it should not be supposed that there existed in mid to late seventeenth-century Britain any well-recognized, much less well-worked-out, notion of self-determination or autonomy. On the contrary, the idea was very much in the process of being shaped. It was not, indeed, until the early nineteenth century that 'autonomy' came in English to have other than a political sense.[3] Nevertheless, it can be shown that the idea of self-determination played a very significant role in the thought of a number of early modern British philosophers and, indeed, that some of these writers advanced versions of a

---

3. Primarily, it seems, as a consequence of Coleridge's Kantian writings. *The Compact Edition of the Oxford English Dictionary* (Oxford: Oxford University Press, 1985), vol. 1, p. 575, gives the first use of 'autonomy' in connection with the will as Coleridge's *Biographia Literaria* (1817). A use of 'autonomy' as early as 1803 to mean political liberty of individual choice is also listed.

thesis we are much more familiar with in Kant: that moral obligation is self-imposed in the practical reasoning of a self-determining agent.[4] The "fact" of obligation to do something consists in this: Were the agent in her practical context to determine her will autonomously, she would "impose" on herself a conclusive motive for acting in that way.

Given the usual picture of modern British moral philosophy, the claim that versions of this Kantian view were represented in Britain during the early modern period may seem surprising. The British moralists are usually divided into two broad categories, and a theory like Kant's fits neatly into neither. One category is the sort of empirical naturalism typified by Hobbes, Cumberland, Francis Hutcheson, and Hume. The other is the kind of rational intuitionism represented by Samuel Clarke, John Balguy, and Richard Price.[5] Although thinkers in each of these categories have been associated with varieties of internalism in ethics, neither category admits of an autonomist internalism or internalism of practical reason of the Kantian sort. Like Hobbes, Empirical naturalists may take the internal turn for reasons we have already noted. Or, like Hutcheson or Hume, they may understand morality to be grounded in a distinctive sentiment in a way that guarantees a (perhaps indirect) link to motive. Rational intuitionists, on the other hand, though they also assert a kind of connection between morality and motive, are not internalists in the present sense, since they do not believe that normativity (obligation) is itself to be understood as internal to the rational will. Rather, they affirm the ancient Platonic doctrine that it is of the nature of the ethical that it cannot be *known* or *perceived* with indifference.[6] And they explicitly deny that what makes a moral claim true, even a claim about obligation, is anything essentially to do with motivation or the will.[7] For rational intuitionists like Clarke and Price, reason is a

4. The primary Kantian texts here are Chapter III of Kant's *Groundwork of the Metaphysics of Morals* and his *Critique of Practical Reason*. For a very helpful discussion of this aspect of Kant's views, see Henry Allison, *Kant's Theory of Freedom* (Cambridge: Cambridge University Press, 1990), especially Part III; and Korsgaard, "Kant's Analysis of Obligation," passim.
5. John Deigh, for example, refers to empiricism and intuitionism as the "two great traditions" of British moral philosophy. See his "Sidgwick on Ethical Judgment," in Bart Schultz, ed., *Essays on Henry Sidgwick* (Cambridge: Cambridge University Press, 1992), p. 241.
6. For Price, see Raphael, *British Moralists, 1650–1800*, vol. 2, p. 194. This has selections from Price's *A Review of the Principal Questions in Morals* (1758). See Chapter 11, n. 16.
7. This claim must be modified with respect to Balguy. See Chapter 11.

purely theoretical faculty that registers a metaphysically independent (normative) order. Empirical naturalists deny any such faculty
or order, but they *agree* with the intuitionists that reason is an entirely
theoretical faculty. *Both* empiricists and intuitionists hold that reason
registers (or infers) facts, whether natural or metaphysical, that are in
no way constituted by it. They recognize, therefore, no such thing as
practical reason in the Kantian sense. Practical reasoning, for them, is
theoretical reasoning in the service of deliberation.[8] Neither intuitionists nor empirical naturalists hold the 'ought' itself to be constituted by practical reason, within the functioning of autonomous
rational will.

Against this background, the claim that the first British moralist to
advance a version of autonomist internalism was Ralph Cudworth
will seem especially surprising, since Cudworth is generally regarded as a precursor of Clarke and Price.[9] But this traditional pic-

---

8. Whether Cumberland can be understood in this way depends on how one understands his claims concerning the relations among desire, rational will, and the
   good.
9. Thus, Martineau placed Cudworth together with Clarke and Price as "dianoetic
   moralists" who held an ultimately "extrinsic ground for the preference involved in
   every moral decision," namely, the concern to mirror the truth: "'We approve the
   Right, because it is *true;* if we did not, we should not be intelligent, but should
   form judgments discordant with the real relations of things.'" James Martineau,
   Types of Ethical Theory (Oxford: Oxford University Press, 1901), vol. 2, p. 425. This
   actually better describes Wollaston than even the rational intuitionists. See Chapter 11.
   Sidgwick says of Clarke that he proceeds "on the lines of Cudworth's reasoning
   rather than of Locke's, . . . that the cognition of self-evident practical propositions
   is in itself, independently of pleasure and pain, a sufficient motive to a rational
   being as such for acting in accordance with them" (*Outlines of the History of Ethics,*
   p. 179). This is true as far as it goes, but Sidgwick fails to recognize that for
   Cudworth, though not for Clarke, the object of cognition is not a metaphysically
   independent normative order but motives inherent in practical reason itself. Thus
   Sidgwick remarks, "According to Cudworth, the distinctions of good and evil
   have an objective reality, cognisable by reason no less than the relations of space or
   number: the knowledge of them comes no doubt to the human mind from the
   Divine; but it is from the Divine Reason. . . . ethical propositions, therefore, are as
   unchangeably valid for the direction of the conduct of rational beings as the truths
   of geometry are" (pp. 170–71). A remark of David Hume's is also relevant in this
   connection: "Father Malebranche, as far as I can learn, was the first that started
   this abstract theory of morals, which was afterwards adopted by Cudworth,
   Clarke, and others; and as it excludes all sentiment, and pretends to found
   everything on reason, it has not wanted followers in this philosophic age." *An
   Enquiry Concerning the Principles of Morals* (1751), in *Enquiries Concerning Human
   Understanding and Concerning the Principles of Morals,* ed. L. A. Selby-Bigge, 3d. ed.,
   with text rev. and notes by P. H. Nidditch (Oxford: Clarendon Press, 1985), p. 197n.
   More recent commentators have more or less accepted this picture of Cudworth
   as a proto-Clarkean. See, e.g., W. von Leyden's edition of Locke's *Essays on the Law*

ture is misleading at best. Cudworth held that the truth of any ethical proposition depends on the practicality of pure reason. And he maintained that morality obligates only because self-determining agents can bring moral motives to bear in their own practical reasoning.[10]

It is understandable how the traditional view of Cudworth emerged. The primary targets of *A Treatise Concerning Eternal and Immutable Morality*, Cudworth's only published work on ethics, were voluntarism and empiricism.[11] Against the voluntarists, Cudworth

of Nature, pp. 57–58; Colman, *John Locke's Moral Philosophy*, pp. 34–38; J. L. Mackie, *Hume's Moral Theory* (London: Routledge & Kegan Paul, 1980), pp. 16–17; and Norton, *David Hume*, p. 27. Not all these writers assert that Cudworth's views were substantially similar to Clarke's in all relevant respects, but they each discuss the two writers without recognizing that Cudworth's rationalism is a practical idealism, whereas Clarke's is not. It should also be noted that Clarke's views are not so easily pigeonholed as this sketch suggests. See, e.g., Sidgwick, *Outlines*, pp. 180–84.

There is one very noteworthy exception to the traditional interpretation of Cudworth, namely, John Passmore's excellent *Ralph Cudworth: An Interpretation* (Cambridge: Cambridge University Press, 1951). As I shall argue, however, Passmore tends to misread Cudworth's many remarks that mere "speculative understanding" or theoretical reason cannot motivate, and attributes to him a theory of action that is more Humean than is warranted. This is another symptom, I think, of the tendency to see modern British moral philosophy as having to fit into either the category of empiricist naturalism or that of rational intuitionism. More on this will follow.

Finally, although Cassirer does not discuss Cudworth much in this context, he makes the intriguing remark that the Cambridge Platonists (including Cudworth) and Leibniz "form two independent movements tending toward the same end; they are two important stages on the way leading from Luther to Kant, from the concept of freedom of the Reformation to the concept of freedom of idealism, from the principle of justification by faith to the principle of the autonomy of the will and of the practical reason." Ernst Cassirer, *The Platonic Renaissance in England*, trans. James P. Pettegrove (Austin: University of Texas Press, 1953), p. 85.

10. Cudworth belonged to a group of philosophers and latitudinarian divines known as the Cambridge Platonists, who attempted to knit together freedom, reason, morality, and love. In addition to Cudworth, these included Benjamin Whichcote, Henry More, and John Smith. Despite broad sympathies of thought, however, none of the rest of these thinkers shared Cudworth's clarity of focus on the foundations of ethics, and none are best read as advancing versions of autonomist internalism. On the Cambridge Platonists, see, in addition to Cassirer's *The Platonic Renaissance in England*, C. A. Patrides, ed., *The Cambridge Platonists* (Cambridge: Cambridge University Press, 1969), which has an especially useful introduction.

11. *A Treatise Concerning Eternal and Immutable Morality* was first published posthumously (Cudworth died in 1688) in London in 1731. A facsimile edition was published by Garland, in New York in 1976. Excerpts are contained in Schneewind, *Moral Philosophy from Montaigne to Kant*, vol. 1, pp. 275–92; Raphael, *British Moralists*, vol. 1, pp. 105–19; and Selby-Bigge, *British Moralists*, pp. 247–66. Further references to book, chapter, and section number of the *Treatise* will be

argued that all things, morality included, "are what they are, not by *Will* but by *Nature*" (1.ii.1). So "nothing is *Morally Good* or *Evil, Just* or *Unjust* by meer Will without Nature," since everything is what it is by nature (1.ii.3). And against the empiricists, he maintained that sense experience without intellect can yield no knowledge. In these respects, Cudworth's project did not differ from the rationalisms represented later by Clarke and Price. As they did, he believed that fundamental moral truths are "eternal and immutable," independent even of God's arbitrary will, and cognizable by the intellect. And as they did, he frequently likened the necessity of fundamental moral propositions to that of mathematical truths: "Omnipotence itself . . . cannot by meer Will make a Body *Triangular*, without having the Nature and Properties of a *Triangle* in it; That is, without having three Angles equal to two Right ones" (1.ii.1). All of this, together with the fact that the *Treatise* was not published until 1731, when Clarke's ideas were still in the air, encouraged a reading of Cudworth's moral philosophy through the lens of Clarke's.

In fact, however, Cudworth made a fundamental distinction between purely speculative intellect and *practical* mind, and asserted that ethical propositions are made true or false by the nature of the latter. This is only implicit in the sole work Cudworth published during his lifetime, the massive tome *The True Intellectual System of the Universe.*[12] But it is explicit in the *Treatise*, even if it is not directly relevant to that work's main aims. Where it is clearest, however, is in Cudworth's manuscripts on freedom of the will, all but one of which remain unpublished to this day.[13] It is there that Cudworth argues

given parenthetically in the text, preceded by *TEIM*, when context requires it. When appropriate, page references to Raphael (vol. 1) will be added, preceded by "R."

12. Ralph Cudworth, *The True Intellectual System of the Universe* (London: Richard Royston, 1678). There are at least two facsimile editions: Garland, New York, 1978 (in two volumes); and F. Fromman, Stuttgart–Bad Cannstatt, 1964. Further references to page numbers of the *System* will be placed parenthetically in the text, preceded when necessary by *TIS*.

13. British Library, Add. Mss. 4978–82. Only one of these (4978) has ever been published: *A Treatise of Freewill*, ed. John Allen (London: John W. Parker, 1838). A facsimile of Allen's edition is included in *The Collected Works of Ralph Cudworth*, vol. 1 (Hildesheim: Olms, 1979). Excerpts can be found in Raphael, *British Moralists*, vol. 1, pp. 120–34. Further references will be placed parenthetically in the text, preceded by *FW*. When appropriate, page references to Raphael's vol. 1 will be included, thus: R. References to other manuscripts in the British Library collection will be to their manuscript and page number, thus: 4980.00. Because spelling in the manuscripts is erratic, I have not tried to retain it.

For a useful discussion of the Cudworth manuscripts, see Passmore, *Ralph*

that morality obligates only because self-determining agents can bring moral motives to bear through their own practical reason.

Actually, there are three separate but interrelated ideas here. First, Cudworth believes, the very existence of a distinction between moral good and evil depends on there being motives intrinsic to perfect intellect. Perfect mind must be practical; it must be determined to *will* some things and not others. Second, we are subject to morality only because we participate in this practical intellect: We have a "superior" reason within us that is a source of moral motivation. And third, as imperfectly rational beings with competing, nonrational motives, who do not necessarily will in accord with superior reason, we can be obligated morally only because we have, in addition to superior reason, a capacity for self-determination. Together these give us "moral free will," making us accountable for determining ourselves by this superior motivational source.

Without a consideration of the manuscripts, it is impossible to appreciate the full significance of Cudworth's distinctions between speculative and practical mind and, especially, between the former and what he calls *practical judgment*, a form of which he identifies with the *will*. Because the manuscripts have not been generally available, it is not surprising that scholars have almost entirely missed the fundamental character of his view.

Cudworth must bear much of the responsibility for the serious misunderstanding of his moral philosophy. None of his voluminous writings on ethics and moral psychology were published during his lifetime, and even his *Treatise Concerning Eternal and Immutable Morality*, published almost fifty years after his death, was a work more in general epistemology than in moral philosophy. When Thomas Birch described the remaining Cudworth manuscripts in his 1743 edition of Cudworth's *System*, he mentioned "A Discourse of Moral Good and Evil, in several folios, containing near a thousand pages," in addition to manuscripts, of comparable length, on liberty and necessity.[14] Of these, only one manuscript, on free will, was subsequently

Cudworth, pp. 107–13. I am indebted to Richard Dees for invaluable help in transcribing Add. Ms. 4980 and the first section of Add. Ms. 4982 (dubbed "4982, Book I" by Passmore). Dees and I were supported by a Research Partnership Grant, for which we are grateful, from the Horace Rackham School of Graduate Studies and the Office of the Vice-President for Research at the University of Michigan.

14. Thomas Birch, "An Account of the Life and Writings of Ralph Cudworth," in Ralph Cudworth, *The True Intellectual System of the Universe*, vol. 1 (London, 1743), p. 32. Also in Cudworth, *True Intellectual System* (London: Tegg, 1843), vol. 1, pp. vii–xxvii. See also Passmore, pp. 107–13.

published, and most of the other materials do not now survive.[15]

It is not that Cudworth failed to *try* to bring his ideas concerning self-determination and its relation to practical mind, judgment, and moral obligation more explicitly before his readers. At the beginning of the Preface to the *System*, he writes that when he "engag'd the Press, [he] intended onely a Discourse concerning *Liberty* and *Necessity*" as necessary to establish the very possibility of genuine moral "*Guilt* and *Blame, Punishments* and *Rewards*." Cudworth's initial concern was indeed to publish something that would establish the necessary conditions for moral accountability or obligation. To say that planning was not Cudworth's forte is, however, severe understatement. He then realized, he tells us, that liberty can be denied on three different grounds. "Democritick" or "atheistick" fatalists, such as Hobbes, maintain that every human act is simply the necessary result of matter in motion, and thereby deny free will. Theists, however, may also deny the liberty necessary for genuine morality, and on two distinct grounds. They may assert "*Divine Fate Immoral*," holding that God's own "Will is no way Regulated or Determined" and that all moral good and evil are mere "*Theticall* or *Positive* things" dependent on God's arbitrary will. Or they may assert "*Divine Fate Morall*," holding that God is essentially good *and* that He has created us without the power of self-determination necessary for moral accountability.

This realization led Cudworth to plan three different books that, taken together, would constitute *The True Intellectual System of the Universe*. The first would refute atheism and "democritick" fate. The second would show that God's nature rather than His arbitrary will forms the basis of morality. And the third would establish that there is "a *Liberty*, or *Sui-Potestas*, in *Rational Creatures*, as may render them *Accountable*," "that we are so far forth . . . *Masters* of our own *Actions*, as to be *Accountable* to *Justice* for them, or to make us *Guilty* and *Blame-worthy* for what we doe Amiss."[16] Suffice it to say that after 899 pages, Cudworth discovered that he had carried out only the first task to his satisfaction. The projected second and third books of the *System* remained unpublished, although the posthumously pub-

15. As Passmore points out, none of the remaining manuscripts on free will corresponds to Birch's description of one of the books that made up Cudworth's *Discourse of Liberty and Necessity*, and what does remain does not seem to compose a continuous work. The *Discourse of Moral Good and Evil* seems to be almost entirely lost.

16. These passages occur on the third and second (unnumbered) pages, respectively, of Cudworth's Preface.

lished *Treatise* is probably a version (perhaps shortened) of the second. The manuscripts on free will must represent various of Cudworth's attempts at the third.

In addition to these failures to bring key elements of his view before his readers, it must also be said that Cudworth's writing is often extremely difficult to penetrate. *The True Intellectual System* is especially heavy with repetition, rhetorical flourish, and gratuitous scholarly quotation. As many commentators have noted, Cudworth's academic style is more that of Renaissance humanism than the plain diction and straightforward argument of such contemporaries as Hobbes, Locke, or even, relatively speaking, Cumberland. It is not surprising that when the *System* was admired, it was as much for scholarly erudition as for philosophical substance. Locke referred to it as a book "wherein that very learned author, hath with such accurateness and judgment, collected and explained the opinions of the Greek philosophers."[17] But Cudworth was by no means merely a quaint antiquarian. A member of the Royal Society, he was well informed about recent scientific developments and, indeed, accepted modern corpuscularism as the correct theory of matter.[18] Moreover, his work on ethics and moral psychology contained the seeds of some of the most important and profound ideas in modern moral philosophy.

Ultimately we shall want to understand the precise character of Cudworth's internal turn, and what led him to take it. It will help, however, to begin with the doctrines of "eternal and immutable morality" for which Cudworth is best known and which may seem far from internalist, to see that, actually, internalism is implicated even there.

ETERNAL AND IMMUTABLE MORALITY

AGAINST MORAL VOLUNTARISM

As I have mentioned, the primary object of Cudworth's famous doctrine of eternal and immutable morality is to counter moral vol-

17. Quoted in Passmore, *Ralph Cudworth*, p. 1. Passmore also there notes that "so sympathetic an interpreter as F. J. Powicke [author of *The Cambridge Platonists* (London: J. M. Dent, 1926)] will not put the importance of Cudworth's writings more strongly than this: 'a rich quarry to which an occasional student has been indebted for apt quotations and curious references.'"
18. As befitted his habits of mind, however, Cudworth steadfastly maintained that current atomic theories of matter were only the most recent versions of a venerable tradition going back to before the Greeks.

untarism or positivism, the view that morality is *"Positive, Arbitrary and Factitious only"* whether this view is advanced by Hobbists or by the "divers Modern Theologers" who hold morality to derive from the will of God (*TEIM.*i.i.1, 5; R.105). Against these views, Cudworth argues that there are three possibilities regarding the meaning of such terms as *"Moral Good and Evil, Just and Unjust, Honest and Dishonest."* Either (1) "they be . . . mere Names without any Signification" or (2) "Names for nothing else, but *Willed* and *Commanded*," or else (3) what they refer to *"cannot possibly be Arbitrary things, made by Will without Nature"* (i.ii.1). Cudworth assumes that not even positivists will be prepared to accept (2), for then 'morally evil' will just mean 'contrary to the sovereign's command,' and 'it is morally evil to disobey the sovereign' will become a mere tautology. The positivist would then be deprived of the ability to assert the rightness of obeying the sovereign as a substantive ethical doctrine.

[I]t was never heard of, that any one founded all his Authority of Commanding others, and others Obligation or Duty to Obey his Commands, in a Law of his own making, that men should be Required, Obliged, or Bound to Obey him. . . . [F]or if they were Obliged before, then this Law would be in vain, and to no Purpose; and if they were not before Obliged, then they could not be Obliged by any Positive Law. (i.ii.3; R.108)

But if (2) is rejected, and if moral terms are assumed to be significant, contrary to (1), then it follows that they have some meaning other than to refer to the fact of will or command. If, therefore, it is right to follow the command of a given sovereign, this must be because of something other than the simple fact that the sovereign has so commanded.[19]

It is consistent with this argument, of course, that there is a single background moral fact, or perhaps a few such facts, concerning the rightness of obeying God and other, earthly, sovereigns, and that all the rest of morality derives from these. But Cudworth may be right not to worry much about this possibility. Once readers have been convinced that the authority of a sovereign, earthly or divine, re-

19. This line of argument has an obvious affinity with G. E. Moore's argument that any attempt to define 'good' commits the naturalistic fallacy. Passmore emphasizes this interpretation on p. 42 and suggests that Cudworth probably believed that positivists are double-minded in something like the same way Moore accused naturalists of being. Both want to assert substantive ethical doctrines but to ground these in a reductive definition. A. N. Prior discusses Cudworth's argument in the context of a study of Moore's presentation of the naturalistic fallacy and its historical predecessors in *Logic and the Basis of Ethics* (Oxford: Oxford University Press, 1949), pp. 13–25.

quires a basis in a background moral fact, they may be unlikely to think the set of moral facts can be restricted to that fact alone. If, for example, we ought to obey God out of gratitude, as Pufendorf urged, then it would seem that ingratitude must be wrong in itself, other things equal.[20] Or, if, as Locke held, God's authority derives from His creative act, then it seems it must be of the nature of creativity that it grounds some title to its products.

The general drift of Cudworth's antivoluntarist arguments in the *Treatise* is to show that moral properties must depend on the nature of things that have them and that natures are "eternal and immutable." If stealing is wrong, it is because it has a nature that makes it wrong. And not even God can make stealing not be wrong by fiat, any more than He can make the angles of a triangle sum to something other than two right angles. To change an action's moral properties it would have to be possible to change its nature without, per impossibile, changing what it is.

We need not worry about the details of this line of thought. Our primary interest is its conclusion, since it may appear to commit Cudworth to a kind of Platonism very different from the sort of position I have been claiming he holds. It may suggest a picture according to which moral properties are entirely independent of their relation to the mind, whether an observer's or an agent's. For example, Cudworth's reasoning may suggest that if we are morally obligated not to steal, that must be due completely to what stealing is, to the nature of an action of that kind, independent of its relation to anyone's mind, including the agent's.

OBLIGATION AND INTELLECTUAL NATURE

That this is not, in fact, Cudworth's view can be seen by considering his own gloss of the doctrine that it is impossible for a person to be obligated "wholly from Will without Nature": "Whereas it is not the meer Will and Pleasure of him that commandeth, that obligeth to do Positive things commanded, but *the Intellectual Nature of him that is commanded*" (1.ii.4; R.109; emphasis added). And he adds that the distinction between cases where we are obligated to do something independent of any command and those where a command does actually obligate "lies wholly in this": "[t]hat there are some things which the *Intellectual Nature obligeth to of it self* . . .; other things there

20. Pufendorf, *On the Law of Nature and Nations*, p. 106.

are which the same Intellectual Nature Obligeth to by Accident only, and hypothetically, upon Condition of some voluntary Action either of our own or some other Persons" (I.ii.4; R.109; emphasis added, except for "of it self").

This is already at odds with the traditional interpretation of Cudworth that is suggested by his arguments against voluntarism. That picture would lead us to expect Cudworth to be saying here that an agent is obligated simply by the nature of, say, the actions he is contemplating, not by something inside him and not by his own intellectual nature or its relation to those actions. Taken by itself, this might not seem to amount to much. Perhaps, encouraged by developments outside his own thought, Cudworth is simply using 'oblige' to refer to something internal to the agent, but in a way that leaves unchanged the thought that what fundamentally matters are moral facts independent of the agent's own mind. He might, for example, be using it to refer to a psychological process of moral cognition in the agent, holding fixed the thesis that what is cognized are independent moral facts concerning what the agent should do.

That possibility is ruled out, however, by the final sentence of the chapter we have been discussing:

And therefore if there were not Natural Justice, *that is,* if the Rational or Intellectual Nature in its self were indetermined and Unobliged to any thing, and so destitute of all Morality, it were not possible that any thing should be made Morally Good or Evil, *obligatory or unlawful,* or that any Moral Obligation should be begotten by any Will or Command whatsoever. (I.ii.6; R.112; emphasis added to "that is")

This passage is remarkable in several ways. First, it is clear that Cudworth considers the power to obligate to be essential to morality. Without obligation there is no "Natural Justice," nor is it "possible that any thing should be made Morally Good or Evil." Second, for Cudworth, morality's power to obligate evidently includes its power to motivate or determine agents. If rational nature were "indetermined and Unobliged to any thing" there would be no obligation. It follows from these first two ideas that, third, the very existence of morality depends on "Rational or Intellectual" nature's having a source of motivation within it – depends, that is, on reason's being genuinely practical. Obligation cannot, therefore, consist in motives provided by the cognition of an independent normative order (as for Platonists and for Clarke, Balguy, and Price), since the very existence of a normative order depends on its already being the case that rational nature has *determinations to will* intrinsic to it. Finally, putting this passage together with the one asserting that when a person is obligated to follow a command what obliges is "the Intellectual Nature of him that is commanded," we can see that Cudworth must think that in order for morality to obligate it has to engage a source of motivation in *the agent's* practical reason.

Already in the second chapter of the first book of the *Treatise*, therefore – the very chapter, indeed, that provides the best case for the traditional interpretation – we have clear evidence that Cudworth's rationalism cannot be, like Clarke's or Price's, a rationalism of purely theoretical reason. There is no reference yet to the idea of free or autonomous agency, but Cudworth plainly asserts that moral obligation requires a source of motivation in the agent's own practical reason.

IDEALISM (WITH MATTER)

Before we consider Cudworth's metaphysics of morals further, we must provide a context for it in his metaphysics more generally. Cudworth accepts the atomic theory of body or matter. An "atomic physiology" performs two important functions in his system. "It renders the Corporeal World Intelligible to us," first. But equally, "it prepares an easie and clear way for the Demonstration of Incorporeal Substances" (*TIS*.48). By clearly delineating the nature of the material as able only to transfer and not to initiate motion, atomism shows why the universe could not be composed of matter alone. Were everything material, there could be no motion; the universe would be Eleatic: "[A]ll would be a dead *Heap* or *Lump*" (*TIS*.829). But the world has motion and, in addition, life, purposiveness, and cogitation. None of these could occur if the universe were entirely material. There must, therefore, be incorporeal as well as corporeal substances.

Cudworth's agreement with modern atomists about the nature of body is not merely dialectical. He applauds the capacity of atomism to explain material phenomena without any recourse to Aristotelian substantial forms or any other "Qualities really existing in the Bodies without, besides the Results, or Aggregates of those simple Elements, and the Disposition of the Insensible Parts of Bodies in respect of Figure, Site and Motion." (*TIS*.7). In particular, he regards it as a substantial advance of the "corpuscular" or "mechanical" philosophy that it can demonstrate that such "sensible *Ideas* of Colours and Tastes, as Red, Green, Bitter and Sweet, formally considered, are only

Passions and Phansies in us, and not real Qualities in the Object without." (*TIS*.9). The only properties really existing in bodies, independent of the mind, are such modifications of matter as are constituted by the "disposition" of its "insensible parts."

Matter is utterly inert, however. And so there must also be incorporeal substances that are "active," "vital," "cogitative," and sources of "internal energy" to explain the existence of motion, life, growth, activity, and thought in the world. These include the mind of God and all created conscious minds, but also what Cudworth calls "plastick nature," a kind of *Life distinct from the Animal*," functioning purposively, through which God can accomplish His creative plan without having to, "as it were with his own Hands, Form the Body of every Gnat and Fly, Insect and Mite" (*TIS*.146, 147). Cudworth's contrast between the incorporeal and the corporeal is thus a contrast between the active and the passive and not, like Descartes's, one between the conscious and the unconscious.[21]

We recall that a prominent theme of the *Treatise* is that knowledge of any truths, including those of ethics, requires the apprehension by the mind of "immutable essences," of what Cudworth also calls "universal rationes or intelligible natures." Not even sense experience is entirely passive, the mere transmission of force by matter, since it also includes a phenomenal appearance and hence a kind of mental activity through the "sympathy" between mind and body (*TEIM*.III.i.2 – 4). Nonetheless, sensory appearances are entirely self-contained and particular, involving no apprehension of anything under a concept. They can therefore have no objective purport and are incapable of truth or falsity. Only an apprehension by the mind under concepts, under "universal rationes" or "intelligible natures," can be knowledge, because only such a state implicitly aims at truth by representing something as having some property.

Sense it self is but the *Passive Perception* of some Individual Material Forms, but to *Know* or *Understand*, is Actively to Comprehend a thing by some Abstract, Free and Universal *Reasonings*. . . . *Sense* which lies Flat and Grovelling in the Individuals . . . is not able to rise up or ascend to an Abstract Universal Notion; For which Cause it never *Affirms* or *Denies* any thing of its Object, because . . . in all Affirmation, and Negation at least, the Predicate is always Universal. (*TEIM*.III.iii.2; R.116)[22]

21. On this point, see Passmore, *Ralph Cudworth*, pp. 20–28.
22. Cudworth also makes some interesting remarks regarding what these days would be called the "normativity of content," viz., that the concepts necessary for knowledge must function as *rules* or standards. E.g.: "[I]f there were Material

Since Cudworth's doctrine of eternal and immutable morality is that a thing's moral properties depend on its eternal and immutable (and intelligible) nature, and thus that morality is itself eternal and immutable, we should now ask what the metaphysical status of intelligible natures is. "If any one demand here, where . . . these Immutable Entities do exist?" Cudworth writes, "I answer, *First*, that as they are considered formally, they do not properly Exist in the Individuals without us" (*TEIM*.iv.iv.4). Atomistic natural philosophy has shown that no substantial forms exist in material bodies. But, he continues, "neither do they exist somewhere else from the Individual Sensibles, and without the Mind." Hence no metaphysical realm of Forms exists independent of mind. Universal natures or essences exist in the mind; they are modifications of (one kind, at least, of) incorporeal, mental substance. Forms are aspects of *forming substance*, of mind:[23] "Wherefore these Intelligible Ideas or Essences of Things, those Forms by which we understand all Things, exist no where but in the Mind it self" (*TEIM*.iv.iv.4).[24] Cudworth remarks that he actually agrees with the nominalist doctrine, which he quotes from Hobbes, that "*'There is nothing in the World'* . . . Universal, but Names" if this be taken to apply only to "Things existing without the Mind"[25] (*TEIM*.iv.iii.15). But he denies that universal natures are not *real*. On the contrary, he thinks they have more reality than the modifications of matter. Writing in particular about such relations as cause and effect and whole and part, he says that though these be "Meer Notions of the Mind and Modes of conceiving in us, that only signify what Things are Relatively to Intellect," this would not mean that these relations "had no Reality at all." "Intellect being a Real Thing, and that which indeed hath more of Entity in it than Matter or Body,

Lines, Triangles, Pyramids, perfectly and Mechanically Exact; yet that which made them such, and thereby to differ from other Irregular Lines, imperfect Triangles and Cubes, could be nothing else but a Conformity to an antecedent Intellectual Idea in the Mind, as the Rule and Exemplar of them; for Otherwise an Irregular Line and an Imperfect Triangle, Pyramid, Cube, are as perfectly that that they are, as the other is" (*TEIM*.iv.iii.9).
 In aid of further establishing that the proper object of knowledge must always be the "Intelligible *Reasons* of things," Cudworth marshals a number of arguments from Plato's *Theaetetus* (*TEIM*.iii.iii.6).

23. Cudworth understands this to have been Plato's view: "[F]or it was very well determined long ago by Socrates, in *Plato's Parmenides*, that these Things are nothing else but *Noemata*" (TEIM.iv.iv.4).
24. And also: "[T]he *Rationes*, Intelligible Essences . . . are Things that cannot exist alone, but together with that Actual Knowledge in which they are Comprehended, they are the Modifications of some Mind or Intellect" (*TEIM*.iv.iv.7).
25. *Lev*.iv.

the Modifications of Intellect must needs be as Real Things as the Modifications of Matter" (*TEIM*.IV.ii.5).[26]

As is often the case with idealism, Cudworth's is driven largely by epistemological considerations. Knowledge of objects is impossible without universal notions. Since these cannot be extracted from experience, they must be prior to it. "Knowledge is a Comprehension of a thing Proleptically, and as it were *a Priori*" (*TEIM*.III.iii.5). And this is possible, Cudworth argues, only if the categories that make knowledge possible are present in the very activity of mind. All knowledge is therefore reflexive. The primary objects of knowledge, universal natures and reasons, are modifications of mind itself:[27] "For to *Know* or *Understand* a thing, is nothing else but by some Inward Anticipation of the Mind, that is Native and Domestick, and so familiar to it, to take Acquaintance with it" (*TEIM*.III.iii.1). The "Intelligible Forms by which Things are Understood or Known, are not Stamps or Impressions passively printed upon the Soul from without, but Ideas vitally protended or actively exerted from within it self" (*TEIM*.IV.i.1). The primary objects of knowledge, universal essences, must therefore be modifications of mind. "The Essence of nothing is reached unto by the Senses looking Outward, but by the Mind's looking inward into it self" (*TEIM*.III.iii.4).

Cudworth's epistemology thus involves a "Copernican Revolution," as Lovejoy pointed out: "Knowledge depends upon the 'conformity of objects to our mode of cognition' rather than upon the conformity of our mode of cognition to objects."[28] Universal natures

---

26. Nor, he adds, is the status of such relations like that of sensible qualities such as being hot or cold, which according to the going theories are not real but are only phantasms in the mind caused by modifications of matter. Unlike these properties, cause and effect and universal natures are part of our going theory of the objective world. (See *TEIM*.IV.5.1; here is one place where Cudworth's idealism comes into conflict with into his dualism.)

27. "Knowledge and intellection doth . . . Intellectually comprehend its Object within it self, and is the same with it. . . . [T]he Intellect and the thing known are really one and the same. For those Ideas or Objects of Intellection are nothing else but Modifications of the Mind it self" (TEIM.III.iii.4).

28. Arthur O. Lovejoy, "Kant and the English Platonists," in *Essays Philosophical and Psychological, in Honor of William James*, edited by members of the Columbia University Department of Philosophy (New York: Longmans, Green, 1908), p. 270. Lovejoy remarks that it "would certainly have been singular" if Kant had not read Cudworth, given that a Latin translation of the *System* was published at Jena in 1733 by J. L. Mosheim, a professor and eventually chancellor of the University of Gottingen, and a second edition was published at Leiden forty years later.

For further discussion of the relation between Cudworth's epistemology and

exist formally by way of mode of cognition – thus does Cudworth's epistemology drive his metaphysics.[29]

Another manifestation of this phenomenon is that Cudworth takes clarity and distinctness of perception to be a *metaphysical* principle, not just an epistemological one; it guarantees not only justification, but truth. "In these Intelligible *Ideas* of the Mind," he writes, "whatsoever is Clearly Perceived to *Be, Is*" (*TIS*.718).[30] Accordingly, he criticizes Descartes's attempt to provide an external warrant for clear and distinct perception in a nondeceiving God as circular.[31] Here again, Cudworth appears to derive metaphysical conclusions from a view about necessary conditions for the possibility of knowledge.

All universal natures or essences, including moral ones, therefore, are modifications of mind. They have reality, Cudworth believes, only so long as mind (specifically, so long as God's archetypal mind, of which all created minds are ectypes) exists.[32] Although he is no theological voluntarist, Cudworth is nevertheless a theological mor-

Kant's see Dugald Stewart, *The Collected Works,* ed. Sir William Hamilton (Edinburgh: T. Constable, 1854–60), vol. 1, pp. 398–99. Martineau criticizes Stewart's views in *Types of Ethical Theory,* vol. 2, pp. 442–43.

It is also noteworthy that J. H. Muirhead called Cudworth the "real founder of British Idealism." *The Platonic Tradition in Anglo-Saxon Philosophy* (London: Allen & Unwin, 1931), p. 35.

29. There is obviously a pressure point in Cudworth's view regarding the nature of the material. Since he argues that we can have knowledge of the nature of matter, as formulated by the atomic theory, and that this must come from the intellect, it must presumably follow that this nature, like all others, is a modification of mind. Thus what looks like a dualism threatens to collapse into a form of transcendental idealism. He might, of course, like Kant, retain an "in itself," but it would seem that his epistemological principles would then require that knowledge of it be impossible.

30. See also *TEIM*.IV.V.5, 9, 12.

31. "For whereas some would endeavour to prove the Truth of their Intellectual Faculties from hence, because there is a God, whose Nature also is such, as that he cannot deceive: It is plain that this is nothing but a Circle, and makes no Progress at all, forasmuch as all the Certainty which they have of the Existence of God, and of his Nature, depends wholly upon the Arbitrary Make of their Faculties" (*TEIM*.IV.V.6).

32. "If therefore there be *Eternal Intelligibles* or *Ideas,* and *Eternal Truths;* and *Necessary Existence* do belong to them; then must there be an *Eternal Mind Necessarily Existing,* since these *Truths* and *Intelligible Essences* of Things cannot possibly be any where but in a *Mind*" (*TIS*.736). "And from hence it is Evident also, that there can be but *One only Original Mind,* or not more than *One Understanding Being Self* Existent; all other *Minds* whatsoever *Partaking* of one Original Mind; and being as it were Stamped with the Impression or Signature of one and the same Seal" (*TIS*.737). See also *TEIM*.IV.IV.

alist. Were there no God, there would be no morality. But then, were there no God, there would be nothing.

From Cudworth's general metaphysics, we may now turn back to his metaphysics of morals. Already we can better understand his remark that when an agent is morally obligated, it is his "Intellectual Nature" which "obligeth" him (*TEIM*.1.ii.4). Whatever an action's being morally good or evil, right or wrong, obligatory or proscribed is more precisely, it is part of intellectual nature – a modification of mind. There is no independent normative order that is somehow disclosed to mind. The fundamental categories and truths of morality are implicit in intellectual activity itself.

By this point it should be obvious that Cudworth's metaphysics of ethics is an idealism of some sort. What I want now to suggest is that, like Kant's, it is a *practical* or *ethical* idealism. Cudworth believes that ethical propositions, specifically those regarding moral obligation, are made true by a distinctively *practical* activity that is intrinsic to intellectual nature – by the existence of pure practical reason. There are three passages in the *Treatise* that say as much explicitly; although it may be possible to discount each taken by itself, once they are read together and in the light of Cudworth's views about God's nature, love, obligation, and freedom of the will, it will become clear that this is the view he has in mind.

We have noted already the first place where Cudworth suggests this view: "[I]f the Rational or Intellectual Nature in its self were indetermined and Unobliged to any thing, and so destitute of all Morality, it were not possible that any thing should be made Morally Good or Evil, *obligatory or unlawful*" (*TEIM*.1.ii.6).[33] The second is a remarkable passage that must be quoted at some length.

[I]t is truly affirmed by the Author of the *Leviathan*, Page 24. *That there is no common Rule of Good and Evil to be taken from the Nature of the Objects themselves*, that is, either considered absolutely in themselves, or Relatively to external Sense only, but according to some other interior Analogy which Things have to a certain inward Determination in the Soul it self, from whence the Foundation of all this Difference must needs arise, as I shall shew afterwards; Not that the Anticipations of Morality spring meerly from Intellectual Forms and notional Idea's of the Mind, or from certain Rules or

33. See the subsection "Obligation and Intellectual Nature," earlier in this chapter.

Propositions, arbitrarily printed upon the Soul as upon a Book, but from some other more inward, and vital Principle, in intellectual Beings, as such, whereby they have *a natural Determination in them to do some Things, and to avoid others*, which could not be, if they were meer naked and Passive things. (*TEIM*.iv.vi.4; R.118, emphasis added to "a natural . . . others")

No rule of good and evil can be relative to "external Sense," but so far this is only what Cudworth thinks he has already established many times over in the *Treatise*. Neither, says Cudworth, agreeing with Hobbes, can an ethical standard be taken from the nature of objects themselves. Of course, Cudworth must agree that no ethical standard can be found in matter. But now he makes it clear that he thinks it cannot be found in the universal natures and essences that are modifications of *theoretical* mind either. Morality does not "spring meerly from Intellectual Forms and notional Idea's of the Mind." If value and morals are to exist, mind cannot be simply theoretical; it must also be practical, determined on the question of what *to do*. There must be in intellectual beings "a natural Determination . . . to do some Things, and to avoid others." Intellect must therefore include determinate volitions or *motives* in its nature; there must be such a thing as pure practical reason.

Cudworth must have thought this an important point if he was willing to enlist his nemesis Hobbes in its support. Cudworth's contrast between the vitality of the "anticipations of morality" and "meer naked and passive things" muddies the waters, since for him mere "Intellectual Forms and notional Ideas of the mind" are themselves forms of mental activity, to be contrasted with the passivity of sense. The crucial point is that they are forms of *theoretical*, rather than *practical*, intellectual activity. The reason for citing Hobbes is that Cudworth agrees with him that value and morals have an intrinsic connection to motive and therefore cannot be grasped by theoretical reason alone. The disagreement with Hobbes is whether this motive is contingent or part of rational nature itself.

All universal essences exist by way of mind, ultimately God's archetypal mind. Thus the existence of morality depends on the existence of God. But notice how Cudworth puts the point in the last of the three passages from the *Treatise*: "[I]t is not possible that there should be any such Thing as Morality, unless there be a God, that is, an Infinite Eternal Mind that is the first Original and Source of all Things, whose Nature is the first Rule and Exemplar of Morality" (*TEIM*.iv.vi.13). God's idea of a triangle must serve as the archetype of triangles, but even if this is a modification of His mind, that does not mean that God's *nature* is "the first rule and exemplar" of triangularity. The reason God's nature is the rule and exemplar of morality is that His nature is itself an ideal of *moral agency*; perfect mind is essentially practical. Cudworth is careful to contrast this view with theological voluntarism. Both take morality to depend on God's existence, but for Cudworth it is grounded determinately in God's nature rather than in His arbitrary will. If God's will were utterly arbitrary, without specific determination, there could be no morality.[34] It is, of course, not because God matches some external standard that He can be said to be morally good, but because His actual will is itself a standard of perfect mind.[35]

LOVE

But what motivation *is* essential to perfect mind? Cudworth does not say in the *Treatise*, but the general shape of his answer is clear from his other writings. In the process of discussing Plato's Form of the Good in the *System*, Cudworth complains that "*Plato* sometimes talks too Metaphysically and Clowdily about it." "Nevertheless," he continues, "he plainly intimates . . . that this Nature of Good which is also the Nature of God, includes *Benignity* in it" (*TIS*.205). Cudworth then writes:

But the Holy Scripture without any Metaphysical Pomp and Obscurity, tells us plainly, Both what is that Highest Perfection of Intellectual Beings, which is . . . *Better than Reason and Knowledge,* and which is also the Source, Life and Soul of all Morality, namely that it is *Love* or *Charity*. (*TIS*.205)

From here he proceeds to quote at length Saint Paul's famous passage on love from the First Epistle to the Corinthians, adding that without love "I have no Inward Satisfaction, Peace or True Happiness" and am "destitute of all True Morality, Vertue, and Grace."[36]

The fundamental ethical motive, essential to perfect Mind, is *love*.[37] Cudworth tells us very little about love's precise character

---

34. "Wherefore according to them [theological voluntarists] there is no pattern or archetypal exemplar of morality in God, and if there be none in him, there can be no natural measure of it in men" (4979.87).

35. This makes it unclear, however, why God would have to exist in order for there to be moral truths; any truth about what a perfect mind would will is presumably independent of whether such a mind exists.

36. "Though I speak with the tongues of men and of angels, and have not charity, I am become as sounding brass, or a tinkling cymbal." 1 Corinthians, 13:1.

37. At one point, indeed, Cudworth speculates "that in a Rectified and Qualified sence, this may pass for true Theology; That *Love* is the *Supreme Deity* and

or what its aim or object is. Although he says love "dispenses it self Uninvidiously," with an equal regard of some sort, he does not try to formulate any such principle as Cumberland's "common good of all rationals." Nor is he particularly concerned with the possibility that love might motivate in conflicting ways or, if unambiguously, in a direction that might conflict with other values such as justice.

None of this should be too surprising. In the first place, the fact that universal benevolence might conflict with other moral concerns such as justice and honesty was not well appreciated until Butler's *Dissertation upon the Nature of Virtue,* some fifty years later. In the second, Cudworth's ethics is fundamentally an ethics of motive and character rather than one of duty and law. In a sermon delivered to a House of Commons sharply divided in 1647 between Presbyterians and Independents, Cudworth naturally enough praised the "silken Knot of *Love,*" which can "tie our Hearts together; though our Heads and Apprehensions cannot meet."[38] But his encomium goes well beyond the political needs of the moment.[39] Love, he says, is the "inward *Soul* and *Principle of Divine Life* . . . that enliveneth and quickeneth, the dead carkasse, of all our outward Performances whatsoever." An ethic of duties uninspired by love is but a *"dead Law of outward Works,* which indeed if it be alone, subjects us to a *State of Bondage."*[40]

But if duties are but "dead laws" without love, they come alive when they derive from love. Cudworth urges that love is itself "the *inward Law* of the Gospel." The "Law of Love" frees us "in a manner from all Law without us, because it maketh us become a *Law unto our selves."*[41] This latter phrase, from Saint Paul's Epistle to the Romans ("For when the Gentiles, which have not the law, do by nature the things contained in the law, these, having not the law, are a law unto

Original of all things: namely, if by it be meant, Eternal, Self-originated, Intellectual Love, or Essential and Substantial Goodness, that having an Infinite overflowing Fulness and Fecundity, dispenses it self Uninvidiously, according to the best Wisdom, Sweetly Governs all, without any Force or Violence . . . and reconciles the whole World into Harmony. For the Scripture telling us, that *God is Love,* seems to warrant thus much to us, that *Love* in some rightly Qualified sence, is *God (TIS.*[123], misnumbered 117). We may recall Cumberland's remarks to a similar effect; see Chapter 4.

38. "A Sermon Preached before the House of Commons," in Patrides, *The Cambridge Platonists,* p. 119.
39. On the importance of love in the theology of Cambridge Platonism more generally, see Patrides, *The Cambridge Platonists,* pp. 36–39.
40. "Sermon," p. 123.
41. Ibid., p. 124.

themselves"),[42] was standardly employed in seventeenth- and eighteenth-century moral and theological discourse to refer to a moral competence rational human beings share independently of their different confessions or revelation. For Cudworth, then, God's love makes morality possible in the first place; without it there would be no distinction between moral good and evil. And because we can participate in this (practical) intellectual nature, *we* can be moral agents. "Love is at once a Freedome from all Law, a State of purest Liberty, and yet a Law too, of the most constraining and indispensable Necessity."[43]

Unlike Cumberland and Locke, who begin their thinking within the framework of natural law, Cudworth's ethics do not start from the problem of obligation. Still, as the passages from the Preface to the *System* show, legitimating moral obligation is a primary purpose behind Cudworth's metaphysical speculations as well as his writings on freedom of the will. Even though his is an ethics of love, his ultimate aim is to argue that love grounds moral obligation. We are obligated, most fundamentally, to give expression to the source of morality we have within, thereby enlivening what would otherwise be the "dead carkasse" of outward acts. The agent's "intellectual nature" is what obligates her, and love is the practical expression of the intellect.

This motivational source is, however, only one necessary condition of moral obligation. The other is what Cudworth calls "free will," the agent's capacity to determine conduct by freely forming her own practical *judgment*.

SELF-DETERMINATION

SELF-DETERMINATION, ACCOUNTABILITY, AND THE WILL

It will be recalled that Cudworth's initial aim in undertaking the *System* was to write a "Discourse concerning *Liberty* and *Necessity*," on the grounds that the absence of liberty takes "away all *Guilt* and *Blame, Punishments* and *Rewards*" (*TIS*.Preface). Only in his manuscripts on freedom of the will, however, does Cudworth finally come to pursue this aim. And what galvanizes his thought is the notion of

42. Romans 2:14. Concerning Butler's important use of this text, see Chapter 9.
43. "Sermon," p. 125.

accountability. It is distinctive of morality that we hold moral agents *accountable* for much of what they do, especially for what we take them to be obligated to do. When we take up an attitude toward, make a judgment of, or take action responding to persons *as responsible* for their acts, we *impute* their acts *to them.* We regard persons as the causes of their own acts, imputing to the person the determination of the act. In so doing, we regard the person as a self-determining agent.

Take the attitudes of blame and commendation, for example. In one sense, someone might blame a defective alarm clock as the cause of his oversleeping. But, Cudworth notes, in so doing he does not "imput[e] to [the clock] its being the cause of its own moving well or ill" (*FW*.1). When "we blame a man for any wicked actions," however, "we blame him not only as doing otherwise than ought to have been done, but also than he might have done, and [we believe?] that it was possible for him to have avoided it, so that he was himself the cause of the evil thereof" (*FW*.1). Our blame takes a *person* as its object. In this way it differs from mere dislike for something a person did, or even for something about a person. Commendation or blame not "only signif[ies] our approbation or dislike of the [acts] themselves . . . but doth also reflect upon the person as the cause of either to himself when it was possible he might not have been so" (4980.31). We take as a condition of commendation or blame's being warranted that *the person* deserves them because *she* was responsible for – the cause of – that for which we blame or commend her.

Morality, then, can only genuinely obligate such agents; it can only bind agents who can determine themselves to act morally. Cudworth uses a bewildering variety of terms to refer to the general capacity for self-determination: "free will," "*sui potestas*," "autexousy," and "autexousious power," among numerous others. The last two are his own coinage, as indeed are many of the rest.[44] Clearly, Cudworth must have felt that the conceptual resources he had inherited were simply inadequate to deal properly with fundamental issues of accountability and responsibility: Specifically, it had not focused sharply enough on the ideas of self-determination and the will he thought crucial for moral obligation.

44. 'Autexousy' and 'autexousious' still appear in the *Oxford English Dictionary* (with citations of Cudworth's *System*), defined as "free will" and "exercising free will," respectively.

One account he found utterly inadequate was Hobbes's. He agreed with Hobbes's critique of faculty psychology that it is as absurd to suppose that there is a faculty of will that wills as it is to think that, say, the faculty of walking walks.[45] It is *the person* who wills. In identifying will as the "last appetite in deliberating," however, Cudworth believed that Hobbes was insufficiently sensitive to his own insight.[46] The will "is no particular appetite," Cudworth objects. It involves "the soul comprehending its whole self" (4982.80). An agent's volition is, he says, her "last practical judgment," using this phrase in his own technical sense to refer to a more or less considered judgment made actively by the agent herself in comprehension, more or less, of her various motives.

Nor is Hobbes's account of deliberation as "nothing but alternate passions where the victory at last falls to that passion whose necessary force is most preponderating" satisfactory.[47] This may accurately describe what precedes the behavior of "brutes," but it ill fits the practical reasoning of a self-determining agent: "[T]here is no . . . thing in them [brutes] that takes notice of all, no reduplicate self-active principle that . . . exerting itself more or less can oversway things one way or the other" (4980.7).

Nor, finally, will it do to conceive of liberty in Hobbes's way as "the absence of external impediments" to the execution of the will.[48] Hobbes's account, whatever its usefulness for other purposes, cannot explain the distinctive freedom of rational agents requisite for moral responsibility, for blame and guilt. "[I]f brutes be supposed to have no other principle of action in them than particular appetites . . ., it seems consequent hereupon that though they may be said to have a liberty to do what they have an appetite unto, when there is no external impediment to hinder them," we will be loath to regard them as morally responsible on that score (4979.1–2).

Cudworth takes there to be two other leading theories in the field besides Hobbes's. One is the idea that after all the agent's beliefs and desires have determined his outlook to whatever degree they can,

---

45. The example is Cudworth's: "to attribute the act of intellection and perception to the faculty of understanding, and acts of volition to the faculty of will, or to say that it is the understanding that understandeth, and the will that willeth. This is all one as if one should say that the faculty of walking walketh, and the faculty of speaking speaketh" (FW.24). For Hobbes, see Sir William Molesworth, ed., *English Works of Thomas Hobbes*, vol. 4, p. 266.
46. *English Works of Thomas Hobbes*, vol. 3, p. 49.
47. This characterization is Cudworth's, at 4980.7.
48. *Lev.*xxi.1.

the agent retains the capacity to will, arbitrarily or indifferently, within a range of options. Indifferency views may differ on the range. Some may hold that an agent's range of options is utterly unrestricted, except, perhaps to those she believes physically possible. Others may hold that an agent can only will an action she holds good, but that she can indifferently choose among these. But these differences do not really matter from Cudworth's point of view. The problem with any indifferency view as a theory of self-determination, Cudworth thinks, is that by disconnecting the agent's act from what she can accept as the best reasons for so acting, it disconnects it from the rational self. The hypothesis that the will is utterly indifferent between its options cannot possibly explain the chosen act as *determined by a rational self.*

[I]f the blind will . . . remains indifferent to follow the last dictate of [the understanding] or not, and doth fortuitously determine itself either in compliance with the same or otherwise, then will liberty of will be mere irrationality, and madness itself acting or determining all human actions. (FW.23)[49]

Some care is needed to get the precise force of Cudworth's remark. First, for the sort of indifferency view Cudworth is considering, the last dictate of the understanding includes the agent's final belief about the relative value of several possible acts. Second (as I shall make clear shortly), Cudworth actually agrees that it is possible to believe, in some sense, that an action would be best to do and still, voluntarily, not do it. He accepts a form of weakness of will. So, with the indifferentists, he accepts that there is a sense in which it is up to a person whether to act rationally or not. Cudworth's point is that the capacity for this kind of freedom cannot be the only thing we must attribute to agents if we are to hold them responsible for not discharging their obligations. We must also attribute to them the capacity for rational self-determination: "Praise and dispraise, commendation and blame, could not be founded in [such] an indifferent free-will whose power and perfection equally consisted in determin-

49. The full passage reads: "But if the blind will does not only at first fortuitously determine the understanding both to exercise and object, but also after all is done remains indifferent to follow the last dictate of it or not, and doth fortuitously determine itself either in compliance with the same or otherwise, then will liberty of will be mere irrationality, and madness itself acting or determining all human actions." Context, however, makes it clear that Cudworth thinks the same objection would apply to a view according to which the indifference of the blind will consists only in an arbitrary choice after the agent had formed whatever beliefs he had about the relative values of options.

ing itself either way and indeed chiefly shined forth in being loose from light and reason" (4980.31). When we blame someone, Cudworth must be thinking, and hold her responsible as a rational moral agent for not doing something that we think there was conclusive reason for her to do, it is not enough that we think what she should have done was within a range of options among which she could arbitrarily have chosen. We must think as well that the good reasons for so acting were reasons *on which she could have acted*. We implicitly attribute to the agent the capacity for rational self-determination, and imply that the proper exercise of this capacity would have resulted in the obligatory act. The indifferency theory cannot be an adequate account of this capacity.

The alternative theory Cudworth finds in the field agrees with the main thrust of this criticism of indifferency, but errs in the opposite direction. It holds that all human action is determined by agents' beliefs about which, of the actions available to them, would be best, and that these beliefs are the necessary result of other external and internal causes.[50] Cudworth admits there is a sense in which action will be explainable as rational on such an account, relative to the beliefs and desires the agent actually had. But it will be explained by a process *in* the person. We will not be able to *impute* the action to *the agent* as rationally determined by himself. This criticism shares a feature with Cudworth's objection to Hobbes's account of deliberation. If rational agents can be held responsible, deliberation cannot simply be something that takes place *in* them, with the agent having no leverage over the shape it takes. It must be something the agent can, in some suitable sense, himself direct.

[I]f speculative and deliberative thought be always necessary in us, both as to exercise and specification then must it be either because they are all necessarily produced and determined by objects of sense from without, according to the doctrine of Democritus and Hobbian atheists, or else because the understanding always necessarily worketh of itself upon this or that object, and passeth from one object to another by a necessary series or train and concatenation of thoughts. (*FW*.61)

In the former case, an agent's practical reasoning is hostage to external circumstance. "But if the latter of these be supposed, then could we never have any presence of mind, no ready attention to emergent occurrences or occasions, but our minds would be always roving or

50. This is the view Cudworth dubs "Divine Fate Morall" in the second page of his preface to the *System*.

134

rambling out, we having no power over them to call them back . . . or fix them and determine them on any certain objects" (*FW*.61–62).

An adequate account of self-determination therefore has to avoid these two extremes. Indifferency cannot account for determination by a rational self. And the view that actions are determined by a "necessary nature" in us lacks, Cudworth thinks, any account of the capacity that agents must have to direct their own practical thinking if they are intelligibly to be held accountable. What is needed, he believes, is an account of the autonomous agent's capacity to undertake and direct *self-comprehensive* ("all things considered") practical thinking voluntarily. Autonomous agents can voluntarily step back from the different perspectives on action provided within their various present desires and beliefs and try to unify their practical situation in a comprehensive view. But this does not mean canceling the motive and doxastic force of individual desires and beliefs and then choosing arbitrarily, as the indifferentists hold. It involves, he thinks, the capacity to get some more or less comprehensive grasp of one's various sources of motivation, so that one comes to a motivationally informed *judgment* of what, all things considered, it would be best to do.

Rational agents cannot, Cudworth believes, do other than what they *judge* best, in Cudworth's technical sense. Even Medea when she killed her children "at that time . . . judged it better to gratify her anger and revenge her husband, than to save her children's lives" (4980.240).[51] A volition just is, Cudworth thinks, the agent's last practical judgment. But in his framework a judgment of the value of options is not the same as the state of the understanding that determines action on the "necessary nature" view. According to that picture, agents cannot do other than what they, let us say, understand to be best. Such a belief or understanding is something an agent *has*. A judgment, for Cudworth, is something an agent himself *makes;* it involves his own more or less self-comprehensive activity. And because he makes it by drawing on his various motivational resources, it is intrinsically motivating.

This, in a sketch, is Cudworth's positive view. Ultimately, as he is fond of pointing out, it makes the capacity of an agent to determine her own conduct consist in the mind's capacity to act not just from itself but also "upon itself" – its capacity to be, as he says, "at once

---

51. Epictetus uses this example in the same context. *The Discourses as Reported by Arrian, The Manual, and Fragments*, trans. and ed. W. A. Oldfather, 2 vols. (Cambridge, Mass.: Harvard University Press, 1979), vol. 1, p. 179.

both agent and patient" – as it directs its own practical thought and as its conduct is determined by the issue of that (4982.4). This is the capacity presupposed, Cudworth claims, by the distinctive imputation of acts to moral agents involved in ascribing moral *obligation*. We must now try to understand the details of his account.

WILL AND PRACTICAL JUDGMENT

Both of the major theories that Cudworth rejects (other than Hobbes's) share the premise that the understanding and the will are two distinct faculties: "[T]he understanding . . . understandeth, and the will willeth" (*FW.* 20). According to indifferentists, the will is free to choose indifferently, whatever assessment of the value of alternative acts the understanding settles on. But the "necessary nature" view, in Cudworth's estimation, also holds the will to be blind, since it maintains that the will blindly follows the understanding's determination of which act would be best.

Now, Cudworth's own view is that agents always will the act they *judge* best; indeed, that the agent's volition is identical with her last practical judgment before acting (4980.55). But there are two important respects in which he takes this claim to differ from the superficially similar thesis of the necessary nature view. First, Cudworth thinks that agents act not on merely speculative or notional beliefs about what it would be best to do but on *practical* judgments, where these are motivational states informed by activating motives and ends. Second, he believes that agents act on practical *judgments*, that is, more or less voluntary assessments that are more or less self-comprehensive of their whole practical situation.

The idea that agents can only do what they think best is, Cudworth writes, "a thing which in some sense is true" (4982.8). But this does not mean that "speculative intellection" can determine action. "[T]he first principle by which good and evil are distinguished is vital and not notional" (4982.9): "[M]ere speculative intellection without any inclination to one thing more than another, without anything of appetite or volition is not the first gate or entry, the first original and beginning of all action in the soul" (4982.10).[52] Were the "hypothesis" that the understanding directly determines the will "true[,]

52. Also: "[T]he discursive understanding is not the first spring of motion and activity in human souls, it is not that which first starts and suggests the ends of life but nature obtrudes this upon us by more simple instincts, the congruities of good arise from something that is vital and not notional" (4979.174).

there needs nothing else to be done in order to virtue but only the informing of a man's speculative understanding concerning the nature of good. . . . [T]here would be no more to do to make a man perfectly good and virtuous than there is to learn the demonstration of some theorem in Euclid" (4982.10).[53] However, the notional belief that a life of virtue is best, or that this virtuous action now is best, is impotent by itself to prompt action. Rather, "vital instincts and inclinations . . . are the spring and source of all vital life and activity." Agents act only when "ends are suggested to us that provoke and incite endeavours and awaken consultation towards the attainment of them" (4982.10). Moreover, "ends and goods are all one, for good is nothing but what is agreeable to ends. . . . It is not speculative knowledge that is the proper rule or judge of good or evil untinctured by anything else, but vital touches, tastes, and savours" (4982.9).

As Passmore emphasizes, these passages contrast sharply with the orthodox, intellectualist interpretation of Cudworth. But although it is true that, for Cudworth, "the instinct comes first," it must also be remembered that Cudworth believes there to be *intellectual instincts*.[54] Just as he distinguishes between the mental contribution to sense experience and pure theoretical mind, so likewise does he distinguish between "animal" passions and appetites and pure *practical intellect*. Sense experience is not completely passive; it involves the active participation of mind in sympathy with the body, without which it could have no cognitive relevance. Likewise with motive and action. Without the active contribution of mind in sympathy with body, brute inclination could hardly bear on the issue of what it would be best to do. Thus "when the sensual appetite strongly inclines to anything, there is a certain light of perception goeth along with the appetite, for that which we desire we always apprehend as good" (4982.37).

In addition to an "animal life" of bodily desires, however, human beings also participate in a "divine life." There are motives essential to pure mind itself. "So in like manner the human soul [has] another principle of life in it superior to the whole animal life . . ., it being . . .

53. Compare this with Molyneux's objection to the account of liberty that Locke presented in his first edition of the *Essay*. See the discussion in Chapter 6.
54. Passmore's remark that "no 'sentimentalist', no upholder of hormic psychology, has ever asserted [the priority of instinct] more firmly than Cudworth" is somewhat misleading, especially in the context of his also saying that Cudworth's psychology is "in some respects Humean." *Ralph Cudworth*, pp. 53, 52. In general, Passmore's chapter on Cudworth's moral psychology is very helpful.

a vital intellectual instinct" (4982.20). Participation in pure practical mind, in the divine life, gives us a source of motivation that is independent of sensual pleasure and desire. When discussing this motivational source in God's nature, Cudworth calls it love. When referring to the same source in human, or imperfect rational, beings, however, his preferred terms are "superior reason" or the principle or dictate of "honesty." Just as the motivational sources of the animal life lead us to view alternatives relevant to them "in a certain light" – namely, *as good* – so "in like manner when the intellectual instinct inclines to honesty, that is not without a certain correspondent light, whereby we apprehend that to be good also, though in another kind" (4982.37).[55] Hence, Cudworth's claim that *speculative* understanding or intellect is motivationally inert does not mean he thinks that all reason or intellect is. On the contrary, this claim signals the distinction between theoretical and practical intellect that we have found fundamental to his thought.

So one difference between Cudworth's thesis that volition is identical with the last practical judgment and the claim of the necessary nature view that the blind faculty of the will always necessarily follows the last evaluative belief of the necessary understanding is that he has in mind a genuinely *practical* judgment rooted in motivating "instincts." The second derives from Cudworth's distinctive use of 'judgment' to refer to the conclusion of a voluntary, "self-comprehensive" process of weighing and balancing. It is the capacity to voluntarily undertake such a process that Cudworth calls "free will."[56]

"[W]e are not," he writes, "merely passive to our own practical judgments and to the appearances of good, but contribute something of our own to them" (FW.38). Human beings can do nothing to affect their fundamental sources of motivation. These are the animal and divine life that together constitute our "necessary nature" (4980.56). Cudworth does think we can, by the habits we develop, affect the prominence these motives come to have for us, but this is nothing we can do, on an occasion, to affect a practical judgment of what to do presently (4980.57, 61). What an agent with free will *can* do is to undertake to get a more or less comprehensive grasp of her own practical situation by self-reflective deliberation. She can thereby af-

---

55. Cudworth also believes that habit – for instance, whether we habitually lead a predominantly animal or divine life – affects the "light" in which we see alternatives (see 4982.9). I shall have more to say on this.
56. Or "autexousy," "*sui potestas*," etc.

fect the "light" in which she views options, or even what options she has in view, as "these may be very different accordingly as we more or less intensely consider or deliberate which is a thing . . . in our own power" (*FW*.38). Thus, "we ourselves finish or determine the last conclusive *visum* or phantasy of good, which is called the last or ruling practical judgment" (4980.239). As Cudworth thinks of it, a practical *judgment* can be made only by agents with free will, agents who can voluntarily exercise the power of self-comprehensive, all-things-considered deliberation (4982.11). "[I]t is made up partly from nature, some natural congruity or other, higher or lower, partly from we ourselves, the soul self-comprehensive or self-active" (4980.239).

GENERIC JUDGMENT

Cudworth treats practical judgment as an instance of a generic "forensic" power to come to conclusions, whether theoretical or practical, where something less than absolute certainty is involved. Just as a judge is called upon to form a considered conclusion, through the weighing of evidence, precedent, and applicable law, in cases that are not crystal clear, so we must decide what to believe or do in situations where truth-guaranteeing clear and distinct perception is not to be had (4980.58). In each of these areas, we are guided by an ideal of *judicious deliberation* – a thoughtful weighing and balancing of competing considerations. Cudworth believes that a being without the power to reflect and consider evidence voluntarily, and thereby shape beliefs, would lack the capacity for error.[57] But it would also lack epistemic responsibility. Similarly, in the moral sphere, the condition of responsibility and fault is the capacity for voluntary self-comprehensive deliberation. Cudworth sometimes uses 'free will' to refer to this general "judging power," whether exercised in the theoretical or the practical realm.

FREE WILL

A person has free will, then, insofar as his "soule" has the "power of intending and exerting itself more or less in consideration and

---

57. "Wherefore if we did always suspend our assents, when we had no clear distinct conceptions of the connexion between the predicate and subject of a proposition, we should never err" (*FW*.40; also 4980.54).

deliberation, when different objects, or ends, or mediums, are pro-pounded to his choice" (*FW.*37). We must distinguish three things here. Free will is a power the agent has to bring conduct under the guidance of the best judgment she can make of what to do. There is, therefore, a difference between *successful* guidance by a correct view of the best available action and free will. Cudworth calls the former liberty, or *sui potens*. This characterizes God. He always has a direct grasp of what is best and necessarily chooses it. He has no need, therefore, of free will or *sui potestas*. Imperfect rational beings, how-ever, have no such intuitive grasp by which they necessarily act. They therefore require free will, the power of an imperfect rational being to make (and act on) sound practical judgments, to lead them to true liberty and the good (*FW.*64–65; 4980.31, 44).

In addition to liberty and free will (the power of rational delibera-tive judgment) there is also, Cudworth thinks, the voluntariness of exercising or failing to exercise this power. Sin or moral fault "is not to be imputed to free will as if it were actively willed by freewill." Rather, it "is nothing but a voluntary deficiency of a good power" (4982.22). As we shall discover, Cudworth believes that whenever a wrongful act can be imputed to an agent as his responsibility, it will be because the agent voluntarily failed properly to exercise free will. By this Cudworth does not mean simply that the obligatory act was something in the agent's power in, say, Hobbes's sense that no exter-nal impediments existed – something the agent could have done if he had wanted. Rather, he means that whereas the agent necessarily judged it better, at the moment, to have done the wrongful act, none-theless "he might have made a better judgment than now he did, had he more intensely considered, and more maturely deliberated, which, that he did not, was his fault" (*FW.*37). Failure to exercise a power that, if properly exercised, would have led to a well-considered volition not to take the wrongful action is blameworthy because the failure was itself within the agent's control. "[T]o deny that a man is blameworthy for inward temerity, in acting in any thing of moment without due and full deliberation, and so choosing the worser is absurd . . . [since] a man [has] this power over himself to consider and deliberate more or less" (*FW.*38). It is always up to us, Cudworth believes, whether or not to exercise free will. Free will is, therefore, a power "to good." It leads to evil only when abused. And this abuse can be faulted because it is voluntary.

Cudworth is at some pains to argue that fault does not result from the active exercise of any power, since he holds that any created power must be "for good" and sin can only be "privation" (4982.40). He is far from wholly successful, however, admitting that "such a being as has a power over itself to intend and exert itself must also have a power (if it be a power) not to do the same" (4980.30). Sometimes Cudworth says that it is a matter of "indifferency" whether an agent voluntarily exercises free will or not. And when he does, he contrasts this indifferency with the sort to which he objects (4980.30, 78). The "acceptable" indifference is one that occurs before the formation of any practical judgment, the unacceptable one after. But it is hard to see how this can really work. If it is a matter of indifference whether an agent exercises free will or not, then how can she be held responsible for failing to do so? Cudworth worried endlessly about the relation between free will and its voluntary but (usually) not free-willed exercise; he evidently found this part of his views less than fully satisfying.[58]

SELF-COMPREHENSIVE SELF-COMMAND

We shall shortly examine further the reasons for Cudworth's confidence that properly judicious deliberation enables an agent to make a correct practical judgment and thus to achieve a practically effective grasp of the considerations that must guide her conduct if it is to be autonomously moral. We should recall here, however, that for Cudworth there is no order of reasons that exists independent of practical mind. The agent's judicious review of reasons is therefore a matter of comprehending sources of rational motivation *within*; it is, he says, "self-comprehensive." Indeed, as we shall see, Cudworth believes it to be a condition of morality's power to create binding obligation that moral agents have a "superior" source of moral motivation within their practical intellect, together with a power of self-determination that engages this motivation. A necessary condition of obligation will therefore be that self-determination be "self-comprehensive."

Cudworth hardly provides any systematic account of the self-reflective practical thinking he thinks free will involves. And he employs a bewildering variety of terms to refer to different "moments" of autonomous agency. Some of these refer to the *effects* of exercising free will or failing to. Thus, free will is a "self-improving," "self-

58. At one point he refers to a "power over this power [free will], if it may be so called" (4980.88).

advancing," "self-impairing," and "self-depressing" power (*FW*.48). Others refer to aspects of self-reflective *deliberation*. Free will is, he says, "self-comprehensive," "self-recollective," and "self-attending"; it is a power to "reflect upon ourselves and consider ourselves."[59] Yet other terms apparently refer to the capacities to *direct* practical thought and to carry out its conclusion. Here Cudworth says that free will is "self-intending" and "self-exerting."[60] Finally, there are terms referring to the whole that he takes the various forms of practical thinking to constitute. Free will is "self-determining" and "self-executive"; it involves "redoubled self-activity" or "duplicity in the soul"; it is the soul "holding itself in its own hand"; and it is that by which moral agents are "agents and patients to themselves" and through which they "exercise an *imperium* over" themselves and "command" themselves.[61]

It is not possible to be much more precise about what Cudworth takes self-comprehensive self-command to be. It is clear he thinks it crucial that, in principle, moral agents can at any point undertake self-reflective deliberation and that they can be vigilant to the need to do so. It is also central that agents can *direct* their deliberation. They not only can voluntarily undertake it but also can determine its extent and direction by their voluntary attention. The mind "is conscious also that it hath a self-active autexousious power to excite and command a full consultation, deliberation, and search" (4982.17). Agents "can consider, speculate, and consult more or less, and therefore when they consider more, they discover reasons to determine themselves otherwise than they should when they had considered less" (4980.66). Finally, it is important in Cudworth's view that by recollecting their various motives more or less comprehensively, agents can come to a *unified* or all-things-considered judgment of what to do that, because it is *informed by* individual desires, enables self-command.

[W]hereas there are in the soul a multiplicity of congruities and lower and higher principles of life and action [here are listed "particular appetites and passions," "inferior and superior reason," and "speculative understanding"], there must of necessity be in the soul one common focus or centre in

---

59. For "self-comprehensive," see, e.g., *FW*.36, 46, 58–59; 4980.1, 78, 240; "self-recollection": *FW*.36, 43; 4979.5; 4980.103; "self-attending": *FW*.44; "reflect upon ourselves": *FW*.71.
60. "Self-intending": *FW*.47; 4980.79; "self-exerting": 4980.79.
61. "Self-determining" and "self-executive": 4982.5, 6; "redoubled self-activity": e.g., 4980.4; "duplicity in the soul": *FW*.45; "holding itself": 4982.76; "agents and patients": 4980.76; "exercise an *imperium*": 4982.5; "command": 4982.76.

which all these lines may meet . . . one thing in which all is recollected and knit together, something that is conscious of all its congruities and capacities both higher and lower . . . which same thing can also wield, steer, guide the whole soul, and exercise a power and dominion over it, arbitrate all difference and determine all strife and discord in it; . . . this can be no other than the whole soul redoubled upon itself. (4979.5)[62]

It should not be assumed in all of this that Cudworth believed that the capacity of human agents to direct the determination of their own wills is unlimited. Far from it: Free will is but "a weak staggering and uncertain power" (4979.39). The human soul is like "a ship under sail moving upon the waters and necessarily carried along with the winds and tide in which the . . . chief pilot himself is carried as well as the other mariners, as being passive to its motion, and yet, not-withstanding, he, sitting at the helm has also some power of deter-mining the motion of that ship in which he is carried on, [and] can direct its course to some port rather than another" (4979.178).[63] Hu-man beings are creatures of habit, and the kind of life we habitually lead affects the practical judgments we are likely to make – "particular actions by little and little contribute every one of them sometimes towards habits of judging and afterwards willing" (4980.57). Moreover, virtue and vice are themselves matters of habit, and free will cannot "despotically command these inclinations and turn itself to good with the same ease as one can nod his head or turn his hand" (4980.33).[64] Still, habits can be changed, and free will pro-vides a window of opportunity for change.

The contingency of free-willed beings is this that though they be fixed in habits of virtue or vice so that there is no probability at present of their acting contrary to them, yet it is not absolutely impossible but that in length of time they may by little and little by different use of their own self-active power loosen and change themselves from either of these habits to the contrary. (4980.39)[65]

In the end, the only practical leverage imperfect rational beings have over their conduct is the power they have to direct their practi-cal thinking. Free will, Cudworth concludes, "is a power which a being hath first over its whole self and therefore consequently and

---

62. Mintz discusses this passage; see Samuel Mintz, *The Hunting of Leviathan* (Cam-bridge: Cambridge University Press, 1962), p. 131.
63. See Passmore's discussion in *Ralph Cudworth*, p. 58.
64. See also 4980.29.
65. By "different use of their own self-active power" Cudworth means not just the power of deliberation before the fact, but also the power of forming and recon-firming standing resolutions after deliberation. See *FW*.44, 73.

secondarily [over] its assents and actions to determine both. It is not first of all a power over external actions as some conceive . . . but it is primarily a power which the whole soul hath over itself" (4980.75).

OBLIGATION, ANIMAL AND MORAL

With Cudworth's account of free will in hand, we can now turn to the question of how it figures in his account of moral obligation. Human beings participate, it will be recalled, in two "stories of life" – the animal life and the divine life. The former is composed of desires, feelings, and experiences arising from our bodily, "animal" nature; the latter, of those instincts of love and "honesty" essential to perfect mind. Now a being might have only animal ends and still have a kind of rationality, one that Cudworth calls "inferior reason." Inferior reason is a self's "larger comprehension of our own utility" (4979.5).[66] Cudworth stresses that this is different from particular animal passions and appetites, even when they are combined with calculative reason individually, since these impel toward their respective objects. Inferior reason, on the other hand, provides a "larger comprehension view of our own private utility," one that is anchored neither to specific desires nor to any particular point in time (4980.6).[67] "Utility" here evidently refers to some comprehensive measure of the satisfaction of *animal* desires only.

A being restricted to animal desires and inferior reason can still have the power of free will, which Cudworth calls "animal free will" (4982.19). Moreover, these materials are sufficient, Cudworth holds, for a kind of "animal" obligation.

[I]t is possible that the soul may be here defective in the exertions of this autexousious faculty . . . in not exerting or continuing sufficient conatus, strength, and vigor but succumbing passively to the urging importunity of the present appetite . . . and then it is conscious to itself that it is faulty and blameworthy, not as guilty of any moral evil properly called sin, [but] be-

66. See also 4982.17.
67. "[T]he inferior reason, which comparing the future with the present dictates more truly and impartially our own private utility" (4979.8). Passmore, although he notes this passage, represents inferior reason as "simply the animal passions in their cooler moments" (*Ralph Cudworth*, p. 56); and he contrasts it with Butler's "self-love." But Cudworth's inferior reason is indeed like Butler's cool self-love, and unlike specific passions, in involving a shift of perspective from the particular passions, however informed by calculative reason, to a point of view that seeks to integrate them "impartially."

cause it was wanting to itself within the sphere of the animal life as to private utility, and hereupon follows . . . regret of mind, self-displeasure. (4982.17)[68]

An agent with animal free will may appropriately consider himself blameworthy for acting contrary to his own private utility since he voluntarily failed to exercise the power of practical judgment, which if properly exercised would have enabled him to determine himself to his greater good. The power of animal free will (together with inferior reason) is necessary for animal obligation, and its proper exercise is sufficient to discharge it. It is not too much, indeed, to say that, for Cudworth, animal obligation itself *consists* in there being conclusive motives to private utility brought into existence by the exercise of animal free will.

Animal free will and inferior reason are, however, insufficient for moral obligation. Cudworth pointedly remarks (with a nod toward Hobbes) that, were human agents only so far equipped, "there is no doubt but they might have societies, polities and laws . . . enforced with punishments and rewards to good purpose, in order to the advantage of private persons and the safety of the whole, which is the very constitution of the Leviathan" (4980.9). But this would not be an "obligation truly moral." "Laws could no otherwise operate or seize upon them than by taking hold of their animal selfish passions . . . and that will allow of no other moral obligation than this utterly destroys all morality" (4980.9). Were these the only sources of motivation available to a person, she would lack any motive to morality in itself, any capacity for moral self-determination. And lacking this, Cudworth holds, moral agents could not be obligated *by morality*, only externally: "[T]he external law promulgated could not otherwise operate or seize upon them but by taking hold upon their natural selfish passions" (4982.19).

In order to have a distinctively moral obligation, an agent must have "moral free will." The contrast between animal free will and moral free will is misleading in one way, since it suggests there are two different kinds of free will, one animal and the other moral. But there is really only one free will in two different motivational contexts. Animal free will is the power of practical judgment conjoined only with animal desires and inferior reason. Moral free will is the same power combined with the distinctive motives of the divine life, together with those of the animal life. "For the better explanation" of moral obligation, Cudworth writes, "it must be first supposed that

68. See also 4980.5–6, 8, 9.

besides the spring of animal life, there is in the soul, a spring or principle of another superior intellectual life" (4982.20).[69] This is the motive Cudworth variously calls "superior reason," "love," the "principle of honesty," and "conscience." It is not in us as God's overflowing love is in Him. God is love essentially and necessarily. But we participate in the divine life and have "a principle of animal life in us besides" (4982.20). So, unlike God, we imperfect rational beings require a power of free will to enable us to guide our lives by this superior motive. We require moral free will.

Since the object of inferior reason is the agent's "private utility," it may seem that Cudworth has in mind something like Cumberland's idea that the agent may determine himself either to his own good or to the good of all, and that moral free will enables him to choose the latter. But this mistakes Cudworth's thought. He never abandons the orthodox Aristotelian framework that the agent's good provides the object of rational pursuit. Sometimes Cudworth characterizes a variety of indifferentism that he is anxious to combat as the view that morality is a matter of indifference to, and no part of, the good of agents who are anything but indifferent to their own good.[70] The contrast between inferior and superior reason, therefore, is not drawn between the good of the agent and the good of all.

Nor is it a difference in *authority* that the agent must herself recognize if she is to regulate herself, such as we shall see in Shaftesbury and Butler. Rather, Cudworth draws the distinction between superior and inferior principles *within* a person's good. It is a distinction between two different sources of intrinsic good to the agent: one, animal and essentially "private" since its object is the agent's own states, the other, "divine" and common because the loving person shares it with others.[71]

Cudworth's view, then, is that the divine life realizes higher, more satisfying goods than does the animal life (4980.59; *TIS*.205). It is a better life not just because of benefits it brings about for others, but intrinsically for the person who lives it. As Cudworth thinks of it, moral free will, the power to comprehend the divine source of motivation within, gives an agent a way of appreciating this. If, consequently, a person fails to make the moral, loving choice, the choice

69. See also FW.31, 59; 4980.53.
70. See 4980.58, 59; 4982.36.
71. See Passmore's chapter "The Good Life" in *Ralph Cudworth*, pp. 68–78, much of which is based on passages from BL Add. Ms. 4983, which the most recent catalogue judges to be only doubtfully the work of Cudworth.

that is intrinsic to the best life she could lead, this can only be because of "slight considerations and immature deliberations" (*FW.*37). And because further deliberation is always in our power, a person may be "blameworthy for inward temerity, in acting in any thing of moment without due and full deliberation, and so choosing the [worse]" (*FW.*38).

THE ACCOUNTABILITY STRAND OF AUTONOMIST INTERNALISM

We need not worry further about the details of this view. The important thing for our purposes is the overall way Cudworth knits together an account of moral obligation with a theory of self-determination. The power of free will is necessary for morality to obligate, and, he thinks, by fully exercising this power a moral agent does all he can be obligated to do. As with his account of animal obligation, it is no exaggeration to say that for Cudworth moral obligation itself consists in there being motives to morality, essentially and not accidentally, that are made practically conclusive by the exercise of the power of self-determination: moral free will.

Cudworth is best viewed as working out the implications, as he saw them, of a notion we found in Culverwell, namely, that because moral obligation involves *accountability*, any being that can be obligated must be capable of "moral government" and, moreover, that proper self-government must invariably coincide with moral demands. Pure practical mind and free will are, for Cudworth, necessary conditions for the very possibility of morality. This might be called the *accountability strand* of the autonomist internalist tradition. Beginning from the idea that moral obligation involves accountability and that this requires both that those morally obligated be self-determining agents *and* that self-determining practical reasoning invariably coincide with moral demands, the accountability strand infers that these are necessary conditions for the very possibility of morality. There can be such a thing as moral obligation only if there is a motivational source within autonomous practical reason that conclusively directs agents to be moral. Moral obligation, this strand concludes, consists in these conclusive motives that are raised by self-determining practical reason.

So far this says only what must hold for there to be such a thing as morality (and moral obligation); it is consistent with the possibility

that there is in fact no such thing. It just says in what moral obligation, should it exist, would have to consist. In effect, this is half of
what has been called the "reciprocity thesis" in Kant's moral philosophy.[72] Kant's reciprocity thesis is his contention that morality and
autonomous rational agency are mutually entailing. One half of the
thesis, the one I am saying is implicated in the accountability view, is
that morality entails autonomous practical reason – more precisely,
that morality entails that only free rational agents can be subject to it
and that the dictates of autonomous practical reason direct compliance with its demands. Again, this is only what must be true in
order for moral obligation to exist. In order to vindicate the proposition that there is such a thing, the other half of the reciprocity thesis
must also hold; that is, it must also be true that there is such a thing as
autonomous practical reason and that it dictates doing what morality
demands.

Cudworth asserts both halves of the reciprocity thesis. It should
now be obvious that he claims the first half, and his theses that pure
mind is practical, that the loving life is the best life for the agent, and
that moral free will enables the agent both to appreciate this truth
and to determine her conduct by it amount to the second half. But
although Cudworth affirms a source of motivation within mind or
reason that gives moral direction, he provides no real argument for it.
He does develop a distinction between will and desire, and a view of
the will as being unlike desire in involving autonomous rational
practical judgment. But his doctrine of animal free will appears to
imply that moral motivation is no part of autonomous rational will as
such, since animal free will is apparently no less autonomous than is
moral free will, by his lights, and it lacks moral motivation. It would
fall to later writers, to Shaftesbury and, especially, to Butler, to argue
that moral direction is inherent in autonomous will itself.

72. Henry Allison, "Morality and Freedom: Kant's Reciprocity Thesis," *Philosophical
Review* 95 (1986): 393–425. See also Allison, *Kant's Theory of Freedom*, Part III.

Chapter 6

Locke: autonomy and obligation in the revised *Essay*

Cudworth's view of moral obligation may seem to contrast with none more sharply than with Locke's. Certainly this is the impression one gets from *Essays on the Law of Nature*. Here morality obligates because its demands emanate from a source that is external and superior to the moral agent; moral obligation is rooted in a juridical relation of superior authority obtaining between God and His creatures. Even so, Locke also implies that what can rationally motivate serves as a constraint on divine command – since God cannot sensibly issue commands that agents will lack rational motives to obey – and thus on moral obligation. And even in the *Essays* he holds that the structure of rational human motives is what makes it necessary for God to institute a system of morality in the first place. It is precisely because human agents would lack adequate motive to act in mutually advantageous ways without supernaturally sanctioned directives that God must establish these. This brings into the picture a connection between obligation and a source of rational motivation. Motivation is no part of Locke's understanding of what moral obligation *is* in the *Essays*, but it is nonetheless central to his account of why there should be such a thing.

By the time of the *Essay*, Locke is even clearer that obligation must connect closely to motive. Leaving out logic and semantics, all knowledge can be divided into theoretical and practical, he now says. And in the latter category he includes knowledge of whatever "Man himself ought to do, as a rational and voluntary Agent, for the Attainment of any End, especially Happiness" (720). Moreover, Locke now defines ethics as "the seeking out those Rules, and Measures of humane Actions, which lead to Happiness" (720). For moral obligation to be part of ethics as thus defined, it must relate to what Locke regards as the agent's sole rational end – her own greatest

149

happiness. Only if moral obligations can be shown to create inescapable motives can what Locke calls "the force of morality" be adequately established.[1]

This, we recall, is Locke's diagnosis of the great failing of those ethical systems that, like Aristotle's, "name this or that action a virtue or a vice" but fail to exhibit any rationally conclusive motive for being virtuous. People may, of course, concatenate simple ideas into complex ones in whatever way they please. But propositions expressed with such ideas will be *practical* truths – part of *ethics* – only if they engage the motives of rational agents. In order for the complex idea of moral obligation to figure in ethics, therefore, it must relate to agents' rational motives.

Thus, although Locke's official view of obligation retains an unreduced normative kernel in the juridical idea of superior authority (even in the *Essay*; see, e.g., 351–52), he plainly feels much the same philosophical pressure in the direction of an empirical naturalist internalism as do Hobbes and Cumberland. That motives created by divinely sanctioned commands derive from a source who rules us with *right* is incidental to the fact that the obligations thereby created are part of practical knowledge and ethics, on their *Essay* definitions. As with Hobbes and Cumberland, the latter fact derives entirely from the commands' inescapable *practical* relevance from a rational agent's point of view.

Appearances to the contrary, therefore, it makes some sense to place Locke's theory of moral obligation within the empirical naturalist internalist tradition of Hobbes and Cumberland. Each hesitates, more or less, to state explicitly and unambiguously that moral obligation consists entirely in there being conclusive motives for being moral that are rationally unavoidable from an agent's perspective. Hobbes retains an intrinsic connection to the transferring of a right; and both Cumberland and Locke frequently insist that the idea of obligation cannot be understood independently of the notion of authoritatively promulgated dictate. Nevertheless, all these writers think that, in the philosophically most important sense, an agent *ought* to act as he is "obligated" to if, and only if, this is dictated by conclusive motives raised through the maximal use of theoretical reason.[2]

1. "Of Ethick in General," in King, *The Life of John Locke*, vol. 2, pp. 129–30. See the discussion of this and related passages in Chapter 2.
2. It will emerge in this chapter that the sense in which Locke thinks the agent's greatest long-run happiness is her sole ultimate rational end is that this is the end

These insights may not seem to soften the contrast between Locke and Cudworth, however, since Cudworth believes that moral obligation requires a distinctively moral motive intrinsic to pure reason *and* that autonomous practical reasoning makes this motive rationally conclusive. Central to Cudworth's internal turn is what I have called the *accountability view*, namely, that only *self-governing* agents can be obligated, and then only through motivation that self-determining practical thinking brings to the fore. Nothing we have yet seen in Locke echoes any of these ideas. And very little did echo them until he came to revise the *Essay* for its second edition (published in 1694).

In the *Essay's* second edition, however, Locke develops a version of the accountability view. Already in the first edition he had affirmed his agreement with "those who cannot conceive, how any thing can be capable of a Law, that is not a free Agent" (76), but the account he gave there of freedom was entirely negative – an "absence of obstacles theory." In the second edition, however, this is completely changed. In his extensive revisions of the chapter "Of Power" (Chap. xxi of Book II), Locke sketches a theory of liberty as self-determined will that is Cudworthian *in detail*.[3] What is more, he also there links obligation to the capacity for self-determination in Cudworth's manner.

Locke remains an egoistic hedonist; so he does not hold that moral obligation requires what Cudworth called *moral* free will: self-determination by distinctively moral motives. Unlike Cudworth, he is not *that* kind of internalist about morality. Morality, he maintains, obligates through the same motives of self-happiness that determine all rational choice. But Locke does hold that for God's commands to be binding, it is insufficient that He simply create sanctions that make obedience to His dictates coincide with self-interest. It is necessary also that moral agents be endowed with the capacity to deliberate and determine their wills by considered practical judgments concerning their best interests. It is necessary, that is, that moral agents have Cudworth's "animal free will." Even though Locke remains in disagreement with Cudworth's doctrine that moral obligation requires a capacity for distinctively *moral* self-determination, in the second edition of the *Essay* he came to agree with the more general idea that morality can obligate an agent only because proper

she would seek if she were maximally and vividly informed by theoretical reason. This is a version of the calm reflective deliberation view.
3. This may well have been no accident, as I discuss in the Afterword to this chapter.

"singing *Faculty*" that sings (242). Finally, Locke insists that a person is free only to act and not to will. Freedom is the power to determine action by will, not to determine the will (247).

Each of these points echoes Hobbesian themes. 'Free' and 'liberty' are abused, Hobbes had said, when applied to anything but "bodies": "From the use of the word *Free-will*, no liberty can be inferred of the will . . . but the liberty of the man" (*Lev.*xxi.2).[8] Second, Hobbes had lampooned faculty discussions of will citing the analogous absurdity of acts of the "ability to dance."[9] Finally, on whether an agent can be free to will, Hobbes had remarked, "I acknowledge this *liberty*, that I *can* do if I *will*; but to say, I can *will* if I *will*, I take to be absurd speech."[10]

The whole thrust of Locke's account in the first edition is that liberty exclusively concerns what happens (or would happen) *after*

---

8. See also *Lev.*v.5.
9. *English Works*, vol. 4, p. 266. Locke gives four analogies: the faculties of speaking, singing, dancing, and walking. In discussing the probability of Cudworth's having influenced Locke's views of freedom and the will, Passmore points out a similarity with the following passage from Cudworth's *Treatise of Freewill*: "[T]o attribute the act of intellection and perception to the faculty of understanding, and acts of volition to the faculty of will, or to say that it is the understanding that understandeth, and the will that willeth . . . is all one as if one should say that the faculty of walking walketh, and the faculty of speaking speaketh, or that the musical faculty playeth a lesson upon the lute, or sings this or that tune. . . . [I]t is really the man or the soul that understands, and the man or the soul that walks, as it is the man that walks . . . and the musician that plays a lesson on the lute" (*FW*.24–25). He then cites the following passage from Locke's *Essay*: "[W]e may as properly say, that 'tis the singing *Faculty* sings, and the dancing *Faculty* dances; as that the *Will* chuses, or that the Understanding conceives . . . it is the Mind that operates, and exerts these Powers; it is the Man that does the Action, it is the Agent that has the power, or is able to do" (*Essay*.242–43). Passmore then remarks, "Unless there is a common source, the inference is irresistible that, even before 1690, Cudworth's unpublished views were not unknown to Locke" (*Ralph Cudworth*, p. 94). Passmore notes that one possible common source might be Hobbes, but he fails to notice that Hobbes uses one of the very examples Locke does. And his passage from Locke also leaves out the third example that Locke and Cudworth have in common: the speaking faculty. The fact is that *all* of Locke's examples appear either in Hobbes's *Of Liberty and Necessity* or in Cudworth's *Treatise of Freewill*; the dancing faculty appears in the former, and the speaking, singing, and walking faculties appear in the latter. I find it hard to resist the conclusion that Locke knew both of these sources. I shall argue later that many of the details of Locke's revised account of freedom are virtually identical to the theory of self-determination Cudworth develops in the manuscripts. Since only one of these, *A Treatise of Freewill*, was ever published, and that a century and a half after Locke's death, the question arises of how Locke could have seen the manuscripts or even known otherwise of the ideas contained therein. More on this in the Afterword to this chapter.
10. *English Works*, vol. 4, p. 240.

volition. If the path from volition to successful execution is free of impediments – if willing is, in given circumstances, sufficient to accomplish the will's object – then a person is free. Otherwise she is not. Having excluded the possibility that freedom has anything to do with how an agent's will is itself determined, Locke turns, in the first edition, to the question of what actually does determine the will. Here is his answer: "If willing be but the being better pleased, as has been shewn, it is easie to know what 'tis determines the Will, what 'tis pleases best: every one knows 'tis Happiness, or that which makes any part of Happiness, or contributes to it; and that is it we call *Good*" (248n). The greatest happiness consists in the greatest pleasure: "[W]hat has an aptness to produce pleasure in us, is that we labour for, and is that we call *Good*" (249n). Doubtless Locke believes that we tend to prefer what actually will produce pleasure. But for our purposes, his crucial claim is that we always prefer what we *believe* will bring the greatest pleasure. "[T]he preference of the Mind [is] always determined by the appearance of Good, greater Good" (256n).

This raises the obvious problem why people choose to do what will make them less happy than they could be. Locke gives two answers in the first edition. One denies that the question arises as often as it may seem when we project our tastes onto others. "[T]he same thing is not good to every Man" – "Study and Knowledge" may make one happy, "Luxury and Debauchery" another (26on). When it comes to *present* pleasure or happiness, human beings cannot possibly ever choose amiss, since our beliefs about current pleasures and pains are incorrigible, and these beliefs, given Locke's definitions of will and preference, constitute volition.[11]

Locke admits that people can choose less than the greatest happiness in view when goods beyond the present are concerned, but only because they are misled by appearances, viewing the future from the perspective of the present. What *"determines the choice* of the Will, and obtains the preference . . . is also only Good *that appears"* (270n); and perspective alters appearance when we consider present and future from "different positions of distance" (275; see also 274, 274n). So, second, he answers that whenever an agent acts contrary to her own greatest good, she does so because of a false belief that what she is doing is actually better.

11. "For the Pain or Pleasure being just so great, and no greater, than it is felt, the present Good or evil is really so much as it appears" (268n).

This leaves it unexplained how beliefs about the good determine preference and so the will. An explanation is at hand for present good, since that is identical with present pleasure, which, according to Locke's definition, is what preference is. In (correctly) judging this good the agent judges a component of her present preference – her being pleased more with, say, continuing her present experience than with not doing so. But there is no such relationship between a belief about absent good and preference. That involves a belief about how pleased one *would* be, and this has no necessary relation to what one prefers now.

There are three main aspects of Locke's first-edition theory of freedom and will on which we shall want to concentrate. First, will is the power to prefer an action to a forbearance, and volition the exercise of this power. Second, preference is in every case determined by the agent's belief about where her greatest good or happiness lies. And, third, liberty is the power to act or forbear as willed.

LIBERTY AND WILL IN THE *ESSAY*, SECOND EDITION

For the second edition of the *Essay*, Locke undertook a massive revision of his chapter on power. In the first edition, II.xxi had some forty-seven sections; in the second, it ran to seventy-three. Many new sections were added, several old sections were replaced, crucial changes of wording were made in remaining old sections, and, in many places old wording took on new meaning in the new context. Locke was obviously aware that his new views of will and liberty would be perceived as significantly different from those the *Essay* had first contained. He remarks on the change in the prefatory "Epistle to the Reader" as well as in the body of the chapter; and in both instances he mentions the objections of another – "a very judicious Friend of mine" – as the occasion for his "stricter review of this Chapter" (11, 282).

The reference appears to be to William Molyneux, who complained in a letter to Locke that the "thread" of liberty and necessity

seems so wonderfully fine spun in your book, that at last the Great Question of Liberty and Necessity seems to Vanish and herein you seem to make all Sins to proceed from our Understandings, or to be against Conscience; and not at all from the Depravity of our Wills. Now it seems harsh to say, that a Man shall be Damn'd, because he understands no better than he does.[12]

Locke responded that he too had thought his "discourse about liberty a little too fine spun" and had wanted to leave it out, but that he had been persuaded by some friends to keep it in. He adds that he showed it "to a very ingenious but professed Arminian," who "frankly confessed he could carry it no farther."[13]

In making a stricter review, Locke says, he "light[ed] upon a very easy, and scarce observable slip I had made, in putting one seemingly indifferent word for another, [and] that discovery open'd to me this present view, which here in this second Edition, I submit to the learned World" (282). He does not say exactly what the change of wording is in the *Essay*, and here begins an intriguing puzzle. In a letter to Molyneux, Locke says his revelatory error was "the mistake of one word (viz. having put things for actions, which was very easy to be done in the place where it is, viz. p. 123. as I remember . . .)."[14] But this is really no help at all. There are two candidate targets for this reference, and in neither does a change from 'thing' to 'action' significantly affect Locke's sense.[15]

Suppose, then, we disregard this answer and try to work out Locke's understanding of the change in his ideas from his remarks in the *Essay*. There Locke describes the "present view" to which he was led by his exchange with his "judicious friend" as follows: "*Liberty* is a power to act or not to act according as the Mind directs. A power to direct the operative faculties to motion or rest in particular instances, is that which we call the *Will*" (282). If we are to find the changed wording in this formulation, the likely candidate is "the Mind directs." In the first edition, will is a power to *prefer* action or forbearance, whereas Locke's new view is that will consists not in a preference an agent *has* for an act but in the agent's power *himself* self-consciously to "direct," "command," or "order" these (236). Still, it is hard to see how this change of words could *initially* have been prompted by Molyneux's objection, since Molyneux's problem could arise even if the rest of Locke's view remained the same. The direc-

12. The letter is dated December 22, 1692. E. S. De Beer, ed., *The Correspondence of John Locke*, vol. 4 (Oxford: Clarendon Press, 1979), pp. 600–601. For a similar objection in Cudworth's manuscripts, see Chapter 5, note 53.
13. *Correspondence of John Locke*, vol. 4, p. 625.
14. Ibid., p. 700.
15. The candidates occur in the original sections xxv and xxviii. See De Beer's discussion, ibid., p. 700n.

tion of the mind might itself always be determined by the appearance of the greatest good, and, if so, it would remain true that all fault and sin proceed "from our Understanding . . . and not at all from the Depravity of our Wills." An agreement with *this* objection should prompt a change in the premise that will, whether it be preference or self-conscious self-direction, is always determined by the agent's beliefs about his greatest good.

And Locke does reject this premise in the second edition. For the first-edition passage asserting that the agent's happiness determines the will, Locke substitutes this:

> To return then to the Enquiry, *what is it that determines the Will in regard to our Actions?* And that upon second thoughts I am apt to imagine is not, as is generally supposed, the greater good in view: But some (and for the most part the most pressing) *uneasiness* a Man is at present under. This is that which successively determines the *Will,* and sets us upon those Actions, we perform. This *Uneasiness* we may call, as it is, *Desire.* (250–51)

This suggests that Locke's first-edition "slip," which he corrects in the second, was something like the substitution of "greatest good in view" for "most pressing present uneasiness" or "desire." But if that be so, we have the reverse of the earlier puzzle. How could this change lead to such radically different views of will and liberty? One could, after all, hold that an agent's preference is determined by the greatest present uneasiness without being moved to a view of the will as self-conscious self-direction, or to Locke's new view of liberty, which I shall describe presently. It would seem that if these changes are to be explained by philosophical stimulation that Locke received, something quite different from Molyneux's objection is required. We must set this intriguing puzzle aside, however, until we get a clearer picture of the dimensions of Locke's new view.

WILL AS SELF-DIRECTING

Locke's full second-edition definition of will runs as follows:

> [W]e find in our selves a *Power* to begin or forbear, continue or end several actions of our minds, and motions of our Bodies, barely by a thought or preference of the mind ordering, or as it were commanding the doing or not doing such or such a particular action. This *Power* which the mind has, thus to order . . . is that which we call the *Will.* (236)

Locke despairs of a clear definition, suggesting that the reader should "reflect on what he himself does, when he *wills*" (240), but he is now certain that *preference* lacks the self-directing element he has come to think central to will.

Preferring which seems perhaps best to express the Act of *Volition*, does it not precisely. For though a Man would preferr flying to walking, yet who can say he ever *wills* it? *Volition*, 'tis plain, is an Act of the Mind knowingly exerting that Dominion it takes it self to have over any part of the Man, by imploying it in, or withholding it from any particular Action. And what is the *Will*, but the Faculty to do this? (240–41)[16]

As Locke now thinks of it, will does not involve self-awareness only in the sense that its object is always some action or forbearance of the self. Volition is an act of the mind *taking itself to have command* over "any part of the Man," through that very act. *Will is the faculty of self-conscious self-command.*

Moreover, Locke now understands will to involve a more or less considered – or, in Cudworth's term, *self-comprehensive* – self-command. He distinguishes *will* from *desire* by noting that a man with "a violent Fit of the Gout" may still desire to be rid of the pain in his feet, though "whilst he apprehends, that the removal of the pain may translate the noxious humour to a more vital part, his will is never determin'd to any one Action, that may serve to remove this pain" (250). The desire's object is simply the removal of pain per se, whereas will intrinsically involves a more or less considered view of alternatives; it involves the mind as self-comprehensive.

Section XXIX of the chapter, in all editions, deals with the question "What determines the will?" In the first edition, as we have seen, Locke's answer is the agent's greatest happiness in view. In the second, however, consonant with his new theory of will, Locke gives this answer: "[T]hat which determines the general power of directing, to this or that particular direction, is nothing but the Agent it self Exercising the power it has, that particular way" (249). And as for what moves the agent to determine his will "to this or that particular Motion or Rest," Locke now denies that it is the "greater good in view." It is, rather, the agent's most pressing present uneasiness or desire. The appearance of good "does not determine the *will*, until our desire, raised proportionably to it, makes us *uneasy* in the want of it" (253). The self-destructive drinker whose "habitual thirst after his Cups" drives him to return to the tavern does so even "though he has in his view" what "he confesses" to be greater goods that he will

16. See also *Essay*.250.

thereby lose (253).[17] Locke thus now accepts Molyneux's point. We are not to be damned for understanding no better than we do.

But if Locke thinks we do not always do what we think is best, why does he persist in saying that "a Man's *will*, in every determination, follows his own Judgment" (265)? In many places Locke asserts that agents invariably choose in accordance with their *judgment* of what course of action will bring the greatest good. Some of these instances are holdovers from the first edition, but many are not; and even the holdovers have to be explained, as Locke could as easily have dropped them. The answer, I propose, is that Locke came to accept a distinction between a merely intellectual belief about which act would be best and a genuinely *practical judgment* with the same content – the same distinction Cudworth had made – and that he connected this to the will just as Cudworth had.[18] This will become clear only when we have had a chance to survey Locke's new view of liberty, which, I shall argue, is a theory of self-determining practical judgment, also after Cudworth's manner.

LIBERTY AS SELF-DETERMINATION

Beginning with the second edition, Locke adds to his first-edition "absence of obstacles" account a discussion of a different species of liberty: the power of deliberative self-determination. Following

17. There is some question about whether Locke ever actually says that we sometimes act contrary to what we regard to be for our greatest *happiness*. Consider, for example: "[A]ll good, even seen, and confessed to be so, does not necessarily move every particular Man's *desire;* but only that part, or so much of it, as is consider'd, and taken to make a necessary part of his happiness" (259). This implies that, although a person can act contrary to a good, he can do so only if he takes it not to be necessary for his happiness. But Locke also draws a contrast between an acknowledgment of absent good, which does not necessarily motivate, and an acknowledgment of "present *happiness*" or its contrary, which does (260). This suggests that it is quite possible for a person to act contrary to his (timeless) happiness. See also: "*Happiness* then in its full extent is the utmost Pleasure we are capable of, and *Misery* the utmost pain" (258).

18. For Cudworth's view, see Chapter 5 of the present volume. In Locke's case, since this judgment actually concerns only the amount of natural good or pleasure that would *result* from various alternatives, there is a sense in which it is misleading to call it a *practical* judgment. It is unlike the sort of practical judgment – a judgment of *reasons to act* – that Butler will argue is necessary for autonomous agency. On this point, see Chapter 10. It is practical in the sense of being inherently motivating.

Yolton, we may call this species "moral liberty."[19] If anything, Locke seems there to think it the more important form of liberty. "In this," he now writes, "lies the liberty Man has" (263). It is "the source of all liberty" (263).

"[T]he greatest, and most pressing [uneasiness]," Locke writes, determines the will to the next action "for the most part, but not always" (263).

> For the mind having in most cases, as is evident in Experience, a power to *suspend* the execution and satisfaction of any of its desires, and so all, one after another, is at liberty to consider the objects of them; examine them on all sides, and weigh them with others. In this lies the liberty Man has; and from the not using of it right comes all that variety of mistakes, errors, and faults which we run into, in the conduct of our lives, and our endeavours after happiness. (263)

The "great privilege of finite intellectual Beings," "the hinge on which turns [their] *liberty*," "the great inlet, and exercise of all the *liberty* Men have," is the "power to suspend any particular desire, and keep it from determining the *will*, and engaging us in action" until we have judiciously examined the alternatives (267, 266, 267, 266). "[H]e that has a power to act, or not to act according as such determination directs, is a *free Agent*" (266).

In its first moment, the power of deliberative decision involves an ability to step back reflectively and thereby to "suspend" the force of present uneasiness in the direction of "the next action." Its second moment consists in a power to survey alternatives with a view to determining the will in the direction of the agent's greatest long-run good or happiness. Owing to *"the weak and narrow Constitution of our Minds,"* present pains and pleasures tend to determine choice out of proportion to their contribution to the happiness of our lives on the whole (276). But future pleasures are no less worth pursuing than present ones, nor future pains less worth avoiding, "since that which

19. See John Yolton, *Locke and the Compass of Human Understanding* (Cambridge: Cambridge University Press, 1970), pp. 147–48. For a generally helpful discussion, see Colman, *John Locke's Moral Philosophy*, pp. 218–34. See also Raymond Polin, "John Locke's Conception of Freedom," in John Yolton, ed., *John Locke: Problems and Perspectives* (Cambridge: Cambridge University Press, 1969), pp. 1–18. For a stimulating if also somewhat breathtaking discussion of autonomy and liberalism in Locke, see Andrzej Rapaczynski, *Nature and Politics: Liberalism in the Philosophies of Hobbes, Locke, and Rousseau* (Ithaca: Cornell University Press, 1987), esp. pp. 113–76. See also Peter A. Schouls, *Reasoned Freedom* (Ithaca: Cornell University Press, 1992), esp. pp. 117–72. This last came into my hands too late to take account of here.

is future, will certainly come to be present; and then, having the same advantage of nearness, will shew it self in its full dimensions, and discover his wilful mistake, who judged of it by unequal measures" (275). To correct these errors of perspective, God gives us an imaginative power to bring distant goods and evils more nearly to mind, so that they can attract or repel us *in proportion to their actual relative value.*

[D]ue, and repeated Contemplation [of an absent good can] giv[e] some relish of it, and rais[e] in us some desire; which then beginning to make a part of our present *uneasiness,* stands upon fair terms with the rest. . . . And thus, by a due consideration and examining any good proposed, *it is in our power, to raise our desires, in a due proportion to the value of that good,* whereby in its turn, and place, it may come to work upon the *will,* and be pursued. (262; emphasis added, except "*uneasiness*" and "*will*")[20]

Locke evidently assumes that future pains and pleasures, when informedly and imaginatively considered with sufficient vividness, will come to have a repulsion and attraction in present deliberation that is equal to their respective hedonic values as experienced.

Taken together, the two moments of suspension and imaginative consideration make up moral liberty: autonomy or self-determination. "The first therefore and great use of Liberty," Locke now writes, "is to hinder blind Precipitancy; the principal exercise of Freedom is to stand still, open the eyes, look about, and take a view of the consequence of what we are going to do, as much as the weight of the matter requires" (279). So there is, after all, "a case wherein a Man is at Liberty in respect of *willing,* and that is the chusing of a remote Good as an end to be pursued" (270).

Central to Locke's picture of self-determination is the idea that agents can make a critical evaluation of alternatives that, because it corrects for narrowness of perspective *in imagination, motivates* choice in the direction of greatest self-happiness as the agent then evaluates this. 'Judgment' is the term Locke consistently uses for this motivating, hence distinctively practical, assessment.[21] Whereas in the first edition he had criticized the liberty of indifference by saying it

---

20. Also: "In this we should take pains to suit the relish of our Minds to the true instrinsick good or ill, that is in things; and not permit an allow'd or supposed possible great and weighty good to slip out of our thoughts, without leaving any relish, any desire of it self there, till, by a due consideration of its true worth, we have formed appetites in our Minds suitable to it, and made our selves uneasie in the want of it, or in the fear of losing it" (268).
21. As had Cudworth; see in Chapter 5, "Will and Practical Judgment."

would be no boon to be able to have volition that is "not determin-able by the Good or Evil, that is thought to attend its Choice" (252n), in the second Locke writes that we should be glad not to have a will that is "not determinable by *its* [the mind's] *last judgment* of the Good or Evil, that is thought to attend its Choice" (264; emphasis added). And: "[W]ere we determined by any thing but the last result of our own Minds, judging of the good or evil of any action, we were not free" (264).

Since Locke now holds both that agents act on their greatest pre-sent uneasiness and that the will is determined by the last practical judgment, he must, like Cudworth, be reserving 'judgment' for the upshot of a (more or less self-comprehensive) weighing and balanc-ing that conclude in a motivating, *practical* assessment of value. He writes, "The result of our judgment upon that Examination is what ultimately determines the Man, who could not be *free* if his *will* were determin'd by any thing, but his own *desire* guided by his own *Judg-ment*" (283).

There are several Cudworthian echoes in Locke's thought that are worth stressing. One is the distinctive, intrinsically practical use of 'judgment'. A practical *judgment* is something a free agent *makes* as a conclusion to practical deliberation.[22] "Judging is, as it were, balanc-ing an account" (278).[23] And once we have made a considered deter-mination of what best to do, "[w]hat follows after that, follows in a chain of Consequences linked one to another, all depending on the last determination of the Judgment, which whether it shall be upon an hasty and precipitate view, or upon a due and mature *Examina-tion*, is in our power" (267). Second, and equally important, Locke connects practical judgment to the *will*. Volition involves the self-

22. Again, see note 18 for a caveat about calling this *practical* judgment. "Judging is a bare action of the understanding, whereby a man, several objects being proposed to him, takes one of them to be best for him. . . . Election . . . is, when a man judging anything to be best for him, ceases to consider, examine, and inquire any further concerning that matter; for, till a man comes to this, he has not chosen, the matter still remains with him under deliberation, and not determined. Here, then, comes in the will, and makes Election voluntary, by stopping in the mind any farther inquiry and examination" (King, *The Life of John Locke*, vol. 2, p. 106, quoted in Colman, *John Locke's Moral Philosophy*, pp. 209–10).

Note, by the way, the remarkable similarity to Hobbes's views about delibera-tion and will, with, of course, the difference that will, for Hobbes, is the last appetite rather than the last practical judgment.

23. The full sentence is: "Judging is, as it were, balancing an account, and determin-ing on which side the odds lies" (278). As I shall argue, Locke uses 'judgment', as did Cudworth, to refer to a more or less comprehensive, or all-things-considered, assessment of what to do *or* what to believe.

comprehensive, unifying activity of the mind, directing action on the basis of some more or less considered survey of alternatives. It is not only in our power to act or forbear as we will. The forming of our wills is also in our hands, since volition is determined by (is?) the last practical judgment of a deliberative process we direct. The judgment itself, Locke now says, is in our power. Thus, third, Locke now believes, as did Cudworth, that free agency primarily involves the agent's ability to direct her own practical thinking.

Fourth (and we shall consider this at greater length presently), Locke agrees with Cudworth that this freedom is a necessary condition for accountability and, therefore, for obligation. Since the determination of the will is up to the agent, he can be held responsible for doing what is not in fact for the best even when in so doing he wills, as he must, in accordance with his present judgment of what is best. "For though his *will* be always determined by that, which is judg'd good by his Understanding, yet it excuses him not; Because by a too hasty choice of his own making, he has imposed on himself wrong measures of good and evil" (271). A "due and mature Examination" of options would have enabled the agent "to raise . . . desires, in a due proportion to the value[s]" of the options, and thereby to make a practical judgment that is correctly reflective of those values (262).[24]

Fifth, like Cudworth, Locke holds that the possibilities of responsibility and fault, both practical *and* theoretical, depend on the same generic power of *judgment.* On the theoretical side, Locke calls judgment the "Faculty, which God has given Man to supply the want of clear and certain Knowledge in Cases where that cannot be had" (653). Lockean knowledge is *"the perception of the connexion and agreement, or disagreement and repugnancy of any of our Ideas"* (525). Frequently lacking certain demonstration, we must, in our "State of Mediocrity and Probationership," make do with probability (652). We have no way of connecting two ideas through a medium that is "constant, immutable, and visible" and can connect them only through mediating ideas that are themselves respectively connected to the two only "for the most part" (654). Judgment, then, "is the thinking or taking two *Ideas* to agree, or disagree, by the intervention

24. Needless to say, Locke is making some pretty optimistic assumptions about the power of what Richard Brandt has called "cognitive psychotherapy" to affect choice. See, e.g., Brandt, *A Theory of the Good and the Right*, pp. 11–12. In section LXIX Locke discusses cases where contemplation, even repeated contemplation, is insufficient to yield correct practical judgments, and some education of the "palate" by relevant experience is required to create the right relish.

of one or more *Ideas*, whose certain Agreement, or Disagreement with them it does not perceive, but hath observed to be frequent and usual" (685).

Theoretical judgment is thus something that an *epistemic* agent *exercises* by thinking about connections that render conclusions more or less probable.[25] Since no such connection is demonstrative, and different connections between the same proposition and differing probabilistic grounds can conflict, the best theoretical judgment must consider all relevant evidence.

Probability wanting that intuitive Evidence, which infallibly determines the Understanding, and produces certain Knowledge, *the Mind if it will proceed rationally, ought to examine all the grounds of Probability,* and see how they make more or less, *for or against* any probable Proposition, before it assents to or dissents from it, and upon a due ballancing the whole, reject, or receive it, with a more or less firm assent, proportionably to the preponderancy of the greater grounds of Probability on one side or the other. (656)[26]

So "[t]he great Excellency and Use of the Judgment" is to take account of "the force and weight of each Probability; and then casting them up all right together, chuse that side, which has the overbalance" (685).

What we find most probable "upon full Examination" we cannot help assenting to. But the proper exercise of theoretical judgment is itself in our hands. And because it is, "Ignorance" and "Error" can be "Fault" (717). Exactly what level of exercise of judgment epistemic agents can reasonably be held responsible for depends on normal capacities.

It being . . . very hard, even for those who have very admirable Memories, to retain all the Proofs, which upon a due examination, made them embrace that side of the question[, it] suffices, that they have once with care and fairness, sifted the Matter as far as they could; and that they have . . . with the best of their Skill, cast up the account upon the whole Evidence. (658)

Thus in the first edition Locke already provides a picture of theoretical judgment and responsibility structured almost identically to

25. Regarding men who "think they have formed right Judgments of several matters; and that for no other reason, but because they never thought otherwise," Locke remarks that those "[t]hat imagine themselves to have judged right, only because they never questioned, never examined their own Opinions" could be as well described as those who "think they judged right, because they never judged at all" (659).

26. Compare Carnap's "total evidence requirement." See Rudolph Carnap, *The Foundations of Probability* (Chicago: University of Chicago Press, 1950), p. 211.

the one he came to stress of practical judgment and responsibility in the second edition. Neither assent nor volition are a matter of indifferent fiat. "[A] man can no more avoid assenting . . . where he perceives the greater Probability" upon a more or less considered examination than he can avoid willing what he judges best as the result of an analogous deliberative process (718). Even so, we are no less responsible for our assents than we are for our volitions, since each results from processes of more or less judicious consideration that it is generally within our power to conduct. "The Foundation of Errour . . . lie[s] in wrong Measures of Probability; as the Foundation of Vice in wrong Measures of Good" (718).

SELF-DETERMINATION AND OBLIGATION

It may be recalled from our discussion in Chapter 2 that when Locke discusses his thesis that *"Morality is capable of Demonstration"* in connection with his idea that moral notions are ectypal rather than archetypal, he says that in "moral Discourses" the natures of the relevant substances (moral agents) "are not so much enquir'd into, as supposed" (516).[27] More specifically, "when we say that *Man is subject to Law:* We mean nothing by *Man,* but a corporeal rational Creature" (516).[28] In his discussion of personal identity, Locke develops this thought, connecting subjection to law to the *imputation* of actions and to the extension of imputation over time. 'Person', he writes, "is a Forensick Term appropriating Actions and their Merit; and so belongs only to intelligent Agents capable of a Law, and Happiness and Misery" (346). The identity of a person over time, he says, "whereby it becomes . . . *accountable,"* presupposes an agent who consciously *"owns* or *imputes* to it *self* past Actions" on the same grounds "that it does the present" (346; emphasis added, except to *"self"*).

Our concern is less with the conditions for diachronic moral agency than for those of the synchronic kind. What matters for our purposes is that Locke thinks no being can be "capable of a Law" unless actions are *imputable* to him. Imputation, we might say, is a necessary condition of *accountability,* and a person can be obligated to do something only if she is accountable for so acting. The crucial point for us is that, by the second edition, Locke believes attributing

27. See Chapter 2, "Demonstration and Moral Ideas."
28. See Ruth Mattern, "Moral Sciences and the Concept of Persons in Locke," *Philosophical Review* 89 (1980): 24–45.

the power of self-determination to an agent is a necessary condition for holding him accountable and thus of his being obligated. Only if an agent has the power to suspend the force of present desire, judiciously deliberate, and thereby determine his will can he be held responsible for doing what is worse even though he may think it better at the time. Only because he has moral liberty can we impute his actions to *him* and hold him accountable for them. "If the neglect or abuse of the Liberty he had, to examine what would really and truly make for his Happiness, misleads him, the miscarriages that follow on it, must be imputed to his own election" (271). A person may therefore "justly incur punishment" even if he never does anything he does not judge best at the time (270–71).[29]

Since moral liberty is the agent's capacity to make distinctively practical all-things-considered judgments of her own good or happiness, it may seem puzzling that Locke holds this to be necessary to moral obligation. What does this power have to do with what makes punishment just? The answer lies, of course, in Locke's view that morality just is a set of commandments that God enforces with eternal sanctions. This is what makes the discussion of the conflict between present and future goods and evils so important for him. Indeed, part of what convinced Locke that it cannot be true that people invariably do what they believe best is the observation that they frequently violate God's commands (255). Even those who are not sure whether God exists must admit there is some probability that He does, and the quantity of eternal good and evil at stake must surely, in the fullness of time, outweigh any of sin's short-term advantages. But whereas morality (God's commands) would make no sense without punishment, punishment itself would be unable to achieve the deterrent effect God desires unless He also endowed us with the capacity to determine choice by our considered judgment of the sanctions we risk.

On Locke's official theory, morality is obligatory because God commands it and He has authority over us. God knows that we can act only for our own pleasure or happiness and that, left to our own

---

29. Locke adds as an example of inference in the fourth-edition version of his chapter on reason (IV.xvii) the reasoning from "*Men shall be punished in another World*" to "*Men can determine themselves*" (672). "For here the Mind seeing the connexion there is between the *Idea of Men's Punishment in the other World*, and the *Idea of God punishing*, between *God punishing*, and *the Justice of the Punishment*; between *Justice of Punishment* and *Guilt*, between *Guilt* and a *Power to do otherwise*, between a *Power to do otherwise* and *Freedom*, and between *Freedom* and *self-determination*, sees the connexion between *Men*, and *self-determination*" (673).

devices without eternal sanctions, we could not avoid mutually disadvantageous conflict. For these reasons, He issues the commands that establish morality. But He cannot *barely* do this, because we would then lack adequate motive to follow them. So He must establish eternal sanctions to give us good reason to follow His commands. But He cannot barely do that either, since we might still lack the power to regulate our conduct by consideration of these motives. So God must also give us moral liberty.

Here, then, is the chain of ideas. Moral obligation requires punishment; punishment requires imputation; and imputation requires self-determination. This, of course, is the same accountability argument that forms the main thread of Cudworth's manuscripts. What is more, when in the *Essay*'s fourth edition Locke adds an example of syllogistic reasoning, he reproduces a version of this very argument: *"Men shall be punished, – God the punisher, – just Punishment, – the Punished guilty – could have done otherwise – Freedom – self-determination"* (673). Thus is the power to determine ourselves, through deliberative practical judgment, necessary if we are to be morally obligated. But if the power of self-determination is necessary for obligation, so also, Locke now thinks, is the proper exercise of this power *sufficient* to discharge obligation. "[W]hen, upon due *Examination*, we have judg'd, we have done our duty, all that we can, or ought to do, in pursuit of our happiness; and 'tis not a fault, but a perfection of our nature to desire, will, and act according to the last result of a fair *Examination*" (263–64). When we have properly exercised the power of self-determination, "we have done our duty, and all that is in our power; and indeed all that needs" (267).

Now, none of this is strictly inconsistent with Locke's official, externalist understanding of obligation. It will perhaps no longer be enough to say that being obligated consists simply in being under a dictate deriving from an authoritative source, even if we add, as Locke usually does, that it would be pointless for such a source to command agents to do what they could not be rationally motivated to do or could not determine themselves to do. In the passages we have just been considering, the possibility of connection to the power of self-determination seems to be operating as a constraint intrinsic to imputability and thus to obligation, and not just through the externally related notion of what God can reasonably believe rational agents will be motivated to do. Even so, Locke might hold a complex view of obligation having two necessary components: first, the existence of a command of superior authority requiring action and, second, the agent's power to determine herself in accordance with this command. Because the latter power will, according to Locke, require sanctions making compliance coincide with agents' long-term interests, along with the power to determine the will by knowledge and consideration of these, sanctions also become intrinsic to obligation, and not just further features that God must put in place if He expects agents to be able to act as they are obligated. Thus Locke now writes:

Morality, established upon its true Foundations, cannot but determine the Choice in any one, that will but consider: and he that will not be so far a rational Creature, as to reflect seriously upon infinite Happiness and Misery, must needs condemn himself, as not making that use of his Understanding he should. (281)

Despite the fact that almost all of what Locke says about morality's relation to self-determination can be accommodated within Locke's usual theory of obligation without flat contradiction, there are several intriguing places where the revised text of II.xxi insinuates a very different, Cudworthian view. Before discussing these, however, it may be worth reiterating the tensions in Locke's more usual position. Suppose that obligation requires the command of a superior authority. We may still ask, What does superior authority itself consist in, such that its commands ought to be obeyed? God has this authority, Locke claims, because He creates and sustains His creatures. But what is the status of *this* claim? Either it is a normative proposition, which still leaves unanswered what the *normativity* of authority, and hence of morality, itself consists in, or it is advanced as a sort of reductive naturalistic account of normativity. But given what Locke says about the *practicality* of ethics, it is hard to see how he can accept any naturalistic account of normativity other than an internalist one. Simply pointing out that certain commands come from a Being who created and sustains us does not thereby make it evident why – or even that – we should or must obey them. On the other hand, if God's creativity is a normative premise necessary for obligation to exist, we are no closer to understanding what normativity (bindingness) itself is.

With these questions in mind, consider the following passage, which I quote at some length:

[T]he highest perfection of intellectual nature, lies in a careful and constant pursuit of true and solid happiness. . . . [W]e are by the *necessity* of preferring and pursuing true happiness as our greatest good, *obliged* to suspend the satisfaction of our desire in particular cases.

This is the hinge on which turns the *liberty* of intellectual Beings in their constant endeavours after, and a steady prosecution of true felicity. . . . For the inclination, and *tendency of their nature to happiness* is an *obligation*, and *motive* to them, to take care not to mistake, or miss it; and so necessarily puts them upon caution, deliberation, and wariness, in the direction of their particular actions, which are the means to obtain it. Whatever necessity determines to the pursuit of real Bliss, the same necessity, with the same force establishes *suspence, deliberation,* and scrutiny of each successive desire. (266– 67; emphasis added, except to "*liberty*," "*suspence,*" and "*deliberation*")

There are several points to note here. First, natural necessity guarantees that the greatest self-happiness is the governing end of any rational being; it is intrinsic to intellectual nature. Second, because it is a necessary *end*, we are under a *practical necessity* to do what will achieve this. "God Almighty himself is under the necessity of being happy" (265). Third, this necessity, Locke says, "obliges" us to use our power of self-determination to will what is likeliest to achieve our necessary end. Finally, fourth, if it be thought that Locke is using 'oblige' to mean practically necessitate, while reserving 'obligation' for a different notion, in something like the way that Hobbes sometimes does, we should note that Locke also says that the necessary determination of rational will to the end of its own happiness is "an obligation and motive." Since "God Almighty himself" is under it, the *necessity* of seeking happiness can hardly be thought to be rooted in Locke's usual theory of obligation. It cannot derive from God's command.[30] Rather, actions that are necessary to achieve her own greatest happiness are *practically* necessary for an agent in the sense that they are necessary to achieve her governing rational end. Unlike in God's, however, it is not in our nature to do automatically what is practically necessary in this sense. But we can determine ourselves so to act by the exercise of our power of suspending desire and forming considered practical judgments. This power makes an agent *obligated,* "answerable to himself," for doing what is practically necessary (271).

This picture is the same, in broad outline, as the kind of autonomist internalism found in Cudworth. Obligation requires that there be necessity operating within the will of a rational being and that she

30. Colman, in the process of pointing out that Locke cannot mean that we are under a causal necessity to pursue happiness, and hence to suspend desire and deliberate, rightly says that 'obligation' signals that Locke means that we *ought* to do these things. Indeed he does, but Locke cannot be viewing this 'ought' as rooted in his official theory of obligation. See Colman, *John Locke's Moral Philosophy,* p. 219.

have a power to determine herself in accordance with such necessities.[31] Nor would Cudworth have disagreed with Locke's formulation of the governing rational motive as the "pursuit of true and solid
happiness." Both agree, moreover, that human beings, though they
be imperfect or "finite intellectual beings" and are therefore not able
to do what is best automatically, nonetheless have a power to will the
good by self-determining practical reasoning. We can step back from
the motivational perspective of present pressing desires, deliberate
from a more or less self-comprehensive point of view, and come
thereby to a will-determining practical *judgment* of our greatest good.
This power is necessary for obligation, and its exercise is sufficient to
discharge it. Effectively, then, to be obligated just *is* to be under the
rational influence of motives raised through the proper exercise of
this power. For a creature with that "great privilege of finite intellectual Beings," "the inclination, and tendency of their nature to happiness is an obligation, and motive" (267).

There remains a stark disagreement between Locke and Cudworth
over Cudworth's claim that love is intrinsic to rational nature as such
and, therefore, necessarily part of the happiness of any rational
being. People differ widely in their tastes, and to inquire whether the
summum bonum consists in "Riches, or bodily Delights, or Virtue, or
Contemplation" makes no more sense than to ask "whether the best
Relish were to be found in Apples, Plumbs, or Nuts" (269). There is,
Locke believes, no Cudworthian moral free will and no *moral* obligation as he understands it. The power of self-determination that un-
derlies the bindingness of morality is animal free will, the power of
an agent to determine himself to his greatest private utility.[32]

CONCLUSION

Locke thus ends up occupying a unique place in early modern thinking about moral obligation. His official view is externalist, locating
obligation in a juridical relation extrinsic to moral agency. At the
same time, significant elements of his thinking make distinctive contributions to the two major internalist traditions under development
in the seventeenth century. In Locke's idea that the "force of morality" and the essential practicality of "ethics" require an intrinsic con-

31. For Cudworth this is no mere *natural* necessity. For Locke?
32. More properly, it *may* be no more than animal free will, since Locke does not rule
   out that love and honesty can make some people happy.

nection to motive, we find a version of empirical naturalist internalism, specifically of the instrumentalist variety.[33] More surprising, no doubt, is Locke's contribution to the tradition of autonomist internalism – a line of thinking far likelier to be carried out in rationalist than in empiricist form. In insisting on a connection between 'ought' and self-determining practical reasoning, and by bringing these into his account of the will, Locke placed himself in the tradition of Cudworth and, later, Shaftesbury, Butler, and, ultimately, Kant, according to whom the bindingness of moral demands is finally to be understood through the agent's capacity to impose authoritative demands *on herself*. This does not mean that Locke was a rationalist or an internalist of practical reason in these respects. On the contrary, for him autonomous or self-determining practical reasoning just is thinking that brings the insights of *theoretical* reason most vividly to mind. And although will, for Locke, somehow involves a conception of internal authority, his moral psychology requires that the latter be motivationally inert.

AFTERWORD: A CUDWORTHIAN INFLUENCE?

Locke's theories of liberty and the will in the revised II.xxi, and their relation to what he has to say there about obligation, have so many parallels with Cudworth's ideas that the question of possible influence inevitably arises. It is known that Locke read and admired Cudworth's *True Intellectual System* and his *Discourse Concerning the True Notion of the Lord's Supper*.[34] But Locke could not have learned anything there of Cudworth's theories of will, self-determination, and obligation. The only place these ideas could be found during Locke's life was in Cudworth's manuscripts. But that is not, it turns out, an irremovable obstacle to Locke's having somehow encountered Cudworth's ideas or, indeed, to his having read them. In the early 1680s, Locke had what Passmore justly calls an "intimate correspondence" with Damaris Cudworth, Ralph Cudworth's daughter.[35]

33. If, as I have suggested, the ground of Locke's claim that the agent's greatest happiness is her sole rational aim is that this is what she would desire if fully and imaginatively informed, then Locke also represents the calm reflective deliberation view.
34. The latter work was published in London in 1642. See Arthur W. Wainwright, ed., *A Paraphrase and Notes on the Epistles of St. Paul to the Galatians, 1 and 2 Corinthians, Romans, Ephesians* (Oxford: Oxford University Press, 1987), vol. 1, p. 14.
35. Passmore, *Ralph Cudworth*, p. 94. Many letters between them survive, the first dated January 6, 1682; see *The Correspondence of John Locke*.

Philosophical ideas are sometimes the subject of these letters, and Damaris Cudworth's own works show her to be an able dialectician.[36] More frequently, though, the letters resonate with romantic banter and intrigue. In 1685, Damaris Cudworth, perhaps tired of waiting for Locke, wrote to him in Holland that she had become Lady Masham. This did not end the close relation between them, however. Indeed, Locke went in 1691 to live at Oates, the home of Lord and Lady Masham and the place where, following his death in 1688, Ralph Cudworth's manuscripts on free will were kept.[37]

There seems to be no direct evidence that Locke read the manuscripts. But the indirect, textual evidence is considerable. Passmore has noted some of it. As regards even the first edition of the *Essay*, there is (1) Locke's attack on indifference and (2) his attack on the

36. Damaris Cudworth Masham's *A Discourse Concerning the Love of God* was published anonymously in 1696, and her *Occasional Thoughts in Reference to a Vertuous or Christian Life*, also anonymously, in 1705. The former is an extended criticism of John Norris on the relation between human love and love of God, and the latter, among other things, a call to women to the study of natural religion.

Occasional Thoughts is particularly interesting for the question of Cudworth's possible influence on Locke. Damaris Cudworth Masham frequently defended Cambridge Platonist doctrines against Locke's objections in the early correspondence, but the view she presents in *Occasional Thoughts* is remarkably Lockean: "Religion [is] (as I shall take at present for granted) the only sufficient ground or solid support of vertue; for the belief of a superior, omnipotent being, inspecting our actions, and who will reward or punish us accordingly, is in all men's apprehensions the . . . only stable and irresistible argument for submitting our desires to a constant regulation, wherein it is that vertue does consist" (pp. 14–15). And "It is indeed only a rational fear of God, and desire to approve ourselves to him, that will teach us in all things, uniformly to live as becomes our reasonable nature" (p. 27, see also pp. 50, 53, and, esp., 78). Insisting on the necessity of moral agents' having a "liberty of acting," she describes this in terms that closely follow the formulations of Locke's revised *Essay*: "[W]hence we can, according to the preference of our own minds, act either in conformity to, or disconformity with, the will of the Creator (manifested in his works no less than the will of any humane architect is in his) it follows, that to act answerably to the nature of such beings as we are, requires that we attentively examine, and consider the several natures of things, so far as they have any relation to our actions" (p. 64).

For a discussion of Damaris Cudworth Masham's thought, see Sarah Hutton, "Damaris Cudworth, Lady Masham: Between Platonism and Enlightenment," *British Journal for the History of Philosophy* 1 (1993): 29–54; also Lois Frankel, "Damaris Cudworth Masham: A Seventeenth-Century Feminist Philosopher," *Hypatia* 4 (1989): 80–90.

37. John Harrison and Peter Laslett, eds., *The Library of John Locke* (Oxford: Oxford University Press, 1971), pp. 57–61. For accounts of the relationship between Masham and Locke, see Maurice Cranston, *John Locke* (Oxford: Oxford University Press, 1985), esp. pp. 217–19, 342–75; and Sheryl O'Donnell, "My Idea in Your Mind: John Locke and Damaris Cudworth Masham," in Ruth Perry and Martine Watson Bromley, eds., *Mothering the Mind* (New York: Hobbes & Meiner, 1984), pp. 27–46.

faculty psychology, and his insistence that it is the agent that wills and not the will.[38] And as regards the second and subsequent editions, Passmore adds (3) Locke's revised definitions of will and volition, (4) his denial that we always do what we (intellectually) think best, (5) his claim that the proper answer to what determines the will is "the mind," (6) his stress on the role of desire, and (7) his claim that it is contradictory to suppose that the will does not follow practical judgment.

As impressive as this list is, it can be extended in important ways. Although this is perhaps implicit in (7), it is worth adding (8) that Locke uses Cudworth's very formula when he says that the will is determined by the "last practical judgment" (e.g., 264, 267). Moreover, (9) like Cudworth, Locke treats practical *judgment* as a distinctive act of the understanding that results from the agent's stepping back from present desires and taking a considered, and self-comprehensive view, and which is necessary for (more or less self-comprehensive) volition. Also, (10) like Cudworth, Locke treats *judgment* as a generic capacity to weigh and balance competing considerations, and draw conclusions, whether practical or theoretical. And (11), just as Cudworth does, Locke holds that epistemic fault is no less chargeable to failure to exercise theoretical judgment than is moral fault chargeable to a failure of practical judgment.

Oddly, Passmore does not mention what is perhaps the most obviously Cudworthian element of Locke's revised II.xxi, namely, (12) his new view of liberty as self-determination, and, in particular, (13) his view that the power to make his own practical judgment – what Cudworth calls "this power over himself" – is that in which an agent's power of self-determination consists. Related to this is (14) that this power is necessary for obligation, (15) that its proper ex-

---

38. Passmore, *Ralph Cudworth*, pp. 91–96. Although at one point Passmore says that unless there is a common source for some of Locke's and Cudworth's examples of faculties, "the inference is irresistible that, even before 1690, Cudworth's unpublished views were unknown to Locke" (p. 94), his considered view is that '[t]he most we can say with certainty" is that Locke's "moral psychology is in many respects very like Cudworth's and perhaps derives from it, directly or indirectly" (p. 95).

On the relation between Cudworth and Locke on criticism of faculty psychology, see note 9. Since Locke did not live at Oates before early 1691, after the publication of the first edition of the *Essay*, the fact that Cudworth's manuscripts were there does not explain these similarities.

For further textual evidence of Cudworth's influence on Locke, see Roland Hall, "New Words and Antedatings from Cudworth's 'Treatise of Freewill,'" *Notes and Queries*, n.s. 7 (1960): 427–32.

ercise is sufficient to discharge obligation, and (16) the suggestion that obligation just is the force of motive raised by the power of self-determination. It is difficult not to be struck by the similarity between the explanations Locke and Cudworth respectively give of why an agent can be held responsible for his acts, despite the fact that he always wills what he judges best. This, Locke writes, "excuses him not: Because by a too hasty choice of his own making, he has imposed on himself wrong measures of good and evil" (271). It is within our power whether "the last determination of the Judgment . . . shall be upon an hasty and precipitate view, or upon a due and mature *Examination*" (267). Now Cudworth: "[H]e might have made a better judgment than now he did, had he more intensely considered, and more maturely deliberated, which, that he did not, was his own fault" (*FW*.37).

Finally, as Roland Hall has noted, (17) Locke's example of syllogistic reasoning, which he added to the *Essay*'s fourth edition, is a formalization of the main argument of Cudworth's manuscripts, namely, that accountability entails self-determination.[39]

Doubtless there are other similarities, but these would seem to be the main ones. A survey of this list makes it difficult not to believe that, although Molyneux may initially have posed the objection that made Locke rethink his views of liberty, will, and obligation, it was Cudworth who provided him with many of the materials for his final view.[40]

39. Hall, p. 432. Since 'self-determination' does not appear in published English before the fourth edition of the *Essay*, and because it does appear in Cudworth's manuscripts, Hall concludes that "we can regard it as established from this passage that Locke read the MS. in the period 1695–1700."

40. Although evidently Cudworth was not the only philosopher who did so. Malebranche termed a person's power to "suspend his love" for any object "and examine with care whether it be truly good" the "principle of our liberty." Nicolas Malebranche, *Treatise on Nature and Grace*, transl. with introduction and notes by Patrick Riley (Oxford: Clarendon Press, 1992), pp. 176–77 (Discourse III, secs. xii–xiii). And Pierre Coste remarked in a footnote to his translation of the *Essay* that section 30 of chapter XXI was aimed at Malebranche (see Nidditch edition, p. 249n). For a discussion of similarities between Locke's views on moral choice and Malebranche's, see Jean-Michel Vienne, "Malebranche and Locke: The Theory of Moral Choice, a Neglected Theme," in Stuart Brown, ed., *Nicolas Malebranche: His Philosophical Critics and Successors* (Assen/Maastricht: Van Gorcum, 1991).

Chapter 7

Shaftesbury: authority and authorship

Even had Locke held unwaveringly that moral obligation consists in a conclusive motive for moral action raised through self-determining practical thought, he would still have been committed to the proposition that the requisite motive can lie only in divinely established supernatural sanction. Finite intellectual nature and the power of self-determination may obligate an agent to her own happiness, but only when combined with supernatural sanctions can these obligate to morality, since only then is a coincidence ensured between rational motive and duty.

From the perspective of Cudworth and the Cambridge Platonists, this amounted to the very denial of morality. "Laws [that can] no otherwise operate or seize upon [agents] than by taking hold of their animal selfish passions" can create no "obligation truly moral," Cudworth had written.[1] A system that "will allow of no other moral obligation than this, utterly destroys morality."[2] Morality purports to obligate in itself, and this is possible only if there are distinctively moral reasons that can decisively guide the practical reasoning of self-determining moral agents. The Cambridge Platonists did not think this requires a source of motivation independent of the agent's good. Rather, their idea was that morally good motives and conduct expressing them are intrinsically beneficial for those who have them.

At the start of the eighteenth century (over a generation later), the Platonists were followed in these ideas by Anthony Ashley Cooper, the third Earl of Shaftesbury. Shaftesbury has been relatively ignored by philosophers of our time, but his thought is pivotal for understanding the development of eighteenth-century ethics, especially

1. Cudworth, British Library Add. Ms. 4980.9.
2. Ibid.

the empiricist sentimentalism of Hutcheson and Hume and the "constructivist" rationalism of Kant. Arguably, Shaftesbury was the first to advance the normative theory of will that would prove so important to the autonomist internalist tradition and, most especially, to Kant.

Shaftesbury's first published work was an edition of sermons of the Cambridge Platonist Benjamin Whichcote, which he introduced with the declaration that those who view ethics as an imposed law restraining our natural bent, "have made *war . . .* on virtue itself."[3] The target of this complaint, if made on the Platonists' behalf, would have been Hobbes and mid-seventeenth-century Calvinist theological voluntarists. Shaftesbury's own sights, however, were set squarely on his former tutor, John Locke.[4] As he would later write:

It was Mr. Locke that struck the home blow: for Mr. Hobbes's character and base slavish principles in government took off the point of his philosophy. 'Twas Mr. Locke that struck at all fundamentals, threw all order and virtue out of the world, and made the very ideas of these (which are the same as those of God) *unnatural,* and without foundation in our minds.[5]

3. This is from the Preface to Shaftesbury's edition of *Select Sermons of Dr. Whichcot* (London: A & J Churchill, 1698). "Dr. Whichcot" is Benjamin Whichcote, the divine who is often considered the founding spiritual influence of the Cambridge Platonists. He published nothing himself, although various of his sermons, discourses, and sayings were published posthumously. Patrides, *The Cambridge Platonists,* includes some selections.
4. Their complicated personal relationship made Shaftesbury's feelings about Locke ambivalent, to say the least. Locke had been secretary to Shaftesbury's grandfather, the prominent Whig politician and first Earl of Shaftesbury. Partly because of the ineffectuality of the second earl (Shaftesbury's father), Locke was made responsible for young Ashley's education. Although the first earl died in political exile and official disgrace, Locke came home after the Glorious Revolution and rose to fame when the *Essay* was published. Moreover, when an annuity Locke had been promised by the first earl, in which Locke himself had already invested, was jeopardized after the first earl's death, Locke asked the grandson to intercede with his parents. Robert Voitle's *The Third Earl of Shaftesbury* (Baton Rouge: Louisiana State University Press, 1984) is the best source for details about this complicated relationship, but Shaftesbury's emotionally charged remarks about Locke in his letters – some of which are in Benjamin Rand, ed., *The Life, Unpublished Letters, and Philosophical Regimen of Anthony, Earl of Shaftesbury* (London: Swan Sonnenschein, 1900) – make one wish more were known. See also Shaftesbury's *Several Letters Written by a Noble Lord to a Young Man at the University* (London, 1714) and *Letters of the Earl of Shaftesbury, Collected into One Volume* (London, 1750).
5. Rand, *The Life of Shaftesbury,* p. 403. References hereafter will be placed parenthetically in the text thus: (*Life.* 403). This was addressed to Michael Ainsworth, the "young man" of *Several Letters Written by a Noble Lord to a Young Man at the University* (see note 4).

Because Locke had made positivism respectable for his contemporaries in a way that Hobbes could not, Shaftesbury thought Locke's ideas a greater threat to moral virtue, as well as to sound moral philosophy. By publishing a collection of Whichcote's sermons eight years after the appearance of the *Essay* (and fifteen years after Whichcote's death), Shaftesbury evidently hoped to enlist Whichcote in virtue's defense. Ultimately, he would have to defend it himself as well.

Shaftesbury believed that in holding moral goodness to concern an agent's internal nature rather than his external behavior or its relation to the commands of external authority, the Cambridge Platonists had correctly identified what morality is most fundamentally about. It is "unaccountable," he writes in his Preface to Whichcote's *Sermons*, "that men who profess a religion where *love* is chiefly enjoined, where the heart is expressly called for, and outward action without that is disregarded . . . should combine to degrade the principle of good nature, and refer all to reward."[6] Sanctions, whether secular or divine, cannot motivate genuine virtue. Moral agents must have a source of moral motivation within as well as the power to determine themselves through it.[7]

Virtue might be held to have "foundation in our minds" in two distinct senses, however. Virtuous motives might be claimed to be *natural* to human beings in some suitable sense, and thus to have a "foundation in our minds" in that sense. Or it might be thought that their property of moral goodness is itself founded "in our minds." Shaftesbury asserts both theses in an interrelated way. Virtuous motives – pity, kindness, and gratitude, for example – are "natural" in that they develop spontaneously in normal human beings, have an important role in the natural order, and figure prominently in the good of agents and patients alike. But so also is the moral goodness of these motives founded in the mind, since it consists, Shaftesbury holds, in their being natural objects of a distinctive natural sensibility that he calls "moral sense." Actually, as we will see, Shaftesbury claims that genuine "virtue or merit" involves not just approved

---

6. *Select Sermons of Dr. Whichcot*, Preface.
7. Although sanctions can play a transitional role for agents who have not yet sufficiently developed their capacity for self-governance. See Anthony Ashley Cooper, Earl of Shaftesbury, *Characteristics of Men, Manners, Opinions, Times*, ed. John M. Robertson, with intr. by Stanley Grean (Indianapolis, Ind.: Bobbs-Merrill, 1964), vol. 2, p. 56. Hereafter, references to this work (referring to the Robertson/ Grean edition) will be placed parenthetically in the text thus: *Char.*II.56.

first-order motives but also the agent's being governed by his own second-order approval through moral sense.

When we rational human agents contemplate "natural affections," Shaftesbury maintains, we reflectively approve them as harmonious and agreeable (*Char*.I.251).[8] Our responding in this way to contemplated virtue is not simply a contingent fact about us. The virtuous is, Shaftesbury believes, a species of the beautiful. We resonate as we do with beauty and harmony because of a kind of sympathy between the creative and formalizing aspects intrinsic to contemplating mind and identical characteristics of mind whose immanence is evidenced by harmonious forms. Since natural affections, for Shaftesbury, are those that have an adaptive systematic role, fitting a creature to his own good and to those of larger natural systems (including his species and the universe as a whole), these affections manifest a creative ordering principle immanent in nature. Any moral agent will reflectively approve natural affections as beautiful, therefore. Virtue supervenes on the self-reflective agent's appreciative contemplation of her natural affections and their place in the natural order.

Shaftesbury thus develops the Cambridge Platonist doctrine that moral goodness is ultimately grounded in creative and practical aspects intrinsic to mind. Moreover, when it comes to morality's normativity, Shaftesbury works out a distinctive version of Cudworth's idea that agents can be obligated to virtue only because they have conclusive motivation for being virtuous when they autonomously determine – or, to use the Shaftesburean term, "author" – their conduct.

There are fascinating differences between Cudworth's and Shaftesbury's respective approaches to obligation. Cudworth was led to link obligation and self-determination because of worries about the relation between obligation and accountability. How can an agent be blamed and held accountable for failing to discharge obligation unless obligations entail the existence of reasons by which she could have determined herself to act as she ought? If obligation just is a conclusive motive for acting created or engaged in the process of self-determination, however, this problem would appear to be solved (although it would, of course, remain an open question

8. *An Inquiry Concerning Virtue or Merit*, the part of *Characteristics* here referred to, was originally published in an unauthorized edition in 1699. A corrected version was published by Shaftesbury in *Characteristicks*, vol. 2 (London, 1711). A second edition of *Characteristicks*, further corrected by Shaftesbury, was published in 1714. There were several other posthumous editions.

whether recognizably moral demands have the requisite status as self-determining motives).

The pattern of ideas connecting obligation with self-determining motivation in Shaftesbury is almost the reverse. Quite unlike Cudworth (or Locke), Shaftesbury holds no brief for the notions of warranted blame or punishment. On the contrary, he is profoundly skeptical of ethical systems in which these ideas figure prominently. He is, however, very much concerned to work out the necessary conditions of an enduring *will* or practical *self*, as well as their relation to the ability to author a life. These conditions include, he argues, that the agent have available a critical standpoint on her own life which she regards as *practically authoritative* and thereby obligating. The recognition of this internal 'ought' is, Shaftesbury claims, a condition of the very possibility of a practical self.

Shaftesbury's relationship to the Cambridge Platonists has not gone unnoticed.[9] Still, most anglophone philosophical commentary has tended to view his ideas retrospectively through the lens of his influence on the empiricist moral sentimentalism of Hutcheson, Hume, and Smith.[10] Sidgwick, for example, treats Shaftesbury as the first moralist to make the empirical study of human mental phenomena the basis of ethics, thereby spawning the ethics of Hutcheson and Hume.[11] But this mostly misses the elements of Shaftesbury's thought that bring him squarely within the tradition that we encountered with Cudworth and that leads toward Kant. Shaftesbury's notion of "moral sense" is very different from Hutcheson's; it is no

9. Cassirer remarked that it was "principally Shaftesbury" who saved "the Cambridge School from the fate of a learned curiosity" and made it a "philosophic force in the centuries to come" (*The Platonic Renaissance in England*, p. 160). See also Ernst Cassirer, *The Philosophy of the Enlightenment*, trans. Fritz C. A. Koelln and James P. Pettegrove (Princeton: Princeton University Press, 1951). Jean-Paul Larthomas, *De Shaftesbury à Kant*, 2 vols. (Lille: Atelier National de Reproduction des Thèses; Paris: Diffusion Didier Erudition, 1985) is also quite good.

10. The influence Cassirer mainly had in mind was that on Kant and German romanticism. An exception to the general anglophone trend is Stanley Grean, *Shaftesbury's Philosophy of Religion and Ethics: A Study in Enthusiasm* (Athens: Ohio University Press, 1967).

11. *Outlines of the History of Ethics*, pp. 184–91. See also Albee, *A History of English Utilitarianism*, p. 58; Martineau, *Types of Ethical Theory*, vol. 2, p. 514; and Thomas Fowler, *Shaftesbury and Hutcheson* (London: Sampson, Low, Marston, Searle, & Rivington, 1882), p. v. Martineau says that Hutcheson worked out Shaftesbury's "fruitful hints and construct[ed] from them a systematical psychology"; Albee, that "it is customary to regard Hutcheson's system as the logical development of Shaftesbury's"; and Fowler maintains that "there are no two of the better-known English philosophers whose writings are so closely related as those of Shaftesbury and Hutcheson."

empiricist's faculty that passively receives ideas and feelings but involves creative and formative powers that Shaftesbury believes are intrinsic to active mind. Like Cudworth, Shaftesbury holds that the very possibility of ethics depends on mind's being inherently creative and practical. And whereas the idea of self-determination plays no fundamental role in the ethics of Hutcheson and Hume, it is, as we shall see, no less central to Shaftesbury's ethics than to Cudworth's.

No doubt one reason Shaftesbury's thought has been insufficiently appreciated by anglophone historians of philosophy, especially in this century, is that he appears to care little for the analytical rigor, systematic clarity, and consonance with developing scientific understanding to which English-based philosophy has predominantly aspired in the modern period. In the terms of Hume's famous distinction between philosophy that seeks to edify and a more scientific sort that seeks "those original principles, by which, in every science, all human curiosity must be bounded," Shaftesbury would seem unequivocally to represent the former.[12] He frequently scorns the metaphysical and epistemological thinking of contemporaries who (like Locke) are stimulated by advances in natural philosophy: "What specious exercise is found in those which are called 'Philosophical Speculations?' The formation of ideas, their compositions, comparisons, agreement and disagreement" (*Life*.267). Such inquiries, he complains, make a person "neither better, nor happier, nor wiser" (*Life*.269).[13] And he is famous for the remark that "the most ingenious way of becoming foolish is by a system" (*Char*.I.189). For Shaftesbury, philosophy is the edifying study of the good – an attempt to find for, or more accurately, *inspire in* the agent a fixed and steady aim necessary for her to project an enduring, integral self.[14]

"There are very few errors in Locke," Diderot wrote in the *Encyclopédie*, "and too few truths in milord Shaftesbury: the former is only a man of vast intellect, penetrating and exact, while the latter is a genius of the first order." "Locke has seen," he continued; "Shaftesbury has created, constructed, and edified. To Locke we owe some great truths coldly perceived, methodically developed, and

---

12. David Hume, *An Enquiry Concerning Human Understanding*, in *Enquiries Concerning Human Understanding and Concerning the Principles of Morals*, ed. Selby-Bigge and Nidditch, pp. 5–16.
13. "Nor," he continues, "more a man of sense or worth; of a more open, free understanding, liberal disposition; a more enlarged mind or a generous heart" (*Life*.269). See also *Char*.I.196.
14. See, e.g., *Char*.II.150–53; *Life*.267.

dryly presented; and to Shaftesbury, some brilliant schemes often poorly grounded, though full of sublime truths."[15] To modern philosophers concerned to understand how morality can be placed consistently with the outlook of naturalistic science, Shaftesbury's writings may seem almost beside the point. Anglophone historians have accordingly been inclined to fasten on those elements that anticipate empiricist moral sentimentalism and ignore the rest. But this is a mistake. Even if Shaftesbury was not primarily motivated by the desire to understand the metaethical question of the normativity of morality, he nonetheless advanced ideas of central relevance to this modern philosophical project.

AN ETHICS OF VIRTUE

The only work of Shaftesbury's that fits orthodox modern philosophical forms is *An Inquiry Concerning Virtue or Merit*, originally published in an unauthorized edition in 1699 and later revised and included in *Characteristicks* (published in 1711). Its first book addresses "what virtue is and to whom the character belongs," and the second, "what obligation there is to virtue, or what reason to embrace it" (1.280). Our ultimate focus will be on this second question; but before we can understand why Shaftesbury thinks virtue is, in a suitable sense, obligatory, we must first grasp what he believes virtue to be.

VIRTUE AND NATURAL AFFECTIONS

Shaftesbury's ethics clearly mark a radical departure from the seventeenth-century tradition of natural law. If the model of law is significantly revised in Cumberland and Cudworth, it is almost entirely absent from Shaftesbury. What makes conduct virtuous and virtue obligating appears to have nothing at all to do with even a reformed idea of law. Rather, morality primarily concerns what Shaftesbury calls the agent's *affections*. A person (or any "sensible creature") is good only if her affections are (1.247). And whether her conduct is right or wrong depends entirely on whether it springs from good or bad affections (1.253). This stands the legislative model

15. Article "Génie," in Denis Diderot, *Oeuvres complètes de Diderot*, ed. J. Assezat and M. Tourneux, 20 vols. (Paris: Garnier Frères, 1875–77), vol. 15, p. 39, translated and quoted by Grean, *Shaftesbury's Philosophy*, pp. x–xi.

on its head. Not only does it make the idea of good affection or character primary and right conduct derivative; it fails even to countenance the possibility that an action might be right though badly motivated or well motivated though wrong.

What makes an affection a good one? Shaftesbury's answer depends on his theory of nature. A good affection is a *natural* one. Indeed, 'natural' frequently functions in Shaftesbury's writings as a synonym for 'good'.[16] Standing behind this identification is a teleological picture of the natural order as an integrated system in which subsystems function together to realize a well-functioning whole. Every species, human beings included, has a natural function. Each has a constitution fitted, indeed designed, to a specific functional role in the "system of all things" or "universal nature." Whether an individual or species is "really" good or ill depends on whether it enhances or detracts from the functioning of the whole (1.246). Nothing is indifferent, since to fail to enhance the whole is to be superfluous, an imperfection (1.246).

Although the logic of his position requires Shaftesbury ultimately to reckon good and ill in relation to the whole natural system, he generally writes as though whether an affection is good or bad in an individual human being primarily concerns how it relates to the flourishing of the human species, which he usually calls the "public interest." Since he sometimes seems to be saying that natural affections have the public interest as *object*, it is important to be clear that his considered view is that natural affections are those that are functionally suited to promote the public interest, regardless of object.[17] What matters, moreover, is not whether the affection, or its degree or expression, *actually* realizes the public good, but whether it is adapted to do so and thus tends to.[18]

In an obvious reference to Hobbes (if not also to Locke), Shaftesbury remarks that a fierce animal who adopts a "tame and gentle carriage" out of fear of his keeper is not really gentle. "A good creature," Shaftesbury writes, "is such a one as by the natural temper

16. For example, "[s]ince it is therefore by affection merely that a creature is esteemed good or ill, natural or unnatural" (1.247).
17. On this point, see Gregory Trianosky, "On the Obligation to Be Virtuous: Shaftesbury and the Question, Why Be Moral?" *Journal of the History of Philosophy* 16 (1978): 289–300. For places where Shaftesbury appears to identify natural affections by their objects, see, e.g., 1.247 and *Life*.1.
18. Hume's theory of virtue agrees with Shaftesbury in this respect. See *A Treatise of Human Nature*, ed. L. A. Selby-Bigge, 2d. ed., with text revised and variant readings by P. H. Nidditch (Oxford: Clarendon Press, 1978), p. 584.

or bent of his affections is carried primarily and immediately, and not secondarily and accidentally, to good and against ill" (1.250). 'Primarily' and 'secondarily' are to be understood functionally. Good affections are those whose primary function is to realize species good.[19] "When in general all the affections or passions are suited to the public good, or good of the species, . . . then is the natural temper entirely good" (1.250).

That natural affections are identified by their being *fitted* to the good of all, rather than by whether their object is the public good, is clear from what Shaftesbury has to say about natural and unnatural degrees of self- and other-love, respectively. Since self-love tends to be "injurious to the society" only when immoderate, he says, only an immoderate degree is unnatural (1.248). Similarly, "even as to kindness and love of the most natural sort (such as that of any creature for its offspring), if it be immoderate and beyond a certain degree," it is unnatural (1.250).[20] "[T]o deserve the name of good or virtuous," Shaftesbury summarizes, "a creature must have all his inclinations and affections, his dispositions of mind and temper, suitable, and agreeing with the good of his kind, or of that system in which he is included, and of which he constitutes a part" (1.280).

VIRTUE AND MORAL SENSE

Having affections adapted to species good is sufficient for the goodness of any sensible creature, but Shaftesbury maintains that "that which is called virtue or merit" can be realized only by a self-reflective rational being (1.251). Only conduct that is suitably related to the agent's "sense of right or wrong" can have merit or be properly virtuous (1.253). For rational beings "capable of forming general notions of things, not only the outward beings which offer themselves to the sense" but also actions and affections can be "fram[ed]" in thought as "rational objects" and contemplated, along with their relation to the rest of nature (1.251, 256). And when natural affections, "being brought into the mind by reflection, become objects, . . . there arises another kind of affection towards those very affections themselves, which have been already felt, and are now become the subject of a new liking or dislike" (1.251).

19. Trianosky points out Shaftesbury's contrast between accidental and natural, but he does not construe this contrast functionally.
20. See also 1.287, 288.

Rational agents have reflective or second-order affections. They regard positively what is natural and good in themselves and are affected negatively by what is unnatural and bad. Shaftesbury dubs this reflective sensibility "natural moral sense" (1.262).[21] What, however, guarantees that rational agents will approve the natural on reflection?[22] And why should their doing so be thought necessary to their having genuine virtue or merit? Fully satisfactory answers to these questions require an examination of virtually the whole of Shaftesbury's thought. At this point we can do no more than sketch some of the systematic connections lying behind these claims.

The mind, [Shaftesbury writes in a famous passage], which is spectator or auditor of other minds, cannot be without its eye and ear, so as to discern proportion, distinguish sound, and scan each sentiment or thought which comes before it. It can let nothing escape its censure. It feels the soft and harsh, the agreeable and disagreeable in the affections; and finds a foul and fair, a harmonious and a dissonant, as really and truly here as in any musical numbers or in the outward forms or representations of sensible things. Nor can it withhold its admiration and ecstasy, its aversion and scorn, any more in what relates to one than to the other of these subjects. (1.251)

Moral goodness is a species of beauty; it is a harmony, proportion, or beauty of the mind.[23] Because the beautiful is a species of the agreeable – we necessarily contemplate it with pleasure – we cannot but approve it. In order to explain why Shaftesbury thinks rational moral agents will reflectively approve the natural, then, we need to explain two connections: that between the natural and the beautiful and that between the beautiful and the agreeable.

We already have a connection between the natural and a purely *formal* conception of beauty. The naturalness of an affection resides in its orderly functioning within the "self-system," the species, and the

21. This is generally acknowledged to be the first use of 'moral sense'. Ernest Tuveson maintains that Thomas Burnet was "the first to formulate the idea of an aesthetic 'moral sense'" in his critical pamphlets on Locke's *Essay* (*Remarks upon an Essay Concerning Humane Understanding in a Letter Address'd to the Author*, published in 1697). As against Locke, Burnet held that "the distinction, suppose of gratitude and ingratitude, . . . is sudden without any ratiocination, and as sensible and piercing, as the difference I feel from the scent of a rose, and of assafoetida" (*Remarks*; assafoetida is a strong-smelling resinous gum found in Central Asia). See Tuveson, "The Origins of the 'Moral Sense'," *Huntington Library Quarterly* 11 (1948): 241–49.
22. Although Shaftesbury apparently allows for the possibility that a rational being might be able to judge that an affection is suited to the public good without actually having any second-order affection for it (see 1.259), he is apparently committed to the view that this is abnormal in rational beings; see, e.g., 1.305.
23. See also, e.g., 1.90–94, 136, 181, 216–18, 227–28, 260, 296; II.268.

universe as a whole, and Shaftesbury thinks that order and function are part of what beauty is. "[B]eauty and truth are plainly joined with the notion of utility and convenience, even in the apprehension of every ingenious artist, the architect, the statuary, or the painter" (II.268). Likewise with the body. Health, which is the "regular course of things in a constitution" – "the harmony and just measures of the rising pulses, the circulating humours, and the moving airs or spirits" – is the "inward beauty of the body" (II.268).[24] Similarly, when the affections function *naturally* they manifest a functional suitability within various subsystems of nature and within the system of nature as a whole. And this suitability to their natural purposes, in particular to the public interest, is beautiful in the same way physical health is. The beauty of each supervenes on suitability, form, and design.

But if the beauty or harmony of natural affections is revealed fully only in their suitability to the public interest and to nature as a whole, how can Shaftesbury also say that the difference between harmony and disorder "is immediately perceived by a plain internal sensation" (II.63)? How can this response be immediate? And how can it involve a sensation? Notwithstanding the term "natural moral sense" and its later elaboration, especially by Hutcheson, Shaftesbury makes it quite clear he means a *cultivated* taste – one that develops, he thinks, only through free *public* critical discourse about the public good and "liberal education."[25] "[A] taste or judgment . . . can hardly come ready formed with us into the world": "Antecedent labour and pains of criticism" are necessary (II.257). And the latter requires a context of liberty and free conversation wherein we "polish one another, and rub off our corners and rough sides by a sort of amicable collision" (I.46). "There is no real love of virtue, without the knowledge of public good. And where absolute power is, there is no public" (I.72). The sense of moral beauty, even if immediate when fully developed, nevertheless results, Shaftesbury believes, from a public liberal critical discourse informed by reflection on the public good.

24. Cf. Hume, *Enquiries*, pp. 244–45.
25. See, e.g., I.125, 218, 273; II.271; *Life*.34, 44. See also Shaftesbury, *Second Characters or the Language of Forms*, ed. Benjamin Rand (Cambridge: Cambridge University Press, 1914), p. 114. This includes materials found among the Shaftesbury papers at the Public Record Office in London. Most interesting philosophically are "Letter Concerning Design" and "Plastics, or the Original Progress and Power of Designatory Art." The passage cited comes from the latter.

This leaves us with the question of how the perception of beauty can involve a sensation, how the mind can *feel* "the soft and harsh, the agreeable and disagreeable" in contemplating affections. In other words, how does Shaftesbury connect the beautiful and the *agreeable*? Granted that the natural manifests a harmony and beauty in the form of its design, what guarantees that contemplating it will be agreeable to any rational being? More specifically, what guarantees that contemplation of moral beauty will produce in rational agents a second-order *approval* of natural affections themselves? Shaftesbury must admit this as a genuine question since he allows that, strictly speaking, the "agreeableness" or "amiableness" may not really be in the acts or affections themselves, or in their natural relations, although their naturalness plainly is intrinsic to the latter. While there may be "no real amiableness or deformity in moral acts," he writes, "there is at least an imaginary one of full force. Though perhaps the thing itself should not be allowed in Nature, the imagination or fancy of it, must be allowed to be from Nature alone" (1.260). Natural affections' suitability to the public good is part of nature, while, strictly speaking, their agreeableness (and their beauty, if amiability is considered part of that) is not – or, at least, is not in the same way. The latter, we might say, is an imagination- or fancy-dependent property. Here we see the seeds of the moral sentimentalism of Hutcheson and Hume.

But this does not mean that beauty is an adventitious projection, or even that pleasure in contemplating it is just a universal reaction contingently rooted in human nature. When Shaftesbury says that the imagination of moral beauty is *from Nature* alone, he means that it is a product of the same organizing rational principle or mind that is immanent in nature, in which we as contemplating, "framing" rational minds sympathetically participate. A number of important Shaftesburean strains come together at just this juncture – his theology, philosophy of nature, and notions of enthusiasm, love, creative inspiration, sympathy, and mind – to create a version of the doctrine of moral sense that is far from the empiricist moral sentimentalism of Hutcheson and Hume. Moral sense unquestionably involves feeling, for Shaftesbury, but it is more accurate to think of him as holding a *rationalist* theory of moral sense.[26] Moral sense involves the creative, framing power of reason, not the passive reception of sensations.

26. Charles Taylor remarks that Shaftesbury is not "a rationalist in the sense that Clarke was": *Sources of the Self*, p. 254. See pp. 248–59 for a generally illuminating account of the main outlines of Shaftesbury's thought.

The form and structure manifested by natural affections, as indeed by all natural beauty in the universe, evidences the design of a unifying creative mind.[27] This is not the God of orthodox Christianity Who transcends nature and consigns mortals to a supernatural heaven or hell[28] but an organizing presence immanent in nature. Shaftesbury's Deity is impersonal but is still a presence we can feel in the operation of nature through our imaginative grasp of harmonious order.

This explains why Shaftesbury describes the *Inquiry* as an attempt to discover the relations between religion and virtue, as well as how far having or lacking opinions on theological matters "may possibly consist with virtue and merit, or be compatible with an honest or moral character" (1.242). A "theist" believes "that everything is governed, ordered, or regulated for the best, by a designing principle or mind, necessarily good and permanent" (1.240). Atheists lack this belief. And "daemonists" make common cause with theists against atheism but hold that divine design is arbitrary, a matter of "mere will or fancy," rather than being determined by ends intrinsic to mind (what Cudworth called "divine fate immoral") (1.241).[29] Since atheism and daemonism conflict with the contemplation of natural affection as aspects of a benevolently designed natural order, they tend to undermine the reflective love or admiration on which virtue or merit supervenes. "For how little disposed must a person be to love or admire anything as orderly in the universe who thinks the universe itself a pattern of disorder?" (1.276). He concludes that "the perfection and height of virtue must be owing to the belief of a God" (1.280).

27. See, for instance, II.112.
28. In a letter to a friend, for example, Shaftesbury heaps scorn on Locke's last letter to Anthony Collins, in which Locke expresses the orthodox (for the time) Christian view that "this life is a scene of vanity" whose main source of satisfaction is the "hopes of another life." This "savours of the good and Christian," Shaftesbury writes. "I should never have guessed it to have been of a dying philosopher." And he adds these sentiments: "Let every one answer for their own experience, and speak of happiness and good as they find it. Thank heaven I can do good and find heaven in it. I know nothing else that is heavenly. And if this disposition fits me not for heaven, I desire never to be fitted for it, nor come into the place. I ask no reward from heaven for that which is reward itself. Let my being be continued or discontinued, as in the main is best" (*Life*.347). For a helpful discussion of Shaftesbury's theological and religious views, see Grean, *Shaftesbury's Philosophy*, Chaps. 4, 5, and 7.
29. All these categories echo Cudworth's dialectic against "atheistical" (or "democritick") fatalism and "divine fate immoral," in *The True Intellectual System of the Universe* – that is, against Hobbesian materialism and theological voluntarism.

Central to Shaftesbury's thinking is his notion of a kind of reasonable *enthusiasm* that, far from conflicting with the rational life, is actually one of its conditions. Shaftesbury is unstinting in his criticism of the sort of sectarian emotionalism generally referred to as "enthusiasm" in late-seventeenth- and early-eighteenth-century England, but he vigorously defends what he calls a "noble enthusiasm" (1.39). The former is irrational or arational; the latter is the result of creative imaginative activity involved in the rational grasp of order and design.

[W]e may . . . presume to infer from the coolest of all studies, even from criticism itself . . . "that there is a power in numbers, harmony, proportion, and beauty of every kind, which naturally captivates the heart, and raises the imagination to an opinion or conceit of something majestic and divine." (II.174)

This is the "inspiration" he calls "a real feeling of the Divine Presence" (1.37).[30] Inspiration by the divine is but a heightened version of our capacity to be moved by beauty and order more generally.

Is there a rational and admired enthusiasm that belongs to architecture, painting, music, and not to this [the order of the universe]? Who is there that is not seized with admiration at the view of any of those ancient edifices, where order and proportion apparent in all the parts, and resulting from the whole, forces in a manner its effect. (*Life.*33)

But if this shows that Shaftesbury believes an admiring imaginative "conceit" or "feeling" accompanies the rational grasp of harmony and order, it does not yet show *why* he thinks this must be so. The answer, I think, is along the following lines. Though the occasion for the agreeable experience of beauty is the contemplation of some designed object – an ancient edifice or the universe – what is really admired is the designing mind that formed the object.

The art then is the beauty? Right. And the art is that which beautifies? The same. So that the beautifying, not the beautified, is the really beautiful? It seems so. . . . "[T]he beautiful, the fair, the comely, were never in the matter, but in the art and design; never in body itself, but in the form or forming power." . . . What is it you admire but mind, or the effect of mind? 'Tis mind alone which forms. (*Char.*II.131–32)

Likewise, the contemplative grasp of beauty itself involves creative, formative powers of mind. "[N]either can man by the same sense or

30. "[I]nspiration may be justly called divine enthusiasm; for the word itself signifies divine presence" (1.38).

brutish part conceive or enjoy beauty; but all the beauty and good he enjoys is in a nobler way, and by the help of what is noblest, his mind and reason" (II.143). The contemplation of beauty thus involves a sharing in, or sympathetic union with, the creative intelligence that formed the beauty contemplated. By this union we are inspired. We are moved by the creative imaginative force that we must suppose formed the order we contemplate and which, in contemplating, we share.[31]

If this sketch is even roughly on the right track, Shaftesbury cannot be thinking of the amiableness of beauty and virtue as a response we simply happen to have to the perception of order and design. "[A]ll sound love and admiration is enthusiasm" (II.129). And the contemplation of beauty elicits enthusiasm by sympathetic union with the beautifying mind behind it. This may help to explain why, when Shaftesbury complained that Locke had "struck at all fundamentals" and had thrown "all order and virtue out of the world," he also said that Locke had made the idea of God, as well as those of order and virtue, unnatural, and then added *that these are all the same idea.*[32] Doubtless this is exaggeration, but what Shaftesbury probably meant was that the latter two ideas, at least, are both dependent on the same reasonable enthusiasm that we can suppose to be intrinsic to the creative ordering principle immanent in the order of nature.[33]

VIRTUE AND SELF-REFLECTIVE MORAL AGENCY

This may explain why rational observers must approve the natural on reflection, but why need an *agent* have this second-order affection in order for *her* to have genuine virtue or merit? Why is natural affection not enough? A glimpse of Shaftesbury's answer comes in the following passage:

Neither can any weakness or imperfection in the senses be the occasion of iniquity or wrong; if the object of the mind itself be not at any time absurdly

31. See 1.6, 8; *Life*.16–22.
32. See note 5 for reference.
33. See, however, 1.266, where Shaftesbury remarks that "it is possible for a creature capable of using reflection to have a liking or dislike of moral actions, and consequently a sense of right and wrong, before such time as he may have any settled notion of a God." Shaftesbury here suggests that the approval of, say, "love to his kind" simply results from that affection with the addition of reflection, presumably by virtue of the fact that the object of the first-order affection is furthered by the object of the second-order one. This picture must be compared with the line of thought I have sketched.

framed, nor any way improper, but suitable, just, and worthy of the opinion and affection applied to it. For if we will suppose a man who, being sound and entire both in his reason and affection, has nevertheless so depraved a constitution or frame of body that the natural objects are, through his organs of sense, as through ill glasses, falsely conveyed and misrepresented, 'twill be soon observed, in such a person's case, that since his failure is not in his principal or leading part, he cannot in himself be esteemed iniquitous or unjust. (I.253)

It is hardly clear in the *Inquiry* itself, but Shaftesbury is relying here on a view of self-critical self-determination very similar to those we found in Cudworth and in Locke's revised *Essay.* Whatever knowledge he might have had of Cudworth's manuscripts, or however he might have been influenced by Locke's revisions, the intellectual source Shaftesbury claims for this idea is Epictetus.[34] Rational agents have a "ruling," "leading," or "governing principle," a *hegemonikon,* by which they act.[35] Although all action is determined by beliefs and desires (here "opinions" and "affections"), rational agents can reflect on and critically assess these, thus determining their conduct by critically determining its determinants. Presently, I shall explore this idea further, along with its relation to Shaftesbury's views about obligation and the self, but what is crucial here is the thesis that a capacity for critical self-reflection gives the agent critical leverage over his opinions and affections that enables self-government.

This is the point of the passage's contrast between an agent whose injuring behavior results from defective "organs of sense" and one

34. Shaftesbury visited Locke and Damaris Masham at Oates during the time when the Cudworth manuscripts were there and, as Passmore points out, was on friendly terms with Damaris Cudworth Masham and was lent books by her. See Passmore, *Ralph Cudworth,* pp. 97–99. For some evidence that Shaftesbury may have read the manuscripts, see note 47. See also Voitle, *Shaftesbury,* pp. 61, 201, 284; Cranston, *John Locke,* p. 352; and the letters from Shaftesbury to Locke in *Correspondence of John Locke.* Shaftesbury's ambivalence about his former tutor reveals itself when he writes about Locke's revisions on liberty: "[H]e made great alterations on these points where, though a *divine* may often waver, a *philosopher,* I think, never can" (*Life*.415). This is from the same letter (November 7, 1709, to General Stanhope) discussed in note 28. Note the continuing contrast between the "Christian" Locke and a genuine "philosopher."

35. I.199, 253; *Life*.113, 130. At *Life*.112, for example, Shaftesbury quotes Epictetus approvingly: "[T]ake care not to injure your own ruling faculty" (*Encheiridion,* chap. xxxvIII). See also note 45.

   For this idea in Epictetus, see, esp., *Discourses,* ed. Oldfather, vol. 1, pp. 9–11, 107, 137–39, 169–71, 223, 263; vol. 2, pp. 15, 29, 41, 43, 65, 85, 185, 207, 263, 329, 333, 349, 525. Shaftesbury also accepts in large measure, though not wholeheartedly, the Stoic idea of valuing only those things that are in one's power. His arguments here, however, do not depend on this.

whose actions derive from opinions and affections that reflect "ab-sur[d] fram[ing]." Sense experience is not within an agent's control, but to the extent that agents have the power of "framing rational objects" and self-critically assessing their opinions and affections, it *is* within their control, in some measure, which opinions and affections determine their conduct. In the former case, "since his failure is not in his principal or leading part, the person cannot in himself be esteemed iniquitous or unjust"; that is, we cannot attribute the defect to *him* rather than, say, to his eyes. In the latter case, Shaftesbury thinks, we can; the defect is in the agent's governing (perhaps more properly, self-governing) principle, and (as we shall see) that is what Shaftesbury thinks the agent, in an important sense, *is*. One reason why a capacity for moral sense and second-order affection is neces-sary for genuine virtue or merit, then, is that we can properly at-tribute these to the agent "in himself" only if they result from a self-governing capacity, and moral sense is required for that. Not that moral sense itself simply is the self-governing capacity. Shaftesbury thinks that rational self-government, even if self-critical, proceeds by reflective consideration of the agent's good, whereas moral sense involves a disinterested reflective affection. Still, as we shall see, moral sense is directly implicated in self-government as Shaftesbury sees it.[36]

Although he does not mention it in this context, Shaftesbury has another rationale for holding that genuine merit requires moral sense, a reason that derives from his idea that the ultimate ground of beauty is beautifying mind. Natural affections are beautiful, but if they are in no way regulated by the agent's moral sense, the mind to which this beauty must ultimately be referred is not the agent's but what is immanent in all of nature. In this case, beauty would be in the agent's mind no differently from what it might be in an ancient edifice or in the workings of a healthy body. In Shaftesbury's terms, the agent's mind would be only the "beautified," not also the "beau-

---

36. "'Tis evident that a creature having [moral sense] in any degree must necessarily act according to it, if it happens not to be opposed, either by some settled sedate affection towards a conceived private good, or by some sudden, strong, and forcible passion" (1.265).

Shaftesbury distinguishes between mistakes of fact and mistakes of right, holding that the latter, but not the former, are a cause of vice (1.254). He evidently assumes that it is broadly within agents' power to avoid the latter; it is within agents' power to cultivate their moral sense and determine themselves to virtue (although not necessarily on any given occasion). Shaftesbury certainly believes the latter. See 1.193; II.271.

tifying." The moral beauty displayed in her mind would be *in* her but, in that sense, would not really be *hers*. If, however, she has a sense of moral beauty and the capacity to shape her conduct and affections by it, she can become not simply a place where beauty is displayed but a creator of moral beauty. She can become the beautifying as well as the beautified; a source as well as an occasion of moral beauty. The "first order of beauty" is that which has "a power of making other forms themselves," or "forming forms" (II.131–132). Merit or virtue, Shaftesbury may be thinking, is moral beauty of the "first order."

THE OBLIGATION TO VIRTUE

We can turn now to Shaftesbury's only explicit treatment of morality's normativity, what he calls the "obligation to virtue." It is quite remarkable that Shaftesbury poses and then discusses the question of whether there is an obligation to be virtuous without any reference to the idea of law or to related notions of accountability, punishment, or blame. He may be the first British moralist to do so. Writers like Hobbes and Cumberland, who did much to naturalize the traditional framework of natural law, still felt the need and use of working within it. And even a philosopher like Cudworth, who rejected so much of legislative ethics' focus on external acts and externally induced motive, was nonetheless concerned to show that there is a "law of love" by which we are appropriately held accountable. By the time of Shaftesbury's *Inquiry*, however, the natural law framework had been so revised from within, and recast from without, that it was possible for Shaftesbury to pose the question of an obligation to virtue in completely nonlegalistic terms without feeling he had to provide any justification for doing so. At the beginning of Book II, he immediately reformulates the issue of the obligation to virtue as "what reason there is to embrace" the virtuous life, sets about answering that question in terms of whether the best (most beneficial) life for the agent is a virtuous one, argues that it is, and ends Book II with the conclusion that there is indeed an "obligation to virtue" – there using the term 'obligation' for only the second time in the book! But whereas he had little use for guilt, moral requirement, and accountability as central moral notions, Shaftesbury was nevertheless concerned to provide an account of why morality is not something we can reasonably ignore. And a reshaped notion of obligation as rationally conclusive motive was available for his use, even if only in passing.

Since Shaftesbury's ethics – unlike, say, Hobbes's or Locke's – lay great stress on other-directed natural affections such as kindness and pity, and since they also provide an important motivational role for moral sense, it may seem odd that he should hold that whether the virtuous life is a reasonable one turns on whether it is likeliest to achieve the agent's good. But although he is certainly no psychological egoist, Shaftesbury *is* a kind of rational egoist. The virtuous life is reasonable, he believes, because it is most in the agent's interest. He does, however, hold that the virtuous life itself involves being motivated by considerations other than the agent's good (at least, so conceived). It involves benefiting others for *their* sakes. Although the rational underpinning of the virtuous life, and thus its obligation, depends on its being best for the agent, a person who in the heat of decision queries his obligation to virtue has "one thought too many."[37]

A man of thorough good breeding, whatever else he be, is incapable of doing a rude or brutal action. He never deliberates in this case, or considers of the matter by prudential rules of self-interest and advantage. He acts from his nature, in a manner necessarily, and without reflection; and if he did not, it were impossible for him to answer his character, or be found that truly well-bred man on every occasion. 'Tis the same with the honest man. He cannot deliberate in the case of a plain villainy. A "plum" is no temptation to him. He likes and loves himself too well. (1.86)

When, however, a rational moral agent does come to reflect on whether she should lead a virtuous life, her own interest or good is the only appropriate standard. "[T]he judgment we are to make of interest, and the opinion we should have of advantage and good, . . . is what must necessarily determine us in our conduct and prove the leading principle of our lives" (1.199). Proper reflection on our interests will lead us to endorse, Shaftesbury believes, a life in which we express a concern for others for their sakes.

Shaftesbury would come to be sharply criticized for his rational egoism by such otherwise friendly successors as Hutcheson and Butler, but it should be recalled that his position here was really no different from that which Cudworth assumed in his manuscripts.

37. The phrase is Bernard Williams's, who uses it to make a similar point in a different context. "Persons, Character, and Morality," in *Moral Luck* (Cambridge: Cambridge University Press, 1981), pp. 17–18.

Cudworth distinguishes between animal and moral obligation, and holds that the latter consists in a distinctly virtuous motive. But this contrast is not between an obligation rooted in the agent's own good and one that is not. Both concern goods to the agent. According to Cudworth, those who, like Hobbes, hold that there is (only) an animal obligation to morality claim that virtue and moral conduct are no more than instrumentally beneficial to the agent. Those who believe that morality is intrinsically obligatory maintain, Cudworth claims, that virtue and moral conduct are intrinsically good for the agent as well as for other beneficiaries.[38]

Shaftesbury's case for the coincidence of virtue and the agent's good is interesting in its own right, but we need not consider it in much detail. The human psyche is a system, he thinks, and if affections have more than their natural strengths, this destroys the balance necessary for a good and happy life.[39] Achieving balance is a delicate matter, and it is often unpredictable what changes an increase or decrease in the level of a given affection will cause elsewhere in the system. Shaftesbury seeks to show that a virtuous character is necessary for psychic balance in general, because it is the only, or the only balanced, way of achieving satisfactions essential to a good human life, and also because virtue is itself balance-enhancing. In the first vein, he argues that satisfactions of mind are likelier to be valuable than physical satisfactions and that, of these, those having to do with natural social affections are of singular importance. Love is the "master-pleasure," and "out of . . . community or participation in the pleasures of others, and belief of meriting well

38. Thus Shaftesbury: "For in this we should all agree, that happiness was to be pursued, and in fact was always sought after; but whether found in following Nature, and giving way to common affection, or in suppressing it, and turning every passion towards private advantage, a narrow self-end, or the preservation of mere life, this would be the matter in debate between us" (I.80–81). For Cudworth, see Chapter 5, "Obligation, Animal and Moral."

39. There is some fudging in Shaftesbury's argument here, since the sort of balance necessary for the agent's own good is in principle independent of the overall balance of nature, whereas whether an affection is natural must ultimately depend on its role in the overall system of nature. The general problem in the background is that Shaftesbury usually writes as though the good of a system – whether an individual human being, the species, or the universe as a whole – is *conceptually* independent of its role in larger systems, even if there is a natural dependence in the order of nature. "[I]f the ill of one private system be the good of others; if it makes still to the good of the general system . . . then is the ill of that private system no real ill in itself" (I.246). Of course, Shaftesbury does believe that the requisite natural dependence exists, but his argument in Book II does not make this premise explicit.

from others . . . would arise more than nine-tenths of whatever is enjoyed in life" (1.295–296, 299). So far, moral sense (hence genuine virtue or merit) plays no essential role, but Shaftesbury also argues that self-reflective rational beings value personal ideals of character highly – indeed, that they stake their very acceptance or rejection of themselves, their pride and shame, on them.[40] And where we desire esteem, what we really want is "deserved esteem" (1.298–302). In both cases, the relevant desires derive from moral sense. Neither an ideal of character nor a conception of what is worthy of esteem is possible without it.

In the second vein, Shaftesbury claims that virtuous affections reverberate throughout the psyche in stabilizing ways. Their distinctive pleasures are likely to be relatively enduring and to add to the pleasures of other affections. The "charm" and cheer of love and fellowship for example, enhances other enjoyments. Additionally, virtuous affections are singularly suited to balance a self-conscious psyche, since whether we are in balance depends importantly on whether we find ourselves to be so. Whether the "self-system" is in tune partly depends on how it sounds to that very self (1.251). Only a virtuous person can have, therefore, a "mind or reason well composed, quiet, easy within itself, and such as can freely bear its own inspection and review" (1.302).

These points are combined with an argument that vicious affections conversely upset balance, and that, as "every reasoning or reflecting creature is by his nature forced to endure the review of his own mind and actions, and to have representations of himself and his inward affairs constantly passing before him," the viciously affected will have their character's dissonance further magnified by its reflection (1.305). Noting that his argument is cast almost entirely in terms of internal, psychological benefit, Shaftesbury concludes by remarking that it survives even Cartesian skepticism.

Nor is it of any concern to our argument how these exterior objects stand: whether they are realities or mere illusions; whether we wake or dream. For ill dreams will be equally disturbing; and a good dream (if life be nothing else) will be easily and happily passed. In this dream of life, therefore, our demonstrations have the same force; our balance and economy hold good, and our obligation to virtue is in every respect the same. (1.337)

40. See, e.g., 1.82–84, 92, 115, 170–71, 251, 268, 302, 306–7, 319; II.138–41, 143; *Life*.21, 23, 60, 66, 105, 113, 117, 120, 143.

AUTHORSHIP AND OBLIGATION

SELF-CRITICAL SELF-DETERMINATION

In discussing Shaftesbury's reasons for holding genuine virtue to require that the agent have a self-reflective moral sense, I mentioned that he relies on an Epictetian version of the doctrine that rational agents can determine their conduct by critically assessing their beliefs and desires. Shaftesbury elaborates, at some length, on the process through which agents can become authors of their lives, both in his Stoic-inspired notebooks (which Rand titled *Philosophical Regimen*) and in *Soliloquy, or Advice to an Author*.[41] Although the latter is nominally addressed to literary authors, Shaftesbury remarks elsewhere that this is "pretence": His real aim is "to correct manners and regulate lives" (II.272). He is concerned to show that through the self-reflective process to which he gives the name "soliloquy" (among other terms), rational agents can author their own conduct.

If rational self-determination is directed toward an agent's good and is necessary, as Shaftesbury believes, to achieve it, it follows that the exercise of this capacity is necessary to fulfill the "obligation" to virtue. From this it need not follow that, like Cudworth or the Locke of the revised *Essay*, Shaftesbury is suggesting that the agent's power to determine himself to his own good has anything to do with what makes him obligated to his own good and hence to virtue. For Locke and Cudworth, obligation requires self-determination because obligation entails accountability, and self-determination is required for that. In Locke's words, "no thing can be capable of a Law, that is not a free agent" (*Essay*.76). Shaftesbury, however, disconnects obligation from law. So he lacks this reason for thinking that the capacity for self-determination is necessary to make virtue obligatory or to explain what obligation itself is.

It would seem, therefore, that although the obligation to virtue and the capacity to author a virtuous life must run along the same tracks

41. *Soliloquy* forms part of *Characteristics*. The notebooks were published, in large part, by Rand in *The Life, Unpublished Letters, and Philosophical Regimen*. Voitle argues that the notebooks are more appropriately titled "Exercises," his translation of Shaftesbury's term *aekhmata*. See Voitle, *The Third Earl of Shaftesbury*, p. 136. Shaftesbury himself actually says, in *Soliloquy*, that were such meditative exercises to be published, no more appropriate title could be found than "Crudities." For an extended discussion of Shaftesbury's notebooks, see Frederich A. Uehlein, *Kosmos und Subjektivität, Lord Shaftesburys Philosophical Regimen* (Freiburg and Munich: Karl Alber, 1976).

for Shaftesbury, they have nothing essentially to do with one another. But whereas Shaftesbury does not assert Cudworth's and Locke's claim that the capacity for self-determination is necessary for obligation, he does implicitly claim that a capacity to bind or *obligate oneself* is necessary for self-determination. An agent can author her conduct, he thinks, only if she can take a standpoint with respect to herself from which she can authoritatively prescribe action for, and thus obligate, herself and then act on these prescriptions *as authoritative and obligating.*

In a moment of self-criticism that is especially harsh even for his notebooks, Shaftesbury writes:

[T]hou hast . . . prostituted thyself and committed thy mind to chance and the next comer, so as to be treated at pleasure by every one, to receive impressions from everything, and machine-like to be moved and wrought upon, wound up and governed exteriorly, as if there were nothing that ruled within or had the least control. (*Life*.114)[42]

The charge is heteronomy. And it is a *charge* (and not a mere ascription of defect), he thinks, because it is open to an agent to be self-governing, to be "ruled within." Like Cudworth and Locke, Shaftesbury rejects the liberty of indifference. "[L]et the will be ever so free, Humour and Fancy, we see, govern it" (1.122). But, also like them, he believes that opinion, humor, and fancy need not themselves be determined "exteriorly." Mature human agents have the power to step back from, critically assess, and thereby affect present beliefs and desires.[43] In this way we can "regulate our governing fancies, passions, and humours" so that, determining the determinants of action, we govern ourselves (1.184). This is the power that Shaftesbury variously calls the "ruling," "leading," or "governing principle."

So far we have a view of the same shape as that of Cudworth and Locke. But Shaftesburean "soliloquy" has some significantly different twists. In contrast to Locke, for whom deliberative reflection focuses entirely on the objects of desire, and Cudworth, who stresses a "self-comprehensive self-recollection" in which an agent deliberates by bringing various motivational sources to mind in a unified way, Shaftesbury describes a kind of self-analytical reality therapy in which an agent seeks an objective picture of the source of

42. Cf. Epictetus, *Discourses*, vol. 2, pp. 41, 71.
43. "What is reason but a power of judging the fancies?" (*Life*.174).

her desires and their place in the natural order with which she then confronts herself. Shaftesbury agrees with Locke that there is no direct correlation between the press of present desire and the real contribution its object would make to the agent's good. Locke's solution, we recall, is to bring desire's present press into line with its object's value (pleasure potential) by imaginatively examining the object's real nature. This strategy may work so long as the original lack of congruence was based on misapprehension. But if, as Shaftesbury believes, the existence and strength of a desire sometimes bears no simple relation to the agent's conception of its object, then it may not. It may be that the desire has a motivational source other than the conception of its object, and if so, correcting the conception may not "correct" the desire.

One instance that concerns Shaftesbury is the case of motivated ignorance, in which a relatively superficial desire is partly explained by another, deeper desire that motivates the first together with the agent's ignorance of its doing so. Getting an adequate conception of the object of the superficial desire in such a case may leave the motive force provided by the secretly motivating desire unaffected. To gain leverage on the latter, an agent must bring the relation to the deeper desire to consciousness.

The very capacity of rational agents to make their own desires an object of awareness may require that a desire be "sly" and "insinuating" if it is actually to motivate. If an agent would be less likely to act on a desire were she to be aware of doing so, then the desire may motivate a more surreptitious pursuit of its object, motivating other desires the satisfaction of which will also tend to satisfy the deeper desire and mask its operation at the same time.

"One would think," Shaftesbury writes, "there was nothing easier for us than to know our own minds, and understand . . . what we plainly drove at, and what we proposed to ourselves, as our end, in every occurrence of our lives" (I.113). But this is not so. Ignorance of some of our desires is motivated by those very desires. "[T]he chief interest of ambition, avarice, corruption, and every sly insinuating vice is to prevent this interview" of ourselves and their consequent discovery. (I.115).[44] Vicious desires, moreover, more frequently speak "tacitly and murmuringly," "by a whisper and indirect insinuation, imperfectly, indistinctly, and confusedly" (*Life*.166). Vanity, for instance, may motivate a desire for political office out of propor-

44. See also I.6, 123.

tion to the attraction this would otherwise have and in such a way that the desire's real motivational source remains hidden.

A different kind of example is the sort of false enthusiasm Shaftesbury sarcastically calls the "inspiring disease" (1.32), as when one catches a feeling, passion, or mood (for example, in a crowd) not by admiration and a desire to emulate but by an "insensible transpiration" from others. Here again desire will be relatively independent of the agent's conception of its object.

What cases of these kinds require, Shaftesbury thinks, is *self-analysis:* the discovery and avowal of desires, and analysis of their causes and mutual relations. So long as an agent can view things only from the point of view of a given desire, she is in its grip. Avowing desire is already a step away from being possessed by it. One now occupies a different standpoint, one from which the desiring view of things can be seen for what it is, the view of things one has by virtue of having the desire.

Because we can change perspective in this way, we can analyze and interrogate ourselves – we can engage in soliloquy or self-converse. Since desires can work through indirection, the first thing one must do is to discover what one's opinions and fancies actually are. This is the part most aptly called soliloquy. Honest and unconstrained soliloquizing may give rise to the expression of desires that would otherwise remain hidden. Privacy, by minimizing the desire to please, helps remove an important obstacle to honesty (1.111). "There is nothing more useful in the management of the *visa*, . . . than to have a sort of custom of putting them into words, making them speak out and explain themselves as it were *viva-voce*, and not tacitly and murmuringly" (*Life*.166).[45] A helpful by-product is a harmless "discharge" of desires whose insinuations might otherwise do damage (1.110–11). The main object, however, is the self-knowledge one gains by listening to what one is saying, the discovery of what it is one actually wants and believes. As "subjects of our own practice" we can "divide ourselves into two parties" and make our thoughts and feelings the object of our own awareness and consideration (1.112). The good sense behind the "Delphic inscription, Recognise yourself" and the ancient idea "that we have each of us a daemon" or "genius" is, Shaftesbury urges, an injunction to "divide yourself, or be two" (1.112–13).

45. And: "[O]ur thoughts have generally such an obscure implicit language, that 'tis the hardest thing in the world to make them speak out distinctly. For this reason, the right method is to give them voice and accent" (1.113).

An agent, having discovered what she desires and believes, is then in a position to ask herself why she does. Often, of course, it will simply be because an object has features she really finds desirable, but not always. So the second step of the process is for the agent to discover the *source* of desire:

Thus I contend with fancy and opinion, and search the mint and foundery of imagination. For here the appetites and desires are fabricated; hence they derive their privilege and currency. If I can stop the mischief here and prevent false coinage, I am safe. "Idea! wait awhile till I have examined thee, whence thou art and to whom thou retainest. Art thou of ambition's train? or dost thou promise only pleasure?" (I.207)[46]

When a desire's strength depends in part on ignorance of its source, or at least on failing fully to recognize it, coming to appreciate its etiology can give the agent a way of affecting its strength in the direction of her overall good.

After scrutinizing desires and their causes, it still remains for an agent to "recollect" himself and place present desires in the context of his most important concerns over time (*Life*.112).[47] This permits a unified considered judgment of what to do that is informed by an accurate picture of desires and beliefs together with their place in the natural order.

Thus at last a mind, by knowing itself and its own proper powers and virtues, becomes free and independent. It sees its hindrances and obstructions, and finds they are wholly from itself, and from opinions wrongly conceived. The more it conquers in this respect (be it in the least particular) the more it is its own master, feels its own natural liberty. (II.282)

We should note a feature of self-converse that further distinguishes it from Lockean practical deliberation. Suppose we think of a Lockean agent "dividing himself" after Shaftesbury's manner. The "more reflective" half, as it were, would make value judg-

---

46. Cf. Epictetus: "For, just as Socrates used to tell us not to live a life unsubjected to examination, so we ought not to accept a sense-impression unsubjected to examination, but should say, 'Wait, allow me to see who you are and whence you come'" (*Discourses*, vol. 2, p. 85). See also *Life*.167.

47. 'Self-recollection' is one of the terms that Roland Hall has listed as appearing in Cudworth's manuscripts on free will earlier than the first use noted by the *Oxford English Dictionary*. Hall gives 'self-improving' as another instance of a term that appears in Cudworth's *FW*, although the *O.E.D.* attributes its first use to Shaftesbury's *Characteristicks*. Roland Hall, "New Words and Antedatings." See also note 34. On the possibility that Shaftesbury read Cudworth's manuscripts, see Passmore, *Ralph Cudworth*, pp. 97–100.

ments in purely hedonistic terms, recognizing no goods as intrinsically higher or lower. It is crucial to Shaftesbury's picture, however, that reflective rational agents recognize (with their moral sense) higher goods on which they stake the value their lives can have for them. Specifically, each person has, as it were, a "better" or "nobler" self – an ideal of character to which she is committed, and on the pursuit of which she stakes her pride and self-respect.[48] This can be, indeed, a powerful reason for shrinking from soliloquy and vulnerability to self-deception.

We may defend villainy, or cry up folly, before the world; but to appear fools, madmen, or varlets to ourselves, and prove it to our own faces that we are really such, is insupportable. For so true a reverence has every one for himself when he comes clearly to appear before his close companion, that he had rather profess the vilest things of himself in open company than hear his character privately from his own mouth. (1.115)

This "close companion" is our "daemon" or "genius": namely, the ideal of self with which we identify and to which we are committed. But commitment to such an ideal, Shaftesbury argues, presupposes acknowledgment of values recognized by moral sense.

And thus as long as I find men either angry or revengeful, proud or ashamed, I am safe. For they conceive an honourable and dishonourable, a foul and fair, as well as I. No matter where they place it, or how they are mistaken in it, this hinders not my being satisfied "that the thing is, and is universally acknowledged; that it is of nature's impression, naturally conceived, and by no art or counter-nature to be eradicated or destroyed." (II.141)

Shaftesburean self-converse thus involves responsibility to a "better self," to a personification of an ideal of character to which the agent is committed. The agent views herself from the standpoint of someone who realizes, or respectably pursues, the ideal of character to which she is committed and, identifying with that, judges what course of action would be best for her, taking account of the higher values on which her self-esteem is staked. Consciousness of being a scoundrel makes life miserable, but that is because one is committed to thinking villainy base, not vice versa. "[W]e can never really blush for anything beside what we think truly shameful, and what we should still blush for were we ever so secure as to our interest" (II.139).

48. See note 40 and, esp., 1.183.

OBLIGATION, SELF-GOVERNMENT, AND
THE UNITY OF THE SELF

More clearly than Locke or even than Cudworth, Shaftesbury conceives of self-determination as self-*regulation* or self-*government*. "How do I govern MYSELF?" "This," he writes in his notebooks, "is a matter, and the only matter" (*Life*.102).[49] Shaftesbury sometimes says that fancy and opinion "govern" the will, but he obviously thinks a rational agent can govern himself through his "ruling principle" in a more robust sense (1.122). For him, soliloquy requires recognizing and subjecting ourselves to the authoritative prescriptions of our better selves. It is a *self-conscious* process of self-guidance by a *normative conception*. In dividing ourselves into two, we erect one as "our counsellor and governor" (1.112). "As cruel a court as the Inquisition appears, there must, it seems, be full as formidable a one erected in ourselves" (1.122). There must be a "superior part which disciplines, instructs, and manages," one with "authority and command" (*Life.* 169).[50] Self-government can thus exist only if there is "due acknowledgment of the superior" or "governing part" (*Life*.130).

As Shaftesbury is envisioning it, therefore, soliloquy works through the agent's recognition of the *authority* of her better self. The agent cannot simply regard its prescriptions as contending with her other fancies in a contest of strength; so long as she does so, she is "governed exteriorly" with her "mind" committed "to chance and the next comer." If her conduct is to be genuinely self-determined, she must recognize a difference *in authority* between the prescriptions of her informed better self and those intrinsic to her individual fancies. She must, in effect, govern herself by a conception of the authority of her own considered better judgment. Shaftesbury does not use the terms in this context, but his view effectively requires that the self-governing agent regard herself as *bound* or *obligated* by her considered better judgment. The self-governing agent must think she *ought* to pursue the course of conduct which, on reflection, she judges best, and, moreover, she must so act *because she thinks she ought to*.

It is illuminating to compare this idea with the sort of externalist voluntarism exemplified by Locke's *Essays on the Law of Nature*. Morality binds us, Locke says there, because it is authoritatively prescribed. Without *authoritative* prescription there can be no obligation.

49. See also *Life*.270.
50. See also *Life*.171.

In a sense, Shaftesbury agrees, but whereas Locke believes that authority derives from outside the moral self, from a superior being, Shaftesbury holds that authority rests within. Moral government is *self*-government, the self's determining its own conduct via a conception of the authority of its considered best judgment. We might thus say that Shaftesbury internalizes morality's normativity by *internalizing authority*. Only if an agent accords prescriptive authority to her considered practical judgment can she govern herself.

Shaftesbury connects the capacity of self-government to the ability to unify and give integrity to a life and to one's agency over time. A consequence of self-obligation is, he says, the "gain[ing of] a Will" (1.123). Only through soliloquy can an agent "be sure of his own meaning and design; and as to all his desires, opinions, and inclinations, be warranted one and the same person to-day as yesterday, and to-morrow as to-day" (1.123). It is "the only way of composing matters in our breast, and establishing that subordinacy which alone could make us agree with ourselves and be of a piece within" (1.113). Identifying self-converse with philosophy itself, Shaftesbury writes: "'[T]is the known province of philosophy to teach us ourselves, keep us the self-same persons, and so regulate our governing fancies, passions, and humours, as to make us comprehensible to ourselves" (1.184).[51] Several distinct claims are in play in these and similar passages. Shaftesbury claims that soliloquy is necessary for the continued existence over time, respectively, of agency and will, self-comprehensible agency, sanity (1.207), and integrity, in the senses both of unity and of truth to one's ideals (1.171). Moreover, he identifies the self with that which enables it to unify itself in these respects: "[W]hat is the person, the self, but the self-knowing, the self-remembering, the self-determining part? And what is this but a mind?" (*Life*.150). If we seek ourselves, "[w]here seek it but in that which *bids seek*, which now seeks, which determines, pronounces, judges of all, makes use of all, governs all? – What is it that now examines about this of self? And according to this then, what am I? . . . [a will], a mind, a judgment" (*Life*.129).

As suggestive as these ideas are, Shaftesbury steadfastly (and characteristically) refuses to develop them in any systematic way. Still, we can safely say that he regards soliloquy as necessary not only for self-determining or "authoring" agency but for a variety of other things that go under the general heading of unifying and unified

51. For similar passages, see 1.185–86, 193–94.

agency. The upshot is that although Shaftesbury is usually anxious to avoid the language of obligation, he nonetheless evidently holds that unified will and agency and the possibility of an authored, integral life themselves depend on an agent's capacity to guide her conduct by a conception of what she ought to do. If, consequently, the term 'obligation' seems almost incidental to Shaftesbury's demonstration of the "obligation to virtue" in the *Inquiry*, his argument there that the moral life is the better life is nonetheless directly relevant to his case in *Soliloquy* that self-determination and unified agency require that the agent bind himself to the (moral sense-informed) judgments of his better self.

A NORMATIVE THEORY OF WILL

There are the seeds here of a very different rationale for autonomist internalism than the accountability view we saw in Cudworth's works and in Locke's revised *Essay*. The final aim of the accountability approach is to vindicate the idea that moral demands have a status that warrants holding those subject to them accountable for violations, since, according to Cudworth and Locke, this is what we convey when we call moral demands *obligations* or consider them to be binding *law*. Since, they argue, only a "free agent" can be "capable of a law," holding a person accountable for violating a demand could be warranted only if there were conclusive reasons for meeting the demand by which the agent could have determined herself to do so. And that would be so only if the agent had a capacity for self-determining practical thinking, the proper exercise of which would have raised determinative motivation to meet the demand. Morality's being obligatory, they conclude, can consist only in the fact (if it is a fact) that ideally self-determining deliberation would yield this motivation.

Shaftesbury, however, is concerned less to vindicate *interpersonal* practices of accountability than to understand the conditions necessary for the very possibility of self-determining agency and unity of the will. And his suggestion seems to be that these include internalizing a conception of authority (if not also of accountability). Only if the agent regards his better self's prescriptions as authoritative and obligating, and acts on them because he so regards them, is unified and self-determining agency possible. Self-determination requires self-*government*, and that requires that the agent be dominantly

205

moved, and his conduct determined, by a normative conception he accepts. We might call this a *normative theory of the will*.[52]

This is not yet a view about what obligation is, and although Shaftesbury does not develop his ideas further in that direction, we can do so. If obligation concerns a distinctively practical necessity, then there may in the end be no room for a distinction between its being the case that a free agent must regard himself as obligated and his being so in fact. By bringing guidance by a conception of norm, authority, and obligation into his theory of the rational will, Shaftesbury opens up the possibility of maintaining, as Kant would later, that morality obligates because free rational wills must act under an "idea of law" (in Kant's phrase) and that this commits an agent to being guided by morality. After all, Shaftesbury believes an agent has a "better self" available for soliloquy only by virtue of her moral sense.

Like the sort of autonomist internalism advanced by Cudworth and suggested by Locke, a view of this sort would hold that the fact of obligation is realized in the motivation of a self-determining agent. The difference would be that, according to a normative theory of the will, the requisite motivation comes from a motivational state that is both distinctive of will and different from the desire for any good, namely, the agent's recognizing a consideration or demand as authoritative.[53]

A normative theory of rational will thus opens the way for a different autonomist internalist vindication of moral obligation than that resulting from the accountability view. Whereas the accountability view asserts the *morality entails free rational will* half of Kant's reciprocity thesis, the idea that guidance by a normative conception is intrinsic to free rational will might be deployed in an attempt to vindicate the *free rational will entails morality* half. For the latter project to work, it would, of course, have to be argued that in being guided by a conception of law, free agents are committed to being guided, more specifically, by moral laws. This would be Butler's project and, of course, Kant's.

52. Compare here Locke's view that will involves "the mind ordering, or as it were commanding" (*Essay*.236).
53. As I mentioned in Chapter 1, Locke's and Cudworth's views of will as self-*command* may require this idea in any case.

Chapter 8

Hutcheson: moral sentiment and calm desire

It has been customary among anglophone scholars, as I have said, to view Shaftesbury's thought retrospectively, through the lens of the empiricist moral sentimentalism his writings inspired in Britain, especially among such Scottish Enlightenment figures as Hutcheson, Hume, and Smith.[1] The young Francis Hutcheson, for example, could find in Shaftesbury's writings many of the doctrines that would prove central to his own moral philosophy: that there is a moral good that fundamentally concerns an agent's motives and is independent of convention, that the morality of acts is derivative from the morality of motives, that moral goodness or virtue depends on a moral sense that is activated when contemplating motives, that this moral sense arises naturally, and that the virtuous affections approved of by moral sense prominently include benevolent concerns, which also arise naturally and which provide a source of motivation independent of self-directed concerns. So important were these ideas to Hutcheson, and so salient was Shaftesbury as their leading contemporary exponent, that Hutcheson appended the following to the title of the first edition of his *Inquiry into the Original of Our Ideas of Beauty and Virtue* (1725): "In which the Principles of the late Earl of Shaftesbury are Explain'd and Defended, against the Author of *The Fable of the Bees*."[2] The latter, of course, was Bernard

1. Albee remarked, for example, that Hutcheson's system is usually seen "as the logical development of Shaftesbury's" (*A History of English Utilitarianism*, p. 58). And Martineau wrote that Hutcheson worked out Shaftesbury's "fruitful hints and construct[ed] from them a systematic psychology" (*Types of Ethical Theory*, vol. 2, p. 514). Note also Fowler's remark that "there are no two of the better-known English philosophers whose writings are so closely related as those of Shaftesbury and Hutcheson" (*Shaftesbury and Hutcheson*, p. v).
2. *The Fable of the Bees* evolved through various versions from 1705 (when it was entitled *The Grumbling Hive: Or, Knaves Turn'd Honest*) until it reached its final form

Mandeville, whose writings early-eighteenth-century British moralists took to pose an egoistic skeptical challenge to morality similar to the challenge Hobbes was taken to have mounted more than a half century before.

It is much too simple, however, to see Hutcheson as primarily engaged in working out Shaftesbury's "fruitful hints" within a systematic, empirical moral psychology and moral philosophy, as Martineau put it.[3] Hutcheson not only disagreed with Shaftesbury in fundamental ways; he understood himself to be doing so. Most important for our purposes, Hutcheson believed that Shaftesbury was mistaken about moral obligation and its relation to moral sense. In addition to an obligation to virtue consisting in the fact that the virtuous life realizes the agent's good, Hutcheson believed there is a distinctively *moral* obligation – one intrinsic to morality and independent of the agent's own good. Hutcheson did not deny the importance of self-interested reasons for leading the moral life. He praised Shaftesbury's project of demonstrating the congruence of virtue and interest as "the principal Business of a moral Philosopher" and asserted throughout his writings that self-interest constitutes *an* obligation to the virtuous life.[4] But he also insisted that moral sense obli-

in 1729. The first edition of the *Inquiry* was published in 1725. Hutcheson dedicated it to Viscount Molesworth, a friend and follower of Shaftesbury. William R. Scott, Hutcheson's biographer, writes that through Molesworth's influence a circle of "earnest young thinkers at Dublin" devoted to Shaftesbury's ideas was established in the early 1720s. Members of this group, including Hutcheson and James Arbuckle, contributed short articles to the *Dublin Journal,* some of which were later collected and published as *Hibernicus's Letters: A Collection of Letters and Essays Lately Published in the Dublin Journal,* edited by James Arbuckle (London, 1729). For an illuminating account of this period, as well as of Hutcheson's life generally, see W. R. Scott, *Francis Hutcheson: His Life, Teaching and Position in the History of Philosophy* (Cambridge: Cambridge University Press, 1900).

3. See note 1.
4. *An Inquiry into the Original of Our Ideas of Beauty and Virtue, in Two Treatises, I. Concerning Beauty, Order, Harmony, Design. II: Concerning Moral Good and Evil,* 5th ed. revised (London, 1753), p. 274. This edition, published after Hutcheson's death, incorporates the text corrections that were collected at the end of the fourth edition (1738), which was the last edition published during Hutcheson's lifetime. The selections from the *Inquiry* reprinted in Raphael's *British Moralists* are from the fourth edition. The (much more extensive) selections reprinted in Selby-Bigge's *British Moralists* are taken from the second edition, printed in 1726. A facsimile of the first (1725) edition exists in the *Collected Works,* vol. 1 (Hildesheim: Olms, 1971). References to the *Inquiry* in the text will be to the so-called second *Inquiry* (concerning moral good and evil); they will give (following the edition number, included only if the passage does not appear [or appear in the same location] in all editions) section and article numbers and, where appropriate, page numbers in Raphael, *British Moralists,* vol. 1. Thus the present reference would be (VII.ii), as the

gates to morality intrinsically. And he argued that self-love provides no more authoritative a reason for acting than does the motive of which moral sense most highly approves: universal calm benevolence. By Hutcheson's lights, Shaftesbury had conceived the moral sense in terms more adequate to aesthetics than to morality, and had characterized the fundamental motive for the virtuous life too similarly to a self-absorbed aesthete's desire to surround himself with pleasing reflections of his own beauty. From its third edition on, the *Inquiry*'s reference to Shaftesbury on its title page was dropped.

In fact, when it comes to understanding Hutcheson's views about morality's normativity, it makes sense to place him not within the tradition of Shaftesbury and Cudworth, for whom the moral bond was intrinsically linked to creative practical reason and the motives of a *self-determining* moral agent, but within the empirical naturalist tradition of Hobbes and Cumberland. (Locke, as I have argued, had a foot in both traditions.) Hutcheson, of course, rejected the egoistic psychologies and voluntaristic metaethics of Locke and Hobbes even more strenuously than he did elements of Shaftesbury's views. But in common with these writers, as with Cumberland, he held fast to the empirical naturalist conception of reason as a wholly *theoretical* faculty. Nor did he hold, as did the autonomist internalists, that a theory of self-determining practical reasoning is essential to an account of morality's normative force. He was especially skeptical of Shaftesbury's thesis that genuine virtue must include the agent's self-direction through moral sense. According to Hutcheson, it is only the moral sense of *observers* that is pertinent to virtue, enabling them to appreciate the moral goodness of first-order moral motives (all forms of benevolence, for Hutcheson). Moral sense's only relevance from an *agent's* perspective, in deliberation, is to exhibit a self-interested concern in being virtuous, namely, to achieve the pleasures of reflecting on one's own virtue.[5] And this motive cannot enhance the agent's virtue.

Although the sentimentalist aspects derive from Shaftesbury, it is Cumberland who stands most firmly behind Hutcheson's thought. In addition to holding that reason is an entirely theoretical faculty,

passage appears in all editions but is not included in Raphael. When context requires identifying a passage as being from the *Inquiry*, edition, section, and article numbers will be preceded by "*In.*"

5. At least, this was his view until *A System of Moral Philosophy*, published posthumously in 1755. For a discussion of an interesting wrinkle in the *System*, see the final section of this chapter.

with no end or practical 'ought' intrinsic to it, both Cumberland and Hutcheson also maintain that the full reflective use of reason elicits benevolent motives for acting no less than self-interested ones. I have called the empirical naturalist approach that argues that morality's normative hold is grounded in the fact that calm, reflective use of reason leads to a motive for acting morally the *calm reflective delibera-tion view*. The idea is not, as in Shaftesbury and Cudworth, that reason is intrinsically creative and practical, with moral motives internal to it. That human beings can be moved by what they discover through empirical investigation about the goods of others – and, on fully calm reflection, by the greatest good of all – is simply a fact about our contingent psychological makeup. But, Cumberland and Hutcheson insist, that we are moved by calm reflection on our own greatest good is also no more than contingent.

As we shall see, Hutcheson's official position about moral *obliga-tion* is that it consists in the sentiment of approval an observer feels in contemplating first-order moral motives. This is a *sentimentalist* rather than a *calm deliberation view* of *obligation*. But that may reflect a semantic decision on Hutcheson's part as much as anything else. For understanding the development of *internalism*, what is more interest-ing is Hutcheson's view that ideally calm, reason-informed delibera-tion leads to the morally best motive (universal benevolence) as well as to the desire for the agent's greatest good on the whole. Morality's authority as rational motive is therefore no less than that of self-love. Here again, a conception of self-determination as the capacity to be guided by comprehensive, authoritative practical judgment is con-spicuously absent. From the agent's point of view, it is simply fortu-nate, a gift from God, that these two ultimate and independent sources of motivation, and their related "obligations," point the same way.[6] The reason why moral philosophy's "principal Business" is to demonstrate a congruence between benevolence and self-love is that there can be, according to Hutcheson's psychology, no deliberative grounds for choosing between them.

NATURALISM AND MORAL SENSE

It is illuminating to view the *Inquiry* as an extended argument that morality can be understood, in all its complexity, within the frame-

6. Cf. Henry Sidgwick's "dualism of practical reason," to be discussed presently.

work of empirical naturalism.[7] Accepting broadly Lockean (if not, Hobbesian) doctrines about the powers of reason and the empirical sources of ideas and knowledge, Hutcheson attempts to show, as against Hobbes and Locke, that morality has a distinctive, irreducible place in nature.[8] Most significant, he argues, a fundamental distinction between moral and natural good can be located naturalistically. What he calls "natural good" is the good of a person (or other sensitive being) – its benefit or welfare.[9] Hutcheson follows Locke in identifying this with pleasure.[10] Moral good, on the other hand, is realized only by the motives of a moral agent and is something we recognize in disinterestedly approving these motives when we contemplate them. Moral good is irreducible to natural good. Nevertheless, Hutcheson is keen to argue, moral goodness is a *natural property*. Whether a motive is morally good is determined by facts

7. For generally helpful discussions of Hutcheson's moral philosophy, see D. D. Raphael, *The Moral Sense* (London: Oxford University Press, 1947); Elmer Sprague, "Francis Hutcheson and the Moral Sense," *Journal of Philosophy* 51 (1954): 794–800; Henning Jensen, *Motivation and the Moral Sense in Francis Hutcheson's Ethical Theory* (The Hague: Nijhoff, 1971); Leidhold, *Ethik und Politik bei Francis Hutcheson;* William T. Blackstone, *Francis Hutcheson and Contemporary Ethical Theory* (Athens: University of Georgia Press, 1965); and Mark Philip Strasser, *Francis Hutcheson's Moral Theory: Its Form and Utility* (Wolfeboro, N.H.: Longwood Academic, 1990). For an account that attempts to understand Hutcheson his Scottish intellectual context, see Alasdair MacIntyre, *Whose Justice? Which Rationality?* (Notre Dame, Ind.: Notre Dame University Press, 1988), pp. 260–80.
8. Hutcheson's comment on a draft of Hume's *Treatise* that it "wants a certain warmth in the cause of virtue" evoked from its author the famous response that one may consider the mind "either as an anatomist or as a painter; either to discover its most secret springs or to describe the grace and beauty of its actions": J. Y. T. Grieg, ed., *The Letters of David Hume* (New York: Garland, 1983), p. 32. But in the terms of this contrast, Hutcheson's own project must surely be likened more to that of the anatomist.
9. In *Illustrations on the Moral Sense,* section I (see notes 10–11 herein), Hutcheson considers an objector who proposes as a reason for approving of "the Pursuit of publick Good" that "[i]*t is best that all should be happy*" and responds: "*Best* is most good: Good to whom? To the *Whole,* or to each *Individual?*"
10. "The Pleasure in our sensible Perceptions of any kind, gives us our first Idea of *natural Good,* or *Happiness;* and then all Objects which are apt to excite this Pleasure are call'd immediately good. Those Objects which may procure others immediately pleasant, are call'd *Advantageous:* and we pursue both kinds from a view of *Interest,* or from *Self-Love*" (In.intro.; R.262). See also *An Essay on the Nature and Conduct of the Passions and Affections. With Illustrations on the Moral Sense,* 3d ed. (London: 1742), p. 2. The *Essay* was first published in 1728: For a facsimile of the first edition, see *Collected Works,* vol. 2. I shall refer to the 3d edition of 1742: facsimile, with an introduction by Paul McReynolds (Gainesville, Fla.: Scholars' Facsimiles & Reprints, 1969). Further references to the *Essay* will be included in the text, preceded by "*EPA*" when necessary, and will be to page numbers in the third edition, with page numbers in Raphael, *British Moralists,* added when appropriate.

of nature and is no less open to empirical investigation than is any issue concerning natural good.

We shall examine Hutcheson's views about the naturalistic basis of moral good and evil presently. Before we do, I want to note why he thinks this task so important. Hutcheson holds that moral good and evil (better: the ideas of "approbation" and "condemnation" that they essentially involve) are fundamental to the system of moral concepts with its full complexity. From these two basic simple ideas he aims to construct every other important moral notion: the morally choiceworthy, obligation, and rights (perfect vs. imperfect, etc.). Placing moral value properly in nature thus provides a naturalistic foundation for the whole moral system.

Later editions of the *Inquiry* begin with the following definition of moral good and evil: "The word MORAL GOODNESS, in this Treatise, denotes our Idea of *some Quality apprehended in Actions, which procures Approbation, attended with Desire of the Agent's Happiness.* MORAL EVIL denotes our idea of *a contrary Quality, which excites Condemnation or Dislike*" (*In*.intro.; R.261). To this Hutcheson adds that "Approbation and Condemnation are probably simple Ideas, which cannot be farther explained." And if this seems to hedge, his definition of moral sense removes any indefiniteness. By moral sense, he says, he means only "*a Determination of our Minds to receive the simple Ideas of Approbation or Condemnation, from Actions observ'd, antecedent to any Opinions of Advantage or Loss to redound to ourselves from them*" (4:1.viii; R.269).[11]

Since he defines a sense as "*a Determination of the Mind, to receive any Idea from the Presence of an Object which occurs to us, independent on our Will*" (1.i; R.264–65), it is the simplicity of approbation and condemnation that stands behind Hutcheson's hypothesis of a moral sense.[12] This definition echoes Locke's distinction between simple and complex ideas. When furnished with simple ideas, Locke says, the understanding can "repeat, compare, and unite them even to an almost infinite Variety, and so can make at Pleasure new complex *ideas*" (*Essay*.119).[13] Simple ideas are precisely those that we cannot

---

11. See also the introduction to *Illustrations on the Moral Sense*: "The Words *Election* and *Approbation* seem to denote simple Ideas known by *Consciousness*; which can only be explained by *synonimous Words*, or by concomitant or consequent Circumstances." Further references to *Illustrations* will be placed in the text as "*IMS*" and will be to section and article number, with page numbers in Raphael, *British Moralists*, vol. 1, added when appropriate. Thus, the present reference is *IMS*.1.i; R.305.
12. But why not two senses – one for approbation and one for condemnation?
13. Cf. Hutcheson's "first" *Inquiry*, 1.ii–iii.

give ourselves at will and that must be given us. So Hutcheson argues against Locke that all moral notions essentially involve simple ideas that are distinctive of morality and are irreducible to any other ideas (including that of natural good): approbation and condemnation.[14]

There are several things to notice about Hutcheson's initial definitions of moral good and evil, and about his project of showing that, so defined, these are part of nature. First, Hutcheson evidently means that what causes approbation or condemnation is the *apprehension* or contemplation of "some Quality" in actions, not the quality directly.[15] Second, moral goodness is a quality of *motives* of action (in the first instance, at least) and thus of actions *as motivated*. As he sometimes puts it, the simple moral ideas arise from contemplating the "Affections of *rational Agents*" (1.i; R.264).

Third, moral value contrasts with "natural good" in two ways. Natural good is simply whatever causes pleasure, either mediately or immediately, but moral good is that the contemplation of which causes approbation. What is morally good is the contemplated quality itself. Now, approbation is a kind of pleasure. So to the extent that moral good actually tends to cause its contemplation and thus the pleasant sensation of approbation, this will make it (mediately) naturally good (for the person who contemplates it).[16] But this does not make moral goodness a species of natural goodness. Something might be no less morally good even if its existence did not *occasion*

14. Only a "strange Love of *Simplicity* in the Structure of human Nature, or Attachment to some favourite *Hypothesis*," Hutcheson writes, "has engaged many *Writers* to pass over a great many *simple Perceptions*, which we may find in ourselves" (EPA.ix–x; R.300). Within these, of course, he includes the simple ideas received by moral sense which he thought Locke had ignored.

15. At EPA.1.i, Hutcheson distinguishes between pleasures that are "simple" and those – including those involved in the perception of moral good and beauty – which "arise only upon some *previous Idea*, or *Image*, or *Assemblage*, or *Comparison of Ideas*." "*Affections, Tempers, Sentiments*, or *Actions*," he continues, "reflected upon in ourselves, or observed in others, are the constant *Occasions* of agreeable or disagreeable *Perceptions*, which we call *Approbation*, or *Dislike*." Like Hutcheson, I will sometimes adopt the convenience of saying that certain motives cause approbation. Hutcheson's terminology is confusing here, since 'simple' in this context plainly contrasts with the Lockean distinction between simple and complex ideas, which he employs in the claim that approbation is a simple idea. Approbation is a simple idea which, though a pleasure, is not a simple one.

16. There are, however, places where Hutcheson *says* that moral goodness is *immediately* good. Thus: "[S]ome Actions have to men an *immediate Goodness*; or, that by a *superior Sense*, which I call a moral one, we approve the actions of others" (*In.* intro.; R.263).

pleasurable contemplation – if, say, it tended not to call attention to itself. And it would not become morally better the more it did.

The other thing distinguishing moral good from natural good in general is that approbation is a *distinctive* pleasure – a simple idea, by Hutcheson's empiricist theory of concepts – and similarly, with appropriate changes, for condemnation. We find when we reflect on the state of mind we are in when we contemplate the "Affections of *rational Agents*" that we are then subject, spontaneously and immediately, to distinctive, simple, pleasing and displeasing ideas: approbation and condemnation.

Finally, Hutcheson says not that moral goodness is the property of causing approbation and love but, rather, that it is whatever quality of actions, if any, that causes approbation (when it is contemplated). He appends to his definition: "[W]e must be contented with these imperfect Descriptions, until we discover whether we really have such Ideas, and what general *Foundation* there is in Nature for this Difference of Actions, as morally Good or Evil" (*In*.intro.; R.261). Empirical inquiry is necessary to see if there is in fact some quality that satisfies the description. If there is, then that, it would seem, is moral goodness.

This suggests that Hutcheson intends his definition to function as a reference fixer, pointing to a certain place in the causal order of nature and identifying moral good with whatever happens to occupy it. Moral goodness would then be whatever quality in fact causes approbation, empirical inquiry being required to discover what that is. His hypothesis is that every quality that causes approbation is, in fact, some form of benevolence. Thus moral good would be the same thing as benevolence (an undeniably natural item). On this reading, benevolence would be morally good even if, contrary to fact, we did not approve it. And being approved by moral sense would turn out to be an inessential feature of being morally good.

There are other places, however, where Hutcheson seems to be denying this and to be thinking of moral goodness as the disposition to cause approbation when contemplated.[17] He sometimes treats beauty as depending on an "internal sense" in this way: "[W]ere there no Mind with a *Sense* of *Beauty* to contemplate Objects, I see not

---

17. In what follows, I am indebted to Nicholas Sturgeon for points made in a reply to my "Hutcheson on the Moral Bond," delivered at the Chapel Hill Colloquium in Philosophy in 1990.

how they could be call'd *Beautiful*."[18] And he gives his readers every reason to think he regards beauty and moral goodness as having the same ontological status. Moreover, he says that the ideas received by both the moral and the internal senses are, like those of "*Colours, Sounds, Tastes, Smells, Pleasure, Pain*," "only *Perceptions* in our Minds, and not Images of any like *external Quality*" (*IMS*.IV; R.318).[19] They thus contrast with the ideas of "*Extension, Motion, Rest*." Of this group, Hutcheson apparently believes, only the latter ideas represent natural features that are independent of our sensory makeup. Finally, Hutcheson considers the possibility that God could have constituted us with a moral sense that approved of "*Barbarity, Cruelty*, and *Fraud*," rather than benevolence, and implies (but does not say) that this would make these traits morally good (*In*.4.VII.xii; R.313).[20]

It will not matter for our purposes whether Hutcheson believed that moral good is identical with benevolence, and that being approved by moral sense is a contingent and inessential feature of it, or that moral good is the property of being such as to "procur[e]" approbation (and the desire for the agent's happiness) when contemplated, and that it is a contingent fact that all and only benevolent motives are morally good.[21] Either way, moral goodness is a feature of the natural order. To convince his readers that this is so, Hutcheson

18. In the "first" *Inquiry*, I.xvi.
19. He does sometimes speak, for example, of a "Perception of *moral Excellence*," as he does also of a "Perception of *Beauty*" (*In*.I.i; R.264). He cannot, however, mean that approbation represents, say, benevolence as having the quality of causing approbation, if only because the approbation is supposed to be a simple idea. And the passage in the text entails that, if approbation represents motives as having some simple, response-independent feature, it will involve us in massive error.
20. Cf. *IMS*.I. Here I am especially indebted to Sturgeon.
21. These issues are central in a burgeoning literature on the question of whether Hutcheson can be considered a moral realist. Much of this debate, I think, has been at cross purposes owing to a lack of agreement on how 'moral realism' should be understood. The debate was introduced by David Fate Norton's challenging but, I think, somewhat unclear claim that Hutcheson was a moral realist, in his *David Hume: Common-Sense Moralist, Sceptical Metaphysician*, pp. 55–93. This provoked vigorous replies by J. Martin Stafford, "Hutcheson, Hume, and the Ontology of Morals," *Journal of Value Inquiry* 19 (1985): 133–51; and by Kenneth P. Winkler, "Hutcheson's Alleged Moral Realism," *Journal of the History of Philosophy* 23 (1985): 179–94. Although I agree with much of the critical case made by these writers, especially with Winkler's, their positive claims are also marred, I think, by some unclarity about what moral realism must be. Norton replied to Winkler's paper in "Hutcheson's Moral Realism," *Journal of the History of Philosophy* 23 (1985): 397–418. William Frankena's famous paper "Hutcheson's Moral Sense Theory," *Journal of the History of Ideas* 16 (1955): 356–75, looms in the background of this controversy.

attempts first to show that we all do experience distinctive pleasurable and painful states of mind when we contemplate certain motives disinterestedly. Second, he argues that every motive that causes approbation and the desire for the agent's good when contemplated either is a form of benevolence (a desire for the happiness of another) or is approved because of its relation to benevolence. And third, he argues that, other things equal, our approbation increases with the extensiveness of benevolence, so that we approve most highly of *universal* benevolence.[22] In every instance, his method is the same: appeal to introspection guided by judiciously selected cases.

If successful, this line of argument establishes that it is a fact of nature that benevolence is morally good, and that universal benevolence is morally best. But what about the other moral ideas? How does Hutcheson propose to understand these within the framework of empirical naturalism? Hutcheson is famous, for example, for being the first to formulate (in English, anyway) the utilitarian dictum that *"That Action* is *best,* which procures the *greatest Happiness* for the *greatest Numbers"* (*In.*III.viii; R.284).[23] Since that an action causes the greatest happiness is a fact about its (mediate) *natural* good, how is this to be related to morality and the moral sense? Moral sense's approval of actions, after all, is based on their motives, not on their consequences. Hutcheson believes, however, that there is a species of moral evaluation of actions within which they are appropriately ranked by their consequences *and* that this species derives from the more fundamental moral evaluation of motive.

Approbation and condemnation, the simple ideas distinctive of morality, arise from an observer's rather than an agent's perspective. It is when we contemplate actions as motivated that we have these ideas. But knowing what motives are morally good does not directly answer an *agent's* question of what to do. As moral agents, Hutcheson believes, we bring moral sense to bear indirectly, "in order to regulate our *Election* among various Actions propos'd" (III.viii; R.283; emphasis added). And it is in this context that he

22. *"Benevolence* is a Word fit enough in general, to denote the internal Spring of Virtue. . . . But to understand this more distinctly, 'tis highly necessary to observe, that under this name are included very different Dispositions of the Soul. Sometimes it denotes a *calm, extensive Affection,* or Good-will toward all Beings capable of Happiness or Misery. . . . [This] first sort is above all amiable and excellent" (*In.*4: III.vi; R.282).
23. Joachim Hruschka argues that Leibniz first formulated the utility principle: "The Greatest Happiness Principle and Other Early German Anticipations of Utilitarian Theory," *Utilitas* 3 (1991): 165–77.

advances the utilitarian formula. It is not difficult to see how he must be reasoning. Moral sense approves most highly of universal benevolence, so the moral question of what to do should be seen against the background of that motive. Moral sense thus "regulate[s] our Election among various Actions propos'd" by how various options would appear against a deliberative background of universal benevolence. That motive, Hutcheson believes, aims at the greatest happiness and, given frictionless circumstances, will achieve it. "$M = B \times A$," he writes in the *Inquiry*'s earlier editions, where M is the "*Moment* of *public Good*," B is the degree of benevolence, and A is the degree of the agent's ability to do good (including, presumably, her knowledge) (2:III.xi). There is thus no inconsistency between Hutcheson's claims that moral sense approves of actions most fundamentally as motivated and that it regulates the choice of acts by means of their consequences. For him, the latter claim derives from the former.

In his later works, Hutcheson makes this point by distinguishing between "formal" and "material" goodness.[24] His definition of 'Formal goodness' is identical with that of 'moral goodness' in the *Inquiry*. An act is materially good, on the other hand, to the extent that it actually brings about the "general good of all." Moreover, Hutcheson is more explicit here about the connection between these, linking them, respectively, with the ways a "good man" would assess conduct before the fact in deliberation (material goodness) and after it (formal goodness), calling these "antecedent conscience" and "subsequent conscience," respectively. Actions are formally (morally) good when motivated by the desire for the greatest natural good; and they are materially (morally) good if they are what this desire would motivate in auspicious circumstances, that is, if they actually achieve the greatest available good overall.

Hutcheson is most explicit about his project of constructing all moral notions out of the two simple, distinctively moral ideas in the *Inquiry*'s Section VII, which he titles: "A Deduction of some *Complex moral Ideas*, viz. of *Obligation*, and *Right, Perfect, Imperfect,* and *External, Alienable,* and *Unalienable*, from this *moral Sense*." We shall ultimately be most interested in his views about obligation, but it is worthwhile pausing to note his derivation of a proto-utilitarian the-

24. *A Short Introduction to Moral Philosophy*, 2 vols. (Glasgow: Robert Foulis, 1747), vol. 1, p. 125; and *A System of Moral Philosophy*, 2 vols. (Glasgow: R. and A. Foulis, 1755), vol. 1, p. 252. Facsimiles of both are contained in vol. 4 and vols. 5–6, respectively, of *Collected Works*. Further page references to the *System* will be placed in the text as "*Sys*" (all such references are to vol. 1).

ory of rights. He begins by reminding his readers of "the *true Original of moral Ideas*, namely, "[t]his moral *Sense* of *Excellence* in every Appearance, or Evidence of *Benevolence*" (VII.i; R.292). "From this Sense too," he writes, "we derive our Ideas of RIGHTS."

> Whenever it appears to us, that a *Faculty of doing, demanding, or possessing any thing, universally allow'd in certain Circumstances, would in the Whole tend to the general Good*, we say, that one in such Circumstances has a *Right to do, possess, or demand that Thing*. And according as this Tendency to the *publick Good* is *greater* or *less*, the *Right* is *greater* or *less*. (VII.vi; R.297)

This is remarkably similar to the theory of rights Mill will offer more than a century later, but it is built on a very different foundation. Both reckon rights to depend on the contribution that practices sanctioning them (constituting Hutcheson's "faculties") would make to the general good. But, as we have seen, this is not yet bedrock for Hutcheson. The moral standing of the general good itself derives from the fact that it is the object aimed at by motives most highly approved by moral sense – motives the contemplation of which "procures" the distinctive simple idea of morality.

Hutcheson is then able to account for traditional distinctions among rights within a utilitarian framework. Rights are perfect (appropriately coercively enforced in every instance), if what they protect is so important to the public good that their universal violation *"would make human Life intolerable"* and if "allow[ing] a violent Defence, or Prosecution of such *Rights*," even outside civil government, has better consequences than "the Violation of them with Impunity" (VII.vi; R.297). Imperfect rights, on the other hand, are those not appropriately enforced with coercion, since "a violent Prosecution of such *Rights* would generally occasion greater *Evil* than the Violation of them." Similarly, the distinction between alienable and inalienable rights depends on whether "a Power . . . to transfer such *Rights* may serve some valuable Purpose" (2: VII.v; 4: VII.vii).

DUALISTIC OBLIGATION I:
THE *INQUIRY* ACCOUNT

We can turn now to Hutcheson's attempts to account for morality's normativity within empirical naturalism, and to his differences with Shaftesbury on this score. It is a measure of how far philosophical speculation about obligation had moved away from the seventeenth-century model of law that when Hutcheson presents his theory of obligation he does not even consider a conception defined in relation to his rule-based conception of rights.

The way Hutcheson presents his views on obligation (if not the views themselves) undergoes an interesting evolution over the course of his writings. We should start at the beginning, therefore, with the first edition of the *Inquiry*. "If any one ask," he there writes, "Can we have any Sense of OBLIGATION abstractly from the *Laws* of a *Superior*? we must answer according to the various Senses of the word *Obligation*" (2: VII.i). 'Obligation' is, he says, ambiguous as between two quite different meanings. One, which we may call *interested obligation*, Hutcheson takes over from Shaftesbury: "*a Motive from Self-Interest sufficient to determine all those who duly consider it, and pursue their own Advantage wisely, to a certain Course of Actions*" (VII.i; R.293).[25] Like Shaftesbury, Hutcheson concludes that in this sense there is, in fact, an obligation to virtue. The virtuous life is the happiest life, bringing the most natural good for the agent, not least because it includes the pleasure, provided by moral sense, of contemplating her own virtue and avoids self-condemnatory pain. Regarding the obligation to virtue in this sense, Hutcheson's view remained fixed and in agreement with Shaftesbury.

It is Hutcheson's second sense of 'obligation' that is of most interest. He is clear throughout his writings that there is a peculiarly moral sense of 'obligation' internal to morality and deriving *directly* from moral sense. We may therefore call this *moral obligation*. Although exactly what Hutcheson understands moral obligation to consist in is initially unclear and subsequently appears to change, he consistently rejects Shaftesbury's view that the sole rational motive for the moral life is its benefit to the agent, even benefit deriving from moral sense.

Hutcheson includes Shaftesbury among "[s]ome other Moralists" who, despite believing that "we are determin'd to perceive some *Beauty* in the Actions of others, and to love the Agent, even without reflecting upon any *Advantage* which can any way redound to us from the Action," nonetheless also hold that "we are excited to perform these Actions, even as we pursue, or purchase *Pictures, Statues,*

25. As, indeed, does Hume in the *Enquiry* (where he coins the term "interested obligation; in the *Treatise* he calls it "natural obligation"). Hume follows Hutcheson in distinguishing between interested and moral obligation. See *An Enquiry Concerning the Principles of Morals*, in Selby-Bigge and Nidditch, eds., *Enquiries*, p. 278; and *A Treatise of Human Nature*, ed. Selby-Bigge and Nidditch, p. 498.

Landskips [landscapes], from *Self-Interest*." These philosophers, he believes, recommend the virtuous life on account of the "secret Sense of Pleasure" we get from contemplating our own virtue (intro.; R.263).[26]

Of course, Hutcheson agreed with Shaftesbury that we feel a disinterested pleasure or pain in contemplating motives in others and, by reflection, in ourselves. Shaftesbury had coined the phrase 'moral sense' to refer to this capacity, and Hutcheson takes both term and idea from him. Still, Hutcheson reads the argument of Book II of Shaftesbury's *Inquiry* as saying that the only way virtue can be justified to an agent considering how to lead a life is through the fact that the virtuous life will be best *for her*. Interpreting this in light of his own hedonistic theory of value, Hutcheson takes this as committing Shaftesbury to recommending virtue primarily on account of the pleasures the virtuous derive from self-reflection.

Directly after the passage just quoted, Hutcheson announces two propositions he will undertake to prove. The first he describes in terms that emphasize his agreements with Shaftesbury: "That some Actions have to Men an *immediate Goodness*; or, that by a *superior Sense*, which I call a *Moral one*, we perceive Pleasure in the Contemplation of such Actions in others, . . . without any View of further *natural Advantage* from them."[27] The second, however, indicates his disagreement. In the first edition he puts it this way: "[W]hat excites us to these Actions which we call *Virtuous*, is not an Intention to obtain even this *sensible Pleasure* . . . but an entirely different Principle of Action from *Interest* or *Self-Love*" (1: intro.).[28] Shaftesbury's view creates an unacceptable gap between the motives of which moral sense approves and those that can give an agent reasons for acting, Hutcheson believed. According to Shaftesbury, only the agent's interests give him reasons, whereas, Shaftesbury and

26. Hutcheson does not explicitly refer to Shaftesbury here, but it is sufficiently clear that he has him in mind. See, e.g., *IMS*.v, where he does mention Shaftesbury as holding that "the Agent has a *moral Sense*, *reflects* upon his own Virtue, *delights* in it, and *chuses* to adhere to it for the *Pleasure* which attends to it."

27. In the preceding paragraph he had summarized the view of "[s]ome other Moralists" (including Shaftesbury) as being that there is "an *immediate natural Good* in the Actions called *Virtuous*." This is puzzling, however, since the immediate *natural* good he has in mind is not part of virtuous action but reflective contemplation of virtuous action.

28. And in the fourth edition: "[T]he *Affections, Desire, or Intention*, which gains *Approbation* to Actions flowing from it, is not an Intention to obtain this *sensible Pleasure* [of self-approbation] . . . but an entirely different principle of Action" (4: intro.; R.263).

Hutcheson agree, the motives we morally approve are disinterested. If such a gap is not to exist, there must be disinterested reasons to act. And if, like Shaftesbury, we understand obligation to consist in rational motive, there must be another obligation to morality other than self-interest.

To writers who, like Shaftesbury, define obligation entirely in egoistic terms, Hutcheson objects (in later editions):

> Let this Definition be substituted, wherever we meet with the words, *ought, should, must,* in a moral Sense, and many of their Sentences would seem very strange; as that the Deity *must* . . . not, or ought not to punish the Innocent, *must* make the State of the Virtuous better than that of the Wicked, *must* observe Promises; substituting the Definition . . . would make these Sentences either ridiculous, or very disputable. (*In.*4: vii.iv; R.296)

Since we use 'ought' and its synonyms "in a moral Sense," trying to reform this use by substituting the interested sense of 'obligation' yields "sentences either ridiculous, or very disputable."

So Hutcheson attempts to identify a second, distinctively moral sense of 'obligation': "*a Determination, without regard to our own Interest, to approve Actions, and to perform them*" (vii.i; R.293). The "*Determination . . . to approve*" presumably refers to moral sense. But what about a "*Determination . . . to perform*"? This suggests that moral sense includes or generates a disinterested motive and that this motive is essential to moral obligation. That thought is encouraged, moreover, by Hutcheson's also saying that God gives us moral sense "to direct our Actions" (i.viii; R.269). How can moral sense function to direct action except through the motivational force it provides? Of course, if moral sense approves in the first instance of motives and not of acts directly, then its approval can motivate only if it is a determination to act from the motives of which it approves in the first instance, and not to act *simpliciter*.

Even if this is the view of moral obligation suggested by these texts – as, indeed, by the way 'obligation' functioned in arguments of fundamental justification during the period, it was not one Hutcheson could ultimately accept. On his mature psychology, which we shall examine in the next section, no motive can have moral good as object. In this he agreed with other empirical naturalists such as Locke and Cumberland. Except for appetites and passions that need have no good in view, every motive aims at natural good, either for self or for other. That this was a significant tendency of his thinking even in the first edition of the *Inquiry* is suggested by texts surrounding those just quoted. Just after he has said that a species of obligation consists in *"a Determination, without regard to our own interest, to approve Actions, and to perform them,"* Hutcheson adds: *"which Determination shall also make us displeased with our selves, and uneasy upon having acted contrary to this Sense."* And farther on: *"*[A]nd we shall be conscious, that we are in a base unhappy State, even without considering any *Law* whatsoever, or any external Advantages lost, or Disadvantages impending from its Sanctions" (VII.i; R.293). Moreover, the full passage from the Introduction is: "[H]e has given us a MORAL SENSE, to direct our Actions, and to give us still *nobler Pleasures;* so that while we are only intending the *Good* of others, we undesignedly promote our own greatest *private Good"* (*In*.I.viii; R.269). The ultimate object of all *these* motives is natural good for the agent.

It is difficult, actually, to work out a single consistent version of the first edition's view of the relations between moral obligation, moral sense, and motivation. "We shall be conscious that we are in a base unhappy State, even without considering any *Law* whatsoever, or any external Advantages lost" suggests that, although both moral and interested obligation consist in motives related to the agent's pleasure, the former concerns an "immediate good" and the latter "external" advantages and disadvantages. But this cannot be the whole of the contrast, since Hutcheson writes of *interested* obligation: "[W]e may likewise have a sense of such *Obligation* by reflecting on this *Determination* of our *Nature* to approve *Virtue,* to be pleas'd and happy when we reflect upon our having done *virtuous Actions,* and to be uneasy when we are conscious of having acted otherwise" (VII.i). And he even adds the "superiority" of this happiness as part of the interested obligation to virtue (compare the "base unhappy State" referred to in the account of moral obligation).

A change of wording in the fourth edition may indicate that Hutcheson's ideas about the relations between moral obligation, moral sense, and motivation underwent some change. In the first edition, we find "this *internal Sense,* and *Instinct* toward *Benevolence,* will either influence our Actions, or else make us very uneasy and dissatisfy'd" (1: VII.i). This appears to attribute two kinds of motivations to moral sense:[29] first, a direct "influence" on our actions that presumably operates through seconding the motives of which it ap-

---

29. Note that if the *"Instinct* toward *Benevolence"* makes "us very uneasy and dissatisfy'd" if we do not act benevolently, the instinct must be part of moral sense and not benevolence itself.

proves, and, second, motives that Hutcheson includes under inter-ested obligation. If the first appearance is correct, Hutcheson is say-ing that distinctively moral obligation consists in the direct motiva-tional influence of moral sense.

In the fourth edition, however, Hutcheson makes a small but sig-nificant change. *"Instinct* toward *Benevolence"* is changed to *"Instinct of Benevolence"* so that the passage now reads: "[T]his *internal Sense,* and *Instinct* of *Benevolence,* will either influence . . ." (4: vii.i). This makes a big difference. It allows the interpretation that what directly motivates is not moral sense at all but benevolence, the motive of which it approves. This, indeed, is the position to which Hutcheson's psychology, worked out in the *Essay on the Nature and Conduct of the Passions and Affections* (1728), ultimately committed him.

INTERLUDE: CALM DESIRES, REASON, AND MORAL SENSE

Hutcheson makes it clear in the *Essay* that he no longer thinks, if he ever did, that moral sense can motivate, even by seconding motives of which it approves. He makes a fundamental distinction between motives – "desires" or "affections" in his terms – and any sensation or perception, including the ideas of moral sense among the latter.[30] The point first comes up in an objection he makes to Locke's account of desire as an "uneasiness." The surrounding context is interesting because it sets the stage for a major thesis of the *Essay:* Ultimate motives include disinterested as well as interested desires.

The Occasion of the imagined Difficulty in conceiving *disinterested Desires,* has probably been from the attempting to define this simple Idea, *Desire.* It is called *an uneasy Sensation in the absence of Good.* [Footnote citing Locke's *Essay*] Whereas *Desire* is as distinct from any Sensation, as the *Will* is from the *Understanding* or *Senses.* This every one must acknowledge, who speaks of *desiring to remove Uneasiness or Pain.* (EPA.24)[31]

Since approbation and condemnation are pleasures or "ideas" re-ceived by a sense, they differ from any motive (desire or affection),

---

30. On this point, see Jensen, *Motivation and the Moral Sense in Francis Hutcheson's Ethical Theory,* p. 87. Hume also distinguishes between the effect of the judgment of vice and virtue on sentiment or "taste" and its effect on motivation. See the discussion in Chapter 10.
31. See also *EPA.*44, 45, 60 and *Sys.*7, 41.

even, it seems, the desire to have, or to act on, motives that are pleasurably contemplated.

The *Essay* virtually begins, indeed, with the claim that desires always have *natural* good, or the avoidance of natural evil, as object. "DESIRES arise in our Mind, from the Frame of our Nature, upon Apprehension of Good or Evil in Objects, Actions, or Events, to obtain for *ourselves* or *others* the *agreeable Sensation,* when the Object or Event is good; or to prevent the *uneasy Sensation,* when it is evil" (*EPA*.7). This may seem like a kind of universalistic psychological hedonism, but although Hutcheson does think every desire or affection has the natural good of someone or other as object, he does not believe every motivational state does. There are springs of actions other than desires and affections – namely, "Passions" and "Appetites" – and these need not aim at any good. In Hutcheson's hands, this amounts to a distinction between motivational states that are sensitive and states that are blind to reason, respectively. Ultimately, Hutcheson's hedonism is more a *rational* than a psychological hedonism.

Typically, passions and appetites are directed "towards Objects immediately presented to some Sense" (*EPA*.29; R.303). And usually they are "attended with a *confused Sensation* either of Pleasure or Pain" and "by some violent bodily Motions, which keeps the Mind much employed upon the present Affair," preventing the consideration of alternatives and thus "all *deliberate Reasoning* about our conduct." (*EPA*.28–29). Since "we have little reason to imagine" that "other Agents have such *confused Sensations* accompanying their Desires," we can get a clear picture of *rational* motive and agency only if we "abstract from them, and consider in what manner we should act upon the several Occasions which now excite our Passions, if we had none of these *Sensations* whence our Desires become *passionate*" (*EPA*.29). The proper focus of a theory of rational agency and will, therefore, is what Hutcheson variously calls "pure" or "calm Desire" or "affection."

Now a favorite doctrine of Hutcheson's *Illustrations,* one later taken up by Hume, was that reason alone can provide no motive to action. Reason is wholly theoretical: "our *Power of finding out true Propositions*" (*IMS*.1; R.307). Although reason is intrinsically inert, Hutcheson nonetheless thinks it can have practical effect when combined with contingent human motivational susceptibilities. It can discover "*exciting Reasons*" for acting: "*Truth*[s] *that sho*[w] *a Quality in the Action, exciting the Agent to do it*" (*IMS*.1; R.308). Because the agent is disposed to desire what she apprehends as good (as a source of pleasure for herself or someone else), this rational apprehension can motivate.

Sometimes Hutcheson states his thesis of the inertness of reason in even stronger terms. In fact, much like Hume, he overstates his case; at least, what he says must be viewed as overstatement from the perspective of his theories of will, rational deliberation, and calm desire.[32] Thus he says that no truth can be an exciting reason "previous to *Affection*" or "*end*" (*IMS*.1; R.308–9). The clear implication of this usage is that exciting reasons are all and only truths about the relation between action and one of the agent's ends or the object of one of her affections. "But are there not," he imagines an objector asking, "also exciting Reasons, even previous to any end, moving us to propose one end rather than another?" (*IMS*.1; R.309). Hutcheson responds that some ends must be ultimate and that, although "*subordinate Ends* may be called *reasonable*" by virtue of their relation to ultimate ends, "as to the *ultimate Ends*, to suppose *exciting Reasons* for them, would infer, that there is no *ultimate End* but that we desire one thing for another in an infinite Series" (*IMS*.1; R.309).

The psychological nature of human beings, however, might contingently be such that discovery of some truths (through reason) can move an agent to adopt something as an ultimate end. This, in fact, is Hutcheson's own position. He holds that we are naturally so constituted that when we apprehend the prospect of pleasure we tend then to desire it, to seek it as end. And he explicitly denies that whenever we do, it is as a means to some further end of good or pleasure in general, whether for self or for others: "We need not imagine any Innate idea of *Good in general*, of *infinite Good*, or of the *greatest Aggregate:* Much less need we suppose any *actual Inclination* toward any of these, as the *Cause* or *Spring* of all particular Desires" (*EPA*.32). What is true, he says, is simply that "we must, by the Constitution of our Nature, desire any apprehended Good which occurs a-part from any Evil," and that *subsequently*, by abstraction, we form an abstract desire for good, both our own and generally (*EPA*.32).

---

32. Thus Hume says, like Hutcheson, that discovering "the prospect of pain or pleasure from any object, we feel a consequent emotion of aversion or propensity," but also, and more famously, that "reason is, and ought only to be the slave of the passions" (*Treatise*, pp. 414, 415). For an important corrective to the usual view of Hume, which emphasizes the latter to the exclusion of the former, see Nicholas Sturgeon, "Hume on Reason and Passion," unpublished manuscript.

Hutcheson's strictures on practical reason in the context of his critique of ethical rationalism in *Illustrations* are familiar aspects of his thought, but they must be balanced against the view of rational deliberation contained in his *Essay* theory of calm desire and the will. Calm desires are precisely those motivational states that arise from a "rational Apprehension of Good or Evil," that is, from reason's discovery of the prospect of pleasure or pain for someone or other (*EPA.*63). The desire or affection does not, of course, result from rational apprehension alone; an appropriate motivational susceptibility or "instinct" is required. But it is important to see that the requisite instinct *embeds a conception of rationality:* It is a disposition to desire private or public happiness when the latter is rationally apprehended. On these grounds Hutcheson refers to calm affection as "rational Desire" (*EPA.*65). And his definition of *will* connects it conceptually to calm desire and the rational apprehension of good: "[t]he *Will,* or *Appetitus Rationalis,* or the disposition of Soul to pursue what is presented as good, and to shun Evil" (*IMS.*1). Finally, he notes that when a desire's object is abstract, such as the desire for a greater (or the greatest) good, this will require the capacity "to reflect and compare the several goods."[33]

Hutcheson lists twenty different "Maxims, or natural Laws of *calm Desire*" (*EPA.*39). These are evidently intended to describe the phenomenon of fully calm desire, that is, desire for good and evil "as they appear to our *Reason* or *Reflection*" without the attendant sensual confusion and violence of the passions (*EPA.*29).

The first two laws define selfish and "Benevolent or *publick*" desires, respectively. When taken exhaustively (as evidently intended), they entail universal hedonism – not as a thesis about all motivation but as a claim about rationally motivating states: the motives of a rational human will.

1. Selfish *Desires* pursue ultimately only the private Good of the Agent.
2. Benevolent or *publick Desires* pursue the Good of others, according to the *Systems* to which we extend our Attention, but with different Degrees of Strength. (*EPA.*39)[34]

---

33. See *EPA.*43 and *IMS.*1, where Hutcheson says that the ultimate ends of our own greatest happiness and the greatest happiness of all would not "occur to us without reflection."
34. For a discussion of Hutcheson's arguments that benevolence is a genuine human motive, and against the egoistic hedonism of John Clarke, see Robert M. Stewart, "John Clarke and Francis Hutcheson on Self-Love and Moral Motivation," *Journal of the History of Philosophy* 20 (1982): 261–78.

It is the third law that states the central idea of Hutcheson's theory of calm desire.

3. The *Strength* either of the *private* or *publick* Desire of any Event, is proportional to the imagined *Quantity of Good* . . . (*EPA*.39)

The other laws elaborate this basic idea in various ways, making it clear that the strength of calm desire depends on total net good or, rather, on *expectable* total net good and that the value of pleasure depends only on its duration and intensity.[35]

On the face of it, there is a problem about how Hutcheson means his theory of calm desire to be understood. For it may seem obviously false that our desires track total expectable net pleasure, even when they are preceded by thoughts of obtainable good or pleasure. To elaborate further an example that Hutcheson mentions himself, we may well desire the happiness of family, friends, and countrymen out of proportion to its value in the universal scheme, even though the former desires result from rational apprehensions of the good of these "narrower systems." And a similar remark might be made about temporal perspective in the intrapersonal case. An agent may have a greater desire for some pleasure in the nearer future than for an exactly equal pleasure in the farther future, even though the former desire is occasioned by an apprehension of the opportunity to obtain pleasure now.[36] That, we recall, was a major factor lying behind Locke's theory of practical judgment.

Hutcheson provides little help with this problem in the *Essay*, but there are remarks in the *System* that suggest what his response might have been.[37]

When the Soul is calm and attentive to the Constitution and Powers of other Beings, their natural Actions and Capacities of Happiness and Misery, and

35. The third law, taken by itself, might seem to be saying only that the strength of calm desires varies in direct proportion to the amount of pleasure for the particular people for whom the pleasure is desired. But even if it is understood in this way, later laws make it clear that what matters is total net good, including all persons.
36. Hutcheson admits some tendency for calm desires to work in this way, but not beyond what can explained in terms of differences in expectation. Thus Law 14 states that "to Beings of *limited uncertain Duration*, the Earliness of Commencement increases the Moment of any Good, according to the Hazard of the *Possessor's Duration*. This may, perhaps, account for what some alledge to be a *natural Disposition* of our Minds, even previous to any Reflection on the Uncertainty of Life, viz., that we are so constituted, as to desire more ardently the *nearer* Enjoyments than the more distant, tho' of equal Moment in themselves, and as certainly to be obtained by us" (*EPA*.41–42).
37. See note 24.

when the selfish Appetites and Compassions and Desires are asleep, 'tis alleged that there is a calm Impulse of the Soul to desire the greatest Happiness and Perfection of the largest System within the Compass of its Knowledge. (*Sys*.10)

The sense, then, in which the strength of calm public desires naturally varies with expectable total net good is that this is the case when the mind is calm and "attentive to the Constitution and Powers of other Beings." "When upon recollection we present to our minds the notion of the greatest possible system of sensitive beings, and the highest it can enjoy, there is also a calm determination to desire it" (*Sys*.50). Likewise, in the intrapersonal case, "there is found in the human Mind, when it recollects itself, a calm determination toward personal happiness of the highest kind it has any notion of" (*Sys*.50).

It is illuminating to view the laws of calm desire, therefore, as embedding an ideal of rational deliberation. They are empirical generalizations, but about an ideal human deliberator whose deliberations are free of the perturbing influence of passion and appetite, and who is perfectly informed about, and attentively considering of, all natural goods in prospect. Passion and appetite, we recall, "prevent all *deliberate Reasoning* about our Conduct" (*EPA*.29). Nothing in the idea of rational apprehension of facts concerning pleasure and pain, Hutcheson thinks, *entails* that private and public calm desires of the appropriate strength will arise from it. But human beings do have these dispositions, as a matter of fact; we are disposed to the most extensive private and public desires, respectively, "when upon Recollection we present to our Minds" the most extensive notions, respectively, of our own happiness and of the happiness of all.[38]

Hutcheson has, then, a much farther-reaching account of the practical role of reason than, taken on its own, the *Illustrations* might suggest. Reason is no mere instrument to ends antecedently given. On the contrary, reason is itself required in order to raise the calm affections – most important, the "two grand determinations" of our nature: "one toward our own greatest happiness, the other toward the greatest general good" (*Sys*.50). Moreover, each of these two dominant calm desires, when properly raised by reason, is "capable

38. Hutcheson certainly believes it possible, in some sense, that the apprehension of possible evil to a creature could lead to a desire to bring it about. Thus he imagines the existence of *"antecedent Minds"* who choose "what *manner of Sense* they would have desired for Mankind": "Had they been *malicious,* as we suppose the Devil, the *contrary Tendency* of the *contrary Sense* would have excited their *Election* of it" (*IMS*.1).

of such strength as to restrain all the particular affections of its kind, and keep them subordinate to itself" (*Sys.*50). Hutcheson thus accepts what, in discussing Cumberland's similar view, we called the *calm reflective deliberation view*. Calm, reason-informed reflection leads to motivation for moral conduct that is unrestricted to antecedently given ends.

To sum up: There are two ultimate independent rational motives or ends – two calm desires that arise from the maximal calm use of theoretical reason: the desire for one's greatest pleasure and the desire for the greatest pleasure for all. Every rational motive is a desire for some natural good for some "sensitive being" or other, but each of the two "grand determinations" (the desire for greatest pleasure for self and the desire for the greatest pleasure for all) rationally trumps all "particular Affections of its kind."

Even with this abbreviated description of his moral psychology we can see why, by the time he wrote the *Essay*, Hutcheson could not have believed that moral sense motivates directly. All rational motives concern the prospects of *natural* good to the agent or to others, whereas moral sense concerns *moral* good, and moral good is no species of natural good. It remains true that moral sense makes possible natural goods that would otherwise not exist – most prominently, Hutcheson believes, the agent's pleasurable contemplation of her own morally good motives.[39] But the motive to realize these goods remains a form of Shaftesburean interested obligation.

Still, Hutcheson also rightly believes that he has sketched in the *Essay* a substantial alternative to Shaftesbury. Shaftesbury included benevolent motivation in human nature but thought it could form no basis for a reflective practical endorsement of the moral life. He was forced to this conclusion, Hutcheson thinks, because he supposed there to be only one organizing motive; only the agent's interest on the whole provides a framework within which she can order her pursuits in a rational way. But it is a central thesis of the *Essay* that agents have a second organizing motive. Just as an agent can order the goods she can realize *for herself* within a conception of her good

39. In the *Essay*, Hutcheson works out a theory of how certain kinds of pleasures can be superior to others (a view already implicit in the *Inquiry*) and defends the superiority of the pleasures of moral sense on this theory. The theory is remarkably like Mill's: "It is obvious that those alone are capable of judging [the value ("intenseness") of a pleasure] who have experienced all the several *kinds of Pleasure*, and have their *Senses* acute and fully exercised in them all" (*EPA*.129). See Mark Philip Strasser, "Hutcheson on the Higher and Lower Pleasures," *Journal of the History of Philosophy* 25 (1987): 517–31.

on the whole, so likewise can she order goods she can realize *for someone or other*. Particular benevolence stands to "calm extensive Benevolence" as the agent's desire for particular goods for herself stands to calm self-love. By the time he wrote the *Essay*, then, Hutcheson believed that agents have a source of disinterested motivation not in moral sense but in its most highly approved *object* (universal benevolence), *and* that this motive is no less rational than the agent's desire for her own greatest happiness. This, presumably, is why he changed "*Instinct* toward *Benevolence*" to "*Instinct of Benevolence*" in his discussion of moral obligation in later editions of the *Inquiry*.

Hutcheson had another route to the conclusion that moral sense cannot directly motivate actions of which it approves. Suppose that desire could have moral good as well as natural good for its object. And assume that moral sense's approval of a motive generates a desire to have and act from that motive. Even were this so, it would not follow that a judgment of moral value, or a sentiment on the basis of which we attribute it, provides even a subsidiary, or seconding, motive to morally good action. Consider, first, how it might. If morally good motives were like Kantian maxims or *principles of action* (like the principle of bearing small sacrifices to aid others in greater need), then there would be no reason why a desire to act on them could not help in motivating appropriately principled action when they apply. But, for Hutcheson, morally good motives are not even implicitly self-regulating in this way. Their ultimate object is never a principled course of action but always a state of affairs: someone's experiencing pleasure. Hutcheson believes all morally good motives are forms of benevolence – a desire for the happiness of others. The morally good person's interest in action is thus purely *instrumental* – her motives look *through* action to the state of the beneficiary's happiness. The virtuous agent has no intrinsic concern, as moral, for how she regulates *conduct*.

The desire to have and act on motives of *this* sort cannot motivate actions that realize this desire. Benevolence is not a motive that can be *adopted* like a Kantian principle of action. Hutcheson makes the point himself in the process of arguing that benevolence cannot derive from self-love: "[W]ere we assured that, whether our Country were happy or not, it should not affect our future Happiness; but that we should be rewarded, provided we *desired the Happiness of our Country*; our Self-Love could never make us now desire the *Happiness of our Country*" (EPA.18). In such a situation we would desire to

desire the happiness of our country, just as the desire to act on benevolent motives might lead us to desire to desire the happiness of
others. But in neither situation would the relevant first-order desire
be generated. Benevolence arises only as a response to the consideration of its *object*, the happiness of others, and then only by the
"frame of our nature."

But what if an agent already has benevolent motives? Might the
desire to act on them not help to motivate morally good action by
seconding these? Not directly. Hutcheson treats the moral goodness
of an action as directly proportional to the intensity and extensiveness of the benevolence realized in it.[40] A desire to act benevolently
might cause one to act when benevolent motives would have been
insufficient by themselves. But that could increase the moral value
above what already existed in the inefficacious benevolent motives
only if it could somehow increase the degree of benevolence itself.
Although it cannot do that directly, it can move an agent to direct her
attention to prospects of natural good that are "naturally apt to raise"
benevolent motives (*EPA*.26). This indirect influence of moral sense
would be no different, however, from the way Hutcheson thinks
interested motives such as the desire to have the pleasure of contemplating one's own virtue or the desire for heavenly reward can
motivate benevolence (*EPA*.26).[41]

Here then are three reasons why Hutcheson was committed to the
view that moral sense cannot directly motivate actions of which it
approves. First, moral sense receives sensation or perception, and
Hutcheson explicitly distinguishes between these and desire. Second, all "calm" desires are for some natural good, either for oneself
or for others, and are never for moral good per se. And, third, actions
are morally good only to the degree they manifest *benevolence* and no
other desire.[42]

Hutcheson combines the latter two considerations in a remarkable
criticism of Shaftesbury's doctrine that virtue requires self-regulation
through moral sense, which he is led to characterize in terms that
Shaftesbury would doubtless have hardly recognized. "SOME alledge, that MERIT supposes, beside *kind Affection*, that the Agent has a
moral Sense, reflects upon his own Virtue, *delights* in it, and *chuses* to ad-

40. See *In*.III.xi; R.285f.
41. I am indebted to Nicholas Sturgeon for reminding me of this.
42. In addition to the primary sense of morally good actions, Hutcheson also holds
    that acts can be morally good *to choose* to the extent that they realize the object of
    universal benevolence: the greatest happiness for the greatest number.

here to it for the *Pleasure* which attends it" (*IMS*.v).[43] Hutcheson's psychology required him to reshape his understanding of Shaftesbury's
view in two significant ways. First, Shaftesbury held that moral sense
motivates. "'Tis evident," he wrote, "that a creature having this sort of
sense [natural moral sense] . . . in any degree must necessarily act
according to it, if it happens not to be opposed" (*Char*.1.265). And
second, although he did hold that reflective rational endorsement of
the virtuous life can proceed only from the perspective of the agent's
interest, he also affirmed that agents have an intrinsic, higher interest
in leading lives of which moral sense approves, and in the harmonious, balanced life it makes possible. But neither a desire for moral
goodness nor a desire for any nonhedonic good for the self makes
psychological sense for Hutcheson. So he is required to understand
Shaftesbury as holding that the additional motive moral sense gives
agents for being virtuous is the desire for the pleasurable contemplation, through moral sense, of their own virtue.[44] And, he remarks,
"[t]his Reflection shews to him a Motive of Self-Love, the joint view to
which does not increase our *Approbation*" (*IMS*.v).[45]

This brings into relief a point that reemerges in various guises in
Hutcheson. For Shaftesbury, as later for Butler and Kant, only a self-

43. Hutcheson refers explicitly to Shaftesbury's *Inquiry* at this point.
44. Hutcheson gives an absolutely scathing description of the position he attributes
    to Shaftesbury and the Stoics: "That this *affectionate Temper* is true Virtue, and not
    that *undisturbed Selfishness*, were it attainable, every one would readily own who
    saw them both in Practice. Would any honest Heart relish such a Speech as this
    from a *Cato* or from an *Æmelius Paulus*? 'I foresee the Effects of this Defeat, my
    Fellow-Creatures, my *Countrymen*, my honourable *Acquaintances;* many a generous
    gallant *Patriot* and *Friend*, *Fathers*, *Sons*, and *Brothers*, *Husbands*, and *Wives*, shall
    be inslaved, tortured, torn from each other, or in each other's sight made subject
    to the *Pride*, *Avarice*, *Petulancy*, or *Lust* of the Conqueror. I have, for my *own
    Pleasure*, to secure agreeable *Reflections*, laboured in their defence. I am uncon-
    cerned in their Misfortunes, their *bodily Tortures*, or more exquisite *Distresses of
    Mind* for each other, are to me indifferent. I am entirely absolute, compleat in
    myself; and can behold their Agonies with as much Ease or Pleasure, as I did
    their prosperity.' This is the plain Language of some boasting *Refiners* upon
    Virtue; Sentiments as disagreeable as those of *Catiline*" (*EPA*.119–20).
45. Thus he turns on its head the Kantian view that morally good conduct must
    proceed from an explicitly moral motive. One reason Kant would later give for
    thinking that morally good action can only be motivated by the sense of duty
    through pure practical reason is that any motivation which "presuppose[s] an
    object (material) of the faculty of desire" "belong[s] under the general principle of
    self-love." *Critique of Practical Reason*, trans. Lewis White Beck (Indianapolis, Ind.:
    Bobbs-Merrill, 1956), pp. 19, 20. But Hutcheson maintains that, on the contrary,
    the only self-consciously moral motive is itself an instance of self-love. If, there-
    fore, morally good actions are not motivated by self-love, they cannot, Hutcheson
    concludes, arise from any motive that derives from moral judgment.

regulating moral *agent* can have genuine virtue or merit. For Hutcheson, however, moral goodness attaches entirely to a motive *in* an agent – indeed, to one whose object is a state of affairs whose realization does not essentially involve self-regulating agency in any way.

DUALISTIC OBLIGATION II:
THE *ILLUSTRATIONS* ACCOUNT

There is, then, no self-consciously moral motivation of which moral sense itself approves. Nor can moral sense motivate directly. The upshot is that if moral obligation is to be a rational motive to morality of which moral sense approves, thereby closing the gap created by Shaftesbury's theory, it cannot be any motive deriving from (or re-quiring) the agent's moral sense itself. Or, alternatively, if moral obli-gation is to be essentially moral, dependent on moral sense, then it cannot be a motive to morally good action. Hutcheson, for reasons he does not make clear, chooses the latter option. Here is the view of obligation he presents in *Illustrations:*

When we say one is obliged to an Action we either mean, 1. *That the Action is necessary to obtain Happiness to the Agent, or to avoid Misery: Or, 2. That every Spectator, or he himself upon Reflection, must approve his Action, and disapprove his omitting it, if he considers fully all its Circumstances.* (IMS.1)

Interested obligation remains roughly as it was, but moral obligation is fundamentally changed, with not even an implicit reference to motive. Hutcheson now says that it simply consists in the reflective *sentiments* of approbation and condemnation.[46]

It might be thought that by claiming moral obligation to consist in the approval and disapproval of moral sense, Hutcheson was no longer disagreeing with Shaftesbury. Granted, Shaftesbury did not *call* the approval or disapproval of moral sense a moral obligation, but that might have been just a semantic difference. Hutcheson took himself, however, to be in substantial disagreement with Shaftesbury even here.

Shaftesbury, it will be recalled, described moral sense as involving generalized second-order affections: "[T]here arises another kind of affection towards those very affections themselves, which have been already felt, and are now become the subject of a new liking or

46. On this point, see Frankena, "Hutcheson's Moral Sense Theory," p. 364.

dislike" (*Char.*1.251). In the first edition of his *Inquiry*, Hutcheson took a broadly similar view, writing that moral sense is *"a Determination of our Minds to receive amiable or disagreeable Ideas of* Actions" (1: 1.viii). Moral good procures approbation, he says; and moral evil, *"Aversion, and Dislike"* (1: intro.). By the *Inquiry*'s third edition (1729), however, Hutcheson is clear that the approval or disapproval of moral sense cannot be understood in such broad terms. He still calls the idea that moral good elicits "approbation," but the effect of contemplating moral evil he now calls "condemnation." And he says of both that they are *simple ideas*, different from those involved in other positively and negatively valenced sentiments. Moral sense, moreover, he defines as "a Determination of our Minds to receive the simple Ideas of Approbation or Condemnation, from Actions observed" (4: 1.viii; R.269). Thus, even if by 1729 Hutcheson held that moral obligation consists in no more than the approval and disapproval of moral sense, he nonetheless also came to understand the latter in very different terms from Shaftesbury's. The moral obligation to avoid moral evil, he now believed, could not adequately be conceived as dislike, aversion, or a negative aesthetic response to evil. The obligation to avoid evil (implicit in the response that defines it *as* moral evil) is *condemnation*, morality's distinctive negative idea. From the third edition on, the *Inquiry*'s subtitular reference to defending Shaftesbury's principles against Mandeville's attacks was dropped.

These points notwithstanding, it is somewhat puzzling that Hutcheson took a *sentimentalist* approach to obligation, since his psychology makes such a sharp distinction between the simple sentiments of moral sense and rational motive, and since he so clearly accepted the *calm deliberation view*, on whose basis Cumberland had concluded that moral agents are obligated by the good of all. In disconnecting obligation from rational motive, Hutcheson implicitly rejected without any evident rationale the understanding of obligatory force that had become so widely accepted in early modern British ethics (especially among empiricist-minded philosophers), even as that understanding continued to underlie his conception of interested obligation.

The account of moral obligation in *Illustrations* could still be said to be an "internal" theory, but not an internalist theory in our sense, because it situates the moral 'ought' within the perspective of an *observer* rather than that of a deliberating *agent*: "[E]very Spectator, or he himself upon Reflection, must approve his Action" (*IMS*.1). The distinctive force of morality reveals itself not within the agent's context of deliberation and choice but when, as spectators, we contemplate and respond to the deliberated actions of others or ourselves.

We might reasonably ask, What, then, does Hutcheson suppose to be the genus of which interested and moral obligation are species? Trivially: obligation. But what, in general, is that? This puzzle deepens when we realize that part of Hutcheson's aim in the *Essay* is to argue that moral motives (those of which moral sense approves) are no less a source of rational motivation than motives of self-interest. Universal benevolence is no less ultimate a calm or reason-informed desire than is self-love, and no less capable of organizing deliberation. Together, they are "two grand determinations." Thus, had he wanted, Hutcheson could have identified moral obligation with benevolence. He could have held that obligation is generally to be understood in terms of rational motive, and also that there exists another obligation in addition to interested obligation – one we might reasonably call moral, since it is approved of by moral sense and is no less authoritative in the deliberations of a rational agent.

In holding that human agents have two independent and incommensurable sources of rational motivation, Hutcheson begins a tradition in British ethical thought that leads to Sidgwick's "dualism of practical reason."[47] Sidgwick, of course, came to view the dualism as a problem. If it is just as rational to seek one's own greatest good as it is to seek the greatest good of all, what can possibly assure us that these equally rational ends do not conflict? What basis can we have for thinking that practical reasons are not in irresoluble conflict, and the moral agent hopelessly divided against herself?

According to the *Essay*'s psychology, a human agent lacks any deliberative perspective from which she can rationally comprehend her two ultimately authoritative sources of reasons. According to "the natural Laws of *calm Desire*," "the *Strength* either of the *private* or *publick* Desire of any Event, is proportioned to the imagined *Quantity of Good*, which will arise from it to the Agent, or the Person for whose sake it is desired" (*EPA*.39). But, though Hutcheson does not address the matter directly, he must think the proportion to be different for

47. Sidgwick himself cites Butler as the source of his idea. "Butler's express statement of the duality of the regulative principles in human nature constitutes an important step in ethical speculation; since it brings into clear view the most fundamental difference between the ethical thought of modern England and that of the old Greco-Roman world." See *Outlines of the History of Ethics*, p. 197. See also William Frankena, "Sidgwick and the History of Ethical Dualism," in Bart Schultz, ed., *Essays on Henry Sidgwick* (Cambridge: Cambridge University Press, 1992), pp. 175–98.

the two cases, private and public. If he did not, since universal benevolence (as Hutcheson understands it) always includes the agent's good as one among others, he should believe that benevolence always overrides self-love when, on reflection, they conflict. But what he says is quite different: "When any Event may affect both the *Agent* and *others*, if the Agent have both *Self-Love* and *publick Affections*, he acts according to that Affection which is *strongest*, when there is any *Opposition* of Interests" (*IMS.1*). And frequently he writes that the greatest obstacle to agents' acting on their natural benevolence is the belief that its object conflicts with the object of self-love.[48]

The Hutchesonian agent evidently cannot balance reasons provided by her own good against those provided by the good of all. She must regard herself as having two utterly incommensurable (indeed, incomparable) kinds of reasons – agent-neutral, moral reasons, having various "moral weights" and related to their own distinctive moral obligation, on the one hand, and agent-relative reasons of personal good, having various "prudential weights" and related to their own distinctive prudential obligation, on the other.[49] Rational deliberation runs out once she reckons the relation of options to each of her ultimate ends. Then, it seems, she can do no more than act on whichever of calm self-love or calm benevolence happens to be stronger, with no judgment possible of which reasons might be weightier, either in a particular case or in general. Her only hope is that these reasons never really conflict. Happily, Hutcheson believes, this is so. By designing human nature so that our greatest pleasures derive from the agent's reflection on her own benevolence and from other pleasures derived from benevolent association with others, God joined calm benevolence and calm self-love together and thereby unified practical reason.

If he discovers this Truth, that "his constant pursuit of *publick Good* is the most probable way of promoting his *own Happiness*," then his Pursuit is truly reasonable and constant; thus both Affections [calm benevolence and calm self-love] are at once gratified, and he is consistent with himself. (*EPA.227–28*)

48. "[T]he only way to give publick Affections their full Force, and to make them prevalent in our Lives, must be to remove these *Opinions of opposite Interests,* and to shew a superior Interest on their side" (*EPA*.viii–ix). See also *EPA*.19, 26, 89.
49. For the distinction between agent-relative and agent-neutral, see Chapter 4, note 34. In calling the agent-neutral reasons of benevolence "moral reasons," I mean only that they are reasons of which moral sense approves – not, of course, that these reasons *involve* moral sense.

Had God not thus joined self-love and benevolence, reasonable conduct in pursuit of one fundamental rational aim would be unreasonable from the perspective of the other. "Truly reasonable" conduct and self-consistency would be impossible.

UNIFYING REASONS AND AGENCY IN THE *SYSTEM*

By the time he wrote the *System*, Hutcheson was evidently dissatisfied with this state of affairs.[50] He continued to accept the *Essay*'s doctrine that will, "the general springs of action in every rational agent," is "a new motion of the soul, distinct from all sensation, perception, or judgment," and that this arises "as soon as any sense, opinion, or reasoning represents an object or event as immediately good or pleasant, or as the means of future pleasure, or of security from evil," either for ourselves or others (*Sys*.7). And he continued to proclaim the ultimate coordinate status of calm self-love and universal benevolence (*Sys*.50). But he no longer found it satisfactory to think that, ultimately, rational deliberation engages no more than these two calm desires.

But here arises a new perplexity in this complex structure, where these two principles seem to draw different ways. Must the generous determination, and all its particular affections, yield to the selfish one, and be under its controll? must we indulge their kind motions so far as private interest admits and no further? or must the selfish yield to the generous? or can we suppose that in this complex system there are two ultimate principles which may often oppose each other, without any umpire to reconcile their differences? (*Sys*.50–51)

The *Essay* doctrine was that there can be no *practical* umpire between calm benevolence and calm self-love. Through moral sense we *approve* of benevolence, but this approbation is, in itself, deliberatively inert. It can give considerations of general happiness no greater weight as *practical reasons*. But if no deliberative umpire is possible, neither is any needed. God has designed a preestablished harmony between self-love and benevolence, and the consistency of rational human agency is thereby preserved.

50. Scott places this between 1734 and 1738, or six to ten years after the first edition of the *Essay/Illustrations*. See Scott, *Francis Hutcheson*, p. 113.

In the *System*, however, Hutcheson writes that this picture "must appear a complex confused fabrick, without any order or regular consistent design" (*Sys*.74). What is more, he adds that its solution requires "a distinct consideration of [the] moral faculty." "By means of it, all is capable of harmony, and all its powers may conspire in one direction, and be consistent with each other" (*Sys*.74).

Commentators frequently note that Hutcheson was much influenced by Joseph Butler's *Sermons* (1726), and nowhere is this more evident than in the *System*, where he appears to take over Butler's idea that the deliberative authority of a faculty can be inferred from its manifest function and design. At points, he even echoes Butler's doctrine that the supreme authority of the moral faculty can be inferred in this way: "This moral sense from its very nature appears to be designed for regulating and controlling all our powers" (*Sys*.61). But it is also clear that he cannot be thinking of moral sense as having the authoritative deliberative role Butler gives to conscience:

This moral faculty plainly shews that we are also capable of calm settled universal benevolence, and that this is destined, as the supreme determination of the generous kind, to govern and controll our particular generous as well as selfish affections; as the heart must entirely approve its doing thus in its calmest reflections. (*Sys*.74)[51]

For Butler, the moral faculty is itself the authoritative deliberative faculty, the seat of practical *judgment*.[52] Only through this "principle of reflection," Butler believes, can an agent regulate her conduct by judging on which motives (principles) – benevolence, self-love, or particular passions – she should act. This is one of the things Butler aims to express by his familiar doctrine that the moral faculty is *authoritative*, namely, that it governs the deliberations of a self-regulating agent. In the *System*, Hutcheson evidently feels the pull of Butler's thesis, but this passage already signals an important difference. The 'this' that Hutcheson says is destined to govern and override all other desires is "calm settled universal benevolence."

Butler sometimes tries to argue for the final deliberative authority of the moral faculty on the basis of its apparent function and

51. Presumably, if "calm settled universal benevolence" is to govern not only particular generous affections but all particular selfish affections, it must also govern calm self-love *should* they conflict. Note also that Hutcheson now describes moral sense as involving "calm reflection," the term he had reserved for the kind of deliberative reflection that elicits reasons to act.
52. See, in Chapter 9, "Conscience, Autonomy, and Self-Authorization."

design.[53] But Hutcheson poses a general objection to any such argument.

> To allege here that, by our reason and reflection, we may see what was the intention of God the Author of our Nature in this whole fabrick of our affections; that he plainly intended the universal happiness, and that of each individual, as far as it is consistent with it; and that this intention should be our rule: that we should therefore restrain and controll, not only all selfish affections, but even all generous particular affections, within such bounds as the universal interest requires: this is true in fact, but does not remove the difficulty, *unless we are first told from what determination of soul, from what motive, are we to comply with the divine intentions?* (*Sys.*51; emphasis added)

Knowledge of the design and function of the moral faculty and benevolence cannot make the moral faculty a *practical* umpire between self-love and benevolence, since it does not yet properly situate the moral faculty with respect to the will.

Hutcheson thus faces a dilemma in the *System*. On the one hand, his theory of the will, continued from the *Essay*, restricts rational motivation to self-love and benevolence and seems to provide no place for genuinely *practical* judgment between these should they conflict. On the other, he wants to hold some version of Butler's position that the moral faculty provides the agent with just such a perspective or, at least, a perspective from which we can see that benevolence should always govern.

As background to Hutcheson's attempt to resolve this dilemma we should note his doctrine, carried throughout his ethical writings, that some natural goods (pleasures) are intrinsically superior to others.[54] Unlike Mill, he does not contrast this intrinsic value with the "intenseness" of pleasure. "[T]he *Value* of any Pleasure, and the *Quantity* or *Moment* of any Pain," he maintains, "is in a compounded Proportion of the *Intenseness* and *Duration*" (*EPA*.127). Hutchesonian "intenseness," however, *includes* Millian quality. There is no measure of it other than by the preferences of mature judges, ideally experienced and sensitive: "It is obvious that 'those alone are capable of judging, who have experienced all the several *kinds of Pleasure*, and have their *Senses* acute and fully exercised in them all" (*EPA*.129). That the pleasures of virtue are more "intense" than all others is

---

53. I discuss in Chapter 9 this line of argument in relation to a different "transcendental argument" Butler makes for the authority of conscience as a necessary assumption for the very possibility of autonomous practical reason.
54. The doctrine is clearest in the *Essay*. See Strasser, "Hutcheson on the Higher and Lower Pleasures."

shown by the fact that "all virtuous Men have given *Virtue* this testimony, that its Pleasures are superior to any other, nay to all others jointly" (*EPA*.130). To this general position Hutcheson ingeniously adds in the *System* the observation that, unlike other higher pleasures, the pleasures of self-approbation are only increased by requiring the sacrifice of other pleasures.

In all other grateful perceptions, the less we shall relish our state, the greater sacrifice we have made of inferior enjoyments to the superior; and our sense of the superior, after the first flutter of joy in our success is over, is not a whit increased by any sacrifice we have made to it. . . . But in moral good, the greater the necessary sacrifice was which was made to it, the moral excellence increases the more. . . . By this sense the heart can not only approve itself in sacrificing every other gratification to moral goodness, but have the highest self-enjoyment. (*Sys*.61–62)[55]

This strengthens his earlier arguments that moral sense makes possible the coincidence of self-love and benevolence. Not only is the agent's reflection on his own benevolence the most important good, it is a good which only *increases* as (and to the degree that) sacrifices in other goods are required.

Still, this does not yet provide Hutcheson the resolution he wants; it makes the deliberative priority of benevolence too dependent on extrinsic factors. So for the first time he declares:

In those cases where some inconsistency appears between these two determinations, the moral faculty at once points out and recommends the glorious the amiable part; not by suggesting prospects of future interests of a sublime sort by pleasures of self-approbation, or of praise. It recommends the generous part by an immediate undefinable perception. . . . And thus, where the moral sense is in its full vigour, it makes the generous determination to publick happiness the supreme one in the soul, with that commanding power which it is naturally destined to exercise. (*Sys*.77)

But the question remains. How, on Hutcheson's scheme, can moral reflection practically recommend benevolence? The issue is not how it *morally* recommends benevolence – that is, how it grounds the attribution of moral goodness, as Hutcheson defines it. The issue, rather, is how it can recommend universal benevolence as having *deliberative* priority, as responding to weightier reasons to act. There simply seems to be no way for moral reflection to play this *practically regulative* role consistently with Hutcheson's theory of the will.

---

55. He adds that this "plainly shews this moral sense to be naturally destined to command all other powers."

But the moral faculty may play a crucial role in recommending benevolence, not by some practically effective endorsement of its reasons as superior to those of self-love but as having a superior *intrinsic natural* goodness to the agent. The *Inquiry* had maintained that the most important value the agent can achieve by benevolence is extrinsic: "[A] virtuous Temper is called *good* or *beatifick*, not that it is always attended with Pleasure in the Agent . . . but from this, that every Spectator is persuaded that the reflex Acts of the virtuous Agent upon his own temper will give him the highest Pleasures" (4: I.viii; R.270). In the *System*, however, Hutcheson writes that in referring to "the peculiar happiness of the virtuous man" he does not mean the "private sublime pleasures in frequent future reflections which recommends virtue to the soul." Rather, "we feel an impulse, an ardour toward perfection, toward affections and actions of dignity, and feel their immediate excellence, abstracting from such views of future pleasures of long duration" (*Sys.*118). And, describing a "class of enjoyments [which] are the *moral*, arising from the consciousness of good affections and actions," he writes:

These joys are different from the sympathetick, which may arise from that happiness of others to which our affections and actions contributed nothing. . . . When we find our own whole soul kind and benign, we must have a joyful approbation: *and a further and higher joy arises from exercising these affections* in wise and beneficent offices. These joys we find the highest and most important both in respect of dignity and duration. (*Sys.*131; emphasis added)

Human agents who have the moral sense in addition to the other natural senses, and who "have their senses acute and fully exercised" in their pleasures, Hutcheson is saying, prefer *actually exercising* morally approved motives, and not just reflecting on their exercise, to all other pleasures.

Rather than providing a *regulative* standpoint from which the agent can make a practical judgment between benevolence and self-love, moral sense helps her to see that no such standpoint is required. Agents with moral sense find the exercise of benevolence intrinsically preferable, even when (indeed, especially when) it conflicts with self-love. So when in the deliberative context agent-neutral considerations of natural good conflict with those of private good, the agent can reflect on the fact that being motivated by the former will be decisively better for her than being motivated by the latter. For reasons we are familiar with, that cannot raise the former motive, but it can, Hutcheson believes, remove an obstacle to its natural operation. Seeing that she stands not to lose but only to gain by benevolence (not just beneficence), she can then give her attention to the good of all and be motivated as it is best for her to be.

Of course, this congruence of the "two grand determinations" remains contingent. It is only because God so fashioned us that things work out this way. Even in the *System*, therefore, Hutcheson relies on a preestablished harmony between self-love and benevolence. Without the contingent connections Hutcheson supposes to exist between these, an agent would be utterly powerless to resolve conflicts between them in a nonarbitrary way.

CONCLUSION

Although Hutcheson may appear to hold in early editions of the *Inquiry*, and later in the *System*, that the moral agent's reflection on his own motives is regulative in providing direct motivation to act on those of which he reflectively approves, in the end his psychology will permit no such view. Nor is this phenomenon restricted to *moral* assessment in any obvious way.[56] On Hutcheson's theory of the will, it is impossible for the agent to have *any* practically effective concern for self-regulation. The desire to act on motives that provide genuine reasons must therefore be as absent from his ideal of the rational agent as is the desire to act on motives of which she can morally approve absent from his picture of the moral agent. For Hutcheson, rational conduct is motivated de facto by the two calm, reflective desires, kept in harmony by Another's hand and not through the agent's own practical evaluation of reasons. The agent cannot be guided by the deliberative weight she takes motives to have, since the desire to act on genuine reasons makes no more psychological sense for Hutcheson than does the desire to act on morally good motives. The only psychologically possible objects of desire (and thus of will) are natural goods.

Despite various close relations to Shaftesbury, the overall thrust of Hutcheson's views on morality's normativity is thus thoroughly different from that of Shaftesbury and Cudworth. Far from simply thinking that moral obligation (or obligation generally) need not link up with a conception of an autonomous or self-determining agent in

56. A "rational sense" on the model of Hutcheson's moral sense would raise all the same issues. (I am indebted to Gregory Velazco y Trianosky for this observation.)

any particular way, Hutcheson finds the very notion of self-determination to be psychologically problematic. For him, moral value is fully realized in a "state-regarding" desire *in* a moral agent rather than by moral agency itself.

Hutcheson's project was that of empirical naturalism – to place morality within an understanding of the world provided by natural science – or, as his Glasgow colleague William Leechman put it, "the science of human nature and morality."[57] The predecessor who was closest to Hutcheson in this respect was Cumberland. Both accepted broad empiricist and naturalist methodological constraints; both believed that the goods of self *and* others provide motives for any rational human will; both thought that God had arranged the congruence of self-love and benevolence; and most important, both accepted the *calm reflective deliberation view*, according to which the practical force of theoretical reason extends beyond the purely instrumental, since calm, reason-informed reflection can involve the apprehension of goods (of self or others) that, given our contingent psychological makeup, raise new motives for acting (including an ultimately authoritative motive of universal benevolence).

Hutcheson and Cumberland also agreed that there is a form of obligation intrinsic to morality and distinct, therefore, from considerations of the agent's own good. But whereas Cumberland located this in the motive of universal benevolence that (they agreed) is morally best as well as no less weighty (at least) in calm, reason-informed deliberation than rational self-love, Hutcheson reserved the moral 'obligation' for a sentiment-based observer's judgment with no direct role to play in deliberation.[58] For Hutcheson, morality's distinctive force is revealed entirely in a spectator's responses of approval or condemnation and not in anything that can bind the will of a moral agent.

57. In his Preface to Hutcheson's *System*, p. xliv.
58. Unlike Hutcheson, Cumberland does think that the question of which ultimate end has deliberative priority can be raised from a standpoint independent of self-love and benevolence themselves and that, from this standpoint, reason recommends benevolence. See Chapter 4.

Chapter 9

Butler: conscience as self-authorizing

Hutcheson argued against Shaftesbury that interest is not the only obligation to virtue. Morality is adequately supported only if it is *intrinsically* normative, with its own distinctive obligation. But Hutcheson also believed that moral obligation consists entirely in an *observer's* sentiment that plays no direct role in agents' deliberations about what *to do*. This led him to reject as well Shaftesbury's doctrine that moral virtue or merit requires explicitly moral self-regulation.

Hutcheson was joined in the first criticism by Bishop Joseph Butler, whose *Fifteen Sermons Preached at the Rolls Chapel* and *Dissertation of the Nature of Virtue* appeared in 1726 and 1736, respectively, and began immediately to exercise an influence on British moral philosophy that has continued ever since.[1] In the Preface to the *Ser-*

---

1. *Fifteen Sermons Preached at the Rolls Chapel* (London, 1726). *A Dissertation of the Nature of Virtue* was appended to *The Analogy of Religion, Natural and Revealed, to the Constitution and Course of Nature* (London, 1736). References to Butler will be to *The Works of Bishop Butler*, ed. J. H. Bernard, 2 vols. (London: Macmillan, 1900). Most of the relevant sermons (I–III and XI, XII) are collected, along with *A Dissertation of the Nature of Virtue*, in Butler, *Five Sermons*, ed. S. Darwall (Indianapolis, Ind.: Hackett, 1983). Passages in the *Sermons* will be referred to by sermon and paragraph number, prefaced by *S*; those from the *Dissertation of the Nature of Virtue* by paragraph number, prefaced by *DV*; and those from *The Analogy of Religion* by part, chapter, and paragraph number, prefaced by *A*.
   Concerning Butler's continuing influence, it is worth noting that the *Sermons* were reprinted more frequently during the nineteenth century than any other work of moral philosophy in English. J. B. Schneewind, *Sidgwick's Ethics and Victorian Moral Philosophy* (Oxford: Oxford University Press, 1977), p. 7. Sidgwick's *Methods of Ethics*, for example, is full of references to Butler. Sidgwick credits Butler with being the source of the idea of the "dualism of practical reason," although it is actually closer to Hutcheson's notion that universal benevolence and calm self-love are the two independent "grand determinations" than to anything in Butler. See Frankena, "Sidgwick and the History of Ethical Dualism." It is from Butler that Sidgwick also takes the idea of the "paradox of egoistic hedonism" – that is, Butler's thesis in Sermon XI that pleasure can best by achieved by not aiming

mons, Butler objected that although Shaftesbury had shown that virtue is "naturally the interest or happiness, and vice the misery, of such a creature as man," this is not the only obligation to virtue (*S*.Preface 26). "[T]he greatest degree of skepticism" concerning virtue's promoting our own good still leaves us under "the strictest moral obligations" (*S*.Preface 27). Like Hutcheson, Butler grounded moral obligation in a "reflex approbation" – what Shaftesbury and Hutcheson had dubbed "moral sense" – but with a crucial difference. Whereas Hutcheson claimed that moral sense can have no direct practical role, Butler insisted that the faculty of reflective approval and disapproval – "conscience," or the "principle of reflection," as he called it – has an intrinsic *practical authority*.[2]

On the second issue between Shaftesbury and Hutcheson – the necessity of the *agent's* having moral sense ("reflex approbation") in order to exemplify genuine virtue or merit – Butler took Shaftesbury's side. Moral agency is impossible without the principle of reflection (*S*.II.8). A morally good agent is one who acknowledges the authority of conscience and governs herself by it. Indeed, Butler argued that Shaftesbury had not taken his own insight seriously enough. Shaftesbury was led to the conclusion that direction by moral reflection is necessary to *a person's* moral goodness because, otherwise, the goodness of her acts or motives cannot be imputed to *her* but only to some motive *in* her. But he nonetheless assumed that self-interest is the unique standpoint of rational deliberation, at least at the most reflective level concerning how to lead one's life on the whole.[3] Moral sense's role, for him, was to indicate the agent's higher interests in an approvable character, so that these could be entered into an assessment of her greatest interest on the whole. Still, this was not the only place where a normative conception entered Shaftesbury's account of moral and rational action, as we saw. Hold-

directly at it – and this opens the way for Sidgwick at the same time to hold utilitarianism as a criterion of right while denying that "universal benevolence is . . . always [the] best motive of action." Sidgwick, *The Methods of Ethics*, p. 413. Butler also stands firmly behind the development of rational intuitionism in the early twentieth century, as evidenced by the fact that Moore made Butler's "Everything is what it is and not another thing" the epigraph for *Principia Ethica*.

2. Butler uses 'conscience' and 'principle of reflection' interchangeably to refer to disinterested, dispassionate reflective approval and disapproval of actions and principles (motives). See, e.g., *S*.I.8, II.8. He usually reserves these terms for an agent's self-evaluation, although he evidently thinks that this is an instance of an evaluation whose objects are not restricted to self. See, e.g., *DV*.2. I shall adopt the expedient of using 'conscience' to refer to both of these.
3. See, in Chapter 7, "The Obligation to Virtue."

ing what I have called a *normative theory of the will*, Shaftesbury also maintained that a necessary condition of the possibility of integral agency and will is the agent's acknowledging the *authority* of her considered judgment of interest so that she can *govern* or *regulate* herself by it. However, Shaftesbury said nothing about the source of this normative conception, nor about what confers authority on self-interest. These he simply assumed.

By Butler's lights, the signal failing of Shaftesbury's *Inquiry* was "[t]he not taking into consideration this authority, which is implied in the idea of reflex approbation or disapprobation" (*S.*Preface 26). Butler agreed with Shaftesbury that self-determining agency involves self-*regulation* and that this is possible only if what explains the agent's actions is a conception of the *authority* that various motives have for her: He agreed, that is, with a normative theory of the will. Only with a normative practical conception regarding which motives or internal promptings she *ought* to act on, which provide her *reasons*, can a being be a self-governing agent. But there is no place to locate such a conception in Shaftesbury's moral psychology other than in moral sense, or in Butler's other than in the principle of reflection or conscience. So, Butler concluded, Shaftesbury simply missed the claim to deliberative authority implied in the very idea of "reflex approbation."

Butler could have made the same complaint in even stronger terms against Hutcheson. Neither calm self-love nor benevolence themselves involve any conception of practical reasons or justification. Self-love is simply the desire for one's own greatest good or happiness, and no thought that this is a reason for acting is intrinsic to it (*DV.*6). And similarly for benevolence. Neither involves any conception of its own deliberative *authority*. But this is precisely what, according to Butler, autonomous agency requires and the principle of reflection or conscience provides. Authority or "superintendency" (*S.*II.14) is part of the very idea of conscience, and whatever authority other principles have the agent must regard as deriving from it. Alone among the elements of our moral psychology, it is addressed to normative questions.

However, even if conscience must, by its very nature, purport to have authority, the question may still be asked whether it has it in fact. One of Butler's most famous claims is that it does. There has long been general agreement about the intended meaning of this claim, which C. D. Broad articulates nicely:

By saying that conscience has supreme authority Butler means that we regard the pronouncements of conscience, not simply as interesting or uninteresting statements of fact, and not simply as reasons to be balanced against others, but as *conclusive* reasons for or against doing the actions about which it pronounces.[4]

To this it might be added that, according to Butler, we do not simply *happen* so to regard conscience's pronouncements; we do so *rightly*.

But if the doctrine of conscience's authority is clear enough, how exactly Butler means to ground this idea is far from clear. In fact, there are at least two different, and somewhat conflicting, lines of thought that lead him to this thesis. One is evident on the surface of the text, even if its philosophical power does not match its prominence. This is the idea that conscience gives us conclusive reasons because we are *designed* to be guided by its directives, and that we function properly only when we are so. A second is, I think, more promising but also more difficult to tease out and formulate, even though it can convincingly be shown to be an important element in Butler's thought. Put very crudely, it holds that the authority of conscience is a condition of the very possibility of an agent's having reasons to act at all, since only a being who has the capacity for maintaining a self-regulated *constitutional* order can have reasons for acting, and this capacity depends on the agent's taking her conscience to be authoritative.

The second line of argument is a version of *autonomist internalism*, asserting, in effect, both halves of Kant's reciprocity thesis.[5] Although there are Clarkean, rational intuitionist elements of Butler's thought, these are absent from his arguments about the authority of conscience. The principle of reflection is, for Butler, a *principle* of action in the early-eighteenth-century sense – namely, a *motivational* source of conduct, like the principles of calm self-love or benevolence. But unlike the intuitionists, Butler does not argue in the *Sermons* that conscience motivates by putting us into contact with metaphysically independent normative facts whose nature it is to move

4. Broad, *Five Types of Ethical Theory* (Totowa, N.J.: Littlefield, Adams, 1965), p. 78. See also Austin Duncan-Jones, *Butler's Moral Philosophy* (Harmondsworth: Penguin, 1952), chap. 3. Wendell O'Brien dissents from this interpretation in "Butler and the Authority of Conscience," *History of Philosophy Quarterly* 8 (1991): 43–57.
5. See Allison, "Morality and Freedom: Kant's Reciprocity Thesis." See also Allison, *Kant's Theory of Freedom*, Part III.

when grasped. His best argument in the *Sermons* is that autonomous agency is possible only on the condition that agents have a capacity for motivating normative judgment (the "principle of reflection"). Conscience's normativity derives from the fact that agents' acknowledging its authority is a condition for the very possibility of autonomous action. Since conscience is also the seat of *moral* judgment, for Butler, this amounts to a claim that the normativity of morality, our being under the "strictest moral obligations," consists in its being the case that fully exercising the capacity for autonomous agency leads to conclusive motives to be moral.

As I remarked in Chapter 1, Butler's autonomist internalism differs from empirical naturalist internalisms in the following respect. The general internalist formula is that *obligation consists in conclusive motives raised through (practical) reasoning.* "Conclusive motive" is, however, ambiguous. For empirical naturalists, reason is entirely theoretical, and owing to their desire to understand normativity in entirely naturalistic terms, "conclusive motive" must be given a de facto reading. For autonomist internalists, the relevant practical reasoning realizes autonomy. Now, it is possible to believe, as did Locke, that autonomous practical reasoning is exhausted by deliberation adequately based in theoretical reason. Autonomist internalism of this sort *coincides* with empirical naturalist internalism, so a de facto reading of "conclusive motive" will be appropriate here also. Butler, however, resists this reductionist impulse. Normative practical notions, he argues, are intrinsic to autonomous *agency*; Butler holds a *normative theory of the will*. Agents can *regulate* or *govern* themselves only if they act on a normative conception they *accept*. But neither, like Clarke, does Butler think that moral *obligation* derives from a normative fact whose existence is independent of the form of practical thinking that makes autonomous agency possible. Rather moral obligation consists in its being the case that an agent would *regard* herself as having conclusive motive de jure – that is, conclusive *reason*, were she to exercise the form of practical thought that makes autonomous action possible.

As in our discussion of Locke, I emphasize that this autonomist line is only one of a very complex set of elements that make up Butler's thought. It is, moreover, in substantial tension with others: with his acceptance of Clarke's theory of eternal fitnesses, his teleological argument for the authority of conscience, and his theology, to name only a few examples. In general, Butler tends to downplay the tensions in his thought, as is shown in the way he mutes the vigorous debate between rationalists and sentimentalists, saying of the principle of reflection that it may be "considered as a sentiment of the understanding, or as a perception of the heart; or, which seems the truth, as including both" (*DV*.1). My main interest in this chapter will be to draw out Butler's autonomist internalism as it reveals itself in various of his arguments and claims. Again, as with Locke, I am not saying that Butler would accept it were he to consider its interactions with other things he also wants to maintain.[6]

Two preliminaries are necessary before we consider this line of thought. One, to which we shall turn in the next section but one, is to examine the teleological/functional argument for conscience's authority, which is more readily apparent in Butler's text. The second, which will occupy us in the next section, is to ponder Nicholas Sturgeon's challenge that the authority of conscience is actually superfluous in Butler's system. Since I shall be arguing that conscience's authority is fundamental to Butler's thought, I will aim to refute Sturgeon. But Sturgeon's argument also provides a context in which to set out preliminary aspects of the second, autonomist line in Butler, specifically, Butler's suggestion that conscience is self-authorizing in some sense. What this amounts to ultimately, I shall later argue, is the claim that, because acknowledging the authority of conscience is necessary for the very existence of an autonomous rational self, conscience is self-authorizing because it is *self-authorizing*.

THE SUPERFLUOUSNESS OF CONSCIENCE?

Given that the supremacy of conscience is generally regarded as the most distinctive element of Butler's moral philosophy, Sturgeon's claim that this doctrine is superfluous is surely the most provocative thesis in recent Butler scholarship.[7] I agree with the orthodox view, so I must show where I think Sturgeon's argument breaks down. But I also think that Sturgeon's analysis succeeds in bringing into relief elements of Butler's view that have been insufficiently appreciated

6. D. D. Raphael emphasizes some of the tensions in Butler's thought in "Bishop Butler's View of Conscience," *Philosophy* 24 (1949): 219–38.
7. Nicholas L. Sturgeon, "Nature and Conscience in Butler's Ethics," *Philosophical Review* 85 (1976): 316–56.

by other commentators.[8] Coming to grips with Sturgeon's argument will enable us to see not only why the authority of conscience is not superfluous but also what Butler sometimes takes the authority of conscience actually to *be*.

It is common ground that according to Butler's moral psychology the human psyche includes a variety of motives or motivational states that are ordered in various ways with respect to one another. These include, in addition to the principle of reflection, the principle of calm self-love, benevolence, and various passions and appetites. Thus, Butler holds that calm self-love is superior to present appetite, and that conscience is also. What is at issue is whether conscience ever dictates conduct in some way other than by approving an ordering of other principles and whether the relative priority of other principles itself depends on the supreme authority of conscience.

In Sermon II, Butler canvasses three senses of 'nature' in the course of arguing that to disobey conscience is to violate the "law of our nature" and, therefore, to do what is unnatural "in the highest and most proper sense" (II.9). Conscience is *a* principle in the human psyche, so obeying it is natural in one sense. But disobedience is also natural in this sense, since it is no less motivated by "some principle in man" (II.5). Second, a principle may be called "natural" because of its strength. But as any action results from the principle strongest at the time, disobedience will not be unnatural in this sense either (II.6). There is, however, a third sense in which, Butler argues, it can be shown that disobeying conscience *is* unnatural. It is possible for an action to be unnatural not because it "go[es] against a principle or desire barely, nor . . . against that principle or desire which happens for the present to be strongest," but because it contravenes a "superior principle" (II.11). There is, Butler maintains, a difference between practical principles that, "not being a difference in strength or degree," is rather "a difference in *nature* and in *kind*" (II.11). Human nature is a *constitution* – its principles form a constitutional order. An

8. Including recent critics of Sturgeon. See Terence Penelhum, *Butler* (London: Routledge & Kegan Paul, 1985), pp. 61–70; and Alan Millar, "Following Nature," *Philosophical Quarterly* 38 (1988): 172n.

For other useful discussions of Butler's ethics in addition to those of Broad, Duncan-Jones, and Penelhum, see T. H. McPherson, "The Development of Bishop Butler's Ethics," *Philosophy* 23 (1948): 317–31, and 24 (1949): 3–22; S. A. Grave, "The Foundation of Butler's Ethics," *Australasian Journal of Philosophy* 30 (1952): 73–89; Raphael, "Bishop Butler's View of Conscience"; Alan White, "Conscience and Self-Love in Butler's Sermons," *Philosophy* 17 (1952): 329–44; and Amélie Oksenberg Rorty, "Butler on Benevolence and Conscience," *Philosophy* 53 (1978): 171–84.

action is thus unnatural "in the strictest and most proper sense" if it *violates* a principle that is *superior* to any by which it is endorsed (II.10). The superior principle, though weaker, nonetheless has *authority*; it is the one that *should govern.*[9] To oppose it is to go contrary to a "law of our nature."

As Butler defines things, therefore, whether conscience has supreme authority *is the same issue as* whether any action contrary to its dictates is thereby made *unnatural in this third sense.* As Sturgeon puts it, "the supremacy of conscience will be that feature of it which renders unnatural *any* action, however motivated, which conflicts with it."[10] What creates problems, as he sees it, is that Butler is also committed to the *full naturalistic thesis:* "that conscience never *favors* or *opposes* any action, except on grounds which include its naturalness or unnaturalness."[11] If this is so, and if conscience is "fully transparent" (if, that is, "the *favor* or *opposition* of conscience is never founded on a mistaken estimate of an action's naturalness"),[12] then the only way an action can be contrary to (or in accord with) conscience is by being contrary to (or in accord with) some other superior principle.[13] So, Sturgeon concludes, it is only in an uninteresting sense that disobeying conscience is always unnatural. Being contrary to conscience is never what *makes* disobedience unnatural; disobedience is always unnatural only because it always violates some *other* superior principle. In Butler's scheme, conscience turns out to be no more than a transparent registrar of the superiority and inferiority of other principles.[14]

Waiving concerns about transparency, the crucial premise of this argument is the full naturalistic thesis. Butler never explicitly states that conscience always bases its judgment on grounds of naturalness, but Sturgeon offers reasons, which we must consider presently, for thinking that Butler is nonetheless committed to it. First, however, we should note that there are passages in which Butler appears explicitly to *deny* the full naturalistic thesis.[15] The most obvious one

9. Thus, after discussing an illustration of reasonable self-love's superiority to a stronger present appetite, Butler writes: "[I]f we will act conformably to the economy of man's nature, reasonable self-love must govern" (II.11). And he sums up this whole discussion thus: "All this is no more than the distinction, which everybody is acquainted with, between *mere power* and *authority*" (II.14).
10. Sturgeon, "Nature and Conscience," p. 319.
11. Ibid., p. 328.
12. Ibid.
13. Ibid., p. 344.
14. Ibid., p. 347.
15. Here I follow Penelhum, *Butler*, p. 62.

occurs in Sermon II itself: "[T]here is a superior principle of reflection or conscience in every man [which] pronounces determinately some actions to be in themselves just, right, good; others to be in themselves evil, wrong, unjust" (II.8).[16] This certainly seems to say that, at least sometimes, conscience approves or disapproves of actions *in themselves* and not on the grounds that they are natural or unnatural (i.e. contrary to some [*other*] superior principle).[17]

The most convincing reason, however, for thinking Butler must believe that conscience sometimes approves and disapproves of actions (and, perhaps, principles) considered in themselves, and not always on grounds of their naturalness, is his whole dialectical strategy in the *Sermons* in arguing for the authority of conscience. Commentators frequently note that Butler introduces the work with a discussion of two different "ways in which the subject of morals may be treated." One is Clarke's method of "inquiring into the abstract relations of things." The second, he says, begins "from a matter of fact, namely, what the particular nature of man is, its several parts, their economy or constitution; from whence it proceeds to determine what course of life it is, which is correspondent to this whole nature" (Preface 12).

Butler accepts both methods, as he makes clear in the *Analogy*, but it is important that in neither work does he appeal to a Clarkean doctrine of eternal fitnesses to establish the *authority* of conscience and hence moral *obligation*.[18] In the *Analogy*, he contrasts "abstract

16. In the *Dissertation*, Butler says that the object of conscience is "actions, comprehending under that name active or practical principles." And he writes that brutes lack conscience because "that will and design, which constitute the very nature of actions as such, are not at all an object of their perception" (*DV.2*).

17. And he may also be taking the same view of some conscientious judgments of principles or principled actions. Sturgeon admits that Butler sometimes *says* that conscience judges actions "in themselves" (e.g., at II.8), but he adds that Butler means in these places to contrast this not with comparing the action to the nature of the agent (in a judgment of naturalness) but with evaluating actions in light of their consequences ("Nature and Conscience," p. 345). No doubt Butler does have this latter contrast in mind, but he seems to be thinking of the former also. For, just two sections later, in discussing what he takes to be a clear example of an unnatural action – a man's rushing into certain ruin for the sake of a present gratification – he writes that this "disproportion arises, not from considering the action singly in *itself*, or in its *consequences*, but from comparison of it with the nature of the agent" (II.10). There seems no reason to suppose, therefore, that when he says in II.8 that conscience assesses certain actions "in themselves" he means only to contrast this with assessing an act's consequences and not also with assessing its naturalness.

18. "[I]n this treatise I have omitted a thing of the utmost importance which I believe, the moral fitness and unfitness of actions, prior to all will whatever" (*A.II.8.11*),

principle" or "abstract truth" with the "matters of fact" from which we can infer divine moral governance of nature and, therefore, motives to morality and religion. "And thus," he concludes, "the *obligations* of religion are made out, exclusively of the questions concerning . . . moral fitness" (*A*.II.8.11; emphasis added). A similar contrast is in play in the *Sermons*, as the Preface passage makes explicit. Here too he attempts to establish "our *obligations* to the practice of virtue" by appealing not to propositions regarding the "abstract relations of things" but to a "matter of fact" (Preface 12; emphasis added). In the *Sermons*, however, the relevant facts concern the constitution of the moral agent – the governance of his *internal* nature rather than the governance of nature as a whole.[19]

These remarks bring out two important points that bear on the full naturalistic thesis and Butler's argument for the authority of conscience. First, Butler evidently accepts the spirit and, perhaps, the letter of Clarke's doctrine that acts can be "in their own nature good and reasonable and fit to be done."[20] Since we may suppose that Butler must think we have some faculty to apprehend intrinsic fitnesses (how else would *he* believe in them?), and since there is no appropriate faculty in his moral psychology other than some form of conscience, we may attribute to him the belief that conscience sometimes endorses or opposes certain actions as fit or unfit in themselves.[21]

The second point is that, although Butler accepts that conscience

Butler says. He writes that the *Sermons* "proceed chiefly in this latter method. The first three wholly" (*S*. Preface 12). This suggests that he thinks he makes some use of the first method elsewhere in the *Sermons*. Whether or not he does in fact, it is clear enough that his argument that conscience is authoritative is meant to proceed wholly by the second method.

19. "Matter[s] of fact" should be read as inside scare-quotes, since Butler's use of this phrase will seem misleading if one has in mind a use familiar from Hume's *Treatise*, bk. III, pt. I, sec. I.

20. Thus Butler writes: "Fidelity, honour, strict justice, are themselves approved in the highest degree, abstracted from the consideration of their tendency" (*S*.XII.31n). The passage of Samuel Clarke's is from *A Discourse of Natural Religion*, published in 1706. See Raphael, *British Moralists*, vol. 1, p. 196. The passage can also be found in Schneewind, *Moral Philosophy from Montaigne to Kant*, vol. 1, p. 298.

21. Butler sometimes uses 'reason' to refer to a capacity that makes moral judgments (see note 38). No doubt this use of 'reason' is not meant to refer to what he usually reserves 'conscience' for, viz., a judgment of the self; and it *may* be that he thinks that reason apprehends fitness and unfitness and that he means to distinguish reason from any form of conscience. Since I know of no evidence for this theoretical possibility, and since it would not much affect my argument, I shall ignore it.

approves certain actions as morally fit in themselves, he nonetheless thinks there exists a further *normative* question, one he is anxious to address in the *Sermons:* namely, why *should* an agent do what his conscience approves of or forbear doing what his conscience opposes? What *reason* (or rational motive) does an agent have to do so? As he puts it at one point, "[A]llowing that mankind hath the rule of right within himself, yet it may be asked, What obligations are we under to attend to and follow it?'" (*S.*iii.5). That conscience tells us what is intrinsically morally fit and unfit may not be a satisfying answer to *this* question, since it can still be asked: Why should an agent do what is morally fit and forbear what is morally unfit? It is Butler's position that an answer to this question about *normativity* can be defended without relying on a doctrine of eternal fitness.

The claim that conscience is authoritative, therefore, is the claim that we are *obligated* to follow it – the political metaphor carries through. In following conscience we follow the "law of our nature" and do what is natural "in the highest and most proper sense" (*S.*ii.9). Thus Butler summarizes his conclusion as "every man is naturally a law to himself, . . . every one may find within himself the rule of right, and *obligations to follow it*" (*S.*ii.4; emphasis added). Since the proposition that following conscience is natural and violating it unnatural is something Butler thinks he has to show, he can hardly think that conscience *always* bases its favoring or opposing of actions on an assessment of their naturalness. If he thought that, he could not even raise the question he is attempting in the *Sermons* to answer: Allowing that conscience favors a given action, why nonetheless should a person so act? What *obligation* exists to do so?[22]

Despite the facts that Butler explicitly denies the full naturalistic thesis and that he must implicitly deny it in taking seriously the question whether there is an obligation to follow conscience, he might still be otherwise committed to it. Sturgeon gives several reasons for thinking this is so, the most interesting of which is his contention that Butler actually relies on the thesis in a crucial argument in Sermon II for, ironically, the authority of conscience itself.[23]

---

22. Terence Penelhum makes a similar argument in *Butler*, pp. 58–65.
23. Two others are that Butler says in the *Dissertation of the Nature of Virtue* that "our perception of vice and ill-desert arises from, and is a result of, a comparison of actions with the nature and capacities of the agent" (*DV.*5), and that he says that virtue "consists in following nature" (*S.* Preface 13) and that whenever conscience approves or disapproves of an action it does so on grounds of its virtue or

First, however, we must note an earlier passage that sets the stage for Sturgeon's interpretation.

Butler's first illustration of the superiority of one principle to another – of how, that is, acting on one of two conflicting principles can "manifest a disproportion, between the nature of a man and . . . an action" making the action unnatural "in the strictest and most proper sense" – is of the man who rushes into certain ruin for the sake of a present gratification (II.10). The disproportion shows that "self-love is in human nature a superior principle to passion" (II.11). Though passion be stronger, self-love should govern. Sturgeon infers from this that Butler believes that one principle can be superior to another independent of their relations to conscience. Of course, if Butler is to hold the full naturalistic thesis he *must* believe this. Conscience can make its judgments of something on grounds of naturalness only if the latter is independent of an endorsement by conscience of that very thing. I shall argue below, however, that Butler may not actually believe that one principle *can* be superior to another independently of their relations to conscience. If he does not, the full naturalistic thesis cannot possibly be attributed to Butler. Regardless, Sturgeon's reasons do not warrant attributing the thesis to Butler in any case. To see this, let us accept for the moment that Butler believes what he appears here to assert, namely, that self-love is superior to passion independent of the relation of both to conscience.

Having made (in II.14) the distinction between *"mere power* and *authority"* – between, that is, a principle's having strength and its being one by which an agent *should* govern himself – Butler goes on to give two arguments for the supreme authority of conscience. The first is simply Butler's thesis that by its very nature conscience must

vice (Sturgeon, "Nature and Conscience," 324–25). Since the *Dissertation* passage explicitly includes "ill-desert," which obviously brings in "comparison of actions with the nature and capacities of the agent" by way of assessing potentially excusing conditions, it does not necessarily bear directly on the full naturalistic thesis. (Here see also Penelhum, *Butler,* p. 68.) And the Preface passage in which Butler says that the *Sermons* are "intended to explain what is meant by the nature of man, when it is said that virtue consists in following, and vice, in deviating from it" occurs just after the section in which he has said that the method he will undertake leads to "our *obligations* to the practice of virtue" from a consideration of "what course of life it is, which is correspondent to this our whole nature" (Preface 12; emphasis added). I agree, therefore, with Penelhum that "Butler's claim that virtue consists in following nature is not intended to help identify what virtue requires, but to help ensure its practice" (*Butler,* p. 61). It is addressed to the "obligation" to virtue, to whether there is reason to be virtuous.

claim authority (11.14). The more interesting argument is a *reductio* Butler mounts at 11.16–17. The problem, as Sturgeon sees it, is that this argument assumes the full naturalistic thesis, thereby undermining its own conclusion.

The argument is a *reductio*. Notice, however, how Butler formulates the premise to be reduced to absurdity: "Let us now turn this whole matter another way, and suppose there was no such thing at all as this natural supremacy of conscience; that there was no distinction to be made between one inward principle and another, but only that of strength; and see what would be the consequence" (11.16). It is important to realize that Butler here appears to treat the natural supremacy of conscience and the existence of any relations of natural superiority as *equivalent*. Most significant for our purposes is that the *reductio* depends on treating the natural superiority of *any* principle to any other as *entailing* the supreme authority of conscience. Absurd consequences follow, Butler argues, from denying that practical principles can differ in "nature and in kind" and not just in strength. But this absurdity can establish *conscience's* supremacy only if the supremacy of conscience itself follows from the natural superiority of any principle. We shall return to this point in the next section but one. It means, in effect, that if there are any reasons for an agent to act at all, her conscience must be authoritative.[24]

Butler apparently regards the possibility that there might be no reasons for acting at all – that principles might differ only in strength and not in relative superiority – as what needs to be ruled out in order to demonstrate conscience's authority. To do so, he considers what believing this would constrain us to think of an action of which we would normally disapprove:

[S]uppose a man guilty of parricide. . . . This action is done in consequence of its principle being for the present strongest: and if there be no difference

---

24. Butler's example in 11.10 and 11.11 of the superiority (in human beings) of self-love to passion and his remark that "without particular consideration of conscience, we may have a clear conception of the *superior nature* of one inward principle to another" may seem to contradict this. I shall argue presently that they need not: "Conscience, Autonomy, and Self-Authorization."

Sturgeon writes that Butler "leaves it unclear which of these two nonequivalent propositions is to be the supposition of the *reductio*" ("Nature and Conscience," p. 321). He acknowledges that, in order for the argument to be relevant to the authority of conscience, Butler has to think that the latter will follow from the existence of any relations of superiority, but finds it "ironic that he should believe this" since the argument commits him to an assumption (the full naturalistic thesis) "which will render superfluous the assignment to conscience of this or any other rank" (321).

between inward principles, but only that of strength; the strength being given, you have the whole nature of the man given, so far as it relates to this matter. . . . Upon comparing the action and the whole nature, there arises no disproportion. (II.17)

He then concludes: "If there be no difference between inward principles, but only that of strength; we can make no distinction between [a parricide and an act of filial duty], considered as the actions of such a creature; but in our coolest hours must approve or disapprove them equally; than which nothing can be reduced to a greater absurdity" (II.17).

Sturgeon argues that Butler can reasonably think we are constrained to approve or disapprove these actions equally only if he accepts the full naturalistic thesis – only if, that is, conscience always bases its judgments on grounds having to do with naturalness. Thinking these actions equally natural would then constrain us to "approve or disapprove them equally." As Penelhum has pointed out, however, this is not strictly correct. The conclusion that Butler draws here is that we would be constrained to approve or disapprove them equally when considering them *as the actions of such a creature.*[25] Even if conscience's judgments of actions *as of an agent* are never independent of considerations of naturalness, it is consistent with this that conscience also approves and disapproves of actions (and, indeed, of principles) considered in themselves. Butler is not therefore, committed by the *reductio* to the full naturalistic thesis.

Even so, it is an important fact that Sturgeon's analysis helps us to see that Butler must be saying here that conscience's judgment of an action, as of an agent of a certain nature, either is based on naturalness or is itself a judgment of naturalness. Though conscience may disapprove of parricide as a kind of action, it cannot sustain disapproval of an agent's parricide that it believes not to have been unnatural. If we believe such an agent was not in a position to *have* good and sufficient *reason* not to kill his parent, Butler thinks, we cannot disapprove of *him,* or *an agent like him,* for doing so. Therefore, if we do disapprove of him, we are committed to thinking there was such a reason. And since if there be no difference between principles but relative strength there will be no such reasons, it follows that if we believe principles differ only in relative strength we cannot consistently disapprove any *agent's* parricide. And if the existence of relations of relative superiority between principles entails the authority

25. Emphasis added. See Penelhum, *Butler,* p. 67.

of conscience, it follows further that we cannot believe that conscience is not supreme and consistently disapprove of any agent's parricide. Denying conscience's authority requires one to forbear conscientious judgments of this kind. This consequence, Butler trusts, we will find absurd.

I said earlier that Butler distinguishes between conscience's approval of an action and there being an *obligation* to follow this "rule of right within" *and* that his argument that in violating conscience we go counter to a law of our nature and thereby act unnaturally is addressed to the latter. The full naturalistic thesis ignores this distinction. It maintains that the grounds that constitute conscience's authority (natural superiority and inferiority) are the very grounds on which conscience invariably initially approves or disapproves of conduct. We have found no good reason to think that Butler believes this, and hence no good reason to believe that his project of establishing the authority of conscience is internally incoherent. At the same time, the present argument suggests that the line between what grounds a judgment of conscience and what grounds conscience's authority, or power to obligate, is not impermeable. Butler assumes in the *reductio* that only if we think that conscience obligates and that violating it is unnatural can we *disapprove of an agent's* doing so. Here, in yet another guise, we find the *accountability view* and the first half of Kant's reciprocity thesis.[26] Butler's reductio amounts to the claim of the accountability strand of autonomist internalism: Morality is staked on the authority of its demands.

Viewed this way, judgments of naturalness constrain conscientious judgments of *agents' acts;* disapproval of an agent's action requires the belief that the action was unnatural. Moreover, Butler's view is evidently not that the latter is merely a necessary ground for conscience's disapproving of the agent's act, but also that the judgment that an agent's action is unnatural *is itself a judgment of conscience.*[27] If this is so, an account of the unnaturalness of violating

---

26. See also Chapter 5, "The Accountability Strand of Autonomist Internalism."
27. Penelhum is somewhat puzzling on this point. He recognizes that there is no faculty other than conscience to make the "judgments of practical philosophy" that he rightly thinks to be what judgments of naturalness amount to for Butler. But he appears to think that Butler is simply here "using the older and more general sense of 'conscience' as 'inward knowledge or consciousness'." And he says that "it may be that Butler does think that an assumption of equality of status between inward principles would disable conscience, and is therefore closer in this passage to committing himself to the Full Naturalistic Thesis than I

conscience – of, that is, the obligation to follow conscience – will itself be adequate only if it simultaneously explains a further *disapproval* of an agent's violating conscience, beyond that already involved in (the agent's) conscientious disapproval of an act or principle in itself.

There are several reasons for thinking that this is indeed Butler's view. First, it is simply unclear how believing an agent's parricide to be unnatural would be necessary to disapprove of it unless either judgments of naturalness are made by conscience or conscience judges as a general proposition that no action is to be disapproved of that is not unnatural.[28] Second, Butler says in Sermon II that his method of establishing an obligation to virtue from "a review of the nature of man" is "to be considered as an appeal to each particular person's heart and natural conscience" (II.1).[29] Third, just after he announces in the Preface that his method will be to establish an obligation "to the practice of virtue" from a "matter of fact" – namely, that vice is unnatural – he remarks that he aims here to agree with "the ancient moralists [who] had some inward feeling or other, which they chose to express in this manner, that . . . [virtue] consists in following nature" (Preface 12). What could such an "inward feeling" emanate from, for Butler, other than conscience? This theme is repeated several times in the following sections, where the doctrine that vice is unnatural is also called an "inward perception" and an "inward conviction" (Preface 13, 16).

All of this makes sense on the assumption that Butler understands the judgment that conduct is natural or unnatural (in "the strictest and most proper sense") to be a judgment of conscience. In addition, there is another powerful reason for thinking Butler would have to take this view, namely, that 'naturalness' as Butler understands it, like 'superiority' and 'authority', expresses a *normative* notion, and there is no other faculty in Butler's moral psychology from which such a normative judgment can issue but some form of conscience

suggest" (*Butler*, p. 68). Butler says clearly that were we to believe that there is no distinction in which principles a person should be governed by, we could not approve or disapprove of his acts differentially, but this does not involve the full naturalistic thesis. That if we believe violating conscience not to be unnatural then we can no longer disapprove of an agent's parricide does not entail that we cannot initially disapprove of parricide as a kind of act considered in itself and independent of grounds of its naturalness.

28. In the second instance, an account of unnaturalness would still have to explain why, if *that* is what unnaturalness is, an agent's act is to be disapproved of only if it manifests it.

29. A caveat is necessary here: See note 30.

itself.[30] Self-love, for example, is simply the desire for one's greatest good; it does not make, in addition, any judgment that one *ought* to pursue one's greatest good.[31] Conscience appears to be the only faculty that can make normative judgments.

If this is so, then it would seem that Butler must suppose that conscience is in some sense *self-authorizing*. But what can this amount to? It is useful to distinguish here between an agent's first-order disapproval, say, of some action and her (or our) second-order disapproval of her doing what she disapproves of as a first-order matter. On the present suggestion, the judgment that disobeying conscience is unnatural would be a second-order disapproval of doing what is the object of a first-order disapproval. But how could any such second-order judgment of conscience establish conscience's *authority*? How can conscience be genuinely self-*authorizing*? There are, of course, the familiar passages in which Butler says that conscience implicitly claims its own authority: "as from its very nature manifestly claiming superiority over all others: insomuch that you cannot form a notion of this faculty, conscience, without taking in judgment, direction, superintendency. This is a constituent part of the idea, that is, of the faculty itself: and to preside and govern . . . belongs to it" (II.14).[32] But again, from the fact that conscience must claim its own authority it does not follow that it has that authority in fact. It is simply unclear how conscience can succeed in *being* self-authorizing

30. "Some form" of conscience because Butler notoriously uses 'conscience' and 'principle of reflection' to refer to a variety of forms of disinterested, dispassionate, reflective evaluative and normative judgments (see note 2). In note 21 I discussed the possibility that Butler thinks of what he sometimes calls 'reason' as a faculty distinct from any form of conscience that perceives intrinsic fitnesses and unfitnesses. But even if this were so, this faculty could not make the sort of normative judgment of *obligation* that Butler's argument requires, since he is abjuring any use of the Clarkean method. (See note 38 for references for Butler's use of 'reason'.)

31. "Every man hath a general desire of his own happiness. . . . The former proceeds from, or is self-love" (S.xi.5). In the *Dissertation* Butler distinguishes between self-love and the judgment that a person ought to promote his interest: "It should seem, that a due concern about our own interest or happiness, and a reasonable endeavour to secure and promote it, which is, I think, very much the meaning of the word *prudence,* in our language; it should seem, that this is virtue, and the contrary behaviour faulty and blamable; since, in the calmest way of reflection, we approve of the first, and condemn the other conduct, both in ourselves and others. This approbation and disapprobation are altogether different from mere desire of our own, or of their happiness, and from sorrow upon missing it. For the object or occasion of this last kind of perception is satisfaction; whereas the object of the first is active behaviour. In one case, what our thoughts fix upon is our condition; in the other, our conduct." I discuss this passage further later on.

32. See also Preface 24, 26, 27; II.8.

even if it must claim to be. To vindicate morality and what he regards as its distinctive faculty, Butler needs to establish the *other* half of Kant's reciprocity thesis: that autonomous agents must regulate themselves (through conscience) by moral demands.

AUTHORITY FROM FUNCTION?

In the next section, we examine Butler's attempt to make this argument with a *normative theory of the will*. In this section, though, we shall first consider some competing strands of his thought. To this point, I have been presenting Butler's argument that the authority of conscience derives from its being the law of our nature, and hence that disobeying it is unnatural, as resting on "the distinction, which everybody is acquainted with, between *mere power* and *authority*" (II.14). The principles of which we are composed differ not just in "strength or degree" but also "in *nature* and in *kind*" (II.11). This is the basis for Butler's third sense of 'natural', the sense in which he aims to show that disobeying conscience is unnatural (II.9, 10). Going against conscience will be unnatural, in this sense, just in case conscience is *in its nature* authoritative. So Butler argues in Sermon II that the very conception of conscience is of a faculty that claims superiority (II.14) and that denying this claim leads to absurdity (II.17).

The ruling metaphor is that of a *constitutional order*, which exists only if there are relations of *authority* – a truth about who is to govern when the claims of political actors conflict. Likewise, our internal nature forms a constitutional order only if there is a truth about which principles should govern when they conflict. In these terms, in arguing that disobeying conscience is unnatural, Butler is maintaining that it is *unconstitutional* – it *"violates,"* as he sometimes says, our internal constitution.

[A]s in civil government the constitution is broken in upon, and violated by power and strength prevailing over authority; so the constitution of man is broken in upon and violated by the lower faculties or principles within prevailing over that which is in its nature supreme over them all. (III.2)[33]

33. See also Preface 12, 14; II.10. And note the following passage from Sermon V of Butler's *Six Sermons Preached upon Public Occasions*: "Let us transfer, each of us, the equity of this our civil constitution to our whole personal character; and be sure to be as much afraid of subjection to mere arbitrary will and pleasure in ourselves, as to the arbitrary will of others. For the tyranny of our own lawless passions is the nearest and most dangerous of all tyrannies." *Works*, vol. 1, p. 267.

Claim to a constitutional role is part of the very concept of con-science. It alone, from its very nature, claims authority and superintendency.

At the same time, Butler has another model of human nature that, although he does not distinguish it, is actually quite different from a constitutional order, namely, that of a *teleological/functional system*. Parts or principles of a functional system can have a kind of ordering, but not one of relative *authority*. Nor is it established by their intrinsic natures. The idea is not that when, say, conscience and an appetite conflict, conscience properly overrides because of its title to govern based on their respective intrinsic natures; rather, it is that the design of the human system is adapted to certain purposes, and that these define an ideal of proper functioning in which conscience overrides appetite when they conflict. On this view of things, although our design and purpose is not *in fact* such that we would be functioning properly if appetite characteristically overrode conscience, there is nothing in the very nature of conscience and appetite to rule this out. There might be a well-designed system adapted to quite different purposes than those for which our design fits us, one whose makeup included conscience and appetites but in which these played different functional roles – in which it was not part of the design that conscience, despite its (intrinsic) superintendent pretensions, should actually superintend.[34]

"Every work both of nature and of art is a system," Butler writes in the Preface to the *Sermons*, "and as every particular thing, both natu-ral and artificial, is for some use or purpose out of and beyond itself, one may add, to what has been already brought into the idea of a system, its conduciveness to this one or more ends" (Preface 14). He then makes his famous analogy between the way a watch is adapted to time telling and the way our system is adapted to what he here claims to be its distinctive end of virtue. Even if we grant Butler's teleological framework, this analogy may seem problematic. We can easily form a notion of the end that watches serve without already having some conception of how they properly function internally. But is it obvious that this is the case with virtue? Is virtue an indepen-dently specifiable "use or purpose out of and beyond" the well-functioning person to which this functioning is adapted? Or is virtue

34. Of course 'superintend' in its occurrence at the end of the sentence must be taken in a *functional* sense. For convenience I shall continue this use; context should make its meaning clear.

dependent on what our proper functioning itself is? If there are problems in this direction, however, Butler is in a position to finesse them to some extent, since he also says that our system is adapted to the good or happiness of the agent and others. And he understands the good in ways that are independent of any ideal of proper functioning.[35]

Like Shaftesbury, Butler distinguishes between principles by their functional roles. *Private* principles are those whose proper functioning in our overall design tends primarily to the good of the agent; *public* principles are those analogously related to the good of others (1.4–7). A principle may have a primary function that makes it public, but with a secondary function to advance the agent's good. Or, alternatively, its primary function may be to further private good and its secondary function to promote public good.[36] Thus, although benevolence is a public principle since its primary function is to promote the happiness of others, Butler argues that it is also part of our design that "the greatest satisfactions to ourselves depend upon our having benevolence in a due degree." And because this is so, "self-love is one chief security of our right behaviour towards society" (1.6). Self-love and benevolence have converse primary and secondary functions.

Butler first discusses conscience's functional role in Sermon I. It is evident, he argues, that conscience restrains us from doing harm and leads us to do good to others. In this way its function is the same as any public principle. So why do we need conscience in particular? For one thing, it can second other public principles when appropriate, and take over when these are insufficient to achieve their purpose by themselves:

Thus a parent has the affection of love to his children: this leads him to take care of, to educate, to make due provision for them; the natural affection leads to this: but the reflection that it is his proper business, what belongs to him, that it is right and commendable so to do; this added to the affection becomes a much more settled principle, and carries him on through more labour and difficulties for the sake of his children, than he would undergo

35. Thus, the object of self-love is said to be "happiness, enjoyment, satisfaction" (xi.5). And "happiness or satisfaction consists only in the enjoyment of those objects, which are by nature suited to our several particular appetites, passions, and affections" (xi.9).

36. As Alan Millar points out, Sermon XI is not simply rhetorical. Butler is required by his teleology to show the coincidence of virtue and interest. See "Following Nature," p. 176.

from that affection alone, if he thought it, and the course of action it led to, either indifferent or criminal. (1.8)[37]

Since in Sermon I Butler is concerned to exhibit conscience "merely as another part in the inward frame of man, pointing out to us in some degree what we are intended for," he takes his discussion of its functional role no farther, reserving for Sermon II an account of "the particular place assigned to it by nature" (1.8).

In the preceding section, I stressed passages from Sermon II in which Butler treats the authority of conscience as resting on our *constitutional* nature. This argument, however, is run alongside other arguments for conscience's authority that depend on treating human nature as a teleological/functional order. And, it must be said, these other arguments are, if anything, more prominent. Indeed, Butler begins Sermon II by establishing terms for his discussion drawn entirely from the latter framework: "As speculative truth admits of different kinds of proof, so likewise moral obligations may be shewn by different methods. If the real nature of any creature leads him and is adapted to such and such purposes only, or more than to any other; this is a reason to believe the Author of that nature intended it for those purposes" (11.1). Here and immediately after, Butler appears to suppose that it would be a sufficient proof of conscience's authority that it have a controlling function in our actual design. This would make conscience's power to *obligate*, to provide conclusive reasons for acting, depend entirely on its functional role. Of course, it may well be that the intrinsic nature of conscience fits it for a "superintendent" role in our overall design. Nonetheless, Butler seems here to be saying, its authority depends directly on the latter and only indirectly on the former.

From Sermon I we have it that conscience is one of several public principles whose function is to motivate us to do good. Sermon II's distinctive dialectical task is to establish that it is not *simply* one such principle among others, designed to lead us to do good when it "happen[s] to be stronger than other principles," but that we are so designed that "the *whole* character be formed upon thought and reflection; that *every* action be directed by some determinate rule, some other rule than the strength and prevalency of any principle or passion" (11.3). So Butler now asks, "What sign is there in our nature

37. Public principles are not of course restricted to forms of benevolence. Nor, Butler is anxious to argue, does conscience approve only of what aims at or produces benefit to others. See, for instance, XII.31n; *DV.*8.

(for the inquiry is only about what is to be collected from thence) that this was intended by its Author?" What evidence does our nature provide, that is, that it has a design in which conscience's function *is* to superintend?

Butler points to evidence of two main sorts. One is that conscience is the only faculty that represents itself as superintendent. Butler mentions the other consideration only briefly in passing, but brief though it may be, it has several profound implications for his overall view. The passage occurs in II.8, where Butler begins to explicate the sense of 'nature' in which he takes Saint Paul to be asserting (in the sermon's text from Romans 2:14) that "the Gentiles *do by* NATURE *the things contained in the law.*" He then quotes from the next verse – "which shew the work of the law written in their hearts, their conscience also bearing witness" – and he remarks that "if there be a distinction to be made between the *works written in their hearts,* and the *witness of conscience;* by the former must be meant the natural disposition to kindness and compassion." This, Butler continues, is the part of our nature on which he has focused in Sermon I, "which with very little reflection and of course leads [a person] to society, and by means of which he naturally acts a just and good part in it, unless other passions or interest lead him astray." But, he then notes, passions and self-love are "themselves in a degree equally natural." And so he concludes: "[S]ince we have no method of seeing the particular degrees in which one or the other is placed in us by nature; it is plain the former, considered merely as natural, good and right as they are, can no more be a law to us than the latter."

Notice first that Butler says here, perhaps more explicitly than he does at any other point, that *neither benevolence nor self-love can itself be a law to human beings.* Some commentators have been tempted to take the view that Butler means to accord self-love coordinate, or perhaps even superior, authority in relation to conscience, but this passage plainly states that self-love cannot be a law to us.[38] Second, Butler

38. The usual bases for this claim are the famous "cool hour" passage at XI.20 and Butler's remark that "reasonable self-love and conscience are the chief or superior principles in the nature of man: because an action may be suitable to this nature, though all other principles be violated; but becomes unsuitable, if either of those are" (III.9). Regarding the former, it is worth noting not only that the passage – "when we sit down in a cool hour, we can neither justify to ourselves this or any other pursuit, till we are convinced that it will be for our happiness, or at least not contrary to it" – is within the scope of the suppositional "Let it be allowed," and not only that the whole discussion is preceded by the remark that "these inquiries, it is hoped, may be favourably attended to: for there shall be all

says that we have no way of determining "the particular degrees in which" various natural principles such as particular passions, self-love, and benevolence are "placed in us by nature." Although we can tell well enough that these all have functions in our design, we have no way of discerning their intended role in any fine-grained way. In particular, he seems to be saying, knowledge of our design does not extend to which principles are to override when they conflict. But if this is so, it follows that when we judge, as Butler believes we rightly do, that a person's putting herself in mortal danger for the sake of a pressing appetite is unnatural, we cannot be basing this judgment on any justified belief about the "particular degrees in which" self-love and appetite "are placed in us by nature." This shows that judgments of the superiority of principles other than conscience cannot be based on knowledge of their *intended* hierarchy.[39]

Butler says that neither benevolence nor self-love can be a law to us, but he evidently also means that neither can any fact about their precise role in our design, or about the role of any other principle (except conscience, as we shall see). We lack access to such truths and cannot, therefore, determine on this basis which principle we should act on when they conflict. There is, then, a *design problem* for creatures who have the same principles we have (exclusive of conscience) but who are similarly ignorant of the details of their design. Such crea-

possible concessions made to the favourite passion, . . . it shall be treated with the utmost tenderness and concern for its interests" (xi.3) but also that the sentence immediately following the "cool hour" passage shows that Butler *rejects* the idea that self-interest is ultimately justifying: "*Common reason* and humanity will have some influence upon mankind, whatever becomes of speculations; but, so far as the interests of virtue depend upon the theory of it being secured from open scorn, so far its very being in the world depends upon its appearing to have no contrariety to private interest and self-love" (xi.21; emphasis added). "Common reason" evidently refers to conscience or the principle of reflection. (This is also supported by other references to "reason"; see, e.g., S.v.3; xii.17.) Thus Butler is suggesting that although conscience is in fact ultimately justifying, nonetheless, because the "favourite passion['s] . . . cause is so universally pleaded (xi.3), people are only likely actually to be virtuous if they can be convinced that it does not conflict with self-interest. For further discussion, see Broad, *Five Types of Ethical Theory*, pp. 79–80; A. E. Taylor, "Some Features of Butler's Ethics," *Mind* 35 (1926): 273–300; Duncan-Jones, *Butler's Moral Philosophy*, pp. 113–15; John Kleinig, "Butler in a Cool Hour," *Journal of the History of Philosophy* 7 (1969): 399–411.

39. Butler gives this as an instance of one principle's being *superior* to another, regardless of the latter's strength; i.e., the former should *govern*. As I have remarked, his argument at that point trades on treating our nature as a *constitutional* system. What the present point would show is that our taking something to have a particular place in our constitutional system is not based on our taking it to have some functional role in our design.

tures are unable to follow the instruction: Act in accordance with your design; make your design a law to yourself.

Butler immediately notes what he thinks solves this problem: "But there is a superior principle of reflection or conscience in every man, which distinguishes between the internal principles of his heart, as well as his external actions; which passes judgment upon himself and them" (II.8). By giving us intuitive judgment of which principles we should follow, as well as of which actions we should perform, God has given us a way of regulating ourselves that does not require a knowledge of the precise place of other principles in our design. He gives us a faculty *representing* itself as properly superintendent, so that it can function properly by superintending. Or, disambiguating 'superintendency', conscience represents itself to us as controlling de jure, so that it can control de facto. Moreover, we are able, Butler thinks, to infer that this is conscience's function and, consequently, that we function properly when we follow it rather than other principles when they conflict. Even if the relative functional priority of other principles is not evident to us, the functional priority of conscience is. Butler therefore concludes:

This gives us a further view of the nature of man; shews us what course of life we were made for: not only that our real nature leads us to be influenced in some degree by reflection and conscience; but likewise in what degree we are to be influenced by it, if we will fall in with, and act agreeably to the constitution of our nature: that this faculty was placed within to be our proper governor: to direct and regulate all under principles, passions, and motives of action. (II.15)

"Proper governor" is neatly ambiguous for Butler's purposes. If it means "what governs (controls) when we function properly, that is, as designed," then it follows from the fact that God designed conscience to override that it is our proper governor. But it could also mean "what has genuine *authority*" in the sense of having *title to rule*. This is the meaning it must have if our nature is to form a constitutional order and if disobeying conscience is to be unnatural in the "strictest and most proper sense." It is difficult to see, however, how any facts about functional design can establish that, since no normative facts follow from them. It is precisely this ambiguity, I think, that leads Butler to run his two metaphors together.

The more interesting possibility, actually, is not that Butler simply confuses the two metaphors but that he holds that the particular kind of teleological/functional system we are designed to be is one that *represents itself* as a constitutional order. But insofar as we so represent ourselves, *we* can hardly take it as a satisfactory argument for conscience's authority that it was designed for this job; nothing follows from that about whether it has genuine title, that is, whether it is superior "in nature and kind" to all other practical principles. A self-regulating constitutional order will give weight to intention and design only insofar as these are relevant *within* a *constitutional* framework. Moreover, if judgments of naturalness are judgments of conscience, then considerations of functional role can be relevant to these only if there is some background normative proposition that makes them so. The bare judgment that conscience is *designed* to superintend is a judgment not of conscience but of the understanding; it is a theoretical finding and by itself determines no conclusion of the "practical discerning power," as Butler calls conscience in the *Dissertation.*

Before we return to considering how Butler might be conceiving of conscience as self-authorizing within an internal constitutional order, we should note one further argument that he makes along teleological lines. Butler frequently compares the function and purpose of elements of our practical nature to bodily functions, specifically, to that of the eyes. Usually he is concerned just to say that the former are no less obvious than the latter, thereby supporting his conclusion that the purpose of conscience is to superintend (II.1). At one point, however, the terms of the analogy are put in an interestingly different way: "Now obligations of virtue shewn, and motives to the practice of it enforced, from a review of the nature of man, are to be considered as an appeal to each particular person's heart and natural conscience: as the external senses are appealed to for the proof of things cognizable by them" (II.1).[40] By the latter proof Butler evidently means an inference of the following sort. We have senses in order to sense things and would not need them unless there were things to be sensed. Since God has given us senses for a purpose, there must be "things cognizable by them." What would be analogous in the practical case?

The most obvious analogy is not one Butler actually makes here – namely, between the relation of things to be sensed to our senses, on the one hand, and the relation of the intrinsic rightness or wrong-

---

40. Note that this suggests that the way in which concluding an obligation to virtue "from a review of the nature of man" involves an "appeal to conscience" may be no more than the way in which sense experience is appealed to in the analogous proof of an external world. See note 27.

ness, or fitness or unfitness, of actions to conscience, on the other. To appeal to that analogy here would be to make use of Clarkean intuitionism in establishing an *obligation* to follow conscience, which Butler is pledged in the *Sermons* to avoid. Here his analogy seems, rather, to be between the cognitive nature of experience – its presenting itself as something to be believed – and the normative nature of conscience – its presenting itself as something *to be obeyed*. In the former case we can generally rely (in a fallible way) on the testimony of the senses, since God would not have given us these for any reason other than to provide us reliable beliefs about the external world. Likewise, the argument might go, God would not have given us a faculty that presents itself as something to be obeyed unless it actually should be obeyed. On this reading, that conscience is designed to superintend is not what makes it authoritative; it is conclusive evidence that it has this authority.

This would leave it an open question how it is that conscience comes actually to *have* authority – what its authority consists in. Maybe intrinsic fitnesses or unfitnesses of actions just are, in their nature, conclusive reasons for acting, and conscience is the faculty through which we have access to these facts. God gives us conscience so we can receive these truths. On this view, the existence of reasons for an agent to act and, consequently, of facts about how she should act will be independent of her conscience. Just as there would still be objects even if we lacked the means to sense them, so there would be facts about how we should act though we lacked any access to them through conscience. So pictured, the authority of conscience would derive from the independent existence of normative practical facts together with the contingent fact that, as God has designed us, conscience is our best access to these.

Even apart from his pledge to avoid reliance on intuitionistic metaphysics in the *Sermons'* argument for the obligation to follow conscience, there are other reasons why Butler cannot ultimately accept this picture; or, at least, it is deeply at odds with other things he says.[41] As we noted earlier, Butler treats the existence of a distinction between justificatory weight and motivational strength as equivalent to the authority of conscience (II.16). This suggests that a being who lacked conscience could not have genuine reasons for acting – there

41. Of course, it might be argued that this argument does not *rely* on intuitionistic metaphysics, since it would amount to an argument to it as the best explanation of our having the moral faculty. No premises regarding eternal fitnesses would be required.

could be no distinction between the motives that she actually acts on and those on which she *should* act. If this is so, conscience cannot simply be a faculty of access to metaphysically independent normative facts. Moreover, Butler says repeatedly that it is only because we have conscience that we can be a "law to [our]selves" and, furthermore, that "the faculty which surveys, approves or disapproves the several affections of our mind and actions of our lives, being that by which men *are a law to themselves*, their conformity or disobedience to which law of our nature renders their actions, in the highest and most proper sense, natural or unnatural" (II.9). But to be unnatural "in the strictest and most proper sense" (II.10) just *is* to be contrary to weightier reasons – to be contrary to motives on which the agent should act. If what makes an action unnatural in this sense, then, is that it is contrary to conscience, this confirms that Butler thinks that a distinction between "*mere power* and *authority*" cannot be drawn with respect to an agent's motives if she lacks conscience (II.8).

CONSCIENCE, AUTONOMY, AND SELF-AUTHORIZATION

These points return us to the line of thought we put aside to explore Butler's natural teleology, namely, the idea that conscience is somehow self-authorizing. We must now consider what this might involve. Partly, the thought must be that since the question whether conscience should be obeyed is irreducibly normative, it can be answered only by a judgment of conscience in some form. This requires a distinction between the judgment that conscience makes of actions and principles, considered intrinsically, and conscience's judgment of naturalness – that is, of what there is reason for the agent to do. Without this distinction, the full naturalistic thesis looms and, along with it, the superfluousness of conscience: An action will never be made unnatural, and therefore contrary to a motive that should have governed, by virtue of being contrary to conscience.[42] Suppose, however, that through conscience we do endorse certain actions and principles, considered intrinsically, and oppose others. We can then ask: What should a person do *given* the endorsements of her conscience and her nature otherwise considered? As I read him, this is the same as Butler's question: What would it be natural for her to do "in the strictest and most proper sense"?

42. On this, see Penelhum, *Butler*, pp. 68–69.

Now if any question concerning what a person should do is a question of conscience, then this must be one also. But it will be a second-order rather than a first-order question. It will be the question: Given my first-order conscientious judgments, along with my other motives, how should I act? Suppose that at this second level an agent approves of her performing acts and acting on principles that she conscientiously endorses at the first level despite their being opposed by other principles, and that she analogously disapproves at this second level of performing acts and acting on principles that she conscientiously opposes at the first level despite their being favored by other principles. If this is so, she will be taking her conscience to be authoritative; she will take it that her conscience should govern when it conflicts with other principles.

In arguing that conscience represents itself as superintendent, Butler is maintaining, in effect, that an agent with conscience will necessarily judge that she should follow it, at least insofar as she is not self-deceived or her judgment is not corrupted in some other way. To have conscience is to be disposed to acknowledge its authority. But again, we may still wonder what *gives* conscience this authority. Perhaps we cannot have conscience without some tendency to believe that it has authority, but we may still query this very belief; we may ask whether it has the authority it claims and, if so, what that authority derives from.[43] Without some showing that conscience is itself rationally inescapable, we will lack any convincing argument that conscience's pretensions are realized.

43. Penelhum's reconstruction of Butler's defense of the authority of conscience is puzzling at just this point. He correctly diagnoses the question of conscience's authority as concerning the justification or reasonableness of following conscience. People who raise it "wonder whether what [conscience] tells them is what they should do" (*Butler*, p. 58). Ultimately, however, Penelhum thinks that Butler is committed to regarding this question as confused, and that the argument "from nature" reinforces this: "It amounts, instead, to the claim that every agent is so constituted by providence that, barring special circumstances, he or she will make the judgments that the principle prompts, and *will recognise them to be better reasons for action* than the presence of lower principles or inclinations with which they conflict. . . . [I]t tells someone who questions whether the dictate of a higher principle really is a better reason for acting than the urgings of a lower one, that he is so made by providence that he knows quite well that it *is* a better reason" (p. 59). This does not address the question of what *makes* considerations of conscience conclusive reasons. And to say, as Penelhum does, that "virtuous action is action done from motives which are implanted in us by providence, and which have a hierarchical relationship" (59) does not help. Whether conscience is superior is precisely what is at issue, and since the relevant hierarchy must be constitutional and not simply functional, it is unclear how any fact about providence can give conscience supremacy of the right kind.

The point can be put in terms of Kant's reciprocity thesis.[44] To this juncture, all Butler can justifiably claim is half of the reciprocity thesis, specifically, that morality (conscience) is staked on its own authority because its judgments entail its authority for a free rational agent. But it is consistent with this that it lacks this authority and, thus, that moral claims are actually ultimately invalid, as Butler says of the parricide in the *reductio* at II.17. In order to vindicate morality, it is necessary to establish the authority that, by its nature, morality claims. And to do that Butler must show the other half of the reciprocity thesis, namely, that the reasons that regulate free rational action dictate acting morally. Now, it seems clear that Butler believes that conscience *is* rationally inescapable, and not just because being governed by it is our intended function. He apparently believes, as well, that the very having of reasons to act itself requires conscience. But why?

Before we can answer this question we must consider an obstacle to interpreting Butler in this way. We recall that Butler's initial example of the superiority of one principle to another – namely, that of self-love in comparison with passions and appetites – seems to be independent of the relation of either to conscience. He compares a "brute creature [who] by any bait [is] allured into a snare, by which he is destroyed" with "a man [who], foreseeing the same danger of certain ruin, [rushes] into it for the sake of a present gratification." After remarking that, though both act on their strongest desire, only the man and not the brute acts unnaturally, he then concludes:

[I]t is manifest that self-love is in human nature a superior principle to passion. This may be contradicted without violating that nature; but the former cannot. So that, if we will act conformably to the economy of man's nature, reasonable self-love must govern. Thus, without particular consideration of conscience, we may have a clear conception of the superior nature of one inward principle to another. (II.11)

This can reasonably be taken as some evidence against the present interpretation. I doubt that it is strong evidence, however. And it is certainly not decisive. For one thing, Butler says that self-love is "in *human* nature a superior principle to passion" and that the action of "a man" who pursues present passion against self-love is unnatural. One difference between human beings and "brute creature[s]" is that we have calm self-love. But that is not the only difference; we also

44. For a discussion, see, in Chapter 5, "The Accountability Strand of Autonomist Internalism."

have conscience. And it may be that Butler is thinking that self-love is superior to passion in *us* because, through conscience, we favor the former over the latter, but that it would not be in a creature who, lacking conscience, could not. Butler does say that we can appreciate the superiority of self-love in human beings "without particular consideration of conscience." But note that he says, "without *particular* consideration of conscience." There is, I think, a perfectly good explanation of why he would have said just this if he believed what he says in the *reductio*, namely, that the natural superiority of any principles at all is equivalent to the authority of conscience.

First-order conscience approves or disapproves not only of acts but also of *principles* (or principled conduct). (See, for example, I.8; II.8.) And Butler holds that self-love is one of the principles we reflectively approve of, at least when it is properly tempered: "It should seem, that a due concern about our own interest or happiness, and a reasonable endeavour to secure and promote it . . . is virtue, and the contrary behaviour faulty and blamable; since, in the calmest way of reflection, we approve of the first, and condemn the other conduct, both in ourselves and others" (*DV*.6). Butler does say that what we are approving of here is "conduct," but he appears to mean conduct motivated by a certain principle – specifically, by "a due concern about our own interest." A second example of a principle approved by conscience is, of course, benevolence.[45]

Now, in the case where conscience disapproves of an act in itself, and not on the grounds that it manifests a disapprovable principle, there will be no other prominent approved motive not to perform the act other than that it violates conscience. In the case, however, where conscience approves of acting on one motive (other than conscience) in preference to another (say, self-love in preference to passion), there *will* be another approved motive for doing so in addition to conscience. In such a case, therefore, there will be some reason to say that we judge that a human being should defer gratification "without particular consideration of conscience" *even if* we would not, on reflection, disapprove of a being's failure to defer gratification if, lacking conscience, *she* lacked any way to judge that self-love should override the desire for present pleasure. In the case Butler is discussing, therefore, it may be a background assumption that conscientious judgment provides a (regulating) motive for the agent to give preference to self-love over passion – a motive necessary for us to disap-

45. See Sermon XII.

prove of her action. But although the agent's conscientious motive can be placed in the background of this case because she has another relevant motive that conscience approves of, this would not be true in the case of an act that conscience opposes intrinsically. The only motive for forbearing might be conscience itself. Although the agent's conscience is always relevant, in the latter sort of case it must be given a "particular consideration" that is unnecessary in the former.[46]

What Butler says about his example, therefore, need not be inconsistent with interpreting him as holding that an agent's having conscience is necessary for her to be capable of acting naturally or unnaturally in the "strictest and most proper sense" or for her principles to manifest relations of superiority or inferiority. Since he explicitly says that conscience is the faculty "by which men *are a law to themselves*" and that "their conformity or disobedience to [this] law of our nature renders their actions, in the highest and most proper sense, natural or unnatural," and since the *reductio* argument for the authority of conscience assumes the latter's equivalence with the very existence of relations of superiority, it is not unreasonable to interpret him as holding that the authority of conscience is equivalent to the existence of reasons for acting, and that if a being were to lack conscience there could be no facts regarding what she should do – no reasons for her to act.

This is not an implausible idea. Consider a being who differed from brutes in having a desire for his own greatest happiness on the whole, a desire brutes presumably lack, but who differed also from mature human beings in not being able to see this latter desire (or its object) as a *superior reason* for acting to the reasons provided by momentary appetites and passions. Suppose that such a being is

---

46. Another passage that presents a similar problem occurs in the Preface to the *Sermons*, where Butler criticizes Shaftesbury for holding that the obligation to virtue depends entirely on the virtuous life's being most in our interest, thereby neglecting the obligation provided by conscience. He there concedes to Shaftesbury that "[supposing] a sceptic not convinced of this happy tendency of virtue, or being of a contrary opinion, . . . leaving out the authority of reflex approbation or disapprobation, such an one would be under an obligation to act viciously; since interest, one's own happiness, is a manifest obligation" (Preface 26). Still, the person in question is someone who has conscience. And Butler holds that conscience approves of prudence. Moreover, when he writes "leaving out the authority of reflex approbation," what he is explicitly excluding is a direct obligation to virtue when it conflicts with interest. Of course, this requires shoehorning, but *any* interpretation of Butler does. I claim only to be describing one strand of his thought.

lured into a snare by a strongly attractive bait. Can we say that he had good reason not to be so lured? Or even that there was such reason *for* him not to be so lured? Since a brute lacks a desire for his own happiness, it will be true that our creature's act is contrary to a desire he has but the brute lacks. But does that mean he has reason to avoid the snare although the brute does not? After all, the brute is presumably frustrating other desires he has also. We may assume that in having a desire for his own happiness, our creature considers that if he takes the bait he will be frustrating many of his desires, including his desire for his own happiness (one *we* regard as superior). What he cannot do is see these *as reasons* not to take the bait, or as better reasons than that provided by present appetite.[47] But if he lacks this capacity, can we really give sense to the idea that his desire for happiness nonetheless gives *him* good reason not to take the bait? Nothing prevents us from saying that self-interest should be given greater weight than current appetite by any agent capable of weighing reasons, including by this being were he so capable, that it would be better for him to avoid the trap, and so on. But that our creature would be acting contrary to reason in taking the bait may still seem mistaken. If it is, then it will be a necessary condition of there being reasons for someone to do something that he could (in principle) acknowledge them and act on them in deliberation. Given the broad outlines of Butler's moral psychology, having a principle of reflection will then be necessary for the existence of practical reasons.

This may still seem a puzzling idea. Even if Butler is bound to think conscience is the faculty through which we make judgments about what we have reason to do, why should he think that the truth of what conscience judges depends on it in this way? Why does the existence of reasons for an agent to act entail even that an agent *have* conscience, much less that it be authoritative? A key to answering this question, I suggest, is to appreciate the central role that the idea of *autonomy* or *self-regulated constitutional order* plays in Butler's thought. What conscience gives an agent is the capacity to guide her life by normative practical *judgment*, and this capacity, Butler seems to be saying, is a condition of the very possibility of autonomous

47. It might be held that this is not really imaginable, since desire itself involves seeing its object as providing a reason, or that the desire for one's happiness does, because it is reflective or second-order. Perhaps, but the creature we are imagining would still lack the capacity to assess these "given" perceptions critically, and, therefore, to make reasons for acting its own. And in any case, it clearly seems possible for someone to want himself to satisfy a particular first-order desire without thinking that he has good reason to do so.

rational (and moral) will and, for that reason, of an agent's having reasons to act.

Butler's preoccupation with autonomy is apparent at the beginning of the Preface to the *Sermons* – indeed, in the very first sentence. "Though it is scarce possible to avoid judging, in some way or other, of almost everything which offers itself to one's thoughts; yet it is certain, that many persons, from different causes, never exercise their judgment, upon what comes before them, in the way of determining whether it be conclusive" (Preface 1). By "judgment" Butler evidently means not simply an assessment of whether something or other is the case but a weighing *of reasons* or justifications for some conclusion. Here, of course, he is discussing the exercise of judgment in guiding belief rather than action. But he is also sounding a general theme he will later repeat for the practical case. Although we can hardly think at all without judging, judgment is something we can exercise more or less, and so our beliefs and actions can be guided more or less by its exercise. Many persons, he continues, frequently desire arguments "for some accidental purpose: but proof as such is what they never want for themselves; for their own satisfaction of mind or conduct in life" (Preface 1). What they seek is *rationalization*, not reasons on which to base their beliefs or conduct.

Butler's rhetorical purpose at this point in the Preface is to spur his readers to the effort he rightly thinks it will take for them to digest the *Sermons* fully. So he tries to convince them that this is not something they are unable to do but only, perhaps, something they are not in the *habit* of doing.

The great number of books and papers of amusement, which, of one kind or another, daily come into one's way, have in part occasioned, and most perfectly fall in with and humour, this idle way of reading and considering things. By this means, time even in solitude is happily got rid of, without the pain of attention. (Preface 3)

Thus people habituate themselves to let things pass through their minds, as one may speak, rather than to think of them. . . . Review and attention, and even forming a judgment, becomes fatigue; and to lay anything before them that requires it, is putting them quite out of their way. (Preface 4)

He concedes that he has no right to demand the attention of his readers but insists that "it is also true . . . that nothing can be understood without that degree of it, which the very nature of the thing requires." And, he adds, "morals, considered as a science . . . plainly requires a very peculiar attention. For here ideas never are in themselves determinate, but become so by the train of reasoning and the place they stand in" (Preface 6).

The general message is unmistakable. Human thought and action can be shaped more or less by the self's own theoretical and practical judgment. At their most heteronomous, people may be habituated simply "to let things pass through their minds . . . rather than to think of them." However, we can, by "review and attention," make *judgments* about what to believe and thereby make our beliefs subject to reasons we *have*. This is even more important in ethics than elsewhere, Butler says. Moral ideas become determinate only by virtue of "the train of reasoning and the place they stand in." We shall return to this remark presently.

The contrast that concerns Butler in the body of the *Sermons* is that between *practical* heteronomy and autonomy. Here self-governance requires a faculty of *practical judgment,* one by which a person can make a judgment of reasons to act and, through so judging, direct her own actions. This, Butler thinks, is what conscience provides. It is the "practical discerning power" (*DV*.1); "judgment, direction, superintendency" are "a constituent part of the idea . . . of the faculty itself" (*S*.ii.14). To the principle of reflection "belongs the adjustment and correction of all other inward movements and affections" (ii.1). In short, conscience is what makes autonomy possible; it is "that by which men *are a law to themselves*" (ii.4).

Why does the capacity for autonomy matter? We recall that Butler concludes the *reductio* with the observation that, if we cannot judge that an agent has a conclusive reason for forbearing an act of which we disapprove, we cannot disapprove *of him* for failing to do so. Unless we can suppose that an agent has a way of determining himself by reasons he has to do what we think he should, we cannot disapprove of his failing to do so.[48] And he must also think that without a capacity for normative judgment (conscience, in Butler's psychology), a person can neither act on nor have reasons for acting at all.

Butler contrasts conduct that can be natural or unnatural in the "strictest" sense with conduct that can only be *heteronomous,* proceeding only from whatever principle *happens* to be strongest. In order for a being's conduct to *accord with or violate its constitution* and be natural or unnatural in the strictest sense, the being must be capable of autonomy, of being a "law to [it]sel[f]." But for this, Butler

48. Or unless he could have by a process of self-determining habituation.

believes, an agent requires conscience. She must be able to draw for herself the distinction between a motive's being strongest and its being one on which she should act, and to determine herself by the latter judgments. In Butler's moral psychology, this is conscience's role. It gives the agent a critical perspective on her own motives through which she can make self-motivating normative judgments.

Significantly, Butler puts the issue of conscience's authority as whether it is natural "to let it govern and guide only occasionally in common with [other principles], *as its turn happens to come, from the temper and circumstances one happens to be in*" or whether "the very constitution of our nature requires, that *we bring* our whole conduct before this superior faculty; wait its determination; [and] enforce upon ourselves its authority" (Preface 24, 25; emphases added). The former alternative would hold true if, as creatures incapable of being a law to ourselves, our conduct could only be heteronomous. If, on the other hand, we can act naturally or unnaturally in the strictest sense, that will be because we can be autonomous, a law to ourselves. And, Butler repeatedly says, it is conscience, and the practical recognition of its authority, that makes autonomy possible. Conscience, for him, is not simply a part of our constitution; it is the very root of self-regulated constitutional order. Without it, the agent can draw no contrast between acting on the strongest motives and acting on the weightiest reasons. "[T]he whole business of a moral agent," Butler concludes, is to "conform [himself] to it."

Here, then, is an explanation for Butler's holding that the existence of reasons for acting entails the authority of conscience. A being can have reasons to act (and hence act naturally or unnaturally in the strictest sense) only if he has the capacity for autonomy, for self-regulated constitutional order. And having conscience and crediting its authority is necessary for that. Only if a being can be a "law to [him]sel[f]" can he conform to or violate his nature in the "strictest" sense, that is, as a constitutional order. "[C]onformity to or disobedience" to conscience thus "renders . . . actions, in the highest and most proper sense, natural or unnatural" (II.9).

Recall now Butler's remark that "morals, considered as a science . . . plainly requires a very peculiar attention" because, unlike those in other "scientific" areas, ethical "ideas never are in themselves determinate, but become so by the train of reasoning and the place they stand in" (Preface 6). What makes ethical ideas unlike those in the natural sciences? The latter become determinate by connection to an independent natural order to which they refer, discovered through naturally reliable empirical investigation. 'Water', to take a familiar example, refers to the natural substance we find in the rivers and lakes, and we make our idea of water more determinate by investigating the nature of this substance. Similarly, Hutchesonian moral goodness, on one reading, is whatever in the natural order "procures approbation," and greater determinacy about it awaits empirical investigation concerning "what general Foundation there is in Nature" for this response.[49] Actually, the point has nothing essentially to do with *natural* reference or investigation. If, as Clarke supposed, moral ideas refer to nonnatural metaphysical properties of eternal fitness, then they could presumably become more determinate as we investigated this independent order. Butler accepts some version of the doctrine of eternal fitness, but he also says that the *obligation* to follow conscience does not depend upon it. This may help to explain his contrast. It suggests he thinks that *normative* ideas refer to no order that is independent of the exercise of autonomous practical reason (conscience) itself.

Butler defines conscience *formally*, not by its connection to an independent order. For him, conscience, unlike the sense of touch, which would not be *touch* unless it was connected to independently existing touchable things, is defined by its formal features. In Sermon I, for example, he takes it as sufficient evidence that someone has conscience that she can reflect (more or less) "coolly" and impartially about actions and principles of action and that, when she does, she comes to an "all things considered," disinterested attitude (I.8).

If conscience is delimited formally, then its authority should derive from these formal features. It is, of course, true that some of Butler's arguments do not depend solely on these: most obviously, his analogy between conscience and the external senses in II.1. And neither, of course, are his teleological/functional arguments independent of considerations of functional role. But Butler has good reasons to be dissatisfied with these latter arguments. From facts about function and design no normative facts directly follow. And an analogy between conscience and the senses ultimately depends upon a Clarkean metaphysical doctrine of the sort Butler is committed to avoiding in establishing moral *obligation*.

According to the autonomy argument, conscience's authority derives from its necessity for self-regulated constitutional order. But how do conscience's formal features fit it for this role? Conscience is

49. See, in Chapter 8, "Naturalism and Moral Sense."

the only principle fit to ground self-regulated constitutional order, because it is the only principle addressed to the defining question of autonomous agency, What should I do? (More universally, What should someone like me do in a situation like this?) Unlike self-love and benevolence, whose objects are *states*, conscience's object is exclusively *conduct* and its regulation. The very feature of reflex approbation that disqualifies it from being a motive in Hutcheson's scheme – its not having natural good as object – is what uniquely qualifies it for authority in Butler's.

Butler typically reserves conscience for instances of self-judgment. But it is clear enough that he thinks this is only an instance of what aims to be, and presents itself as, a disinterested, dispassionate, and informed attitude toward universal questions of conduct: what a person should do in a kind of situation, what motives a person should act from, and so on.[50] It is not unreasonable to attribute to Butler the view that each of these features is necessary for normative practical judgment. The only evaluative judgment one can make from the perspective of self-interest, for example, is what would be best from the standpoint of one's own interests. But that is simply a *different question* from what one *should do*, even if a person should do what is in her interest. And similarly for the other features. In having these features, Butler is arguing, conscience is the only part of our moral psychology able to make normative judgments and, therefore, able to ground a self-regulating constitutional order. The principle of reflection enables an agent to step back from actual motives (principles of action) and ask: What motive should I act on? Which provides me with the weightiest reasons? Faced with a snare whose bait attracts him more strongly than he desires his own happiness, he has a kind of agential leverage that the demiagent we considered earlier has not. Having a principle of reflection, he can approve of his acting on the latter desire and disapprove of his acting on the former, judging that self-love is superior to appetite – that his own happiness is a weightier reason for acting than any satisfaction the bait offers.

It is important to see why Butler thought normative judgments of conscience can have a motive force that Hutcheson thought impossible. For Hutcheson, as for Cumberland, agency is entirely *transparent* and *instrumental*. Deliberation looks *through* conduct to *states* (natural goods) that the agent aims to bring about. For Butler, however, agency has an internal defining aim quite distinct from the desire for

50. See notes 2, 21, and 30.

any such state. Agents are, as such, concerned with how they conduct themselves, with *self-regulation*. Similarly, the object of moral approbation is quite different for Butler from what it is for Hutcheson. What Hutchesonian moral sense approves of is a motive *in* the agent, not anything about how an agent with that motive conducts herself. That is one reason Hutcheson thinks that moral sense cannot itself motivate. It can only approve the strength of virtuous motives (benevolence) in the agent, and its approval will not affect *that*.

To see the contrast, we may imagine a Hutchesonian agent in whom self-love and benevolence are in conflict. Reflecting on her motives in the context, we may imagine that she approves more of her benevolent motive than she does of her self-interested one. But this could provide her with a motive to *act* on her benevolent motive only if, somehow, it could increase her benevolence. If the relative strengths of benevolence and self-love remain the same, then so will the moral goodness of her act. So the fact that she approves more of benevolence can provide her with no motive to *do* what benevolence directs. It is no reason to act. For Butler, on the other hand, the object of reflective approval is always agency and action. In considering a conflict between self-love and appetite via the principle of reflection, the agent approves of *acting* on the former rather than the latter – judges the former to be a superior principle *of action*, responsive to weightier reasons for acting. And since the defining aim of an agent's having conscience is to act on superior principles – that is, on the best reasons – this approval can then motivate such action. Acting on superior principles because they are superior is precisely her defining aim.

Butler does not think that an agent can on every occasion bring himself to do what he judges he should. Conscientious approval gives the agent some practical leverage on his actions, but only some. On any given occasion, present habits may overpower the motivational force of conscientious judgment. But if habit can overpower conscience, it is also something an agent can make use of to realize self-determination. In the *Analogy*, Butler lists "attention, industry, self-government" as among the traits a person can acquire through practice (*A*.1.5.4).

If each of the formal elements of conscience is necessary for normative judgment, what guarantees that they are jointly sufficient? There may, however, be only two remaining possibilities. One is that some formal feature other than universality, impartiality, dispassionateness, and informedness is necessary for normative judgment. But if that is so, nothing prevents including it in a formal account of conscience.[51] The other possibility is that normativity is not a purely procedural matter. As we normally suppose about the epistemology of natural science, the truth of what we are attempting to judge can outstrip our best procedures. But if the authority of conscience is to be established without reference to any connection to an independent (normative) order, this possibility would appear to be ruled out.

CONCLUSION

What I have been calling Butler's autonomist line is a version of *autonomist internalism.* Conscience's dictates are obligatory because the fullest exercise of the capacity for autonomy yields conclusive motive to act as it directs. Again, "conclusive motive" should not be given a de facto reading here, as in Locke. Butler holds a *normative theory of the will* according to which autonomous agency and will involve self-*regulation* by a normative conception that the agent herself accepts. What makes moral demands authoritative for an agent is that were the agent fully to exercise her capacity for autonomous practical reason, she would herself *regard* them as practically conclusive de jure.

Normativity thus derives from a motivational source that makes self-regulation possible. Of course, this is only the beginning of a line of thought, and it remains in tension with others that are in some ways more prominent, especially Butler's teleological/functional narrative. Resting conscience's authority on its essential role in a self-regulating constitutional order disconnects it from anything having to do either with functional role or with some independent order of normative fact. And once this is done, there is nowhere else for normativity to be grounded other than in the direction of that which makes self-regulation possible, namely, conscience itself.

To develop this line of thought would be to attempt to establish the second half of Kant's reciprocity thesis, namely, that free practical reason entails morality. Holding a normative theory of the will, as do Kant and Shaftesbury, Butler maintains against Hutcheson that a being with desires and instrumental reason, or even with calm self-love and benevolence, is not yet a free rational agent. That requires as well the possession of a normative conception by which the agent

---

51. This is Kant's approach, as I discuss briefly in Chapter 11.

can govern her own conduct. And conscience, the seat of this conception, is also the seat of moral demands.

This gives Butler a way of defending a view of moral obligation
that, as Hutcheson had wanted, is intrinsic in morality but, unlike
Hutcheson's "observer" theory of moral sense, ties it to authoritative
motivation. It is, however, apt to raise as many questions as it answers. What assures the coincidence of moral and rational authority
in Butler is that conscience is simultaneously the source of both. But
why should that be? Also, basing the authority of conscience on its
role in autonomous practical reason will seem precarious if conscience itself consists of contingent *responses* – "sentiment[s] of the
understanding" or "perceptions of the heart" – that are simply *given*
in practical experience, passively received because of the way God
has fashioned our psyche (xII.31n).[52] If this is the source of conscientious judgment, then the coincidence between moral laws and laws
of practical judgment will seem to be accomplished by a *Deus ex
machina:* one perhaps more sophisticated than Hutcheson's, but one
no less objectionable.[53]

52. How Butler can believe this and also subscribe to a doctrine of eternal fitnesses is
   puzzling.
53. This opens the way for a criticism of Butler's version of autonomist internalism
   similar to the rationalists' criticism of Hutcheson's theory of moral sense. Although Cudworth and Hutcheson had complained against the voluntarists that
   their view gave morality a kind of contingency and arbitrariness by basing it in
   God's will, Hutcheson was himself criticized along similar lines. John Balguy
   argued that Hutchesonian moral sense and benevolence are but "instincts" or
   "affections," making virtue "of an arbitrary and positive nature." John Balguy,
   The Foundation of Moral Goodness (London: 1728; facsimile edition, New York:
   Garland, 1976), pp. 5, 8–9. Reprinted in Raphael, *British Moralists*, vol. 1, p. 390.
   Further references to this work will be placed parenthetically in the text, preceded by *FMG*. But to the extent that conscience's responses are simply part of
   contingent human nature, whether divinely ordained or not, it would seem that
   its dictates will be no less contingent. Perhaps worse from the standpoint of
   autonomy, even though the object of Butlerian conscience is autonomous will, the
   source of its dictates is entirely outside the will of a free rational agent. (Christine
   Korsgaard makes a similar criticism of Humean moral sentiment in "Normativity
   as Reflexivity: Hume's Practical Justification of Morality," delivered at the meetings of the Hume Society at the University of Lancaster in the summer of 1989.)

Chapter 10

Hume: norms and the obligation to be just

Butler and Hutcheson provide radically different vantage points on the role of autonomy and reason in action and the moral life. Hutcheson carries forward an empiricist tradition – one including Hobbes, Cumberland, and Locke – that holds agency to be entirely instrumental. Every motive is a desire for some naturally good *effect* of action, usually some pleasurable state of the agent or of someone else.[1] Reason's task is exclusively theoretical: to inform the agent of means to these desired end states or of natural goods of which she may have been insufficiently aware, giving rise to new desires or new levels of desire. What human agents learn from this use of reason (contingently) presents itself, within the deliberative context, as a kind of directive or dictate to take necessary means or to desire new natural goods. But there is nothing more to normativity than this appearance under these conditions, or, perhaps, than the contingent fact that human agents are motivated in these ways. This might be thought to have the effect of explaining normativity away, at least as a fundamental ethical concept. For all these writers, *practical* ethics can proceed entirely in terms of natural good and evil: the valuable and disvaluable states action can bring about. No further normative practical notion (of a reason for acting, for example) is required by deliberating agents or by any ethics addressed to them.

This is most obvious in Cumberland and Hutcheson. Hutchesonian calm deliberation exclusively concerns natural goods and is organized into two independent structures by the two ultimate calm motives – self-love and universal benevolence – desires for the greatest good for ourselves and for everyone, respectively. Only the invis-

1. Every motive, that is, that provides a reason. For Cumberland and Hutcheson, passions and appetites need have no good as object.

ible hand of divine providence gives unity to human agency, since we lack any deliberative normative perspective from which to judge what to do if these should conflict. Cumberland provides a place to raise this question but argues that it reduces to which is the better end. And, owing to his instrumental conception of *agency* (though not of reason), he is bound to construe that issue as Which is the better *state:* the agent's own happiness or the greatest happiness of all? This makes the conflict a walkover for Cumberland. The greatest universal happiness is the better state, since it contains more natural good.

Even Locke treats all practical normative questions as issues about natural good, despite the centrality of self-determination to his thinking about agency and obligation. I stressed his emphasizing a kind of practical judgment in autonomy, but that is misleading in the present context. Lockean agents determine themselves solely by judgments about their own natural good (happiness) in prospect.[2] They require no normative practical notions beyond these, Locke believes, because there are no rational motives other than desires for self-happiness. Judgments of their own good are inherently motivating – according to Locke, the only inherently motivating judgments that agents can make.

When it comes to the normativity of *morality* in the empirical naturalist tradition, we find the following internalist options: Locke and Hobbes argue that human agents have conclusive self-regarding motives for moral conduct. Cumberland holds that universal benevolence is a rationally conclusive motive to be moral, since the greatest happiness of all is the "best end." Hutcheson maintains that benevolence is in human agents as rationally conclusive as any motive, but no more so than self-love – and claims as well that distinctively moral obligation consists not in any motive but in the approving sentiment of moral observers.

All these options hold that the motive to be moral derives entirely from desires for natural goods and aversions to natural evils. According to none does moral obligation involve a motivational source intrinsic to agents' normative practical judgments – judgments about what one should do – that are irreducible to any judgment about naturally good and evil effects of action, and whose motive force is thus independent of desires for and aversions to such effects. This is the major point of contrast with Butler's doctrine of the authority of

2. See, in Chapter 6, "Liberty as Self-Determination," especially note 18.

conscience. For Butler, action does not result simply from motives *in* an agent. Rather, agents act *on* reasons: Their own critical endorsement of considerations *as* reasons makes a difference to what they do. That is why agency requires the principle of reflection.

The same dialectic holds in the moral sphere, as Butler sees it. What we morally approve about persons are not only motives *in* them – forms of benevolence, for example. Nor do all considerations that bear on what a person morally should do concern the naturally good effects of action. Against Hutcheson, Butler famously argued that we "condemn falsehood, unprovoked violence, [and] injustice . . . abstracted from all consideration, which conduct is likeliest to produce an overbalance of happiness or misery" (*DV*.8). Just as plural sources of reasons necessitate some standpoint from which we can come to a critically reflective, all-things-considered judgment of reasons, so likewise do plural moral grounds demand such a standpoint for moral judgment. *Moral* agency requires a principle of reflection, and real virtue attaches not, as with Hutcheson, to some motive or motives *in* the agent but to the agent *herself* insofar as she regulates herself through conscience.

The contrast between Butler and Hutcheson on the psychology and normativity of morals is instructive background against which to consider the views of David Hume. Perhaps no philosophical writer in early modern Britain, if not in the whole history of English-speaking philosophy, is more subtle, creative, and difficult to pin down to orthodox categories than Hume. This is particularly so in the present context. On the one hand, the influence of Hutcheson on Hume was profound. Hume's metaethic, like Hutcheson's, was a kind of sentimentalism, and both held the object of moral sentiment always to be states internal to the moral agent – motives and character – rather than external conduct. Indeed, Hume's virtue ethics went Hutcheson's one better. Whereas Hutcheson thought that moral sense can derivatively evaluate options for "election," Hume's ethics feature no such evaluations of acts from the agent's point of view.[3] Humean moral sentiment always has motive and character as objects; it is invariably an observer rather than agent phenomenon: "[W]hen we praise any actions, we regard only the

---

3. This, again, is the source of Hutcheson's utilitarianism. Moral sense approves of acts that achieve the greatest happiness of the greatest number because it approves of the motive that aims at this.

References to Hume's *Treatise of Human Nature* will be to the edition by Selby-Bigge cited in Chapter 7, note 18; references will be placed parenthetically in the

motives that produced them. . . . The external performance has no merit. We must look within to find the moral quality" (*THN.477*).

Hume also agreed with Hutcheson in maintaining the empiricist (instrumentalist) theory of WILL. "The will," he writes, "exerts itself, when either the good or the absence of the evil may be attain'd by any action of the mind or body" (*THN.439*; see also 399). By 'good' and 'evil' he means pleasure and pain, respectively (*THN.439*; see also 276, 399, 438). The doctrine that an agent's defining aim is a concern to regulate himself by good reasons, this being irreducible to any desire for natural goods, had been put forward by the rational intuitionists in addition to Butler. Balguy, for instance, had argued that "[t]he end of rational actions, and rational agents, consider'd as such, is reason and moral good" (*FMG.48*). Against the view in its intuitionist garb, Hume famously objected that reason is incapable of providing any motive (*THN.413*), forcefully repeating Hutcheson's antirationalist critique in the *Illustrations*. And as for Butler's thesis of the authority of conscience, Hume complained to Hutcheson, whom he thought dangerously close to accepting Butler's idea in his later work, that moral sense is "but an instinct or principle, which approves of itself upon reflection, and that is common to all of them."[4]

Finally, Hume accepted Hutcheson's distinction between, and his respective accounts of, interested and moral obligation. (Hume calls the former "natural obligation" in the *Treatise*, 498.) Hume's "moral obligation," like Hutcheson's, derives entirely from an observer's response to contemplated character, not from anything (to use Cumberland's words) that "can superinduce a *Necessity* of doing or forbearing any thing, upon a Human Mind deliberating upon a thing future" (*TLN.233*).

Despite these Hutchesonian elements, when Hume comes to discuss *justice* and the obligation to be just, the richness and complexity of his thought outrun his usual categories, giving him a much more interesting view and a distinctive place in early modern thinking about obligation. Although to be consistent with his brand of virtue ethics Hume must continue to hold that the moral obligation to justice fundamentally concerns character – the *virtue* of justice

text, preceded by *THN* when appropriate. References to *An Enquiry Concerning the Principles of Morals* will be to the edition by Selby-Bigge cited in Chapter 5, note 9; references will be placed parenthetically in the text, preceded by *ECPM* when appropriate.

4. This is from a letter from Hume to Hutcheson. John H. Burton, *The Life and Correspondence of David Hume* (Edinburgh: William Tait, 1846), pp. 148–49.

rather than just acts – this latter involves a motivational state quite unlike any other Humean virtue: agents' regulating conduct by rules they accept as authoritative.

Actually, justice is only one example of a virtuous trait or motive that Hume thinks cannot be reduced to some form of benevolence. As against Hutcheson, Hume argued that moral sentiment is not really a distinct sense or original instinct (*THN.*473). Rather, moral approval works by sympathy with traits' and motives' usual effects, and many besides benevolence tend to produce natural good. What makes justice unique in the present context is the pressure Hume's account puts on the theory of will common in the empiricist tradition. What is distinctive about just persons, Hume tells us, is not their seeking some good or avoiding some evil "by any action of the mind or body" but their *regulating* themselves by *rules* (of property, transfer, and promise) they regard as "sacred and inviolable" (*THN.*533). This affects in fascinating ways Hume's account of the obligation to be just.

PUZZLES ABOUT JUSTICE

As soon as one starts to sort out Hume's views about obligation in the *Treatise,* especially in relation to what he there says about justice, various puzzles arise. Here are several:

1. The very idea of obligation, Hume says, depends – as do those of justice, right, and property – on mutually advantageous conventions having already been "enter'd into" (490–91). "Those . . . who make use of the word . . . *obligation,* before they have explain'd the origin of justice, or even make use of it in that explication, are guilty of a very gross fallacy, and can never reason upon any solid foundation" (491). Several pages later, however, Hume announces that since he has "fully explain'd" the "*natural* obligation to justice, viz., interest," it remains to demonstrate the "*moral* obligation," evidently meaning by the latter the sentiment of moral approbation toward justice and disapprobation toward injustice (498). If the idea of obligation depends on convention, then since neither the moral sentiment nor the motive of self-interest does, how are we to understand Hume's referring to both as *obligations* to the practice of justice?

2. Sometimes Hume appears to treat 'justice' (and 'honesty') as a term of moral approbation. Thus, following his general argument that "the first virtuous motive, which bestows a merit on any action,

can never be a regard to the virtue of that action" (478). Hume applies this argument to the special case of justice. The "honesty and justice" of restoring a loan, he says, "can never be a regard to the honesty of the action. For 'tis a plain fallacy to say, that a virtuous motive is requisite to render an action honest, and at the same time that a regard to the honesty is the motive of the action" (480). At other points, however, Hume treats 'justice' (and 'honesty') as morally neutral, defined by mutually advantageous rules concerning possessions, transfer, and promise. And he there supposes that whether justice is a virtue – or whether, as he also puts it, there is a moral obligation to be just – is something that must be established. We must ask, he says, "*Why we annex the idea of virtue to justice, and of vice to injustice*" (498). So is the idea of virtue annexed to justice or contained within it?

3. The moral obligation to justice, again, consists in the sentiment of approbation and disapprobation toward justice and injustice, and love and hatred toward the just and unjust, respectively. But none of these sentiments or emotions can be a direct motive to action, according to Hume, since, for one thing, the object of moral approbation is always a motive and never an "external performance."[5] Nonetheless, Hume also writes that, for example, " 'tis evident we have no motive leading us to the performance of promises, distinct from a sense of duty. If we thought, that promises had no moral obligation, we never shou'd feel any inclination to observe them" (518).[6] This suggests that we are morally obligated and, through this realization, motivated to perform just *acts* in the first instance, even though, if moral obligation consists in approbation, and if approbation can never have external conduct as object, this cannot be.

4. As I mentioned above, Hume generally takes the view that ("by an *original* instinct") will aims at some good (i.e., pleasure) in prospect (438–39, 399). But it is important to his view that justice is a rule-regarding rather than a good-regarding virtue. Unlike benevolence

5. At least this is so when what is approved is a "virtuous action" (478). Other "mental qualities" than motives can be approved also.

   On the intrinsic motivating power of moral sentiment, it is worth noting that Hume remarks that moral sentiment is "a fainter or more imperceptible love or hatred" (614) and that love and hatred are "always follow'd by" motivating desires but do not themselves include them (367). On the impotence of the moral sentiment to motivate directly, see Charlotte Brown, "Is Hume an Internalist?" *Journal of the History of Philosophy* 26 (1988): 69–87. I shall discuss this further presently.

6. Cf. "[W]e have naturally no real or universal motive for observing the laws of equity, but the very equity and merit of that observance" (483; see also 479).

and self-love, the trait of justice *itself* aims not at any good to self or others but at regulation by mutually advantageous rules (even though moral sentiment and self-interest both endorse the trait for its usefulness). How, then, is voluntary just conduct possible?

Puzzles 2–4 combine in Hume's astonishing remark that we have "no real or universal motive for observing the laws of equity, but the very equity and merit of that observance; and as no action can be equitable or meritorious, where it cannot arise from some separate motive, there is here an evident sophistry and reasoning in a circle" (483).[7] Taken literally, this says that justice is not simply puzzling but paradoxical.

No interpretation can dissolve all these puzzles. They result, I believe, from Hume's trying to combine the following three positions: (*a*) his deeply insightful account of justice (as realized both in social practice and in the motivation of moral agents), (*b*) the fundamental principle of his virtue ethics (that the direct object of moral approbation and disapprobation is always some trait of character), and (*c*) his theory of the will as invariably aiming at some prospective good or the avoidance of some prospective evil. Hume could have held (*b*) and (*c*) (as Hutcheson had) had he not made the important discoveries about justice that today we regard as among his most important contributions. This account (*a*) is, however, incompatible with (*c*).

HUMEAN JUSTICE

Despite what will emerge as fundamental differences, Hume and Hutcheson agree that an adequate account of justice and rights must be rule-consequentialist.[8] Where they disagree starkly is in Hume's

---

7. Hume's manuscript amendment to the original edition of the *Treatise* adds "naturally," which Nidditch includes in his edition thus: "[W]e have naturally no real or universal motive. . . ." This does not appear in the Selby-Bigge edition.

    Since Hume concludes that "unless . . . nature has establish'd a sophistry" the sense of justice must be artificial rather than natural, we can see why he was drawn to add "naturally" where he did. But it really does not help. As long as the motive that renders an act equitable or meritorious is regard for equity or merit, this is "evident sophistry and reasoning in a circle" whether the source of the motive be natural or artificial (*THN*.483).

    I have been helped here by reading some of Rachel Cohon's papers on "Hume's circle."

8. "Whenever it appears to us that a Faculty of doing, demanding, or possessing any thing, universally allow'd in certain Circumstances, would in the Whole tend to the general Good, we say, that one in such Circumstances has a Right to do,

belief that justice is a virtue quite independent of benevolence that aims not directly at any good but at complying with generally benefi-cial rules. Hutcheson assumes that violating such rules "is always exceedingly evil, either in the immediate, or remote Consequences of the Action" (*In.*VII.ix).⁹ By his lights, right-defining rules can enter into agents' deliberations only as *summary* rules (in Rawls's sense), guiding benevolence, the master virtue. And "Justice, . . . if it has no regard to the Good of Mankind . . . is a Quality properer for its ordinary Gestamen, a Beam and Scales, than for a rational Agent" (*In.*II.i).¹⁰

possess, or demand that Thing" (*In.*VII.vi). For Hume, of course, the conventions of justice must actually be established, and their consequences must be good for everyone, not just overall. Nonetheless, Hutcheson and Hume are in agreement that justice and rights can be recommended only on grounds of the consequences that generally attend their establishment.

9. This passage actually asserts this to be true of violating "perfect rights."

10. This passage occurs at the end of a remarkable paragraph in which Hutcheson critically reviews in similar fashion the cardinal Aristotelian virtues. This may begin a tradition of utilitarian criticism of intuitive or commonsense morality that reaches maturity in Sidgwick's *Methods of Ethics*. For the distinction between the "summary" versus the "practice" conception of rules, see John Rawls, "Two Concepts of Rules," *Philosophical Review* 64 (1955): 3–32. Note, by the way, that what I am calling Hutcheson's "rules of right" is appropriately viewed as sum-mary rules only insofar as they enter into determining right action. The way rules actually enter into Hutcheson's definitions of rights is more like a practice rule.

Even had Hutcheson come to believe that benevolence can conflict with a desire to abide by (mutually beneficial) rules that structure just practices, he would, quite unlike Hume, have had powerful systematic reasons for holding that benevolence should then prevail. For one thing, benevolence is morally good, Hutcheson believed, not because of its effects but because moral sense approves of it (and only it) intrinsically. This is probably a secular version of the Christian idea that love begets love. On the Christian roots of Hutcheson's thought, see Leidhold, *Ethik und Politik bei Francis Hutcheson*. Moral sense also approves (derivatively) of beneficial acts and of establishing beneficial conven-tions, but that is because these are what benevolence, the immediate object of its approval, motivates. I discuss this aspect of Hutcheson's thought, in comparison with Hume's theory of the moral sentiment, in "Hume and the Invention of Utilitarianism," in M. A. Stewart and J. Wright, eds., *Hume and Hume's Connexions* (Edinburgh: Edinburgh University Press, forthcoming). The moral goodness of benevolence is thus fundamental for Hutcheson; good consequences have moral relevance only because they are that at which benevolence aims. And even if, as Hume argues, agents' regulating themselves by (mutually beneficial) rules of justice as a general practice has better effects, that has no tendency to establish the moral goodness of motivational states of the agents who are so regulated. For another, since Hutcheson believes that any rational desire or motive must aim at some good for someone if just persons are concerned to comply with mutually advantageous rules, then, since the object of this concern is no good as such, Hutcheson must regard it as more like an appetite or a passion than a rational motive. It can enter into rational deliberation only insofar as its object is related to the good.

For Hume, however, a convention of justice arises when members of a society communicate their common interest in "regulat[ing] their conduct by certain rules" (most prominently, by abstaining from the possessions of others) (*THN*.490), and come actually to do so – when, that is, they establish mutually advantageous *practices*, and come to regard the rules structuring them as *practice rules*, in Rawls's sense.

> I observe, that it will be for my interest to leave another in the possession of his goods, *provided* he will act in the same manner with regard to me. He is sensible of a like interest in the regulation of his conduct. When this common sense of interest is mutually express'd, and is known to both, it produces a suitable resolution and behaviour. (490)

This, Hume concludes, "may properly enough be call'd a convention or agreement betwixt us" (490). Slowly, by gradual accretion, the common sense of interest and resolve spreads through society until enough members regulate their conduct by the rule of property, "upon the supposition, that" similar rule-required actions are "to be perform'd" by others (490).

The latter construction brings out nicely the prescriptive/predictive aspects of the situation. From an external standpoint, each expects that, by and large, others will in fact regulate their conduct, and regulates himself on that expectation. But it is also crucial for Hume that the rules come to have for each what Hart called an "internal aspect" – that each regard the rules prescriptively.[11] If the expectation were simply *that* others will in fact regulate their conduct, rather than an expectation *of* them (applying also to oneself), then this could give no one a basis for regulating her own conduct. Only for a person who is resolved to regulate her conduct by mutually advantageous rules if others do (and thus who regards the rules prescriptively on that condition) would the knowledge that others will in fact regulate their conduct provide any ground for conforming herself. Such a person, we might say, regulates her conduct by a *metarule of cooperation*: Regulate your conduct by mutually advantageous rules (of promise, transfer, and property) so long as others do.

Note how the conditional works in the passage set out above. Hume is not saying that each expresses to others the prediction that if they abstain from his possessions, then it will be in his interest to abstain from theirs. What each expresses to others is the sense that it

---

11. On the "internal aspect" of rules, see H. L. A. Hart, *The Concept of Law* (Oxford: Oxford University Press, 1961), pp. 55–57.

will be in his interest to follow a certain rule: Abstain if others do. Or perhaps: Follow mutually advantageous rules provided others do.

As we shall see below, Hume is somewhat ambivalent in the *Treatise* concerning the relation between regulating conduct by rules of justice and acting for the good, either the agent's own or the public's. But whatever the exact relation, Hume appears to consider justice a distinct virtue, and thus a trait of character distinct from any focused on the goods of self or others – for example, from prudence or benevolence. And he seems to be saying that what is distinctive about this virtue is the just person's regulation of her conduct by rules that define the practices of property, transfer, and promise. Just persons, he tells us, "lay themselves under the restraint" of these rules (499, 532); "strict[ly]" "regulate their conduct" by them (490, 534); "impos[e]" on themselves these "general inflexible rules" and regard them as "sacred and inviolable" (499;533). Each person, he writes, must "fix an inviolable law to himself, never, by any temptation, to be induc'd to violate" it (501).[12]

What this *says* is that just persons regard the rules of justice *as normative*, conditional on others' doing so. They conditionally treat these rules, or perhaps the metarule of cooperation, as authoritative, as *in themselves* giving reasons – indeed, conclusive reasons – not to take the property of others, to keep their promises, and so on. In one sense of the word, therefore, just persons would appear to regard the fact that something belongs to another, or that the rule of property requires forbearance, as a *motive* – i.e., a ground or a reason – for not taking it.[13]

The problem, of course, is that this motive (or a motivating acceptance of it) can find no place in Hume's theories of action and will as

12. What Hume actually says here is that no one should ever violate "those principles, which are essential to a man of probity and honour." But these are violated precisely by (knowingly) violating the rules of justice (501).

Sometimes, as in this passage, Hume seems to be assuming that agents can "impose" or "fix" rules by which they then regulate themselves – something, apparently, like the Kantian idea that agents can freely adopt maxims. Nothing that I say about the way rule regulation figures in Hume's account of justice depends on this assumption. My interest is in the state of rule regulation itself, and in its difference from motivation by desires for goods (including those that will be realized by having the disposition of rule regulation).

13. Hume uses 'motive' sometimes to refer to a reason for acting (as in: "What reason or motive have I to restore the money?" [479]) and sometimes to refer to a motivational state of the agent (as in: "[A]ll virtuous actions derive their merit only from virtuous motives, and are consider'd merely as signs of those motives" [478]).

advanced in the *Treatise*.[14] The "perception of pain and pleasure," Hume writes, is "the chief spring and moving principle of all . . . actions" (118). 'Perception' is ambiguous here as between two different ways in which pain and pleasure "mak[e] their appearance in the mind" (118). They appear in person, as it were, as impressions; and since "impressions always actuate the soul," they can then cause action directly (118). Touching the hot stove, I pull back. Or testing the pleasantly warm tub water, I immerse myself further. But *ideas* of pleasure and pain also arise in the mind, including of pleasures and pains that would result from possible actions. When these are sufficient in force and vivacity to constitute beliefs, they come to have a "like influence on the passions" as do pleasurable and painful impressions (119; see also 414). So believing pleasure will result if I immerse myself in the tub can have an effect similar to that of the pleasurable impressions of testing the water. And the belief that touching the stove will cause pain can result in an aversion to doing so. "'Tis from the prospect of pain or pleasure," Hume writes, "that the aversion or propensity arises towards any object" (414). Evil and good ("or in other words, pain and pleasure") "consider'd simply" give rise to aversion and desire, respectively (439). And "the WILL exerts itself, when either the good or the absence of the evil may be attain'd by any action of the mind or body" (439).

Hume's theory of action thus not only employs the traditional idea that the will invariably aims at the good; it also interprets that idea hedonistically and egoistically. Desires and aversions arise from the prospect of pleasure or pain, respectively, for the agent. Hume recognizes that this theory will not work in all cases. Indeed, he says that "direct passions *frequently* arise from a natural impulse or instinct, which is perfectly unaccountable" and unconnected to any thought of pain or pleasure (439; emphasis added). As examples he gives "the desire of punishment to our enemies, and of happiness to our friends," and such bodily appetites as hunger and lust (439). To these should be added some of Hume's "calm passions": "instincts originally implanted in our natures, such as benevolence and resentment, the love of life, and kindness to children" (417). Pleasure and pain are still connected to these passions, but through their satisfaction, not

14. Hume discusses will and the causes of human action at three places in the *Treatise*: "Of the influence of belief," in Book I (118–20); "Of the influencing motives of the will," in Book II (413–18); and "Of the direct passions," in Book III (438–39). I am greatly indebted to David Aman and Rachel Cohon for discussion of points in these sections.

because they are caused by the idea of some pleasure or pain for the agent (439).

Hume does not tell us what he takes the will to aim at in such cases. Resenting an injury, I desire to punish my enemy and see an opportunity to do so. If, however, will can exert itself only when a good (pleasure) or the absence of an evil (pain) to the agent is attainable, then my motive can only be something like the satisfaction of my desire to punish, rather than, say, that he deserves it or that this will lay him low (or the judgment that one of these is so). On the other hand, if the will can have the same object as these "nonstandard" direct passions, then it can aim directly at an enemy's (deserved) unhappiness. Since Hume appears to be assuming that the will exerts itself to attain the object of desire or the absence of the object of aversion, it is hard to see how he can avoid the latter possibility once he has admitted the existence of nonstandard direct passions. If this is right, Hume will be committed to revising his theory of action and the will quite independently of anything he says about the just person's regulation of her conduct by conventionally established rules of property, transfer, and promise.

We shall return presently to the relations between the virtue of justice, regulation by the rules of justice, and the motives to just conduct. We should note here, however, a further textual problem in understanding Hume's talk about rule regulation. When Hume discusses "what reason or motive" there is to just acts when the rules of justice have been established and people have been "train'd up according to a certain discipline and education" in the practices of property, transfer, and promise, what he says is not that this consists in any ground mentioned in the rules or in (what just persons take to be) the (conditional) authority of the rules. Rather, Hume cites as the "civiliz'd" motive to justice in those who "have the least grain of honesty, or sense of duty and obligation," the "regard to justice, and abhorrence of villainy and knavery" (479). And by this he means moral approbation of justice and disapprobation of injustice – that is, what he later calls the moral obligation to justice (498; see also 483, 518). As I shall argue below, however, since the direct object of approbation or disapprobation is always some mental quality ("all virtuous actions derive their merit only from virtuous motives" [478]), the "regard to justice and abhorrence of villainy and knavery" must be directed toward the virtue and vice of justice and injustice, respectively. It will follow that, unless justice involves "a sophistry" (483), the virtue of justice must itself involve some motivational state other than the regard to justice.[15] This, I shall ultimately argue, is nothing other than the just person's regulation of her conduct by the rules of justice.

THREE SPECIES OF OBLIGATION

We are now in a position to appreciate the sense Hume must have in mind when he says that the concept of obligation arises only *after* the conventions establishing the rules of justice have been "enter'd into." (490–91).[16] As I mentioned at the outset, neither natural obligation (the motive of self-interest) nor moral obligation (the sentiment of approbation) requires background conventions to be intelligible. Granted, the only place Hume uses 'natural obligation' is in connection with justice, but that is not the only place he uses the concept. Twice he refers to the motive of self-interest as obligating in contexts that have nothing to do with conventions and justice (312, 314). And even if he had not called the motive of self-interest an obligation in any other context, it would not follow that the idea somehow depends on background conventions.

Likewise with moral obligation. Hume uses 'moral obligation' in a context that has no special connection to the justice conventions (479), but again, it would not matter were he never to have done so. The concept he has in mind evidently depends in no way on convention. "[W]hen any action, or quality of the mind, pleases us *after a certain manner*, we say it is virtuous; and when the neglect, or nonperformance of it, displeases us *after a like manner*, we say that we lie under an obligation to perform it" (517). The moral obligation is created by an approving or disapproving moral sentiment. And even if the only thing moral sense ever disapproved were violation of the rules of justice, it would not follow that it is necessary to explain the conventional origins of justice in order to explain the idea of moral

15. Note that even if approbation of justice were to involve something like a desire to perform just acts (and an aversion to injustice), these direct passions would also be nonstandard by Hume's theory of action and will. Note also that nothing here affects Hume's thesis that every action proceeds from a passion. What is at issue is whether all action-motivating passions are desires for some good.
16. Hume generally uses 'convention' to refer, not to the rules by which people agree to regulate themselves but to the state of agreement itself. The rules, he says, "deriv[e]" from the convention (490).

obligation.[17] After all, Hutcheson, from whom Hume borrows the ideas of natural and moral obligation, gives convention no role whatsoever.

So what can Hume mean? He must have some third concept in mind. And we can see pretty clearly what it must be; he must be referring to a notion of obligation defined through the rules of justice (or their acceptance) themselves. Rules are in their nature directive. The rule of property, for example, directs agents to abstain from others' possessions. It requires that agents so abstain, and if they do not they violate the rule. We might say, meaning nothing more, that it obligates them to abstain.

Here we should recall Hart's distinction between the internal and external aspects of rules.[18] From an external point of view, we may say that the rule of property obligates abstinence from others' possessions, meaning only to convey the content of the rule without endorsement. But if we *accept* the rule or norm as a basis for regulating conduct, then from an internal standpoint we shall not simply be reporting that this is what the rule requires; we shall be saying, as we might put it, that this is what the person really ought (or is obligated) to do, at least other things being equal. The external claim requires a background rule in the obvious sense that it is a claim *about* a rule (from the outside). Were there no rule of property, for example, there would be no rule obligation to report. But internal-standpoint claims do not similarly refer to rules as part of their very content. They assert nothing about any rule. Someone who accepts the rule or norm of property, and says from the internal standpoint that people are obligated to abstain from the possessions of others, makes a normative claim that *expresses* the rule, or perhaps his acceptance of it.[19] But a claim with the very same content could be made were there no *established* rule of property or conventions of justice at all.

An external-standpoint rule obligation claim, therefore, requires reference to a rule for its very intelligibility, but an internal-

17. I take this to refute David Gauthier's speculation that "moral obligation, for Hume, arises from a coincidence between an object of our moral sentiments and an object of our reflective interests." "David Hume, Contractarian," *Philosophical Review* 88 (1979): 28. Annette Baier makes a similar suggestion: "Hume seems to require that, for something to be a moral obligation, it must first satisfy the test of self-interest which convention imposes." *A Progress of Sentiments* (Cambridge, Mass.: Harvard University Press, 1991), p. 243. See also Baier, "Hume and Social Artifice," *Ethics* 98 (1988): 757–78.
18. See note 11.
19. On the idea that accepting a norm is a distinctive motivational state that normative judgments express, see Gibbard, *Wise Choices, Apt Feelings*, pp. 55–82.

standpoint claim does not. Still, we can understand why Hume would think there is a sense in which even the normative claims that agents make when they accept a rule are not really intelligible without an existing background convention. Hume clearly regards the attitude that self-regulators take toward the rules of justice as *reasonable* only so long as enough others share it. And what makes this possible, he thinks, is the publicly expressed common sense that it serves mutual advantage, that is, the existence of what he calls a convention.[20]

For Hutcheson, we recall, there are no act-regarding virtues. All virtuous motives are "kind affections," desires for the good of others. And any rational motive is a desire for some good to self or others. The Humean virtue of justice, however, aims at no condition or state to which it regards action as instrumental. Rather, it is like Butlerian conscience in this respect: It aims at action, or the governance of action, itself. This is, as I have noted, a significant departure from Hutcheson. But it is also important that for Hume it is the *only* act-regarding virtue, because it is the only case in which the motivational state of rule regulation is supported by mutually advantageous conventions. No such state is natural; it arises only as a result of a convention, through publicly expressed mutual advantage.

Hume, then, recognizes three species of obligation: those he calls "natural" and "moral" and the one we have called norm obligation or *rule obligation*. Although, on its face, the third concept has nothing essentially to do with rational motive, I shall claim that a central piece of Hume's account of justice is that just persons are rationally motivated by their acceptance of the rules of justice, and that this motivation is not itself a species of any desire for the good, either for themselves or generally.[21]

JUSTICE, MOTIVE, RULE, AND GOOD

Again, Hume says clearly that rules of justice are established only when individuals come to *regulate* their conduct by these rules (490, 499, 532, 533, 534). They "lay themselves under the restraint of such

20. "[A convention] is only a general sense of common interest; which sense all the members of the society express to one another, and which induces them to regulate their conduct by certain rules" (490).
21. Although Hume also holds rule regulation to be supported by both self-interest and moral approbation and thinks that these depend on that motivational state's furthering private and public interest, respectively.

rules" (499), "impose" them on themselves (533), and "suppos[e them] to be sacred and inviolable" (533). It is hard to see how to interpret these remarks in any way other than as entailing that rules of justice are established only when individuals come to treat rules of justice as having authority in their deliberations – when, that is, they give them independent weight (indeed, conclusive independent weight), thereby deliberating on a basis different from their own good (or, for that matter, the public good). Nonetheless, Hume appears to take the position in the *Treatise* that what the rules of justice require is invariably extensionally equivalent with enlightened self-interest. If so, then Hume may well be saying in the *Treatise* that enlightened self-interest invariably leads to compliance with rules of justice despite their intensional inequivalence, so that agents can actually "regulate" themselves by these rules without giving them independent deliberative weight.

Hume certainly says there that it is only because each person can expect to gain by the existence of rule-structured practices of property, transfer, and promise that each has reason to establish them. "To the imposition then, and observance of these rules, both in general, *and in every particular instance,* they are at first mov'd only by a regard to interest; and this motive, on the first formation of society, is sufficiently strong and forcible" (499; emphasis added). Once the "common sense of interest" is mutually expressed, moreover, no more is needed "to induce any one of them to perform an act of justice, who has the first opportunity" (498). Each sees that doing so will become an example of good will to those equally prepared to follow the rules if others do, and this makes it advantageous for her to do so. "On the first formation of society," when each appreciates the "disorder and confusion" that result from "every breach of these rules," self-interest dictates observing the rules "in every particular instance" (499). When the circle of interagents is sufficiently small and the rules are insufficiently well established, the personal costs of flouting them are likely to be high; the situation will resemble not a one-shot Prisoner's Dilemma but an iterated form of a game that changes the payoffs to make justice and self-interest coincide.[22]

Were this situation to continue, agents could successfully comply with rules of justice by following their own interests. Hume does not

22. See Francis Snare, *Morals, Motivation, and Convention: Hume's Influential Doctrines* (Cambridge: Cambridge University Press, 1991), pp. 297–302; Robert Axelrod, *The Evolution of Cooperation* (New York: Basic, 1984); and Philip Petitt, "Free Riding and Foul Dealing," *Journal of Philosophy* 83 (1986): 361–79.

expect it to, but in the *Treatise*, at any rate, the reason is apparently not that he thinks that when "society has become numerous, and has increas'd to a tribe or nation," individuals can sometimes actually gain by violations, but that he thinks the interests individuals have in maintaining order are there "more remote" and ones they "may frequently lose sight of," so that they come to follow a "lesser and more present interest" (499).[23] In a larger, more anonymous setting, the "consequences of every breach of equity seem to lie very remote, and are not able to counterballance any immediate advantage, that may be reap'd from it. They are, however, never the less real for being remote" (535). Before the mutual acknowledgment of a shared interest in establishing rule-structured practices of property, transfer, and promise, self-interest "is the source of all injustice and violence" (480). But once there is a convention, "a general sense of common interest," this is sufficient to make self-interest the servant of justice. When society becomes sufficiently numerous, individuals may tend to lose sight of their real interests, but these continue to dictate abiding by the rules of justice in every case.

Because Hume stresses that the primary benefits of justice for individuals are benefits they reap from the *practice*, from the "whole plan or scheme" (497), and because he says that "single acts of justice may be contrary, either to public or private interest" (497), it may seem that he is willing to allow in the *Treatise* that justice does occasionally conflict with the agent's interest, that it is possible for individuals to act unjustly and "free ride" on the just actions of others. In this passage, however, Hume is excluding from the consequences of individual just acts any compliance they may cause by others.[24] "A single act of justice is frequently contrary to *public interest;* and were it to stand alone, without being follow'd by other acts, may, in itself, be very prejudicial to society" (497). So the "somewhat singular" connection Hume asserts in the *Treatise* between the rules of justice and

23. I am indebted to Rosalind Hursthouse for stressing this to me. On this point, and the importance of *THN*.535, see David Gauthier, "Artificial Virtues and the Sensible Knave," *Hume Studies* 18 (1992): 407, 410; also Barry Stroud, *Hume* (London: Routledge & Kegan Paul, 1977), pp. 204–18. It is not clear, by the way, that Hume must be understood (as Gauthier understands him) as implying that injustice is invariably disadvantageous when he writes, "nor do men so readily perceive, that disorder and confusion follow upon every breach of these rules, as in a more narrow and contracted society" (499). He may be implying that, or he may be allowing the possibility that these consequences are sometimes not there to be perceived. The former is surely more likely, however, given the passages just discussed in the text.
24. On this point, see Gauthier, "Artificial Virtues and the Sensible Knave," p. 407.

self-interest is not, as we might expect from recent discussions of the free rider problem, that though the "whole plan or scheme" is essential to promoting mutual advantage, individual acts of justice may be contrary either to the agent's or to the public interest. Hume's point at 497 is that, considering all consequences other than those that run through the rule-structured practices of property, transfer, and promise, individual acts of justice may do more harm than good. Once we include these practice-mediated effects, however – for example, that trust may be threatened and others therefore less likely to comply – then, Hume appears to believe in the *Treatise*, it is invariably in the agent's interest to comply. The "singular connection" is that it is only because others are likely to comply only if one does – that their compliance with rules of justice is among the consequences of one's compliance – that each individual agent's complying with the rules of justice invariably has the best consequences.

As far as the *Treatise* goes, therefore, it would appear that Hume's talk of agents' regulating themselves by the rules of justice need not be taken too seriously. Compliance with these, or with what I have called the metarule of cooperation, is invariably dictated by self-interest once the common sense of interest in establishing just practices has been mutually expressed. Individuals comply with these rules only because others do, but this latter consideration functions for them not as a condition for giving intrinsic weight to these rules, nor as the antecedent of an intrinsically weighty metarule of cooperation, but as the fact that one had better comply since others are likely to comply only if one does, the good consequences of their compliance being consequences of one's compliance as well.

MORAL OBLIGATION, MOTIVE, AND ACT

Still, even in the *Treatise* Hume says that just practices will be stable among interagents sufficiently numerous to constitute a "tribe or nation" only if they have some motive to comply *other* than self-interest. Prudence will continue to dictate compliance, but when the bad consequences of injustice are sufficiently remote, persons are far likelier to be attracted by "lesser and more present interest[s]" (499), so some other motive is necessary to generate adequate support for just practices. The problem is that Hume says that the requisite motive is the sense of duty or moral obligation, and this, as I have said, requires some other motive as *its* object.

Indeed, Hume holds that the sense of duty is not simply a fail-safe device but is the motive uniquely appropriate to justice. "[W]e have naturally no real or universal motive for observing the laws of equity," he writes, "but the very equity and merit of that observance" (483).[25] And: "'tis evident we have no motive leading us to the performance of promises, distinct from a sense of duty. If we thought, that promises had no moral obligation, we never shou'd feel any inclination to observe them" (518). Justice's having merit, being a duty, and being morally obligatory all come to the same thing for Hume, namely, that justice is the object of moral approbation and injustice the object of moral disapprobation (477, 498–500, 517). But approbation and disapprobation always take some "mental quality" as direct object. An "external performance" – for example, an action that complies (extensionally) with a rule of justice – "has no merit" in itself. So a just action can acquire merit only derivatively, by evidencing a meritorious motive (483–84). It follows that "no action can be equitable or meritorious, where it cannot arise from some separate motive" (483) – specifically, some motive other than the sense of merit, duty, or moral obligation.

These ideas seem to be in irreconcilable conflict. How can Hume both hold the fundamental thesis of his virtue ethics, that the sense of duty cannot be the "first virtuous motive" (478) of justice or any other virtue, and also think that it is the only "real or universal motive for observing the laws of equity" (483)? This conflict has led some commentators to the conclusion that Hume cannot really mean to maintain his distinctive virtue ethics when it comes to justice. Although with the natural virtues it is clear that what we approve is some motive or mental quality that might be manifested in various actions, when it comes to the artificial virtues what is approved in the first instance, and thus is morally obligatory, is *actions* themselves: those required by the rules of justice.[26] In this section, I shall argue that this interpretation faces numerous obstacles. To avoid these, justice must be treated, like every Humean virtue, as having moral qualities only as "a mental quality," specifically, as a motivational state. Seeing things this way, however, will leave the substantial question what this motivational state can be, especially since what is

25. On "naturally," see note 7.
26. J. L. Mackie makes this suggestion in *Hume's Moral Theory*, p. 80, as do Francis Snare, *Morals, Motivation, and Convention*, pp. 192–201, and Rachel Cohon, "Hume's Difficulty with the Virtue of Honesty," unpublished.

distinctive about justice in Hume's view is the way a sense of obligation is supposed to enter into it.

According to any plausible interpretation of Hume's ideas, the
moral obligation to justice is supposed to derive from the fact that
sympathy with the usual effects of justice and injustice leads to moral
approbation of justice and moral disapprobation of injustice, respectively (479; see also 483, 518). And it is uncontroversial that the
relevant consequences are (at least primarily) consequences of acts of
justice and injustice. What is at issue is whether Hume thinks that,
uniquely with justice (and the artificial virtues more generally), the
proper objects of moral approbation and disapprobation are kinds of
acts or whether he holds that with both artificial and natural virtues
the object of moral sentiment is a mental quality of which an "external performance" is only a sign.

Since Hume puts forward the thesis that "all virtuous actions
derive their merit only from virtuous motives, and are consider'd
merely as signs of those motives" at the very outset of Part II ("Of
Justice and Injustice"), and since it is the centerpiece of his argument
that justice is an artificial virtue, it is hard to see how he can mean it
not to apply to the case of justice (478). But perhaps we should not
conclude from this directly that Hume denies that acts of justice and
injustice can be morally approved or disapproved in themselves.
After all, common sense distinguishes analytically between evaluations of persons and their characters (and of actions as signs of
these), on the one hand, and evaluations of acts as things to do, on
the other. Hume could be saying that "merit" concerns the former
while believing that another category of moral evaluation concerns
the latter.[27] This thought might be encouraged by the account he
gives of moral obligation in his discussion of promising: "[W]hen
any action, or quality of the mind, pleases us *after a certain manner*, we
say it is virtuous; and when the neglect, or non-performance of it,
displeases us *after a like manner*, we say that we lie under an obligation to perform it" (517). Perhaps Hume's view is that whereas merit,
virtue, and vice all concern mental qualities of the agent in the first
instance, *moral obligation* primarily concerns acts – "external performances." And if just *acts* can be morally obligatory, then perhaps the
just person is moved actually to follow the rules of justice by this
conviction or sentiment.

This passage notwithstanding, however, Hume makes no prin-

27. I am indebted here to Rachel Cohon and Nicholas Sturgeon.

cipled distinction between the categories of virtue and vice, merit and demerit, on the one hand, and duty and obligation, on the other. He does not say that the (moral) motive to justice is the sense of duty or obligation as opposed to a sense of merit and virtue. Rather: "the very equity and merit" of just acts is the only "real or universal motive for observing the laws of equity" (483). Hume includes the category of moral obligation, moreover, within the scope of the thesis that links the moral quality of an action to that of its motive: "But tho', on some occasions, a person may perform an action merely out of regard to its moral obligation, yet still this supposes in human nature some distinct principles, which are capable of producing the action, and whose moral beauty renders the action meritorious" (479). Whenever we require an action, he says, "we always suppose, that one in that situation shou'd be influenc'd by the proper motive of that action, and we esteem it vicious in him to be regardless of it" (478).

How thoroughgoing Hume's commitment is to this thesis can be illustrated by his discussion of the rare instance in which "the sense of morality or duty [can] produce an action, without any other motive" (479). Whenever we approve of a motive or principle in human nature,

a person, who feels his heart devoid of that principle, may hate himself upon that account, and may perform the action without the motive, from a certain sense of duty, in order to acquire by practice, that virtuous principle, or at least, to disguise to himself, as much as possible, his want of it. (479)

By "the action" here, Hume evidently means an action characteristic, and thus ordinarily a sign, of a virtuous motive or "mental quality." If what the sense of duty (later in the paragraph: "regard to its moral obligation") motivates is acting *in order to* acquire a virtuous principle by practice or to sustain ignorance of its lack, then the object of moral duty or obligation must be having the virtuous principle itself.

Were Hume to maintain that just acts are morally obligatory (by his definition) independent of the agent's state, and that this approbation is what directly motivates just acts after the "first formulation of society," he would face numerous problems. Most obviously, he would have to abandon the fundamental principle of his virtue ethics, that all merit derives from "mental qualities." But, second, it is not obvious that Hume could count a moral approbation of just acts that was independent of their relation to a state of the agent as any kind of motive to justice. One reason is that the way Humean ap-

probation motivates is indirectly, through the agent's hatred or esteem of himself on account of his qualities.[28] Approbation or disapprobation are "nothing but a fainter and more imperceptible love or
hatred" (614). And only insofar as the objects of approbation and
disapprobation are qualities in the agent will they be related to love
and hatred in the right way. Knowing that someone performed a
kind of act that we regard unfavorably does not yet connect the act to
her in a way that reflects on her as an appropriate object of love or
hatred. Thus, although Hume is willing to allow that approbation
and disapprobation can as a psychological matter be transferred by
association from thing signified to sign (479), in order to motivate
through self-esteem or self-hatred the object of moral sentiment must
be some quality in the person.[29]

Additionally, in a manuscript amendment to the *Treatise*'s original
edition, Hume makes it clear that he thinks moral approval of justice
is an insufficient motive to just acts in any case.

Thus *Self-interest* is the original Motive to the *Establishment* of Justice: but a
Sympathy with *public* Interest is the Source of the *moral* Approbation, which
attends that Virtue. This latter Principle of Sympathy is too weak to controul
our Passions; but has sufficient Force to influence our Taste, and give us the
Sentiments of Approbation or Blame. (670; see also 586)[30]

A third and final point: The idea that moral approbation of just acts
can directly motivate agents conflicts no less with Hume's official
theory of the will than does the suggestion that agents are motivated
by their acceptance of mutually advantageous rules. If will exerts
itself only when "the good or the absence of the evil may be attain'd"

28. See, for example, 479. On this point, see Brown, "Is Hume an Internalist?"
29. Hume's official psychological view is that love and hatred always have some
    other person as object, their self-correlates being pride and humility (329).
30. Moral judgment's influence on the passions is, of course, an important theme of
    Hume's (457). But this is fully explainable by the natural, if indirect, psychologi-
    cal mechanisms linking moral judgment to motivation via the pleasurable and
    painful moral sentiments and love and hatred. Hume's famous objection against
    the rationalists that they are in no position to "prove *a priori*, that [their favored]
    relations, if they really existed and were perceiv'd, wou'd be universally forcible
    and obligatory" is sometimes offered as proof that he thinks that moral judgment
    is intrinsically action guiding (466). But Hume regards this complaint as apt here
    precisely because the rationalists, maintaining that morality derives from rela-
    tions between ideas and not from impressions, hold it to consist in "immutable
    measures of right and wrong [that] impose an obligation, not only on human
    creatures, but also on the Deity himself" (456). They therefore are committed to
    explaining a relation between morality and motivation that is universal and a
    priori. A contingent natural connection will not do for their purposes, though it
    will for Hume's.

by an action, then it will not be moved by moral obligation per se. At most, the agent will be moved to follow the rules of justice by the thought that doing so will enable him to avoid painful contemplation of (his own) injustice. If somehow he could do injustice without having to contemplate it, this would give him no reason not to.

JUSTICE AS AN AGENT STATE

If the moral obligation to justice derives from our approbation and disapprobation of justice and injustice as states of the agent, respectively, the question obviously arises, which states are they? Hume never says explicitly, so the interpretive problem is to work out indirectly what it might be.[31] David Gauthier suggests that in the *Treatise* Hume holds that the virtue of justice is nothing other than self-love ("the interested affection") "redirected towards its fuller satisfaction through its own restraint by the conventionally instituted laws of society."[32] Hume rejects the possibility that "a concern for our private interest or reputation is the legitimate motive to all honest actions" (480) in arguing that justice is an artificial virtue, but that is on the grounds that *before* the convention arises "self-love . . . is the source of all injustice and violence" (480). And as we have seen, Hume holds in the *Treatise* that once the sense of common interest has been mutually expressed, a person appropriately mindful of justice's long-term benefits and able to weigh them properly with "lesser and more present interests" (499) will always have an adequate motive of interest to comply with its rules. Hume has a name for the trait that enables a person to act in her greater long-term interest when that requires forgoing lesser, more immediate interests: "strength of mind" (*THN.*418; see also *ECPM.*205, 239).[33]

Suppose we take Hume to hold that suitably enlightened self-

31. No doubt, this should count as some evidence that Hume is (at least) ambivalent between carrying through his ethics of virtue in the case of justice and treating justice as an underivative property of acts – if not, indeed, that he holds the latter view.
32. Gauthier, "Artificial Virtues and the Sensible Knave," p. 413.
33. In the course of arguing that there is no agent state of justice, and thus that Hume holds that the moral obligation to justice motivates through self-hatred for lacking what we mistakenly believe to be such a natural state, Knud Haakonssen writes that "it is hardly likely that Hume thought self-interest, as a general character trait, morally approved by men" (*The Science of a Legislator* [Cambridge: Cambridge University Press, 1981], p. 35). But there is no doubt that Hume thinks strength of mind is a virtue.

interest, or strength of mind, is the motivational state distinctive of the just person. If self-interest invariably dictates compliance with the rules of justice, as Hume appears to believe in the *Treatise*, then a fully informed strong-minded person will invariably comply. Moreover, we can understand on this hypothesis how someone lacking this trait might be moved by the sense of duty or moral obligation to act justly in situations where he otherwise would not. If lesser, more immediate interests incline him to act unjustly, he may still reflect, contemplate his lack of a strong mind, and "hate himself upon that account" (478). And this will give him an additional, and more immediate interest in acting justly than he would have had if he did not disapprove of weak-mindedness, since by so acting he will be encouraging a trait of which he would be proud "or, at least, disguis[ing] to himself, as much as possible, his want of it" (479).

Now whereas this shows how an obligation to justice other than the natural obligation (self-interest) can figure in motivating justice as a backup if the virtue of justice is strength of mind, it does raise various puzzles, even in the *Treatise*. First, although Hume's general view is that virtues include various kinds of "mental qualities," he says at the beginning of his discussion of justice that "all virtuous actions derive their merit from virtuous *motives*" (478; emphasis added). This suggests that the agent state of justice involves a distinctive motive to just acts. But on the current proposal, the motive of just acts is simply enlightened self-love.

Second, it is hard to explain on this proposal the prominence Hume gives to a distinctive motivational source (and thus to obligation) in the case of justice and the other artificial virtues. I have already mentioned Hume's remarks in the *Treatise* that the sense of moral obligation is the only "real or universal motive for observing the laws of equity" (483).[34] and that "if we thought promises had no moral obligation, we never shou'd feel any inclination to observe them" (518). In "Of the Original Contract," Hume makes clear that what he has in mind here is nothing less than a fundamental difference between natural and artificial virtues:

All *moral* duties may be divided into two kinds. The *first* are those, to which men are impelled by a natural instinct or immediate propensity, which operates on them, independent of all ideas of obligation. . . .

---

34. Again, the Nidditch edition adds that this is "naturally" the only such motive. See note 7.

The *second* kind of moral duties are such as are not supported by any original instinct of nature, but are performed entirely from a sense of obligation.[35]

If Hume thinks strength of mind is the trait we admire in the just person, and also that enlightened self-interest invariably dictates complying with rules of justice, then it is odd that in his description of the just person's motivating reasons he would give a prominent role to a sense of any obligation to justice other than the "natural obligation" of self-interest.[36]

Third, it is a mystery why Hume should say that there is *any* idea of obligation that is "unintelligible" before the "convention, concerning abstinence from the possessions of others, is enter'd into" (490). Neither natural obligation nor moral obligation requires conventions to be understood. On the present suggestion, the idea of natural obligation would be adequate to capture the practical thinking of the just person, and that of moral obligation would suitably explain the evaluative thoughts of observers of justice and injustice and of agents as observers of themselves. So why does Hume think there is any idea of an obligation to justice that requires the existence of convention in order to be understood?

I claimed earlier that Hume's remarks about the unintelligibility of obligation before the existence of a convention make sense if we take him to be speaking of *norm* or *rule obligation*. The convention in question is a sense of common interest in regulating conduct by rules of justice (or, perhaps, by what I called the metarule of cooperation). Each communicates to the other his sense that it is in his interest to accept and abide by the rule of abstinence "*provided* he [the other] will act in the same manner with regard to me" (490). Again, this is not a prediction that if others abstain, then it will be in one's interest to do so. Of course, Hume believes that it is in each person's interest to encourage others to abstain by abstaining as an example, but that is a different matter. Rather, it is an expression that it is in one's interest to *accept* and *follow* a conditional rule or norm: Abstain if others do. On this hypothesis, there would indeed be a sense of

35. David Hume, *Essays, Moral, Political, and Literary* (Edinburgh, 1741; 2d ed., 1741; 3d ed., 1748), ed. with foreword, notes, and glossary by Eugene F. Miller, with variant readings from the 1889 ed. by T. H. Green and T. H. Grose (Indianapolis: Liberty Classics, 1987), pp. 479–80.
36. It should be noted here that Hume's contrast between natural and artificial virtues in "Of the Original Contract" brings in natural as well as moral obligation. Unlike artificial virtues, natural virtues operate "independent of all ideas of obligation, and of all views, either to public or private utility" (*Essays*, p. 479).

'obligation' for which Hume believes people would have no use before the convention, before the expression of common interest in regulating themselves by the rule – namely, rule obligation.

Still, although Hume speaks as though participants in a rule-structured practice of justice genuinely regulate themselves by rules they accept, regarding them as authoritative (and overriding), what he really seems to think in the *Treatise* is that self-interest always provides an adequate deliberative basis. Only metaphorically do just persons "regulate" themselves by the rules; their motive is always given by enlightened self-interest.

JUSTICE AND THE SENSIBLE KNAVE

By the time he wrote the *Enquiry*, however, Hume was no longer prepared to say that justice is invariably advantageous:

[A] man, taking things in a certain light, may often seem to be a loser by his integrity. And though it is allowed that, without a regard to property, no society could subsist; yet according to the imperfect way in which human affairs are conducted, a sensible knave, in particular incidents, may think that an act of iniquity or infidelity will make a considerable addition to his fortune, without causing any considerable breach in the social union and confederacy. (*ECPM*.282)

Hume now appreciated what we have come to call the "free rider problem" – or, at least, its appearance. People "may think" that occasionally they benefit more by injustice, even in the long run, since, owing to the "imperfect way in which human affairs are conducted," a single injustice may not cause "any considerable breach in the social union and confederacy."

Nor, Hume must have believed, is this *mere* appearance; if it were, he would answer the knave differently than he does. The knave's position is to regard "honesty is the best policy" as a "good general rule" that is nonetheless "liable to many exceptions" and that "he . . . conducts himself with most wisdom, who observes the general rule, and takes advantage of all the exceptions" (282–83). If Hume really believed at this point that, despite appearances, justice is invariably advantageous, he would have tried to correct the knave's beliefs about the consequences of injustice. Indeed, even if Hume believed the knave is right that particular unjust acts may actually be advantageous, but nonetheless thought it disadvantageous, because too risky, to execute a policy of making exceptions to the rules when doing so appears advantageous, he, like Hobbes, could still have recommended inflexible conformity to the rules of justice solely on the grounds that it is the most advantageous general policy. But Hume did neither of these things. Although he did point to ways in which knaves may be betrayed by their own frailties, the overall burden of his response is quite different. He despaired of adequately answering a knave who can regard the rules of justice as no more than strategically valuable: "If his heart rebel not against such pernicious maxims, if he feel no reluctance to the thoughts of villainy or baseness, he has indeed lost a considerable motive to virtue" (283). If, that is, there were no moral obligation to justice – if normal human beings did not disapprove of knavery – then we might lack an adequate motive to justice. It is only the moral sentiment and our tendency to love and hate ourselves on the strength of our virtue and vice that give us moral interests that make the just life advantageous: "Inward peace of mind, consciousness of integrity, a satisfactory review of our own conduct; these are circumstances, very requisite to happiness, and will be cherished and cultivated by every honest man, who feels the importance of them" (*ECPM*.283; see also *THN*.501).

Hume does not say why the uncertainties and dangers inherent in the knave's strategy would be insufficient in themselves to warrant treating the rules of justice as inflexible constraints, but we can see some problems that would develop. Even if an agent lacking moral interests can be convinced by a Hobbesian argument that she would be better off were she so to treat the rules of justice as a matter of general policy, there will inevitably be cases where the most advantageous policy will dictate what she reasonably believes to be less advantageous acts. How, in such cases, is she to deliberate? She knows that she is better off in general if she deliberates by justice rule regulation. But she may also have good reason to think that in this case she will be better off violating the rules. The same reasons that recommend that she generally deliberate by rule regulation also recommend that she violate. In such circumstances, her practical convictions may prove unstable.

Moral interests counteract this instability. Prone to self-esteem or self-hatred through inescapable reflection on our own character, and deeply concerned with the approval of others, we have more at stake in violating the rules of justice. "After the opinion, *that a merit or demerit attends justice or injustice,* is once firmly establish'd among mankind," the interest in our reputation (than which nothing "touches us more nearly") comes to depend more on "our conduct, with relation to the property of others" than on anything else. "For this reason," Hume concludes, "every one, who has any regard to his character, or who intends to live on good terms with mankind," must fix the rules of justice as an "inviolable law" (*THN*.501). Likewise, if we did not think that infidelity to promises was vicious (contrary to moral obligation), "we never shou'd feel any inclination to observe them" (518).[37] But because we do, anyone who makes use of the conventional signs of promising "is immediately bound by his interest to execute his engagements" (522). The moral interests in integrity, reputation, and so on that support regulating conduct by the rules of justice, therefore, do not also support acts that violate these rules.

Thus, whereas in the *Treatise* Hume appears to believe that self-interest invariably dictates justice, by the time of the *Enquiry* he has abandoned this view, having come to think that, with large numbers, occasional injustice can be advantageous owing to the free rider problem. Any doubt about Hume's having recognized the free rider problem (finally, at least) is removed by the following passage from "The Origin of Government":

All men are sensible of the necessity of justice to maintain peace and order; and all men are sensible of the necessity of peace and order for the maintenance of society. Yet, notwithstanding this strong and obvious necessity, such is the frailty and perverseness of our nature! . . . Some extraordinary circumstances may happen, in which a man finds his interests to be more promoted by fraud or rapine, than hurt by the breach which his injustice makes in the social union. But much more frequently, he is seduced from his great and important, but distant interests, by the allurement of present, though often very frivolous temptations.[38]

But if this is so, the virtue of justice cannot be strength of mind, since that will sometimes dictate injustice. Adding in the moral interest in avoiding self-hatred does not help; indeed, it exacerbates the problem.

So the problem reemerges: *What agent state is the virtue of justice?* Even apart from the "sensible knave" passage, there are several problems with taking it to be strength of mind, as we noted at the end

37. Cf. "Of the Original Contract," in *Essays*, p. 480.
38. "Of the Origin of Government," in *Essays*, p. 38. This first appeared in the edition of 1777. It did not appear in any edition of the *Essays* published during Hume's lifetime.

of the last section. And the knave passage is flatly inconsistent with the proposal, in any case.[39]

Hume continues in the *Enquiry* to emphasize his theme that justice involves *regulation by rules*. Rules "found requisite" for society's subsistence are "immediately embraced" (*ECPM*.192; see also 193). And men's "understanding and experience tell them that [their] combination is impossible where each governs himself by no rule, and pays no regard to the possessions of others" (307; see also 305, 306). But if self-interest does not invariably dictate compliance, Hume's claims that just practices are established when "the whole scheme or system [is] concurred in by the whole, or the greater part of society" (304) and that this involves just persons regulating their conduct by the rules of justice, "lay[ing] themselves under the restraint of such rules" (*THN*.499) and regarding them as "sacred and inviolable," now commit him to the virtue of justice's being a motivational state distinct from enlightened self-interest or strength of mind. Since he cannot now think that rule regulation is reducible to the pursuit of interests in maintaining rule-structured practices viewed *externally*, Hume's continuing talk of acceptance of ("embrac[ing]": *ECPM*.192) and regulation by rules must now be taken seriously. And this requires interpreting Hume as holding that just persons regard the rules *internally* as agents. They take them to have a normative relevance to their conduct distinct from a consideration of any good or evil that "may be attain'd by any action of the mind or body" (*THN*.439).

Just persons acquire the "habit of justice." They are determined to follow the rules of justice, and although their original motive for being so determined is self-interest, they continue "without recalling, on every occasion, the reflections, which determined [them]" (*ECPM*.203).[40] But rules of justice enter into the determination of their conduct differently from the way in which general rules and habit usually operate in Humean psychology, where "we extend our motives beyond those very circumstances, which gave rise to them,

---

39. Note, however: "Had every man sufficient *sagacity* to perceive, at all times, the strong interest which binds him to the observance of justice and equity, and *strength of mind* sufficient to persevere in a steady adherence to a general and a distant interest, in opposition to the allurements of present pleasure and advantage; there had never, in that case, been any such thing as government or political society, but each man, following his natural liberty, had lived in entire peace and harmony with others" (*ECPM*.205).

40. There is a problem, of course, about how one could come to *accept* a norm out of self-interest.

and form something like *general rules* for our conduct." Usually "these rules are not perfectly inflexible, but allow of many exceptions" (*THN*.531). The rules of justice, however, "are unchangeable . . . by particular views of private or public interest" (532). They "are artificially invented for a certain purpose, and are contrary to the common principles of human nature, which accommodate themselves to circumstances, and have no stated invariable method of operation" (532–33). The convention that establishes the rules of justice depends, indeed, on a mutual recognition of the "disorders that result from following their natural and variable principles," *including* "natural" general rules (533). And the convention, again, is the shared recognition of a mutual interest in *regulation* by the "inflexible" rules of justice. "I see evidently, that when any man imposes on himself general inflexible rules in his conduct with others, he considers certain objects as their property, which he supposes to be sacred and inviolable" (533; emphasis added).

These thoughts could be developed in different ways. Perhaps justice (the agent state) involves regulation by specific rules of property, transfer, and promise, and this is a virtue only if enough others have it. Or perhaps justice involves conditional regulation by these specific rules – conditional, that is, on enough others' doing so also. Or perhaps just persons regulate themselves by a metarule of cooperation that dictates following mutually advantageous rules so long as others do. For our purposes, the differences between these do not matter. All have in common the notion that just persons regulate themselves by rules they regard as authoritative. And the crucial point is that by the time of the *Enquiry* there seems to be no way to understand such claims other than as positing an agent state distinct from the desire to promote any good.[41]

If we take the virtue of justice to consist in the agent's regulating herself by the relevant rules (or her disposition to do so), we can solve various puzzles of Hume's text. For example, Hume can thereby avoid the circle involved in claiming that, as with any virtue, there must be a "first virtuous motive" of justice other than the sense of duty, and that the sense of duty is the "only real or universal motive for observing the laws of equity." If the virtue of justice is the

---

41. The sensible knave's point that noncompliance is occasionally advantageous for the agent can be extended to the case of the public interest in ways that Hume's own examples suggest (*THN*.497; *ECPM*.306). Again, for a contemporary (to us) example of a view that norm acceptance is a distinctive psychological state, see Gibbard, *Wise Choices, Apt Feelings*, pp. 55–83.

motivational state of rule regulation, then the object of the moral sentiment can be specified noncircularly. Justice, the virtue, consists in the trait of justice rule regulation as realized in the agent's practical reasoning. And its being morally obligatory or virtuous consists in an observer's approbation of this trait generated by Humean association and sympathy. When the observer thinks about the beneficial effects of the trait (including those of the "whole plan or scheme" of which it is an ineliminable part), sympathy turns ideas of contemplated pleasure into a pleasurable sentiment.

We can also explain on this hypothesis why Hume lapses into speaking as though just *acts* are themselves morally obligatory *and* why he gives a substantial motivational role to the moral sentiment in explaining just action in our "civiliz'd state." Hume believes that in the case of justice, and in that case only, what is morally approved is a motivational state whose direct object is a kind of act. Unlike such natural virtues as benevolence or parental concern, the virtue of justice is no aspect of the heart, no emotion or desire that takes some state or condition (such as another's welfare) as object and that arises only by involuntary response. A parent lacking in the naturally virtuous parental responses can drag himself out of bed in the middle of the night to tend a sick child out of a sense of moral obligation, according to Hume, only in the hope thereby of creating circumstances in which virtuous parental feeling will in time arise. The virtue of justice, on the other hand, is a disposition not to an emotional response that might be *reflected* in action but to a form of practical reasoning that is *realized* in the decision to abstain from unjust acts on the ground that it is required by the rules of justice. Someone who approves of the virtue despite lacking it himself can be motivated by his moral interest in being just to follow the rule, to perform just acts, hoping to acquire "by practice" the stable trait of governing himself by it without appeal to this interest. Strictly speaking, what is morally obligatory is the agent's mental quality of rule regulation, not just acts themselves. But the direct object of this state, unlike that of other virtuous principles, is a kind of act. Uniquely with justice, therefore, it is *almost* true that the just act is itself morally obligatory, regardless of its relation to a virtuous principle.

If we regard the moral obligation to justice as consisting in moral approbation of the "mental quality" of justice, and identify the latter with rule regulation, we can explain why Hume would still *say* that the motivation to be just depends on the moral obligation to justice. The latter, on the present suggestion, is generated (through sympathy) by contemplating the beneficial consequences of general justice rule regulation. Holding psychology fixed, justice (rule regulation) would fail to be approved only if its normal consequences were not beneficial. But if that were so, it could not be mutually advantageous. So a person disposed to act on mutually advantageous rules, so long as others do, would be disposed to act on the rules of justice only if justice is morally obligatory.

But this does not explain why Hume says that, uniquely with the artificial virtues and justice in particular, virtuous actions are "performed entirely from a sense of obligation" ("Original Contract," p. 480; see also *THN*.483, 518). It is an important part of my case, of course, that it *would* explain it if he there meant "rule obligation." But what he seems to have in mind in these passages is moral obligation: the sense of the "merit" of just action (*THN*.483).

The interpretation I am suggesting must attempt to explain this away as confusion. It is indeed crucial to Hume's distinction between the artificial and natural virtues that only the former are performed from a sense of obligation. But the relevant obligation cannot be the moral obligation, because that depends in no way on artifice and convention. The notion of obligation that is "unintelligible" without convention is rule obligation. The convention, we recall, is the jointly acknowledged mutual interest in regulating conduct by the rules of justice – that is, in regarding the rules of justice as authoritative and obligating. So the relevant virtue – justice as an agent state – is realized when agents act because they so regard the rules – that is, from a sense of (rule) obligation. The only sense of obligation that can enter uniquely into artificial virtues, therefore, is rule obligation. Because it does not fit with his usual categories, however, Hume confusedly asserts that it is the moral sentiment that uniquely motivates artificially virtuous acts. And that is what lands him in the circle.

As far as I can see, any alternative to this interpretation requires Hume to hold that the virtue of justice involves either error or a sense of "sophistry" that he thinks the insight that justice is conventional should enable us to see beyond. If, for example, we take Hume's remarks that the sense of merit is the motive distinctive of justice, then either we are involved in the circle or else we must suppose that just actions can have merit, and thus be morally obligatory, as "external performances."[42] The former is the sophistry of which we are to

42. See note 26.

be disabused by understanding the conventional roots of justice (*THN*.483). And although the latter is given psychological support by an association of ideas between "thing signify'd" (virtuous motive) and "sign" (virtuous action), this also involves error, since "the external performance has no merit" (483, 477). "To find the moral quality" of any action, "we must look within" (477). We cannot do this "directly," so we "fix our attention on actions, as on external signs" (477).

Another possibility would be to hold that the virtue of justice consists not in an accurately informed strength of mind but either in a tendency to overestimate the disadvantages of injustice sufficiently so that, conjoined with a strong mind, it leads to invariable compliance with justice's "inflexible" rules[43] or, perhaps, in a tendency to imagine vividly and dwell on disadvantageous consequences of injustice out of proportion to their importance in what the agent (accurately) believes to be her long-run interest.[44] Both alternatives implicate the just person in error. Either she mistakenly believes that injustice is invariably disadvantageous, or else she does not believe this but dwells disproportionately, in her practical thinking, on distant disadvantages. The latter involves no cognitive mistake, only the same kind of vice (the mirror image) that Hume laments when people lacking strength of mind give greater weight in deliberation to lesser, more immediate interests.

Finally, there are Haakonssen's and Gauthier's error-theoretic proposals. Taking his cue from Hume's curious description of promising as including a feigned willing of an obligation, Haakonssen constructs Hume's position as follows.[45] In order for us to regard justice as a virtue, we must suppose that there is a "first virtuous motive" to justice – one that we would approve of and would hate ourselves for lacking. But there is no such motive. So we feign its existence and hate ourselves for lacking it, with this then giving us motive to act justly – either because we also imagine we might acquire this motive by practice or because we want to maintain the fiction that we have it. Gauthier rejects this account for the *Treatise*, since enlightened self-interest can function there as the "first virtuous motive," but he

43. Something like this is suggested in Marcia Baron, "Hume's Noble Lie: An Account of His Artificial Virtues," *Canadian Journal of Philosophy* 12 (1982): 539–55.
44. I am indebted to David Aman for this suggestion.
45. Knud Haakonssen, *The Science of a Legislator*, pp. 30–35. Haakonssen emphasizes that this is his own construction and not anything to which Hume is explicitly committed.

suggests that the sensible knave passage makes something like it necessary.[46] In order for the moral obligation to justice to help motivate just actions, we must at least believe there to be a first virtuous motive of justice. The sensible-knave passage commits Hume to denying that it can be enlightened self-interest, and this, Gauthier thinks, is the only real contender. The sole remaining possibility is that we pretend otherwise, hate ourselves for lacking the pretended motive, and act to convince ourselves either that we have it or that we are on the way to acquiring it.

The best way for Hume to avoid the possibility that justice involves some kind of error is to hold that the moral obligation to justice consists in moral approbation for the trait of justice, and that this consists in the just person's disposition to engage in a form of practical reasoning substantially different from any countenanced by his official theory of the will, namely, by regulating her conduct by rules she regards as authoritative. It is, as he puts it in "Of the Original Contract," "a *regard* to the property of others" that is morally obligatory, not acts considered independent of this regard.[47]

CONCLUSION

On this interpretation there is a resultant congruence in the case of justice between the three things Hume identifies as forms of obligation. First, Hume's approach is distinguished most sharply from Hutcheson's by the idea that justice is realized by social practices that require a different concept of obligation from either Hutchesonian natural or moral obligation: rule obligation. The just person does not act simply from desire for the good; she regulates her conduct by rules of justice. In accepting these, she regards action falling under them as what she ought or must do. She can, of course, step back from her acceptance of these norms and consider that critically. When she does so from the general point of view, the evident benefits of the "whole plan or scheme" lead to moral approval (the moral obligation). Critical endorsement results also from the perspective of her own good, not least because moral sense gives her interests in her own character. Rawls's distinction between justifying a practice and justifying a particular action falling under it can thus be drawn *within*

46. Gauthier, "Artificial Virtues and the Sensible Knave," pp. 401–28.
47. *Essays, Moral, Political, and Literary,* p. 480.

the just agent's practical reasoning, as well as within the social practice it helps to realize.[48]

Hume never deduces the consequences for his theories of agency and will of the idea that justice requires individuals to regulate their conduct by rules they recognize as authoritative. It is, however, inconsistent with the empiricist theory he inherited from Hutcheson. There is no denying, of course, that empirical naturalism is the major source of inspiration for Hume's moral philosophy. Ultimately, however, Hume found that he could not adequately account for justice in the terms that tradition had bequeathed to him. He needed to avail himself of the idea that agents can choose an action not because that action may be instrumental in achieving natural goods, but because it is mandated by a a normative principle they accept. As we have seen, this idea was much closer to the autonomist internalisms of Shaftesbury and Butler than to anything in Hobbes, Cumberland, or Hutcheson.

48. "Two Concepts of Rules," p. 3.

Chapter 11

Concluding reflections

Hume drew more radical, skeptical conclusions from an empirical naturalist conception of reason than did Hutcheson (his theory of justice to one side). If reason is, as both agreed, exclusively theoretical, concerned only with "the discovery of truth and falsehood" (*THN*.458; *IMS*.1; R.307), then, since no action can be literally true or false, neither, strictly, can any be reasonable or unreasonable. It is not "contrary to reason," Hume famously concluded, "to prefer even my own acknowledg'd lesser good to my greater" (*THN*.416). This conflicts with a calm reflective deliberation view as articulated by Hutcheson and Cumberland. A person acts "*reasonably*," Hutcheson claimed, when, upon considering the "various Actions in his Power" in light of "*true Opinions* of their *Tendencies*," he "chuses to do that which will obtain the highest Degree of *that*, to which the *Instincts* of his Nature incline him" (*IMS*.1). Because calm, informed reflection leads beings with our psychological makeup to desires for their own greatest good and for the greatest good of all, self-love and universal benevolence are the "two grand determinations" of human will, structuring rational human deliberation. Hume accepted that the pursuit of lesser goods may result from a failure of theoretical reason, but he thought that reason is violated only when there is false judgment, and "even then 'tis not the passion [or action], properly speaking, which is unreasonable, but the judgment" (*THN*.416; see also 413–18, 458–60). Nor does the pursuit of a lesser good entail that the agent has judged falsely. "A trivial good may, from certain circumstances, produce a desire superior to what arises from the greatest and most valuable enjoyment" (416). So although Hume spoke, as did Hutcheson, of a form of obligation consisting in the agent's greatest good ("natural" or "interested obligation"), he did not share Hutcheson's and Cumberland's project of naturalizing obligation via the calm reflective deliberation view – or, at least, he did not regard that project in the same way.

Similarly, although no philosopher has been more widely proclaimed than Hume as the source of the instrumental theory of rational action and, as well, of the idea that normativity can be theorized as instrumental rationality, Hume's own view was that, strictly speaking, failing to take necessary means to ends is no more contrary to reason than is the pursuit of lesser goods. He did accept that, as a matter of contingent fact, instrumental "irrationality" is usually accompanied by false belief, but then, he thought, it is the belief and not the action that is unreasonable. And even here Hume called neither the believer nor her believing unreasonable, but only the belief itself, and that simply because it is false (*THN*.415, 416, 458). So again, although he and Hutcheson began from the same premise that (to quote now Hutcheson) "Reasonableness must denote . . . *Conformity to true Propositions, or to Truth*" (*IMS*.1), Hume was prepared to draw more skeptical conclusions about the reasonableness or unreasonableness of action. "[S]*ubordinate ends* may be called *reasonable*," Hutcheson wrote, because they are means to achieving the agent's ultimate ends.

None of this means, of course, that Hume thought that either instrumental thinking or calm reflection lacks a significant role in human action or in our thought about it. The point is, rather, that Hume wanted to be clear that, once the empirical naturalist conception of reason is accepted, any accounts of normativity it can ground must be frankly *revisionist*. Neither instrumental nor calm reflective deliberation theories can capture the idea of a "dictate of reason" (Hobbes's language in *Lev.*.xv.41), nor should they attempt to. For the empirical naturalists, reason cannot strictly *dictate* or counsel anything; it is not inherently practical. Viewed this way, empirical naturalist internalisms offer what Hume called (in a different context) "sceptical solutions" to the problem of normativity.[1] On the one hand, they assert that there is no such thing as normativity as traditionally conceived, but they argue, on the other, that many of the

1. In sect. V of *An Enquiry Concerning Human Understanding*, "A Sceptical Solution of These Doubts." See *Enquiries*, pp. 40–55. This attempts to resolve, without dogma, the "sceptical doubts concerning the operations of the understanding" that Hume raises in sect. IV, namely, those connected with causal and inductive reasoning. For a discussion of skeptical solutions in a different context, see Saul Kripke, *Wittgenstein on Rules and Private Language* (Cambridge, Mass.: Harvard University Press, 1982), esp. pp. 66–69, 84–86.

traditional conception's functions are served just as well by a sufficiently close substitute that can be based in a philosophically respectable way – normativity as instrumental rationality or as calm, reflective deliberation.

There is no overestimating the power of this philosophical program, whose wide and deep influence continues to the present day.[2]
Still, even Hume feels the attraction of a more robust notion of normativity than any that can be supplied by a reductionist or reforming
naturalism – at least, by those of his time. When he describes just
persons as "regulat[ing] their conduct" by rules they regard as "inviolable law" (*THN*.490, 534, 501) – abiding by them even when there
is, on balance, personal and public cost – it is hard to imagine that he
would be pleased to accept naturalist substitutes for the normative
notions to which he helps himself. The bindingness that Hume says
just persons regard rules of justice as having can hardly be reduced
to just acts' invariable usefulness in achieving desired natural goods,
since these persons regard the rules as binding even when they think
this is not the case.

Justice is but one especially compelling example of a common-
sense moral demand that requires conduct on grounds other than its
beneficial consequences. A continuing worry many have felt about
the empirical naturalist program in ethics is that it will be unable to
account for the normativity of such norms and thus for an important
part of commonsense morality. In revising normativity it will force
an unacceptable revision of moral common sense. Of course, one
naturalist response has been to say, "So much the worse for common
sense." Perhaps it should be revised in these respects.

No doubt an even greater and more abiding worry, however, has
been the suspicion that no reductive or reforming naturalist theory
can account for the kind of normativity morality must have
generally – whether the correct moral theory be consequentialist or
deontological – if it is to be supported adequately. Lying behind this
concern is the thought that gives rise to the accountability strand of
autonomist internalism found in Cudworth and Locke: A person can

---

2. As, for example, in the work of Richard Brandt and Peter Railton. See Brandt, *A
Theory of the Good and the Right*, esp. pp. 10–23, 149–62; Railton, "Naturalism and
Prescriptivity," *Social Philosophy and Policy* 7 (1989): 151–74. Recent approaches of
this sort are discussed in Darwall, Gibbard, and Railton, "Toward *Fin de siècle*
Ethics," pp. 174–80.

intelligibly be held accountable for having violated moral demands only if there were conclusive reasons against her so acting, reasons on which she could, in principle, have acted.

Morality, as a system of accountability, differs in this way from other systems of rules incorporating penalties for violations. It is no part of a game such as tennis, for example, that players are accountable for violations such as foot faults or failing to place serves within the service lines. The rules merely impose specified penalties. If, however, we think it central to morality that people are accountable for meeting moral demands, then we will see moral criticism and punishment not just as penalties incurred for infractions of rules but as implying judgments of normative (justifying) reasons that will be hard to contain within a circumscribed "moral" sphere. Can the idea of accountability be sustained if, when we confront a person who infringes a moral requirement and tell him that the fact that *he* benefits is inadequate justification, we are nonetheless forced to admit that, whereas it is inadequate "moral reason," it is nonetheless, unqualifiedly, a perfectly adequate reason for his actions? If someone can convince us that the best reasons recommended acting as he did, then it would seem he has sufficiently accounted for his action.[3]

The most we can apparently hope from instrumentalist or calm, reflective deliberation theories of normativity is that fully informed and vivid consideration of the deliberative context will invariably lead to the choices morality demands. But despite Hutcheson's optimism, that seems unrealistic. And even if contingent features of our desires somehow ensured this happy result, that would still not be enough unless we thought morality's demands are also conditional on those very features. If, therefore, morality requires an account of normativity that guarantees moral agents conclusive reason to comply with its demands, reforming or reductive naturalisms will seem inadequate to the task.

No doubt, much of the dissatisfaction that many have felt toward naturalistic approaches to normativity derives from this sense and from the related conviction, described by Kant in his *Critique of Practical Reason*, that the very considerations that make an action morally obligatory must also be conclusive reasons for acting – reasons on the

3. Here I borrow some thoughts from my review essay of Samuel Scheffler's *Human Morality*: Darwall, "Human Morality's Authority," *Philosophy and Phenomenological Research*, forthcoming.

basis of which we can *act*.[4] But the problem remains: Is there a philosophically adequate account of normativity that can vindicate this conviction? This would require that both halves of Kant's reciprocity thesis hold. It would have to be the case *both* that moral obligation entails the existence of conclusive reasons for acting by which the obligated agent can freely determine herself *and* that free rational agency is realized, in these contexts, only by action on these reasons.[5] The accountability strand springs from the former conviction, namely, that morality's credit depends on the promissory note that the requisite reasons for acting exist. But what stands behind that? Why think that the other half of the reciprocity thesis holds?

By the eighteenth century's end, Kant would derive his own autonomist internalist answer from his distinctively *formalist* version of what I have called the *normative theory of the will*. Free rational will involves determination under a normative conception, specifically, Kant says, under the "idea of laws."[6] Agents choose rationally and freely when they choose acts *as dictated by principles* they regard as valid *universally*, for all rational agents. But what, then, is it for a principle to *be* valid for all rational beings? What is it for a practical law to exist? Here Kant relies on a form-matter distinction that, it might be argued, is fundamental to a fully developed autonomist internalism. It is inconsistent with what he calls the "autonomy of the will" – rational will's being a law to itself – that the will's final determining ground be *either* a desire for some "matter" (a state to which action is instrumental) *or* an intuition of independent normative facts that are somehow given to it.[7] Rational agents can fully

---

4. *The Critique of Practical Reason*, Ak. p. 30, trans. L. W. Beck, p. 30. This is sometimes called the "fact of reason." For a discussion, see Allison, *Kant's Theory of Freedom*, pp. 230–49.
5. See, in Chapter 5, "The Accountability Strand of Autonomist Internalism," for a discussion of Kant's reciprocity thesis and references.
6. "Everything in nature works in accordance with laws. Only a rational being has the power to act *in accordance with his idea* of laws – that is, in accordance with principles – and only so has he a *will*. Since *reason* is required to derive actions from laws, the will is nothing but practical reason." Kant, *Groundwork of the Metaphysics of Morals*, Ak. p. 412, trans. Paton, p. 80.
7. "Autonomy of the will is the property the will has of being a law to itself (independently of every property belonging to the objects of volition)" (*Groundwork*, Ak. p. 440). "Here bare conformity to universal law as such (without having as its base any law prescribing particular actions) is what serves the will as its principle, and must so serve it if duty is not to be everywhere an empty delusion and a chimerical concept" (*Groundwork*, Ak. p. 402). "If a rational being can think of its maxims as practical universal laws, he can do so only by considering them as

(and autonomously) ground their conduct in the *idea* of law, he argues, only by acting exclusively on principles they can *prescribe* as universal law, because the principles are suited (formally) to be universal law. And the only way they can do that, he says, is by restricting themselves to acting on principles they can *will as law*.[8] This commits free rational agents to the Categorical Imperative: "Act only on that maxim [principle] through which you can at the same time will that it should become a universal law."[9] Since the Categorical Imperative is the fundamental principle of morality, according to Kant, moral agents are thereby assured of conclusive reasons for acting as morality demands. Moral demands are grounded in the Categorical Imperative, and rationally autonomous action is possible only if agents ultimately determine their conduct by that fundamental principle.

The conclusion of a book on the British moralists is no place to attempt to interpret and evaluate these difficult, and in some ways deeply puzzling, aspects of Kant's ethics. It may help to set the British contributions to the project of forging a link between obligation and autonomy in an illuminating context, however, to consider them briefly in relation to Kant. As I have just said, Cudworth's and Locke's accountability arguments were intended to establish one half of Kant's reciprocity thesis, namely, the claim that moral obligations can exist only through reasons by which moral agents can freely determine themselves. It was Cudworth whose thinking was both more original here and far closer to the line Kant would ultimately pursue. But both Cudworth and Locke aimed to establish the existence of moral reasons, the other half of the reciprocity thesis, in ways that Kant would have found objectionable. This is most obviously true of Locke, for whom autonomous practical thinking brings agents into contact with motives for being moral that are both *independent* of the exercise of autonomy and *extrinsic* to morality. Only

principles which contain the determining grounds of the will because of their form and not because of their matter" (*Critique of Practical Reason*, Ak. pp. 26–27).

8. "Since I have robbed the will of every inducement that might arise for it as a consequence of obeying any particular law, nothing is left but the conformity of actions to universal law as such, and this alone must serve the will as its principle. That is to say, I ought never to act except in such a way *that I can also will that my maxim should become a universal law*" (*Groundwork*, Ak. p. 402; see also *Critique of Practical Reason*, Ak. pp. 23–30). This, no doubt, Kant's most daring and most problematic move. For an excellent discussion, see Korsgaard, "Kant's Analysis of Obligation," pp. 311–40.

9. *Groundwork*, Ak. p. 421.

thanks to God's arranging the coincidence of moral demand with long-run happiness are there reasons for meeting moral demands by which agents can determine themselves. Cudworth's thinking was much closer to Kant's. For Cudworth as for Kant, ethics is possible only if pure reason can be practical. But pure practical reason, Cudworth held, is not autonomy but love. Its object is, in Kantian terms, material rather than formal. God's perfect mind is benevolent, but only we, not God, need "autexousy," which functions in roughly the way Locke's freedom does, though without the hedonism. We require the capacity to recollect ourselves and our motives in order to remind ourselves in a practically effective way that the loving life is the happiest life, so that we can act on moral (loving) reasons, reasons whose existence in no way depends on the exercise of autonomy.

Cudworth discovered the path that led to Kant's view of morality as "laws of freedom." But other important elements leading to the Kantian picture were the following ideas encountered in Butler and, to some significant extent, in Shaftesbury: First, autonomous practical reason is *itself* a source of motivation that is irreducible to the desire for any good. (This is an aspect of a *normative theory of the will* and, hence, of an account of self-*regulation* as opposed [merely] to self-determination.) Second, agents exercise their capacity for autonomous practical reason fully only if they acknowledge moral demands as overriding reasons for acting. And third, *because* this is so, moral demands actually *are* overriding reasons to act. Butler's autonomist line advances all three of these propositions. Shaftesbury's account of the unity of the will commits him to the first, but although he accepts that moral agents have conclusive reason to be moral, that is because, like Cudworth, he thinks that leading a moral life is most in their interest. For Shaftesbury, agents reflectively regulate themselves only by reasons deriving from their own good.

Since the normative theory of will also figured prominently in the externalist rational intuitionisms of Clarke, Balguy, and, later, Richard Price, it illuminates the way this idea worked within the autonomist internalisms of Shaftesbury and, especially, Butler to compare that with its role in eighteenth-century British rational intuitionism. This will also provide a better picture of the relation of the intuitionists to Kant.

Because the intuitionists insisted on a necessary connection between the perception of a moral demand (and its grounds), on the one hand, and motivation, on the other, we must remind ourselves what makes them externalists in our terms. To put the matter briefly, the intuitionists accepted the first and second of the three propositions above, but they rejected the third. They accepted, that is, that autonomous agency involves a source of motivation different from the desire for any (natural) good, and they accepted that someone exercises (fully) the power of autonomous agency only if she recognizes moral reasons as overriding; but they denied that this is what *makes* moral reasons overriding.

This is best seen by considering the analogy Clarke and Balguy drew between action and *belief*. It is sometimes said that truth is normative for belief, because truth is the internal object of the psychological state we call "belief."[10] Beliefs, so to say, *aim* at truth; they aim to track the way things really are. They have a "representative quality," as Hume put it (*THN*.415). Because belief has truth as internal object, to be a reason to believe something just is to be evidence of the truth of that belief. That is what a reason for believing something is; no more, no less. But if evidentiary relations between propositions do not themselves depend on anything internal to believers, and if facts concerning what ought to be believed (theoretically normative facts) consist in these (*modulo,* perhaps, what evidence is available), then so also will theoretically normative facts be "external."

Despite the externality of the theoretically normative, however, we can easily see why the perception of reasons for believing (as reasons) necessarily tends to affect a person's beliefs. That is a consequence of the nature of belief. We need attribute to someone no further desire to believe truths to explain why her beliefs tend to change in response to evidence. Her psychological states would not be beliefs unless they did.

The case of belief shows how it is possible to combine an externalist account of normativity with the sort of necessary connection between the *perception* of reasons and "motivation" that is frequently called internalist.[11] And this is exactly what happens with the rational intuitionist account of practical normativity. Both Clarke and Balguy suppose that action has an internal object in just the way belief does.[12] Actions aim at being "right," "fit," and in accordance with "reason and moral good" (*FMG*.45, 48). Whereas belief aims to

---

10. In what follows, I am indebted to J. David Velleman, "The Possibility of Practical Reason," unpublished manuscript.
11. Obviously, I am using "motivation" metaphorically in the case of belief.
12. Except that Balguy and Clarke believe that action involves incompatibilist freedom. We may ignore this difference, however.

track the facts in general, action aims to track immutable ethical facts concerning the fit and unfit. So just as the perception of reasons for belief necessarily affects belief tendencies, so also does the perception of facts concerning what is fit and unfit necessarily affect motivations or action tendencies. "The same Necessity," Balguy writes, "which compels Men to *assent* to what is *true*, forces them to approve what is *right* and fit," approval being a motivational state that gives rise to action "where-ever it is not over-ruled by another more powerful" (*FMG.*45).[13]

This picture requires a realm of ethical fact that is independent of the activity of autonomous practical reason. As with belief, the practicality of reason judgments – their capacity to motivate – is explained by supposing action to involve psychological states whose function is to track this independent reality. For Balguy and Clarke, therefore, the practicality of practical reason is no different from that of theoretical reason.[14]

Sometimes Clarke and Balguy put their ideas in ways that seem more internalist than this suggests. Thus Balguy identifies "internal obligation" with the *"State of the Mind into which it is brought by the Perception of a plain Reason for acting,"* that is, by the intuition of what is fit and reasonable (*FMG.*31). Likewise, Clarke calls the "Judgment and Conscience of a Man's own Mind, concerning the Reasonableness and Fitness" of an action, "the truest and formallest *Obligation."* And he says that someone who violates the golden rule, acting to-

13. Compare Clarke: "The only difference is, that *Assent* to a plain speculative *Truth*, is not in a Man's Power to withhold; but to *Act* according to the plain *Right and Reason* of things, this he may, by the natural Liberty of his Will forbear." Samuel Clarke, *A Discourse Concerning the Unalterable Obligations of Natural Religion* (London: J. Knapton, 1706), I.3. Also in *Works of Samuel Clarke*, 4 vols. (London: J. and P. Knapton, 1738), vol. 2, p. 614. Facsimile edition, New York: Garland, 1978. Further references will be placed parenthetically in the text, preceded by *Discourse.*

14. The comparison with another eighteenth-century British rationalist position, that of William Wollaston, is instructive here. Wollaston argues in *The Religion of Nature Delineated* (London, 1722) that actions aim to represent reality – but the natural and social world of ordinary life rather than the intuitionists' normative metaphysical order. For Wollaston, immoral actions are contrary to reason for the simple reason that they assert plain falsehoods. Thus, he thought that theft is contrary to reason because the thief implicitly asserts that what he takes is not the property of another, and that is false. Wollaston's rationalism might be called *reductive,* since it seeks to reduce moral categories to those of truth and falsehood. From even this cursory description it should be clear, by the way, that Hume's "refutation" of Wollaston in the *Treatise* is directed at a straw man (*THN.*461–62n). For selections from *The Religion of Nature Delineated,* see Raphael, *British Moralists*, vol. 1, pp. 239–58.

ward others as he would not have them act toward him, is guilty of a contradiction similar to that of someone who asserts that one thing is equal to another but that the second is not equal to the first (*Discourse*.1.3). But Clarke's more usual practice is to ground obligation (and reasonableness) in eternal relations of fitness and unfitness that reason can grasp in the same way it grasps mathematical relations.[15] And it is clear in Balguy also that even if he reserves the term 'obligation' for the motivating state of perceiving a reason for acting, reasons for acting themselves depend on nothing internal to the agent; they consist of independent normative facts of fitness and unfitness (*FMG*.10, 12). Not surprisingly, when the later intuitionist Richard Price came to discuss Balguy's view, he remarked that the state of mind to which Balguy referred is "the *effect* of obligation perceived, rather than *obligation itself*."[16] For the intuitionists, practical normativity ultimately consists in an independent metaphysical order.

Autonomist internalism, by contrast, holds that practical normativity has no metaphysical status independent of agency, since it depends upon autonomous practical thinking. An intuitionist such as Balguy *can*, like Butler, object against Hutcheson that his account of virtue makes it "a blind Pursuit of the *Instinct*" rather than the result of "a *Rational Determination*" (*FMG*.21). And, as we have seen, he can hold that rational agency is unlike the intelligent pursuits of objects of instinct in requiring determination by a normative conception – a conception of reasons to act and of what one ought to do, all things considered. But unlike autonomist internalism, rational intuitionism does not hold that the truth or validity conditions of such a conception – what makes it the case that something is a reason to act, or that someone ought to do something – have anything to do with the conditions for autonomous will. The former are determined by the eternal relations of fitness and unfitness.

In all its forms, autonomist internalism is a theory of practical normativity. To be obligated, it holds, is for there to be conclusive motives that can be raised by autonomous deliberation. This is true whether the relevant motives are held to derive from the agent's greatest pleasure, as with Locke; from a good involving rationally creative loving relations or aesthetic enjoyments, as in Cudworth; or

15. Samuel Clarke, *A Demonstration of the Being and Attributes of God* (London, 1705), XII. In *Works of Samuel Clarke*, vol. 2. Facsimile, New York: Garland, 1978.
16. Price, *A Review of the Principal Questions in Morals* (London, 1758), ed. D. D. Raphael (Oxford: Clarendon Press, 1974), p. 114.

from a judgment of the authority of first-order motives, as in Shaftesbury, Butler, and Kant.[17] What distinguishes this last version is the normative theory of will – the idea that rational will involves self-*regulation:* self-determination under a normative conception. This is what is required, Butler maintains, to capture the idea of an agent who can step back from her various desires – for example, from her desires for her own good and for the goods of others, or of all conceived impartially – and ask which she should act on.

Again, this is common ground with the intuitionists. But what gives authority to the agent's judgment of reasons for Clarke and Balguy is that these reliably track independent normative facts. Butler's autonomist line avoids any reliance on such an order of eternal fitness. It attempts a "transcendental deduction" of the authority of conscience as a necessary condition for the very possibility of a kind of *internal* order: autonomous agency or self-regulated internal constitution. Since free rational will – self-determining constitutional order – is possible only if the agent has a way (procedurally) of making normative judgments and guiding herself by them, the authority of her judgments follows from this. We could not even seriously raise the question of whether there is reason to follow conscience unless we had the capacity to answer it affirmatively and be guided practically by that answer. Its being the case that we ought to follow conscientious judgments is a consequence of their essential role in autonomous rational will. Whereas the intuitionists take practical reasoning and action to have an implicit *material* aim, namely, to track independent normative facts, autonomist internalists take the implicit aim of practical reasoning to be entirely *formal* – guidance by considerations that we can reflectively endorse, thereby realizing autonomy.

From the standpoint of autonomy, however, there is a serious weakness in Butler's doctrine of the authority of conscience. According to Butler, as I mentioned at the end of Chapter 9, conscience's approvals and disapprovals are, from the agent's perspective, simply given.[18] But though rational autonomy may be impossible without conscientious approval or disapproval, it can hardly depend on the particular conscientious attitudes one happens to find in oneself. How, moreover, are we to regard someone who does not share our

17. Again, Shaftesbury holds, uniquely in this group, that the agent's overall interest is the uniquely authoritative motive.
18. Christine Korsgaard makes a related criticism of Hume's theory. See her "Normativity as Reflexivity."

attitudes? What Butler says about the parricide in his *reductio* argument for the authority of conscience in Sermon II implies that he is committed to holding that a person cannot be obligated unless *that person* can, in principle, determine herself conscientiously to act as obligated (the accountability strand). But that requires not only that she have a principle of reflection but that it issue in the same judgments. And what can guarantee convergence in conscientious judgments for every agent, especially if, as Butler sometimes suggests, human conscience's dictates depend on God's solution to a contingent problem of social engineering, namely, the problem of which conscientious dictates are likeliest to achieve the happiest whole (*S*.xii.31n)?

Butler is thus subject to an objection of the same sort that the rational intuitionists raised against Hutcheson, namely, that his theory makes virtue "of an arbitrary and positive nature . . . entirely depending on instincts, that might originally have been otherwise" (*FMG*.5, 8–9). Butlerian conscience differs from Hutchesonian instincts in having conduct and principles as object, rather than states to which action is only instrumental, but it is like them nonetheless in having its *content* fixed contingently rather than by anything internal to the functioning of autonomous practical reason itself. It cannot possibly explain the existence, therefore, of any obligations under which all rational moral agents might be thought to stand, independent of their different given motivations, simply through their capacity for autonomous will. It is not surprising, therefore, that later thinkers who, like Richard Price, stressed the universal bindingness of morality tended to interpret Butler as a rational intuitionist.

When Kant wrote the so-called Prize Essay of 1763, he found something close to Butler's approach about as satisfactory as any he could then think of. There he calls obligation "the primary concept" of ethics, and he distinguishes it from the prescription of necessary means to ends – what he will later dub "hypothetical imperatives" – whose "necessity indicates no obligation at all."[19] Genuine obligation requires a "formal ground," he says, distinct from any such purpose.[20] But at this point Kant maintains that the requisite formal

---

19. *Enquiry Concerning the Clarity of the Principles of Natural Theology and Ethics* ("Prize Essay," 1763), trans. by G. B. Kerferd and D. E. Walford, in *Kant: Selected Pre-Critical Writings and Correspondence with Beck* (Manchester: Manchester University Press, 1968), p. 31. I am indebted to Christine Korsgaard's discussion in "Kant's Analysis of Obligation," p. 313.
20. Ibid.

ground is provided by "the rule: do the most perfect possible by you." And he adds that, since this does not by itself determine any "particularly definite obligation," we require in addition something like the moral feelings that "Hutcheson and others have provided."[21]

Actually, it is fair to say that by the time of the Prize Essay Kant had not yet thought as far in connecting obligation to autonomy as Butler had in his doctrine of the authority of conscience. But what would enable Kant to do that, Rousseau's doctrine in *The Social Contract* that agents realize autonomy only when they obey a law that they prescribe for themselves, also helped him to glimpse a potential solution to the problem that beset Butler's autonomist line.[22] A practical or moral law *cannot* be *given* to *autonomous* agents, Kant concluded – for example, through a Butlerian conscience. Rather, self-regulating agents must be able to prescribe the law to themselves; anything else is heteronomy. Because a genuine law binds all autonomous agents, a principle cannot be prescribed *as law* unless it can be prescribed by any such agent from a suitably general point of view, the standpoint of a "realm of ends" in which an agent "abstract[s] from the personal differences between rational beings" and considers what principles he can will to govern the conduct of all rational agents.[23] Only by regulating himself by principles meeting this condition can an agent be "subject only to *laws which are made by himself* and yet are *universal.*"[24]

But if Kant first encountered in Rousseau the idea that obligation involves self-imposed (yet general) law, we can now appreciate that this was hardly the first attempt to understand practical normativity as grounded in the conditions for autonomous will. From Cudworth's first attempts to work out a conception of autonomy, through his and Locke's accountability linkage to obligation, to

21. Ibid., pp. 33, 34.
22. "We might, over and above all this, add, to what man acquires in the civil state, moral liberty, which alone makes him truly master of himself; for the mere impulse of appetite is slavery, while obedience to a law which we prescribe to ourselves is liberty." Jean-Jacques Rousseau, *The Social Contract*, I.viii (Amsterdam, 1762), trans. G. D. H. Cole, in *The Social Contract and Discourses*, rev. and augmented by J. H. Brumfitt and John C. Hall (London: Dent, 1975), p. 178. For an account of Rousseau's influence on Kant, see Ernst Cassirer, *Kant's Life and Thought*, trans. by James Haden (New Haven: Yale University Press, 1981), esp. pp. 86–90, 235–36. See also Cassirer, *Rousseau, Kant, Goethe: Two Essays*, trans. James Gutmann, Paul Oskar Kristeller, and John Herman Randall, Jr. (Princeton: Princeton University Press, 1963).
23. *Groundwork*, Ak. p. 433.
24. Ibid., Ak. p. 432.

Shaftesbury's and Butler's normative theories of autonomous will and authoritative motivation, this project was a profoundly important strand of early modern British moral thought, even though it is also one that historians of ethics have heretofore all but ignored.

Works cited

CLASSICAL AND EARLY MODERN PRIMARY SOURCES

Aquinas, Saint Thomas. *De Regno*. In *On Law, Morality, and Politics*. Edited by William P. Baumgarth and Richard J. Regan, S.J. Indianapolis: Hackett Co., 1988.

Aquinas, Saint Thomas. *Summa Contra Gentiles*. 1259–1264. In *Basic Writings of Saint Thomas Aquinas*. Edited by Anton C. Pegis. New York: Random House, 1945.

Aquinas, Saint Thomas. *Summa Theologica*. 1265–1273. In *Basic Writings of Saint Thomas Aquinas*. Edited by Anton C. Pegis. New York: Random House, 1945.

Aristotle. *The Nicomachean Ethics*. Translated by W. D. Ross. New York: Oxford University Press, 1980.

Balguy, John. *The Foundation of Moral Goodness*. London, 1728. Facsimile edition, New York: Garland, 1976.

Butler, Joseph. *The Analogy of Religion, Natural and Revealed, to the Constitution and Course of Nature*. London, 1736. Included in *The Works*, vol. 2.

Butler, Joseph. *A Dissertation of the Nature of Virtue*. Appended to *The Analogy of Religion*. London, 1736. Included in *The Works*, vol. 2.

Butler, Joseph. *Fifteen Sermons Preached at the Rolls Chapel*. London, 1726. Included in *The Works*, vol. 1.

Butler, Joseph. *Six Sermons Preached upon Public Occasions*. London, 1749. Included in *The Works*, vol. 1.

Butler, Joseph. *The Works of Bishop Butler*. Edited by J. H. Bernard. 2 vols. London: Macmillan, 1900.

Calvin, Jean. *Institutio Christianae Religionis*. Geneva, 1559. *The Institutes of the Christian Religion*. Translated by F. L. Battles. Philadelphia: Westminster, 1961.

Clarke, Samuel. *A Demonstration of the Being and Attributes of God*. London, 1705. In *The Works*, vol. 2, pp. 516–577.

Clarke, Samuel. *A Discourse Concerning the Unalterable Obligations of Natural*

Religion, and the Truth and Certainty of the Christian Revelation. London: J. Knapton, 1706. In *The Works*, vol. 2, pp. 579–733.

Clarke, Samuel. *The Works of Samuel Clarke.* 4 vols. London: J. & P. Knapton, 1738. Facsimile, New York: Garland, 1978.

Cudworth, Ralph. Manuscripts on freedom of the will. British Library, Additional Manuscripts, nos. 4978–82.

Cudworth, Ralph. "A Sermon Preached before the House of Commons." In *The Cambridge Platonists.* Edited by C. A. Patrides. Cambridge: Cambridge University Press, 1969, pp. 90–127.

Cudworth, Ralph. *A Treatise Concerning Eternal and Immutable Morality.* London, 1731. Facsimile edition, New York: Garland, 1976.

Cudworth, Ralph. *A Treatise of Freewill.* Edited by John Allen. London: John W. Parker, 1838. Facsimile edition included in *The Collected Works of Ralph Cudworth*, vol. 1. Hildesheim: Olms, 1979.

Cudworth, Ralph. *The True Intellectual System of the Universe.* London: Richard Royston, 1678. Facsimile editions, Stuttgart–Bad Cannstatt: F. Fromman, 1964; New York: Garland, 1978.

Culverwell, Nathaniel. *An Elegant and Learned Discourse of the Light of Nature.* London, 1652. Facsimile edition, New York: Garland, 1978. Also edited by Robert A. Greene and Hugh MacCallum. Toronto: University of Toronto Press, 1971.

Cumberland, Richard. *De Legibus Naturæ Disquisitio Philosophica.* London, 1672. *A Treatise of the Laws of Nature.* Translated by John Maxwell. London, 1727. Facsimile, New York: Garland, 1978.

Diderot, Denis. *Oeuvres complètes de Diderot.* 20 vols. Edited by J. Assezat and M. Tourneux. Paris: Garnier Frères, 1875–77.

Epictetus. *The Discourses as Reported by Arrian, The Manual, and Fragments.* Translated and edited by W. A. Oldfather. 2 vols. Cambridge, Mass.: Harvard University Press, 1979.

Gay, John. *A Dissertation Concerning the Fundamental Principle and Immediate Criterion of Virtue. As Also, the Obligation to, and Approbation of It. With Some Account of the Origin of the Passions and Affection.* "Prefix'd" to William King, *Essay on the Origin of Evil.* London, 1731.

Grotius, Hugo. *De Jure Belli ac Pacis.* Amsterdam, 1625. *The Law of War and Peace.* Translated by Francis W. Kelsey. New York: Carnegie Endowment for International Peace, 1925.

Hobbes, Thomas. *De Cive.* London, 1642. *De Cive, the English Version, Entitled in the First Edition, Philosophicall Rudiments Concerning Government and Society.* Edited and translated by Howard Warrender. Oxford: Clarendon Press, 1983.

Hobbes, Thomas. *The Elements of Law, Natural and Politic.* London, 1640. Edited by Ferdinand Tönnies. 2d ed. London: Cass, 1984.

Hobbes, Thomas. *The English Works of Thomas Hobbes.* Edited by Sir William Molesworth. 11 vols. London: John Bohn, 1839–45.

Hobbes, Thomas. *Leviathan.* London, 1651. There are several editions; two prominent ones (1) Richard Tuck, editor. Cambridge: Cambridge University Press, 1991; (2) Edwin Curley, editor. Indianapolis, Ind.: Hackett, 1994.

Hobbes, Thomas. *The Questions Concerning Liberty, Necessity, and Chance.* In *The English Works of Thomas Hobbes,* vol. 5.

Hobbes, Thomas. *A Treatise of Liberty and Necessity.* London, 1654. In *The English Works of Thomas Hobbes,* vol. 4.

Hume, David. *An Enquiry Concerning Human Understanding.* London, 1748. In *Enquiries.*

Hume, David. *An Enquiry Concerning the Principles of Morals.* London, 1751. In *Enquiries Concerning Human Understanding and Concerning the Principles of Morals.* Edited by L. A. Selby-Bigge. 3d. ed., with text revised and notes by P. H. Nidditch. Oxford: Clarendon Press, 1985.

Hume, David. *Essays, Moral, Political, and Literary.* Edinburgh, 1741; 2d ed., 1741; 3d ed., 1748. Edited with foreword, notes, and glossary by Eugene F. Miller, with apparatus of variant readings from the 1889 edition by T. H. Green and T. H. Grose. Indianapolis, Ind. Liberty Classics, 1987.

Hume, David. *The Letters of David Hume.* Edited by J. Y. T. Grieg. New York: Garland, 1983.

Hume, David. *A Treatise of Human Nature.* London, 1739, 1740. Edited, with an analytical index, by L. A. Selby-Bigge. 2d. ed., with text revised and variant readings by P. H. Nidditch. Oxford: Clarendon Press, 1978.

Hutcheson, Francis. *Collected Works of Francis Hutcheson.* 7 vols. Hildesheim: Olms, 1969–71.

Hutcheson, Francis. *An Essay on the Nature and Conduct of the Passions and Affections. With Illustrations on the Moral Sense.* London, 1728. 2d ed., 1730; 3d ed., 1742. Facsimile edition (of 3d ed.), with an introduction by Paul McReynolds: Gainesville, Fla.: Scholars' Facsimiles & Reprints, 1969. Facsimile edition (of 1st ed.) also in *Collected Works,* vol. 2.

Hutcheson, Francis. *An Inquiry into the Original of Our Ideas of Beauty and Virtue, in Two Treatises. I: Concerning Beauty, Order, Harmony, Design. II. Concerning Moral Good and Evil.* London, 1725. 2d ed., 1726; 3d ed. 1729; 4th ed., 1738; 5th ed., revised, 1753. Facsimile (of 1st ed.) in *Collected Works,* vol. 1.

Hutcheson, Francis. *A Short Introduction to Moral Philosophy.* 2 vols. Glasgow: Robert Foulis, 1747. Facsimile edition in *Collected Works,* vol. 4.

Hutcheson, Francis. *A System of Moral Philosophy,* 2 vols. Glasgow: R. and A. Foulis, 1755. Facsimile edition in *Collected Works,* vols. 5–6.

Kant, Immanuel. *Enquiry Concerning the Clarity of the Principles of Natural Theology and Ethics* ("Prize Essay," 1763). In *Kant: Selected Pre-Critical Writings and Correspondence with Beck.* Translated by G. B. Kerferd and D. E. Walford. Manchester: Manchester University Press, 1968, pp. 3–35.

Kant, Immanuel. *Grundlegung zur Metaphysik der Sitten.* Riga, 1785. *Groundwork of the Metaphysics of Morals.* Translated by H. J. Paton. New York: Harper & Row, 1964.

Kant, Immanuel. *Kritik der praktischen Vernunft.* Riga, 1788. *The Critique of*

Practical Reason. Translated by Lewis White Beck. Indianapolis, Ind.: Bobbs-Merrill, 1956.

King, Peter. *The Life of John Locke, with Extracts from His Correspondence, Journals, and Common-Place Books.* 2 vols. London: Henry Colburn & Richard Bentley, 1830.

Locke, John. *The Correspondence of John Locke,* vol. 4. Edited by E. S. De Beer. Oxford: Clarendon Press, 1979.

Locke, John. *An Essay Concerning Human Understanding.* London, 1690. 2d ed., 1694. Edited by Peter H. Nidditch. Oxford: Oxford University Press, 1975.

Locke, John. *Essays on the Law of Nature.* Edited and translated from the Latin by W. von Leyden. Oxford: Clarendon Press, 1954. Edited and translated as *Questions Concerning the Law of Nature* by Robert Horwitz, Jenny Strauss Clay, and Diskin Clay. Ithaca: Cornell University Press, 1990.

Locke, John. *A Paraphrase and Notes on the Epistles of St. Paul to the Galatians, 1 and 2 Corinthians, Romans, Ephesians.* 2 vols. Edited by Arthur W. Wainwright. Oxford: Oxford University Press, 1987.

Locke, John. *The Reasonableness of Christianity.* London, 1695. Edited, abridged, and introduced by I. T. Ramsey. Stanford, Calif.: Stanford University Press, 1958.

Locke, John. *Two Tracts on Government.* Edited, translated, and with an introduction by Philip Abrams. Cambridge: Cambridge University Press, 1967.

Locke, John. *Two Treatises of Government.* London, 1698. Edited with an introduction and notes by Peter Laslett. Cambridge: Cambridge University Press, 1988.

Malebranche, Nicolas. *Treatise on Nature and Grace.* Translated with an introduction and notes by Patrick Riley. Oxford: Clarendon Press, 1992.

Mandeville, Bernard. *The Fable of the Bees: Of Private Vices, Publick Benefits.* 6th ed. London, 1729.

Masham, Damaris Cudworth. *A Discourse Concerning the Love of God.* London, 1696.

Masham, Damaris Cudworth. *Occasional Thoughts in Reference to a Vertuous or Christian Life.* London, 1705.

Plato. *The Republic.* In *The Collected Dialogues.* Edited by Edith Hamilton and Huntington Cairns. Princeton: Princeton University Press, 1961.

Price, Richard. *A Review of the Principal Questions in Morals.* London, 1758. Edited by D. D. Raphael. Oxford: Clarendon Press, 1974.

Pufendorf, Samuel. *De Jure Naturæ et Gentium.* Lund, 1672. *On the Law of Nature and Nations.* Translated by C. H. Oldfather and W. A. Oldfather. Oxford: Oxford University Press, 1934.

Rousseau, Jean-Jacques. *Du contrat social.* Amsterdam, 1762. *The Social Contract.* Translated by G. D. H. Cole. In *The Social Contract and Discourses.* Revised and augmented by J. H. Brumfitt and John C. Hall. London: Dent, 1975.

Shaftesbury, Anthony Ashley Cooper, 3d Earl of. *Characteristicks of Men,*

Manners, Opinions, and Times. 3 vols. London, 1711. 2d ed., 1714. Edited with notes by John M. Robertson and introduction by Stanley Grean. 2 vols. Indianapolis, Ind.: Bobbs-Merrill, 1964.

Shaftesbury, Anthony Ashley Cooper, 3d Earl of. *Letters of the Earl of Shaftesbury, Collected into One Volume.* London, 1750.

Shaftesbury, Anthony Ashley Cooper, 3d Earl of. *The Life, Unpublished Letters, and Philosophical Regimen of Anthony, Earl of Shaftesbury.* Edited by Benjamin Rand. London: Swan Sonnenschein, 1900.

Shaftesbury, Anthony Ashley Cooper, 3d Earl of. *Second Characters or the Language of Forms.* Edited by Benjamin Rand. Cambridge: Cambridge University Press, 1914.

Shaftesbury, Anthony Ashley Cooper, 3d Earl of, editor. *Select Sermons of Dr. Whichcot.* London: A. & J. Churchill, 1698.

Shaftesbury, Anthony Ashley Cooper, 3d Earl of. *Several Letters Written by a Noble Lord to a Young Man at the University.* London, 1714.

Suarez, Francisco. *De Legibus ac Deo Legislatore.* 1612. Translated as *A Treatise on Laws and God the Lawgiver* by Gwladys L. Williams, Ammi Brown, and John Waldron, with certain revisions by Henry Davis, S. J., and an introduction by James Brown Scott. In *Selections from Three Works of Francisco Suarez, S. J.,* vol. 2. Oxford: Clarendon Press, 1944. Reprinted as vol. 20 of Classics of International Law by Carnegie Endowment for International Peace.

Whichcote, Benjamin. *Select Sermons of Dr. Whichcot.* Edited by Anthony Ashley Cooper, 3d Earl of Shaftesbury. London: A. & J. Churchill, 1698.

Wollaston, William. *The Religion of Nature Delineated.* London, 1722. Facsimile edition, Delmar, N.Y.: Scholars' Facsimiles & Reprints, 1974.

ANTHOLOGIES OF PRIMARY SOURCES

Patrides, C. A., editor. *The Cambridge Platonists.* Cambridge: Cambridge University Press, 1969.

Raphael, D. D., editor. *British Moralists: 1650–1800.* 2 vols. Oxford: Clarendon Press, 1969. Reprint, Indianapolis, Ind.: Hackett, 1991.

Schneewind, J. B., editor. *Moral Philosophy from Montaigne to Kant: An Anthology.* 2 vols. Cambridge: Cambridge University Press, 1990.

Selby-Bigge, L. A., editor. *British Moralists, Being Selections from Writers Principally of the Eighteenth Century.* 2 vols. Oxford: Oxford University Press, 1897. Reprinted in one volume with a new introduction by Bernard H. Baumrin. Indianapolis, Ind.: Bobbs-Merrill, 1964.

SECONDARY SOURCES AND RECENT PHILOSOPHY

Albee, Ernest. *A History of English Utilitarianism.* London: Allen & Unwin, 1957; originally published 1901.

Allison, Henry. *Kant's Theory of Freedom*. Cambridge: Cambridge University Press, 1990.

Allison, Henry. "Morality and Freedom: Kant's Reciprocity Thesis." *Philosophical Review* 95 (1986): 393–425.

Annas, Julia. *The Morality of Happiness*. New York: Oxford University Press, 1993.

Anscombe, G. E. M. *Intention*. 2d ed. Ithaca: Cornell University Press, 1963.

Axelrod, Robert. *The Evolution of Cooperation*. New York: Basic, 1984.

Baier, Annette. "Hume and Social Artifice." *Ethics* 98 (1988): 757–778.

Baier, Annette. *A Progress of Sentiments*. Cambridge, Mass.: Harvard University Press, 1991.

Baron, Marcia. "Hume's Noble Lie: An Account of His Artificial Virtues." *Canadian Journal of Philosophy* 12 (1982): 539–555.

Barry, Brian. "Warrender and His Critics." *Philosophy* 43 (1969): 117–137.

Barry, Brian, and Russell Hardin, editors. *Rational Man and Irrational Society*. Beverly Hills, Calif.: Sage, 1982.

Blackstone, William T. *Francis Hutcheson and Contemporary Ethical Theory*. Athens: University of Georgia Press, 1965.

Brandt, Richard. *A Theory of the Good and the Right*. Oxford: Oxford University Press, 1979.

Brink, David O. *Moral Realism and the Foundations of Ethics*. Cambridge: Cambridge University Press, 1989.

Broad, C. D. *Five Types of Ethical Theory*. Totowa, N.J.: Littlefield, Adams, 1965.

Brown, Charlotte. "Is Hume an Internalist?" *Journal of the History of Philosophy* 26 (1988): 69–87.

Burton, John H. *The Life and Correspondence of David Hume*. Edinburgh: William Tait, 1846. Facsimile, New York: Garland, 1983.

Carnap, Rudolph. *The Foundations of Probability*. Chicago: University of Chicago Press, 1950.

Cassirer, Ernst. *Kant's Life and Thought*. Translated by James Haden. New Haven: Yale University Press, 1981.

Cassirer, Ernst. *The Philosophy of the Enlightenment*. Translated by Fritz C. A. Koelln and James P. Pettegrove. Princeton: Princeton University Press, 1951.

Cassirer, Ernst. *The Platonic Renaissance in England*. Translated by James P. Pettegrove. Austin: University of Texas Press, 1953.

Cassirer, Ernst. *Rousseau, Kant, Goethe: Two Essays*. Translated by James Gutmann, Paul Oskar Kristeller, and John Herman Randall, Jr. Princeton: Princeton University Press, 1963.

Colman, John. *John Locke's Moral Philosophy*. Edinburgh: Edinburgh University Press, 1983.

Cranston, Maurice. *John Locke*. Oxford: Oxford University Press, 1985.

Curley, Edwin. "Reflections on Hobbes: Recent Work on His Moral and Political Philosophy." *Journal of Philosophical Research* 15 (1990): 169–250.

Darwall, Stephen. "Harman and Moral Relativism." *Personalist* 58 (1977): 199–207.

Darwall, Stephen. "Hume and the Invention of Utilitarianism." In *Hume and Hume's Connexions*. Edited by M. A. Stewart and J. Wright. Edinburgh: Edinburgh University Press, forthcoming.

Darwall, Stephen. *Impartial Reason*. Ithaca: Cornell University Press, 1983.

Darwall, Stephen. "Internalism and Agency." *Philosophical Perspectives* 6 (1992): 155–174.

Darwall, Stephen, Allan Gibbard, and Peter Railton. "Toward *Fin de siècle* Ethics: Some Trends." *Philosophical Review* 101 (1992): 115–189.

Deigh, John. "Sidgwick on Ethical Judgment." In *Essays on Henry Sidgwick*. Edited by Bart Schultz. Cambridge: Cambridge University Press, 1992, pp. 241–258.

Driscoll, Edward A. "The Influence of Gassendi on Locke's Hedonism." *International Philosophical Quarterly* 12 (72): 87–110.

Duncan-Jones, Austin. *Butler's Moral Philosophy*. Harmondsworth: Penguin, 1952.

Falk, W. D. "'Ought' and Motivation." *Proceedings of the Aristotelian Society* 48 (1947–48): 492–510. Reprinted in *Ought, Reasons, and Morality: The Collected Papers of W. D. Falk*. Ithaca: Cornell University Press, 1986.

Forsyth, Murray. "The Place of Richard Cumberland in the History of Natural Law Doctrine." *Journal of the History of Philosophy* 20 (1982): 23–42.

Fowler, Thomas. *Shaftesbury and Hutcheson*. London: Sampson, Low, Marston, Searle, & Rivington, 1882.

Frankel, Lois. "Damaris Cudworth Masham: A Seventeenth-Century Feminist Philosopher." *Hypatia* 4 (1989): 80–90.

Frankena, William. "Hutcheson's Moral Sense Theory." *Journal of the History of Ideas* 16 (1955): 356–375.

Frankena, William. "Obligation and Motivation in Recent Moral Philosophy." In *Essays in Moral Philosophy*. Edited by A. I. Melden. Seattle: University of Washington Press, 1958, pp. 40–81.

Frankena, William. "Sidgwick and the History of Ethical Dualism." In *Essays on Henry Sidgwick*. Edited by Bart Schultz. Cambridge: Cambridge University Press, 1992, pp. 175–197.

Gauthier, David. "Artificial Virtues and the Sensible Knave." *Hume Studies* 18 (1992): 401–428.

Gauthier, David. "David Hume, Contractarian." *Philosophical Review* 88 (1979): 3–38.

Gauthier, David. *The Logic of Leviathan*. Oxford: Clarendon Press, 1969.

Gibbard, Allan. *Wise Choices, Apt Feelings*. Cambridge, Mass.: Harvard University Press, 1990.

Grave, S. A. "The Foundation of Butler's Ethics." *Australasian Journal of Philosophy* 30 (1952): pp. 73–89.

Grean, Stanley. *Shaftesbury's Philosophy of Religion and Ethics: A Study in Enthusiasm*. Athens: Ohio University Press, 1967.

Works cited

Haakonssen, Knud. "Divine/Natural Law Theories in Ethics." In *The Cambridge History of Seventeenth-Century Philosophy.* Edited by Michael Ayers and Daniel Garber. Cambridge: Cambridge University Press, forthcoming.

Haakonssen, Knud. "Moral Philosophy and Natural Law: From the Cambridge Platonists to the Scottish Enlightenment." *Political Science* 40 (1988): 97–110.

Haakonssen, Knud. "Natural Law and Moral Realism: The Scottish Synthesis." In *Studies in the Philosophy of the Scottish Enlightenment.* Edited by M. A. Stewart. Oxford: Oxford University Press, 1990, pp. 61–85.

Haakonssen, Knud. *The Science of a Legislator.* Cambridge: Cambridge University Press, 1981.

Hall, Roland. "New Words and Antedatings from Cudworth's 'Treatise of Freewill'." *Notes and Queries,* n.s. 7 (1960): 427–432.

Hampton, Jean. *Hobbes and the Social Contract Tradition.* Cambridge: Cambridge University Press, 1986.

Hardie, W. F. R. "The Final Good in Aristotle's Ethics." *Philosophy* 40 (1965): 277–295.

Hare, R. M. *The Language of Morals.* Oxford: Clarendon Press, 1952.

Harman, Gilbert. "Moral Relativism Defended." *Philosophical Review* 84 (1975): 3–22.

Harrison, John, and Peter Laslett, editors. *The Library of John Locke.* Oxford: Oxford University Press, 1971.

Hart, H. L. A. *The Concept of Law.* Oxford: Oxford University Press, 1961.

Hood, F. C. *The Divine Politics of Thomas Hobbes.* Oxford: Clarendon Press, 1964.

Hruschka, Joachim. "The Greatest Happiness Principle and Other Early German Anticipations of Utilitarian Theory." *Utilitas* 3 (1991): 165–177.

Humberstone, I. L. "Direction of Fit." *Mind* 101 (1992): 59–83.

Hutton, Sarah. "Damaris Cudworth, Lady Masham: Between Platonism and Enlightenment." *British Journal for the History of Philosophy* 1 (1993): 29–54.

Irwin, T. H. "The Metaphysical and Psychological Basis of Aristotle's Ethics." In *Essays on Aristotle's Ethics.* Edited by Amélie Oksenberg Rorty. Berkeley and Los Angeles: University of California Press, 1980, pp. 35–53.

Jensen, Henning. *Motivation and the Moral Sense in Francis Hutcheson's Ethical Theory.* The Hague: Nijhoff, 1971.

Kavka, Gregory. *Hobbesian Moral and Political Theory.* Princeton: Princeton University Press, 1986.

Kavka, Gregory. "The Rationality of Rule-Following: Hobbes' Dispute with the Foole." *Law and Philosophy,* in press.

Kavka, Gregory. "Right Reason and Natural Law in Hobbes's Ethics." *Monist* 66 (1983): 120–133.

Kirk, Linda. *Richard Cumberland and Natural Law: Secularisation of Thought in Seventeenth-Century England.* Cambridge: James Clarke, 1987.

Kleinig, John. "Butler in a Cool Hour." *Journal of the History of Philosophy* 7 (1969): 399–411.

Korsgaard, Christine. "Kant's Analysis of Obligation: The Argument of *Foundations* I." *Monist* 73 (1989): 311–340.

Korsgaard, Christine. "Normativity as Reflexivity: Hume's Practical Justification of Morality," paper delivered at the meetings of the Hume Society at the University of Lancaster, Summer 1989.

Korsgaard, Christine. "Skepticism about Practical Reason." *Journal of Philosophy* 83 (1986): 5–25.

Korsgaard, Christine. *The Sources of Normativity*, The Tanner Lecture on Human Values, Clare Hall, Cambridge University, November 1992.

Kripke, Saul. *Wittgenstein on Rules and Private Language*. Cambridge, Mass.: Harvard University Press, 1982.

Larthomas, Jean-Paul. *De Shaftesbury à Kant*. 2 vols. Lille: Atelier National de Reproduction des Thèses; Paris: Diffusion Didier Erudition, 1985.

Leidhold, Wolfgang. *Ethik und Politik bei Francis Hutcheson*. Freiburg: Alber, 1985.

Lenz, John. "Locke's Essays on the Law of Nature." *Philosophy and Phenomenological Research* 17 (1956): 105–113.

Leyden, W. von. *Hobbes and Locke: The Politics of Freedom and Obligation*. New York: St. Martin's, 1982.

Lloyd, S. A. *Ideals as Interests in Hobbes's "Leviathan."* Cambridge: Cambridge University Press, 1992.

Lovejoy, Arthur O. "Kant and the English Platonists." In *Essays Philosophical and Psychological, in Honor of William James*. Edited by members of the Columbia University Department of Philosophy. New York: Longmans, Green, 1908.

McDowell, John. *Projection and Truth in Ethics*. Lindley Lecture, University of Kansas, 1987.

McDowell, John. "Values and Secondary Qualities." In *Morality and Objectivity: A Tribute to John Mackie*. Edited by Ted Honderich. London: Routledge & Kegan Paul, 1985, pp. 110–129.

MacIntyre, Alasdair. *After Virtue*. Notre Dame, Ind.: University of Notre Dame Press, 1981.

MacIntyre, Alasdair. *Whose Justice? Which Rationality?* Notre Dame, Ind.: Notre Dame University Press, 1988.

Mackie, J. L. *Ethics: Inventing Right and Wrong*. Harmondsworth: Penguin, 1977.

Mackie, J. L. *Hume's Moral Theory*. London: Routledge & Kegan Paul, 1980.

McPherson, T. H. "The Development of Bishop Butler's Ethics." *Philosophy* 23 (1948): 317–331; 24 (1949): 3–22.

Martineau, James. *Types of Ethical Theory*. 2 vols. Oxford: Oxford University Press, 1901.

Martinich, A. P. *The Two Gods of "Leviathan": Thomas Hobbes on Religion and Politics*. Cambridge: Cambridge University Press, 1992.

Mattern, Ruth. "Moral Sciences and the Concept of Persons in Locke." *Philosophical Review* 89 (1980): 24–45.

Works cited

Millar, Alan. "Following Nature." *Philosophical Quarterly* 38 (1988): 165–185.
Mintz, Samuel. *The Hunting of Leviathan*. Cambridge: Cambridge University Press, 1962.
Moore, G. E. *Principia Ethica*. Cambridge: Cambridge University Press, 1966.
Muirhead, J. H. *The Platonic Tradition in Anglo-Saxon Philosophy*. London: Allen & Unwin, 1931.
Nagel, Thomas. *The Possibility of Altruism*. Oxford: Clarendon Press, 1970.
Norton, David Fate. *David Hume: Common-Sense Moralist, Sceptical Metaphysician*. Princeton: Princeton University Press, 1982.
Norton, David Fate. "Hutcheson's Moral Realism." *Journal of the History of Philosophy* 23 (1985): 397–418.
O'Brien, Wendell. "Butler and the Authority of Conscience." *History of Philosophy Quarterly* 8 (1991): 43–57.
O'Donnell, Sheryl. "My Idea in Your Mind: John Locke and Damaris Cudworth Masham." In *Mothering the Mind*. Edited by Ruth Perry and Martine Watson Bromley. New York: Hobbes & Meiner, 1984, pp. 26–46.
Olson, Mancur. *The Logic of Collective Action*. Cambridge, Mass.: Harvard University Press, 1971.
Parfit, Derek. *Reasons and Persons*. Oxford: Clarendon Press, 1984.
Passmore, John. *Ralph Cudworth: An Interpretation*. Cambridge: Cambridge University Press, 1951.
Penelhum, Terence. *Butler*. London: Routledge & Kegan Paul, 1985.
Petitt, Philip. "Free Riding and Foul Dealing." *Journal of Philosophy* 83 (1986): 361–379.
Platts, Mark. *Ways of Meaning*. London: Routledge & Kegan Paul, 1979.
Polin, Raymond. "John Locke's Conception of Freedom." In *John Locke: Problems and Perspectives*. Edited by John Yolton. Cambridge: Cambridge University Press, 1969, pp. 1–18.
Porter, Noah. "Marginalia Locke-a-na." *New Englander and Yale Review* 47 (1887): 33–49.
Powicke, F. J. *The Cambridge Platonists*. London: J. M. Dent, 1926.
Prior, Arthur. *Logic and the Basis of Ethics*. Oxford: Oxford University Press, 1949.
Railton, Peter. "Facts and Values." *Philosophical Topics* 14 (1986): 5–31.
Railton, Peter. "Moral Realism." *Philosophical Review* 95 (1986): 163–207.
Railton, Peter. "Naturalism and Prescriptivity." *Social Philosophy and Policy* 7 (1989): 151–174.
Rapaczynski, Andrzej. *Nature and Politics: Liberalism in the Philosophies of Hobbes, Locke, and Rousseau*. Ithaca: Cornell University Press, 1987.
Raphael, D. D. "Bishop Butler's View of Conscience." *Philosophy* 24 (1949): 219–238.
Raphael, D. D. *The Moral Sense*. London: Oxford University Press, 1947.
Rawls, John. "Two Concepts of Rules." *Philosophical Review* 64 (1955): 3–32.
Rorty, Amélie Oksenberg. "Butler on Benevolence and Conscience." *Philosophy* 53 (1978): 171–184.

Works cited

Sayre-McCord, Geoffrey, editor. *Essays on Moral Realism*. Ithaca: Cornell University Press, 1988.

Scheffler, Samuel. *Human Morality*. New York: Oxford University Press, 1992.

Schneewind, J. B. "Kant and Natural Law Ethics." *Ethics* 104 (1993): 53–74.

Schneewind, J. B. "Natural Law, Skepticism, and Method." *Journal of the History of Ideas* 52 (1991): 289–308.

Schneewind, J. B. "Pufendorf's Place in the History of Ethics." *Synthese* 72 (1987): 123–155.

Schneewind, J. B. "The Use of Autonomy in Ethical Theory." In *Reconstructing Individualism: Autonomy, Individuality, and the Self in Western Thought*. Edited by Thomas C. Heller, Morton Sosna, and David E. Wellbery. Stanford, Calif.: Stanford University Press, 1986, pp. 64–75.

Schouls, Peter A. *Reasoned Freedom*. Ithaca: Cornell University Press, 1992.

Scott, William Robert. *Francis Hutcheson: His Life, Teaching and Position in the History of Philosophy*. Cambridge: Cambridge University Press, 1900.

Sharp, Frank Chapman. "The Ethical System of Richard Cumberland and Its Place in the History of British Ethics." *Mind* 21 (1912): 371–398.

Shaver, Robert. "Grotius on Skepticism and Self-Interest." *Archiv für Geschichte der Philosophie*, forthcoming.

Sidgwick, Henry. *The Methods of Ethics*. 7th ed. London: Macmillan, 1967.

Sidgwick, Henry. *Outlines of the History of Ethics for English Readers*. 6th ed., enlarged. Boston: Beacon, 1964.

Skinner, Quentin. *The Foundations of Modern Political Thought*. 2 vols. Cambridge: Cambridge University Press, 1978.

Smith, Michael. "The Humean Theory of Motivation." *Mind* 96 (1987): 36–61.

Snare, Francis. *Morals, Motivation, and Convention: Hume's Influential Doctrines*. Cambridge: Cambridge University Press, 1991.

Sprague, Elmer. "Francis Hutcheson and the Moral Sense." *Journal of Philosophy* 51 (1954): 794–800.

Sprute, Jurgen. "John Lockes Konzeption der Ethik." *Studia Leibnitiana* 17 (1985): 127–142.

Stafford, J. Martin. "Hutcheson, Hume, and the Ontology of Morals." *Journal of Value Inquiry* 19 (1985): 133–151.

Stevenson, Charles. "The Emotive Meaning of Ethical Terms." In *Facts and Values*. New Haven: Yale University Press, 1963, pp. 10–36.

Stevenson, Charles. *Ethics and Language*. New Haven: Yale University Press, 1944.

Stewart, Dugald. *The Collected Works of Dugald Stewart*. Edited by Sir William Hamilton. 11 vols. Edinburgh: T. Constable, 1854–60.

Stewart, Robert M. "John Clarke and Francis Hutcheson on Self-Love and Moral Motivation." *Journal of the History of Philosophy* 20 (1982): 261–278.

Strasser, Mark Philip. *Francis Hutcheson's Moral Theory: Its Form and Utility*. Wolfeboro, N.H.: Longwood Academic, 1990.

Strasser, Mark. Philip. "Hutcheson on the Higher and Lower Pleasures." *Journal of the History of Philosophy* 25 (1987): 517–531.

Works cited

Stroud, Barry. *Hume*. London: Routledge & Kegan Paul, 1977.

Sturgeon, Nicholas L. "Nature and Conscience in Butler's Ethics." *Philosophical Review* 85 (1976): 316–356.

Taylor, A. E. "The Ethical Doctrine of Hobbes." In *Hobbes Studies*. Edited by Keith Brown. Oxford: Blackwell Publisher, 1965, pp. 35–55.

Taylor, A. E. "Some Features of Butler's Ethics." *Mind* 35 (1926): 273–300.

Taylor, Charles. *Sources of the Self*. Cambridge, Mass.: Harvard University Press, 1990.

Trianosky, Gregory. "On the Obligation to Be Virtuous: Shaftesbury and the Question, Why Be Moral?" *Journal of the History of Philosophy* 16 (1978): 289–300.

Tuck, Richard. "Grotius, Carneades, and Hobbes." *Grotiana*, n.s. 4 (1983): 43–62.

Tuck, Richard. "The 'Modern' Theory of Natural Law." In *The Languages of Political Theory in Early-Modern Europe*. Edited by Anthony Pagden. Cambridge: Cambridge University Press, 1987, pp. 99–119.

Tuck, Richard. *Natural Rights Theories*. Cambridge: Cambridge University Press, 1987.

Tuveson, Ernest. "The Origins of the 'Moral Sense'." *Huntington Library Quarterly* 11 (1948): 241–249.

Uehlein, Frederich A. *Kosmos und Subjektivität, Lord Shaftesburys Philosophical Regimen*. Freiburg and Munich: Karl Alber, 1976.

Vienne, Jean-Michel. "Malebranche and Locke: The Theory of Moral Choice, a Neglected Theme." In *Nicolas Malebranche: His Philosophical Critics and Successors*. Edited by Stuart Brown. Assen/Maastricht: Van Gorcum, 1991.

Voitle, Robert. *The Third Earl of Shaftesbury*. Baton Rouge: Louisiana State University Press, 1984.

Warrender, Howard. *The Political Philosophy of Hobbes*. Oxford: Clarendon Press, 1957.

White, Alan. "Conscience and Self-Love in Butler's Sermons." *Philosophy* 17 (1952): 329–344.

White, Nicholas. "The Imperative, the Attractive and the Repulsive: Sidgwick and Modern Views of Ancient Ethics." In *Essays on Henry Sidgwick*. Edited by Bart Schultz. Cambridge: Cambridge University Press, 1992, pp. 311–330.

Wiggins, David. *Needs, Values, and Truth: Essays in the Philosophy of Value*. Oxford: Blackwell Publisher, 1987.

Williams, Bernard. "Internal and External Reasons." In *Moral Luck*. Cambridge: Cambridge University Press, 1981, pp. 101–113.

Williams, Bernard. "Persons, Character, and Morality." In *Moral Luck*. Cambridge: Cambridge University Press, 1981, pp. 1–19.

Winkler, Kenneth P. "Hutcheson's Alleged Moral Realism." *Journal of the History of Philosophy* 23 (1985): 179–194.

Yolton, John. *John Locke and the Way of Ideas.* London: Oxford University Press, 1956.

Yolton, John. *Locke and the Compass of Human Understanding.* Cambridge: Cambridge University Press, 1970.

Index

Index

perfectionism, 26–7
Petitt, Philip, 299n
Plato, 3, 4, 10, 128
Platts, Mark, 45n
Polin, Raymond, 161n
Porter, Noah, 41n
Powicke, F. J., 117
practical judgment; *see* judgment, practical
practical reason; *see* reason, pure practical
practicality of ethics; in Cumberland, 85–8, 105; in Locke, 44–9, 51, 149–50, 169
preference in Locke, 152, 156–7, 159
Price, Richard, 10, 19, 21, 111–2, 114, 120–1, 325–8, 330
principle of reflection; *see* conscience in Butler
Prior, A. N., 18n
Prisoner's Dilemma, 74–5, 93–4, 299
Pufendorf, Samuel, 4, 13n, 119

Railton, Peter, 10n, 11n, 12n, 321n
Rand, Benjamin, 177n, 197
Rapaczynski, Andrzej, 161n
Raphael, D. D., 1n, 211n, 249n, 250n
rational intuitionism; *see* intuitionism, rational
Rawls, John, 291, 317–18
realism, moral 11–12, 215n
reason: empiricist conception of theoretical, 15–7, 112, 150, 248, in Cumberland, 107, in Hobbes, 58, 81, in Hume, 319–20, in Hutcheson, 209, 211, 224, 229, 243, 284, 319–20, in Locke, 172; inferior, in Cudworth, 142, 144–5; pure practical, in Cudworth; 112–15, 120–1, 126–30, 137–8, 147–8, 325, dualism of, 98, 235, in Shaftesbury, 187, 189–90; superior, in Cudworth, 115, 138, 141–2, 144 146–7
reasons for acting; *see* motive, rational
reciprocity thesis; *see* Kant, Immanuel, reciprocity thesis in
reductionism, naturalist, 15; in Cumberland, 83–7, 97, 102–3, 105–8, 319–20
reflection principle; *see* conscience in Butler
relativism, moral, 11
rights in Hutcheson, 218; *see also* creation, right of; nature, right of
Rorty, Amelie Oksenberg, 250n
Rousseau, Jean-Jacques 1, 331

rule obligation in Hume; *see* obligation, rule, in Hume
rule regulation in Hume, 288–9, 295–6, 298, 308–15, 317, 321
rules of justice in Hume, 288–9, 295, 297, 299–302, 308–9, 312–13

sanctions: in Cumberland, 88–9; in Locke, 36, 38–9, 42–6, 49, 167
Scheffler, Samuel, 12n, 322n
Schism and Occasional Conformity acts, 7
Schneewind, J. B., 1n, 8–9n, 14n, 24n, 63n, 107n, 244n
Schouls, Peter A., 161n
Scott, William R., 208n, 237n
Selby-Bigge, L. A., 1, 20–1
Selden, John, 24, 80n
self, unity of; *see* will, unity of
self-deception and self-knowledge in Shaftesbury, 199–201
self-determination: 8n, 16–20, 110, 324–5; in Butler, 284 (*see also* self-regulation, in Butler); in Cudworth, 130–44, 151–2, 174–5; Hutcheson on, 244; in Locke, 158–75, 199, 285; in Shaftesbury, 179, 181, 190–2, 197–206, 244
self-love: in Butler, 250, 251n, 252n, 255, 256n, 260, 263, 265–6, 273–4, 282; in Hume, 288, 290, 299, 306–9, 311; in Hutcheson, 223–33, 239–43, 246, 284, 319
self-regulation, 18–20, 325, 329; in Butler, 246, 248–9, 253, 275, 277–8, 280–2, 286; in Shaftesbury, 203–6; *see also* will, normative theory of
sentiment, moral; *see* moral sense
sentimentalism, empiricist moral, 16, 21, 180, 182, 187, 207; *see also* moral sense (sentiment), in Hume *and* in Hutcheson; sentimentalist view of normativity
sentimentalist view of normativity: in Hume, 287–9, 295–8, 301–8, 310, 314–15, 317; in Hutcheson, 208–10, 219–23, 233–6, 243–4, 285, 297
Shaftesbury, Anthony Ashley Cooper, 3rd Earl of, 16n, 21–2, 176–8; Butler on, 244–6, 263, 274n; Hutcheson on, 218–21, 229, 231–3, 242; and normative theory of will, 18–20, 96, 177, 203–6, 245–6, 282, 325, 329, 332; and self-regulation, 172, 203–6
Sharp, Frank Chapman, 82n, 96n